T0207478

Lecture Notes
in Business Information Processing 450

Series Editors

Wil van der Aalst
RWTH Aachen University, Aachen, Germany

John Mylopoulos
University of Trento, Trento, Italy

Sudha Ram
University of Arizona, Tucson, AZ, USA

Michael Rosemann
Queensland University of Technology, Brisbane, QLD, Australia

Clemens Szyperski
Microsoft Research, Redmond, WA, USA

More information about this series at https://link.springer.com/bookseries/7911

Adriano Augusto · Asif Gill ·
Dominik Bork · Selmin Nurcan ·
Iris Reinhartz-Berger · Rainer Schmidt (Eds.)

Enterprise, Business-Process and Information Systems Modeling

23rd International Conference, BPMDS 2022
and 27th International Conference, EMMSAD 2022, Held at CAiSE 2022
Leuven, Belgium, June 6–7, 2022
Proceedings

Editors
Adriano Augusto 🆔
The University of Melbourne
Carlton, VIC, Australia

Asif Gill 🆔
University of Technology Sydney
Ultimo, NSW, Australia

Dominik Bork 🆔
TU Wien
Vienna, Austria

Selmin Nurcan 🆔
University Paris 1 Pantheon-Sorbonne
Paris, France

Iris Reinhartz-Berger 🆔
University of Haifa
Haifa, Israel

Rainer Schmidt
Hochschule für angewandte Wissenschaften
München
Munich, Germany

ISSN 1865-1348   ISSN 1865-1356 (electronic)
Lecture Notes in Business Information Processing
ISBN 978-3-031-07474-5   ISBN 978-3-031-07475-2 (eBook)
https://doi.org/10.1007/978-3-031-07475-2

This Springer imprint is published by the registered company Springer Nature Switzerland AG
The registered company address is: Gewerbestrasse 11, 6330 Cham, Switzerland

Preface

This book contains the proceedings of two long-running events held alongside the CAiSE conference relating to the areas of enterprise, business-process, and information systems modeling: the 23rd International Working Conference on Business Process Modeling, Development and Support (BPMDS 2022) and the 27th International Working Conference on Exploring Modeling Methods for Systems Analysis and Development (EMMSAD 2022).

The two working conferences had a joint keynote given by Raimundas Matulevičius, Professor of Software Engineering at the Institute of Computer Science of the University of Tartu, Estonia.

This year both conferences were held in Leuven, Belgium, during June 6–7, 2022. More information on the individual events and their selection processes can be found on the following pages.

BPMDS 2022

BPMDS has been held as a series of workshops devoted to business process modeling, development, and support since 1998. During this period, business process analysis and design have been recognized as a central issue in the area of information systems (IS) engineering. The continued interest in these topics on behalf of the IS community is reflected by the success of the previous BPMDS events and the recent emergence of new conferences and workshops devoted to the theme. In 2011, BPMDS became a two-day working conference attached to the International Conference on Advanced Information Systems Engineering (CAiSE). The goals, format, and history of BPMDS can be found on the website http://www.bpmds.org/.

The BPMDS working conference deals with and promotes research on business process modeling, development, and support, and has been a platform for a multitude of influential research papers. In keeping with its tradition, the working conference covers a broad range of theoretical and application-based research on BPMDS.

The intention of BPMDS is to solicit papers related to business process modeling, development, and support in general, using quality as the main selection criterion. As a working conference, we aim to attract papers describing mature research, but we still give place to industrial reports and visionary idea papers. To encourage new and emerging challenges and research directions in the area of business process modeling, development, and support, we have a unique focus theme every year. Papers submitted as idea papers must be relevant to the focus theme, thus providing a mass of new ideas around a relatively narrow but emerging research area. Full research papers and experience reports do not necessarily need to be directly connected to this theme (although they still need to be explicitly relevant to BPMDS).

The focus theme for the BPMDS 2022 idea papers, Reflections on Human-human Interaction and Responsibility in a Virtual Environment, reflects the abundance of virtual environments in all domains of our lives. Technologies are here and abundant. Are we ready to use these technologies in an extremely connected world where false information spreads faster than the truth with detrimental consequences? Are we mature enough to process the information as fast as the computers provide it? What is the meaning of a "like" in a professional environment when the "thing" which has been "liked" was not precisely read or understood? How should we enhance business process engineering, modeling, and management to master this increasingly complex new deal? How could/should human-computer interfaces support the issues related to increasing reflexes (fast clicks) to the detriment of reflection? How shall we consider the *quality* of the collected data by the means of logs, clicks, events? A pilot who is using a flight simulator during her training is aware that this is a virtual and fictitious platform, and she is confident that she will use the competencies she is acquiring in this virtual and fictitious environment later in the physical world; the new competencies will be partly due to the mistakes made using the flight simulator. On the other hand, is the surfer, who likes or comments in an online social network, totally aware that she acts in the "real world" (not a fictitious one) when she clicks? Is she aware of her *responsibility*?

Virtual does not mean fictitious. Using virtual environments expands our capabilities/frontiers of action in the real world ("real" in opposition to "fictitious"). For example, using voice-based assistants such as Amazon Alexa allows integrating people who have been excluded (because of their handicap) by graphical user interfaces from using software systems so far. Digital technologies enable the creation of new business models. An important factor to accomplish this is the provision of information on these resources and evaluation of their *quality*. Both can only be accomplished by collecting this information with digital means. Consequently, we are more and more drastically responsible for what we produce as information.

Organizations and the world are going through huge transformations due, in large part, to information technologies and their direct and indirect impacts. These transformations impact frontally the information systems, which support the business processes of organizations and therefore the actors in carrying out their activities/missions. The speed of organizational and societal transformations requires continuous improvement and innovation processes. *Creativity* and *responsibility* are determining factors and require detailed and multi-faceted knowledge of the problem to handle and of the context. The unpredictability of the related transformations (and more particularly their detrimental effects) requires more than ever a systemic vision in (i) the engineering and governance of information systems and (ii) the engineering and architecture of business processes ecosystems, the latter have to support.

The opportunities for evolution and transformation assume the ability to capture, store, organize, search, and analyze large volumes of information and put us in front of many new challenges: meeting and mastering the requirements of volume, speed, variety, veracity, the value of data, compliance with data protection laws, and full awareness of (and responsibility for) the components of the new VUCA (volatility, uncertainty, complexity, and ambiguity) world. We are all responsible as engineers, researchers, professors, and citizens. We need human intelligence more than ever.

Is there a risk of losing control of a situation due to the unpredictability of detrimental effects? Do we have conceptual and technological means to identify behavioral misuses and the corresponding patterns? Cambridge Analytica, a professor killed after an organized series of fake news in social networks, the United States Capitol attack, a university that is ransacked following a flash organization via social networks requiring two months of repair and maintenance, ...

Society 5.0, with its opportunities and threats, has the finality to strengthen the potential of cyber-physical-social relations in promoting the improvement of the quality of life of all people through a super smart society[1].

Driven by these thoughts, we have proposed a challenge to the authors of two promising submissions to (i) present their work as a poster during BPMDS 2022 and then (ii) to co-operate around a hot problem statement, to be identified together during BPMDS, taking into account the feedback of participants. Extended abstracts of these two promising works are included in this volume. The first piece of research work is about the exploitation of "raw" time series data as inputs of (process) mining. The approach could be generic enough to be used in any discipline producing raw sensor data in terms of time series. The second is about a maturity model for industry 4.0.

BPMDS 2022 received 18 submissions from authors in 13 countries (Austria, Australia, Brazil, Canada, the Czech Republic, Germany, India, Italy, the Netherlands, Slovakia, Slovenia, South Africa, and Switzerland). The management of paper submission and reviews was supported by the EasyChair conference system. Each paper was reviewed by at least three members of the international Program Committee. Eventually, seven high-quality full papers, two short papers, and two posters were selected.

The accepted papers cover a wide spectrum of issues related to business process development, modeling, and support, and also fit with this year's focus theme, Reflections on Human-human Interaction and Responsibility in a Virtual Environment, even though none of these papers were submitted as an idea paper. They are organized under the following section headings:

- Actual and Perceived Challenges
- Business Process Modeling
- Understanding Collaboration: One issue, many perspectives
- Event Logs ... Why it Deviates?

We wish to thank all the people who submitted papers to BPMDS 2022 for having shared their work with us, as well as the members of the BPMDS 2022 Program Committee who made a remarkable effort in reviewing submissions.

---

[1] Serpa, S., Ferreira, C.M., Sa, M.J., Santos, A.I. Digital Society and Social Dynamics. Services for Science and Education, UK, August 2020.

We also thank the organizers of CAiSE 2022 for their help with the organization of the event. We also thank IFIP WG 8.1 for its sustainable support and Springer, in particular Ralf Gerstner and Christine Reiss, for their assistance during the production of the proceedings.

April 2022   Selmin Nurcan
Rainer Schmidt
Adriano Augusto

EMMSAD 2022

The objective of the EMMSAD conference series is to provide a forum for researchers and practitioners interested in modeling methods for systems analysis and development (SA&D) to meet and exchange research ideas and results. The conference aims to provide a home for a rich variety of modeling paradigms, including software modeling, business process modeling, enterprise modeling, capability modeling, service modeling, ontology modeling, and domain-specific modeling. These important modeling paradigms, and specific methods following them, continue to be enriched with extensions, refinements, and even new languages, to address new challenges. Even with some attempts at standardization, new modeling paradigms and methods are constantly being introduced, especially in order to deal with emerging trends and challenges. Ongoing changes significantly impact the way systems are analyzed and designed in practice. Moreover, they challenge the empirical and analytical evaluation of the modeling methods, which contributes to the knowledge and understanding of their strengths and weaknesses. This knowledge may guide researchers towards the development of the next generation of modeling methods and help practitioners to select the modeling methods most appropriate to their needs.

This year, EMMSAD 2022 continued its tradition and accepted papers in five tracks that emphasize the variety of EMMSAD topics: (1) Foundations of modeling and method engineering – chaired by Jolita Ralyté and Janis Stirna; (2) Enterprise, business process, and capability modeling – chaired by Jānis Grabis and Paul Grefen; (3) Information systems and requirements modeling – chaired by Roman Lukyanenko and Marcela Ruiz; (4) Domain-specific and knowledge modeling – chaired by Tiago Prince Sales and Arnon Sturm; and (5) Evaluation of modeling approaches – chaired by Renata Guizzardi and Oscar Pastor. More details on the current and previous editions of EMMSAD can be found at http://www.emmsad.org/.

In total, 30 submissions were received from authors in 17 countries (Australia, Austria, Belgium, Brazil, Canada, Denmark, Estonia, France, Germany, Israel, Italy, the Netherlands, Pakistan, Spain, Sweden, Switzerland, and the USA). The division of submissions between the tracks was as follows: three submissions related to foundations of modeling and method engineering, six related to enterprise, business process, and capability modeling, seven related to information systems and requirements modeling, nine related to domain-specific and ontology modeling, and five related to evaluation of modeling approaches. After a rigorous review process, which included three reviews per submission (and a meta-review written by a track chair for submissions with conflicting reviews/scores), 14 high-quality papers, comprising 11 long papers and three short papers, were selected.

Foundations of modeling and method engineering

- Simon Hacks, Sotirios Katsikeas, Engla Rencelj Ling, Wenjun Xiong, Jérôme Pfeiffer and Andreas Wortmann. Towards a Systematic Method for Developing Meta Attack Language Instances.

Enterprise, business process, and capability modeling

- Mario Nolte and Monika Kaczmarek-Heß. Enterprise Modeling in Support Of Transparency in the Design and Use of Software Systems.
- Marco Pegoraro, Merih Seran Uysal, Tom-Hendrik Hülsmann and Wil van der Aalst. Uncertain Case Identifiers in Process Mining: a User Study of the Event-Case Correlation Problem on Click Data.
- Ben Roelens and Louise Tierens. The Integration of Process Simulation within the Business Architecture.

Information systems and requirements modeling

- Simon Curty, Felix Härer and Hans-Georg Fill. Blockchain Application Development Using Model-Driven Engineering and Low-Code Platforms: A Survey.
- Renata Guizzardi, Glenda Amaral, Giancarlo Guizzardi and John Mylopoulos. Eliciting Ethicality Requirements Using the Ontology-based Requirements Engineering Method.
- Steven Alter. Agent Responsibility Framework for Digital Agents: Roles and Responsibilities Related to Facets of Work.
- Thomas Derave, Tiago Princes Sales, Frederik Gailly and Geert Poels. A Method for Ontology-Driven Minimum Viable Platform Development.
- Juan Antonio Gómez-Gutiérrez, Robert Clarisó and Jordi Cabot. A Tool for Debugging Unsatisfiable Integrity Constraints in UML/OCL Class Diagrams [short paper].

Domain-specific and knowledge modeling

- Azzam Maraee and Arnon Sturm. Towards Simplification of ME-Maps.
- Omar ElAssy, Rik de Vendt, Fabiano Dalpiaz and Sjaak Brinkkemper. A Semi-automated Method for Domain-Specific Ontology Creation from Medical Guidelines.
- Elena Planas, Salvador Martínez, Marco Brambilla and Jordi Cabot. Towards Access Control Models for Conversational User Interfaces [short paper].

Evaluation of modeling approaches

- Charlotte Verbruggen and Monique Snoeck. Exploratory study on students' understanding of multi-perspective modelling.
- David Mosquera, Anastassios Martakos and Marcela Ruiz. Experiences from Developing a Web Crawler Using a Model-driven Development Tool: Emerging Opportunities [short paper].

We wish to thank all the authors who shared their work with us, as well as the members of EMMSAD 2022 Program Committee for their valuable reviews in the difficult times of the COVID-19 pandemic. Special thanks go to the track chairs for their help in EMMSAD advertising and the review process. Finally, we thank the organizers of CAiSE 2022 for their help with the organization of the event, IFIP WG 8.1 for its support, and Springer staff (especially Ralf Gerstner and Christine Reiss).

April 2022

Iris Reinhartz-Berger
Dominik Bork
Asif Gill

BPMDS 2022 Organization

Program Chairs

Adriano Augusto	University of Melbourne, Australia
Selmin Nurcan	University of Paris 1 Panthéon-Sorbonne, France
Rainer Schmidt	Munich University of Applied Sciences, Germany

Steering Committee

Ilia Bider	Stockholm University and IbisSoft, Sweden
Selmin Nurcan	University of Paris 1 Panthéon-Sorbonne, France
Rainer Schmidt	Munich University of Applied Sciences, Germany
Pnina Soffer	University of Haifa, Israel

Program Committee

Saïd Assar	Institut Mines-Télécom Business School, France
Marco Bajec	University of Ljubljana, Slovenia
Judith Barrios Albornoz	University de Los Andes, Venezuela
Karsten Boehm	FH Kufstein Tirol, Austria
Cristina Cabanillas	University of Seville, Spain
Claudio di Ciccio	Sapienza University of Rome, Italy
Dirk Fahland	Eindhoven University of Technology, The Netherlands
Renata Guizzardi	Federal University of Espírito Santo, Brazil
Amine Jalali	Stockholm University, Sweden
Paul Johannesson	Stockholm University, Sweden
Kathrin Kirchner	Technical University of Denmark, Denmark
Marite Kirikova	Riga Technical University, Latvia
Agnes Koschmider	Kiel University, Germany
Sander J. J. Leemans	RWTH Aachen, Germany
Henrik Leopold	Kühne Logistics University, Germany
Jan Mendling	Humboldt-Universität zu Berlin, Germany
Haralambos Mouratidis	University of Essex, UK
Michael Möhring	Munich University of Applied Sciences, Germany
Oscar Pastor	Universitat Polytechnica de Valencia, Spain
Gil Regev	EPFL and Itecor, Switzerland
Hajo Reijers	Utrecht University, The Netherlands
Colette Rolland	University of Paris 1 Panthéon-Sorbonne, France
Michael Rosemann	Queensland University of Technology, Australia
Shazia Sadiq	University of Queensland, Australia
Stefan Schönig	University of Bayreuth, Germany
Samira Si-Said Cherfi	CNAM, France

Pnina Soffer	University of Haifa, Israel
Amy Van Looy	Ghent University, Belgium
Irene Vanderfeesten	Open University of the Netherlands, The Netherlands
Han van der Aa	Humboldt University of Berlin, Germany
Barbara Weber	University of St. Gallen, Switzerland
Moe Thandar Wynn	Queensland University of Technology, Australia
Alfred Zimmermann	Reutlingen University, Germany

Additional Reviewers

Edoardo Marangone	Sapienza University of Rome, Italy
Yemna Sayeb	Université de la Manouba, Tunisia
Tianwa Chen	University of Queensland, Australia
Alexander Kraus	Humboldt University of Berlin, Germany

EMMSAD 2022 Organization

Program Chairs

Dominik Bork   TU Wien, Austria
Asif Gill   University of Technology Sydney, Australia
Iris Reinhartz-Berger   University of Haifa, Israel

Track Chairs

Jānis Grabis   Riga Technical University, Latvia
Paul Grefen   Eindhoven University of Technology, The Netherlands
Renata Guizzardi   University of Twente, The Netherlands
Roman Lukyanenko   HEC Montreal, Canada
Oscar Pastor   Universitat Politècnica de València, Spain
Tiago Prince Sales   Free University of Bozen-Bolzano, Italy
Jolita Ralyté   University of Geneva, Switzerland
Marcela Ruiz   Zurich University of Applied Sciences, Switzerland
Janis Stirna   Stockholm University, Sweden
Arnon Sturm   Ben-Gurion University, Israel

Program Committee

Raian Ali   Hamad Bin Khalifa University, Qatar
Joao Paulo Almeida   Federal University of Espirito Santo, Brazil
Said Assar   Institut Mines-Telecom Business School, France
Giuseppe Berio   Université de Bretagne Sud and IRISA, France
Alexander Bock   University of Duisburg-Essen, Germany
Drazen Brdjanin   University of Banja Luka, Bosnia and Herzegovina
Sjaak Brinkkemper   Utrecht University, The Netherlands
Jordi Cabot   ICREA - UOC (Internet Interdisciplinary Institute),
                              Spain
Tony Clark   Aston University, UK
Sybren De Kinderen   University of Luxembourg, Luxembourg
Marne de Vries   University of Pretoria, South Africa
Rebecca Deneckere   Centre de Recherche en Informatique, France
Mahdi Fahmideh   University of Southern Queensland, Australia
Michael Fellmann   University of Rostock, Germany
Christophe Feltus   Luxembourg Institute of Science and Technology,
                              Luxembourg
Peter Fettke   DFKI and Saarland University, Germany
Hans-Georg Fill   University of Fribourg, Germany
Frederik Gailly   Ghent University, Belgium

Mohamad Gharib	University of Tartu, Estonia
Georg Grossmann	University of South Australia, Australia
Cesar Gonzalez-Perez	Incipit-CSIC, Spain
Simon Hacks	University of Southern Denmark, Denmark
Martin Henkel	Stockholm University, Sweden
Jennifer Horkoff	Chalmers University of Technology, Sweden
Manfred Jeusfeld	University of Skövde, Sweden
Elena Kornyshova	CNAM, France
Georgios Koutsopoulos	Stockholm University, Sweden
Thomas Kuehne	Victoria University of Wellington, New Zealand
Birger Lantow	University of Rostock, Germany
Tong Li	Beijing University of Technology, China
Qin Ma	University of Luxembourg, Luxembourg
Patricia Martin-Rodilla	Spanish National Research Council, Spain
Raimundas Matulevicius	University of Tartu, Estonia
Andreas L. Opdahl	University of Bergen, Norway
Jose Ignacio Panach Navarrete	Universitat de València, Spain
Francisca Pérez	Universidad San Jorge, Spain
Klaus Pohl	University of Duisburg-Essen, Germany
Geert Poels	Ghent University, Belgium
Pilar Rodríguez	Universidad Politécnica de Madrid, Spain
Ben Roelens	Open University of the Netherlands, The Netherlands
Kurt Sandkuhl	University of Rostock, Germany
Monique Snoeck	KU Leuven, Belgium
Stefan Strecker	University of Hagen, Germany
Yves Wautelet	KU Leuven, Belgium
Hans Weigand	Tilburg University, The Netherlands
Carson Woo	University of British Columbia, Canada
Anna Zamansky	University of Haifa, Israel

Additional Reviewers

Abasi-Amefon Affia	University of Tartu, Estonia
Hitesh Dhiman	Technische Hochschule Ostwestfalen-Lippe University of Applied Sciences and Arts, Germany
Kristina Rosenthal	University of Hagen, Germany
Mari Seeba	University of Tartu, Estonia

Trustworthy Information Systems: Modelling Security, Privacy and Forensics in Business Processes (Keynote Abstract)

Raimundas Matulevičius

University of Tartu, Estonia
raimundas.matulevicius@ut.ee

The broad application of information systems requires that the communicated information be reliable, secured, private and used according to the intended purpose. Thus, the need for trustworthy information systems where information creation, communication and storage are done reliably and securely is more than an option. Security-by-design and privacy-by-design methods support the development of secure, private and reliable information systems. However, one can't achieve system security and reliability to the full extent. The trustworthy information systems should be designed so that it would be possible to eventual dispute occurrences of incidents.

Business process model and notation (BPMN) has become a de-facto standard for presenting and analysing business processes. Recent extensions suggest various means to create security- and privacy-aware business process models. It also helps develop the forensics controls to explore the security and reliability incidents within business processes. This talk will focus on three business process modelling aspects: (1) security risk management, (2) private information leakage management, and (3) forensic-ready business process modelling.

Security risk management allows us to explain protected organisations' assets, their potential security risks, and countermeasures to mitigate these risks. The talk will illustrate how one can apply BPMN to capture and explain security risk management concepts in business processes.

Although BPMN is well suited for explaining stakeholder collaboration and its support by the information system, managing the sensitive information and decreasing its leakages remain important system design activities. The talk will present how one can use BPMN and introduce privacy-enhancing technology to mitigate information leakages to third parties.

However, it is not possible to entirely mitigate incidents happening through the business processes. This nature necessitates designing forensic-ready information systems and providing a rationale for security and privacy countermeasure design. The talk will present the forensic-oriented constructs and how one can use them to create forensic-aware business processes. The forensic-based extensions introduced to BPMN are done based on the analysis of the security risks and estimates of information leakages. Forensics controls can produce pieces of evidence while investigating information breaches.

Short Bio of Speaker

Raimundas Matulevičius received his Ph.D. diploma from the Norwegian University of Science and Technology. Currently, he is a Professor of Information Security position at the University of Tartu (Estonia). His research interests include security and privacy of information, security risk management, and model-driven security. His publication record includes more than 100 articles published in peer-reviewed journals, conferences, and workshops. Matulevičius is a principal researcher in the SPARTA H2020 project (task: Privacy- by-Design) and several the Erasmus+ projects, including Safeguarding against Phishing in the age of 4 Industrial Revolution (CyberPhish) and A Blueprint for Sectoral Cooperation on Blockchain Skill Development (CHAISE).

Contents

Actual and Perceived Challenges (BPMDS 2022)

Process Mining Challenges Perceived by Analysts: An Interview Study   3
   Lisa Zimmermann, Francesca Zerbato, and Barbara Weber

Towards Process-Oriented IIoT Security Management: Perspectives
and Challenges 18
   Stefan Schönig, Markus Hornsteiner, and Christoph Stoiber

Business Process Modeling (BPMDS 2022)

RBPMN - The Power of Roles for Business Process Modeling
with BPMN 29
   Tarek Skouti, Frank J. Furrer, and Susanne Strahringer

A Complementary Analysis of the Behavior of BPMN Tools Regarding
Process Modeling Problems 43
   João Vitor de Camargo, Nicolas Mauro de Moreira Bohnenberger,
   Vinicius Stein Dani, José Palazzo Moreira de Oliveira,
   Encarna Sosa-Sánchez, Gregor Polančič, and Lucineia Heloisa Thom

**Understanding Collaboration: One Issue, Many Perspectives
(BPMDS 2022)**

A Technique for Collaboration Discovery 63
   Flavio Corradini, Barbara Re, Lorenzo Rossi, and Francesco Tiezzi

Understanding Process Management in Non-profit Organisations
Without Formal Business Process Management. 79
   Chezre Fredericks and Lisa F. Seymour

Event Logs - Why it Deviates? (BPMDS 2022)

Deviance Analysis by Means of Redescription Mining. 91
   Martin Käppel, Engjëll Ahmeti, and Stefan Jablonski

Detecting Context Activities in Event Logs 108
   Yang Lu, Qifan Chen, and Simon K. Poon

Event Log Generation: An Industry Perspective 123
   Timotheus Kampik and Mathias Weske

Foundations of Modeling and Method Engineering (EMMSAD 2022)

Towards a Systematic Method for Developing Meta Attack Language
Instances   139
   Simon Hacks, Sotirios Katsikeas, Engla Rencelj Ling, Wenjun Xiong,
   Jérôme Pfeiffer, and Andreas Wortmann

Enterprise, Business Process, and Capability Modeling (EMMSAD 2022)

Enterprise Modeling in Support Of Transparency in the Design and Use
of Software Systems   157
   Mario Nolte and Monika Kaczmarek-Heß

Uncertain Case Identifiers in Process Mining: A User Study of the
Event-Case Correlation Problem on Click Data.   173
   Marco Pegoraro, Merih Seran Uysal, Tom-Hendrik Hülsmann,
   and Wil M. P. van der Aalst

The Integration of Process Simulation Within the Business Architecture   188
   Ben Roelens and Louise Tierens

Information Systems and Requirements Modeling (EMMSAD 2022)

Blockchain Application Development Using Model-Driven Engineering
and Low-Code Platforms: A Survey   205
   Simon Curty, Felix Härer, and Hans-Georg Fill

Eliciting Ethicality Requirements Using the Ontology-Based Requirements
Engineering Method   221
   Renata Guizzardi, Glenda Amaral, Giancarlo Guizzardi,
   and John Mylopoulos

Agent Responsibility Framework for Digital Agents:
Roles and Responsibilities Related to Facets of Work   237
   Steven Alter

A Method for Ontology-Driven Minimum Viable Platform Development   253
   Thomas Derave, Tiago Prince Sales, Frederik Gailly, and Geert Poels

A Tool for Debugging Unsatisfiable Integrity Constraints in UML/OCL
Class Diagrams.   267
   Juan Antonio Gómez-Gutiérrez, Robert Clarisó, and Jordi Cabot

Domain-Specific and Knowledge Modeling (EMMSAD 2022)

Towards Simplification of ME-Maps.   279
   Azzam Maraee and Arnon Sturm

A Semi-automated Method for Domain-Specific Ontology Creation
from Medical Guidelines   295
  Omar ElAssy, Rik de Vendt, Fabiano Dalpiaz, and Sjaak Brinkkemper

Towards Access Control Models for Conversational User Interfaces   310
  Elena Planas, Salvador Martínez, Marco Brambilla, and Jordi Cabot

Evaluation of Modeling Approaches (EMMSAD 2022)

Exploratory Study on Students' Understanding of Multi-perspective
Modelling   321
  Charlotte Verbruggen and Monique Snoeck

Experiences from Developing a Web Crawler Using a Model-Driven
Development Tool: Emerging Opportunities   336
  David Mosquera, Anastassios Martakos, and Marcela Ruiz

Posters

Process Mining for Time Series Data.   347
  Tobias Ziolkowski, Agnes Koschmider, René Schubert,
  and Matthias Renz

Towards an Information Systems-driven Maturity Model for Industry 4.0. . . .   351
  Francesco Leotta, Jerin George Mathew, Flavia Monti,
  and Massimo Mecella

Author Index   355

Actual and Perceived Challenges
(BPMDS 2022)

Process Mining Challenges Perceived by Analysts: An Interview Study

Lisa Zimmermann[✉], Francesca Zerbato, and Barbara Weber

Institute of Computer Science, University of St. Gallen, St. Gallen, Switzerland
Lisa.Zimmermann@unisg.ch

Abstract. Process mining analysts need to work with event data to discover (business) processes, interpret results and report meaningful conclusions. Although process mining tools are constantly enhanced and advanced techniques are developed to enrich the functional scope in the field, little is known about the individual needs of analysts and the issues they face while conducting process mining projects. This paper aims to close this gap by uncovering perceived challenges occurring in practice. Based on an interview study with 41 participants, we identify and describe 23 challenges, spanning different project phases and directly affecting the work of process mining analysts. We discuss whether methods and techniques exist that can help to overcome these challenges and where further research is needed to devise new solutions and integrate existing ones better into process mining practice.

Keywords: Process mining · Challenges · Interview study · Process analysis · Work practices

1 Introduction

In the last two decades, the interest of companies to leverage, analyze and monetize their data has massively grown. Therefore, analysts are required to acquire, wrangle and explore data, build a statistical data model and report the obtained results [20]. Especially in the area of process mining [18], where specific algorithms are applied to event data to discover and improve (business) processes, the need for trained analysts familiar with different process mining tools is growing [9]. Although there is an increasing demand to attract analysts to work in process mining, little effort is made to better understand their ways of working [10] and particularly, how they approach the analysis phase [21].

With introducing their research framework, vom Brocke et al. [2] have just recently directed researchers towards the consideration of different levels in analyzing and contributing to the field. Particularly relevant to the context of this paper is the individual level they propose, in which attention is drawn to the "effects of process mining on people's interaction and mode of work".

However, individual entry hurdles and aspects hindering the implementation of process mining projects remain largely unconsidered in the research community so far. In this paper, we try to close this gap by shedding light on these,

A. Augusto et al. (Eds.): BPMDS 2022/EMMSAD 2022, LNBIP 450, pp. 3–17, 2022.
https://doi.org/10.1007/978-3-031-07475-2_1

so far unknown, aspects. In particular, we address the following research question (RQ): **"What are the challenges perceived by individual process analysts during a process mining project?"**. With this research question, we complement the previously published results from [11], who identified challenges in the context of process mining on the organizational level.

Having a comprehensive overview of existing process mining challenges allows us to better understand where there is a need to develop support for the daily work practices of analysts. In this way, the risk of a process mining initiative to fail could be mitigated and analysts would be supported to work efficiently.

To answer the research question, we analyzed data from a semi-structured interview study conducted with 41 process mining analysts from academia and industry. The interviews were conducted in the scope of a broader study during which all participants were asked about the challenges they have already experienced and those they perceive in process mining in general.

As an outcome of this paper, we present a catalog of 23 challenges perceived by individual process mining analysts. Then, we discuss whether approaches exist that can be applied in process mining and reflect on avenues for future research to devise novel solutions or integrate existing ones better into practice to support process analysts.

The rest of the paper is structured as follows. In Sect. 2, we discuss related work. Section 3 presents the research method and in Sect. 4 findings are reported, organized by the project phases they relate to. Then, we discuss the findings and limitations of our work in Sect. 5 and conclude the paper in Sect. 6.

2   Related Work

Our research focuses on challenges reported by individual process mining analysts. Therefore, we build upon existing work on (i) process mining challenges as well as more generally (ii) on challenges reported by data analysts in related fields, such as exploratory data analysis (EDA).

To our knowledge, there is no publication to date that explicitly reports challenges stated by process mining analysts regarding their individual perceptions during an analysis task. However, since general, technical and organizational challenges in process mining have already been reported selectively in other papers, our work is related to them.

One of the first publications in the field explicitly listing challenges is the process mining manifesto [18]. The authors describe 11 rather broad and generic shortcomings across all levels of process mining (e.g. "C2: Dealing with Complex Event Logs with Diverse Characteristics"), motivating researchers to develop and enhance algorithms and methods in different areas. Especially "C11: Improving understandability for Non-Experts" is closely connected to research at the individual level of process mining and remains topical. About six years later [13] reviewed the process mining literature and examined whether the challenges outlined in [18] remain open. Their findings show that despite the wealth of research published in the field over the years, none of the reported challenges have been satisfactorily and exhaustively solved. In [12], the authors report challenges of applying process mining in the healthcare domain, remarking some of the challenges of [18], such as the issues related to concept drift and data quality, but also reflecting on the needs of healthcare organizations, such as the involvement of patients and health stakeholders in process mining projects. Somewhat domain agnostic, [11] published their results of a Delphi Study focusing on opportunities and challenges associated with the use of process mining in enterprises. Based on their survey, the authors identified 32 challenges, three of which are extremely relevant in terms of their support from experts: *"Lack of management support"*, *"Poor data quality"* and *"Complex data preparation"*.

Next to related work on process mining challenges, we considered papers reporting challenges of individual data analysts in general. For example, the authors of [8] conducted semi-structured interviews with 35 data analysts to better understand the enterprise analysts' ecosystem and their challenges. They discuss challenges emerging in 12 different areas during five analysis phases. The authors in [20] follow a comparable method to [8] and extended previous work by the aspect of exploration within the data analysis.

Even though our work focuses on the identification of individual challenges, the boundaries between individual and organizational challenges may not be strictly separable for the individuals interviewed in our study. Therefore, we will compare our results to those of [11] and [8] in Sect. 5 and highlight where our work extends the reported results.

3   Research Method

In this section, we describe the design of our study and outline key aspects of the interview data collection and analysis.

Study Design. To investigate challenges perceived by analysts during a process mining project (cf. research question in Sect. 1), we followed a qualitative approach. Specifically, we designed an interview study as part of a broader observational study during which participants engaged in a realistic process mining task. The task served as an anchor for the interviewees to reflect upon a concrete analysis and challenges emerging in their work practices. To participate in our study, we required participants to: (i) have analyzed at least two real-life event logs in the past two years and (ii) be knowledgeable of at least one of the process mining tools available for the task.

Materials. We designed the process mining task to observe participants as they analyze the road traffic fine management event log [3] guided by a high-level question. The focus of the task was on the mining and analysis phase [5], i.e., we provided participants with a ready-to-use log for their analysis and allowed them to use one or more of the available process mining tools. The interview protocol consisted of semi-structured questions grouped into four parts: (i) activities and artifacts; (ii) goals; (iii) strategies; and (iv) challenges. All the questions were designed to be asked twice: the first time in the context of the process mining task; the second time regarding the participants' general work practices.

Execution. We recruited participants in our professional networks and via snowball sampling [6]. We collected the data in the summer of 2021 via virtual meetings with the participants. A few days before the meeting, we administered a background questionnaire to gather information about the participants' demographics, process mining experience and expertise. On the day of the meeting, we supervised the process mining task and conducted the interviews in a semistructured way, complementing our interview protocol with questions prompting participants to describe their work experiences within their current organization.

Participants. Overall, 41 people (21 practitioners and 20 academics) from 27 different organizations participated in our study. On average, the participants reported 4.5 years of experience in process mining and most of them indicated experience in related areas, such as data science and business intelligence. 11/20 academics also indicated experience in the process mining industry.

Data Validation and Analysis. Initially, we watched and transcribed the video recordings of the whole session and assessed data quality. On average, each session lasted 83 min, 30.5 min of which were dedicated to the interviews.

For the analysis, we followed a coding approach based on grounded theory [14], coding the whole interview in three rounds, with a focus on the questions asking explicitly about challenges. We considered all statements of the interviewees referring to perceived difficulties or obstacles arising when conducting process mining analyses, similar to the definition provided by [11]. First, we focused on analyzing participants individually and fragmented the text using "in-vivo" and open coding [14] to capture core concepts related to challenges. Then, we used axial coding to refine codes and aggregated them into categories. Finally, we relied on selective coding to focus on the most frequent categories and find relationships among them until we achieved saturation. As a threshold for selecting the final set of challenges, we considered the categories supported by at least 4 participants. Each coding round was conducted by one author and was followed by a check that the other authors conducted independently to ensure consistency. All the authors collaboratively contributed to revising and refining the codes. As a result, we obtained 23 challenges supported by 371 participants' statements. Since the challenges were related to different phases of process mining projects, we organized them along the phases described in [5].

The interested reader may find supplementary material including the interview questions, participants' details and the final coding scheme at https://doi.org/10.5281/zenodo.6422094.

4 Findings

In this section, we present the 23 challenges resulting from our analysis, organized in project phases ranging from "Defining Research Question", "Data Collection" and "Data Pre-Processing" over "Mining & Analysis" to "Stakeholder Evaluation" and "Implementation" [5]. In Fig. 1, we provide an overview of all the challenges. We did not identify any challenge for the "Implementation" phase, in which process improvement measures identified from previous phases are implemented. Four of the 23 identified challenges are considered overarching since the corresponding statements are associated with several project phases.

For each challenge, we report its name and the number of participants mentioning it. We indicate the count of practitioners (P) and academics (A) in the form of #/41 (P = #, A = #). For direct quotes, we note the participant ID (p#).

4.1 Defining Research Question

The first phase of a process mining project is characterized by planning the analysis and defining the research question [5]. 15/41 (P = 8, A = 7) participants reported three different challenges related to this phase.

The first challenge is named **"Question Formulation" (C1)**. 10/41 (P = 6, A = 4) participants stated that having a question is important because otherwise *"you can spend hours and hours doing something that doesn't have an impact"* (p24). However, the identification of a goal for the analysis and related research questions is perceived as difficult: *"it is very often hard to identify the correct question"* (p36). Analysts either struggle with the formulation of the questions, lack specifications from the process owner or report that the prescribed question is too broad or too narrow to enable a meaningful analysis. For example, p24 reported that he *"felt limited"* in one of his analyses because *"in this case [the question] was already specified"*.

The following challenge, **"Access and Use of Process Mining Tools" (C2)** was mentioned by 6/41 (P = 3, A = 3) participants. It includes problems related to the required infrastructure and access to process mining software. Participants reported that organizations *"do not have the tools implemented"* (p22) or that they are *"not sure how these tools can be applied"* (p25). In addition, participants also mentioned that usability *"is always an issue everywhere in our tools"* (p24) and often prevents them from using a certain tool.

Identifying the **"Process Mining Suitability" (C3)** was perceived as challenging by 4/41 (P = 3, A = 1) participants. It was pointed out that for *"a lot of the questions you don't need process mining to answer or you can use process mining as a tool in the toolbox where you have a lot of other tools that you use around"* (p12). It is considered difficult to identify process-mining-specific use cases and convince others about the usefulness of applying process mining. For example, p11 stated that *"it is hard for process mining consultants to convince people that it is something we should have, a new process mining project targeting this and that"*. As a result of these concerns, it is reported that process mining projects are not pursued or stopped in an early stage. Participant p34 stated that he analyzed event logs *"much less than I wanted to do and than it would be useful"* because stakeholders *"are not ready to start process mining studies"*.

Phase	ID	Challenge	Description The code combines statements related to perceived challenges ...	No.
Defining Research Question	C1	Question Formulation	...due to either **performing the project based on an external, prescribed goal**, due to working with a **loosely defined goal** or a **lack thereof** and covers **perceived challenges during the formulation of questions.**	10
	C2	Access and Use of Process Mining Tools	...due to the **unavailability of a process mining tool**, due to a **missing governance to structure the tool usage in the organization** or due to a **general low usability** which results in avoiding the application of a process mining tool.	6
	C3	Process Mining Suitability	...associated with the **application and selection of process mining as a suitable method** for a task. Covers the application of process mining on the individual level as well as its general application and governance in an organization.	4
Data Collection	C4	Data Extraction	...during the **retrieval, i.e., identification and extraction,** of event data from any kind of source.	11
	C5	Data Availability	...of **having enough data available for the analysis project.** This also covers the problem of process steps being conducted outside of the system from which data is available.	9
	C6	Data Access	...due to **missing permissions (legal, regulatory, organizational) to access the data.**	6
	C7	Source System & Data Structure Knowledge	...during the data collection **due to missing knowledge** about the **data structure** and the **source system** from which data is extracted (e.g., relational databases).	4
Pre-Processing	C8	Data Transformation	...during the **preparation of a process mining conformant event log** based on raw event data. It specifically covers **adding attributes or activities** to the event log and **finding the correct level of aggregation** depending on the case key.	17
	C9	Data Quality	...due to **low data quality** either in the **final event log** or already in the **raw data.**	15
	C10	Data Validation	...during **checking data accuracy** or the **suitability for process mining.**	5
Mining & Analysis	C11	Tool Knowledge	...associated with the **use of a specific process mining tool.** This covers **a lack of familiarity with the tool** or **not having the tool used for a long time.**	18
	C12	Event Log & Data Model Understanding	...associated with the **comprehension of the event log and the data model.** Also, covers **missing insights about the data structure** or problems caused by the **absence of elements they are used to** in a data model.	15
	C13	Process Mining Techniques	...related to **missing or insufficient supported functionalities of specific process mining tools** or in general including **missing support for combining certain functions and methodologies.**	14
	C14	Access to Additional Information	...due to a **lack of information or missing access** of the process analysts to this information.	10
	C15	Process Visualization	...due to a **misleading visualization of the event log** in form of a **directly-follows graph (DFG)** which can be found e.g., in the data map (Disco) or in the variant explorer (Celonis).	8
	C16	Analysis Experience	...due to a **subjective low level of prior experience as a process analyst.**	7
	C17	Analysis Focus	... of **maintaining the big picture** of the analysis **despite the available details.**	6
Evaluation	C18	Conclusions & Question Answering	... of **answering the research questions** and **drawing conclusions** based on the process discovery.	8
	C19	Recommendations & Next Steps	...of formulating a **concrete recommendation** or **deriving concrete next steps** to foster the improvement of the process.	4
All Phases	C20	Process Domain Understanding	...due to **a lack of/partial domain knowledge** or **unfamiliarity with domain-specific terminology** used in the documentation or activity and attribute descriptions.	22
	C21	Collaboration with Stakeholders	...during the communication due to **mismatching expectations, lack of understanding, different process perspectives and different backgrounds** of the process analysts and the business and IT stakeholders.	15
	C22	Business Process Complexity	...due to the **inherent complexity of business processes** and the dependencies among them.	10
	C23	Enablement / Training	...due to a **lack of available training opportunities** or **challenges while conceptualizing trainings.**	9

Fig. 1. Overview of all 23 identified challenges organized by process mining project phases [5]. For each challenge, we report a numeric ID identifying the challenge, its name, its description and the number of participants (No.) reporting the challenge.

4.2   Data Collection

In the "Data Collection" phase, the main goal is to understand and extract the data required for the process mining project [5]. In total, 23/41 (P = 14, A = 9) participants reported challenges related to this phase.

During **"Data Extraction"** (**C4**), which was reported to be challenging by 11/41 (P = 6, A = 5) participants, event data is extracted from source systems in which the process is executed. Participants stated that data extraction is time-consuming and that there are issues due to strong dependencies on third parties, such as IT departments. Analysts need to invest into *"explaining to the partners what [they] really need from them and what [they] really need from the data to be able to start"* (p15), which makes *"getting the total data sometimes the biggest challenge"* (p31). Additionally, participants emphasized challenges while identifying the right data (*"how do you find the data that you need in these huge databases?"* [p16]) and while consolidating the data from different sources.

When the data itself can be extracted, 9/41 (P = 6, A = 3) interviewees reported that **"Data Availability"** (**C5**) is a challenge in their projects. It includes the problem of having sufficiently comprehensive data to enable meaningful analyses. For example, p35 described: *"we had less or not enough event data to check because the process has been changed. And we didn't have that many cases and it wasn't enough to say if the process is working or not"*. Participants also reported that process steps are executed outside of the information systems. For example, when *"at the end you have maybe a letter that goes out and, in that case, to have a digital footprint of the whole process, is very difficult"* (p26). Ultimately, process mining *"is limited to what was recorded by the system"* (p8).

"Data Access" (**C6**) is required to determine what data should be collected but also to be able to understand the data. 6/41 (P = 5, A = 1) of the interviewed analysts described that they experienced challenges in their projects due to missing access to the raw data. They pointed out that legal restrictions or company internal data security/privacy policies limit access to data, making it challenging to get *"permission to get access to the data"* (p11). And indeed, the GDPR[1] and even stricter local regulations of personal data can limit process mining use cases [7].

Furthermore, specifically for practitioners, it is important to understand the functionality of the source system and the underlying database structure. For **"Source System & Data Structure Knowledge"** (**C7**) 4/41, (P = 4, A = 0), participants reported difficulties in understanding database models and were lacking *"system knowledge if it's not SAP and the standard process"* (p9). They experienced these difficulties because analysts are often *"not an expert on the system and the settings there"* (p9).

4.3   Data Pre-Processing

The "Data Pre-Processing" phase focuses on the creation of the event log. For this purpose, data quality is assessed and the process events are created [5], which

---

[1] https://www.gdpr.eu.

contain at least the case ID, event description, and event timestamp. Further information can be added as required [18]. 24/41 (P = 12, A = 12), i.e., more than half of the interviewees, reported challenges related to this phase.

The predominant category of challenges in this phase is **"Data Transformation" (C8)**, supported by 17/41 (P = 9, A = 8) participants. It was reported that data transformation is a *"very big part of each process mining initiative"* (p1), although *"it's not straightforward to put them in a process or in an event data or a XES format"* (p18; referring to data retrieved from an ERP System). Besides these general issues, there are more specific, subsidiary challenges related to adding event or attribute information to the event log/data model and finding the right aggregation level for the events. Participants reported that it feels like a *"philosophical question of which activities to add"* (p39) and that not having defined appropriate events is problematic because *"if you don't have those activities, it can be quite hard to yeah, to refine your analysis"* (p14) later on.

The challenge of **"Data Quality" (C9)** was raised by 15/41 (P = 6, A = 9) participants from our study. Interviewees reported that data pre-processing is *"quite challenging because the industrial data, the sensor data... sometimes the quality is very poor"*, and that *"data quality and event log quality are the most important challenge for the further analysis"* (p28). Data quality issues can be manifold, but *"noise in the data"* (p16), problems in the format of the date fields and missing timestamps were particularly prominent in our interviews.

Closely related to poor data quality is also the assessment of data quality, referred to as **"Data Validation" (C10)**, to ensure that data are correct, complete and representative of the process to be analyzed. 5/41 (P = 3, A = 2) participants reported that it is time-consuming *"to check if the data is ok and accurate"* (p35) and that validation is an important step not only in process mining but also in many data-based analysis methods because *"you will always get an answer but the data will not tell you that the answer is invalid"* (p12).

4.4   Mining and Analysis

In the "Mining & Analysis" phase, analysts apply process mining techniques to explore event logs [5]. 38/41 (P = 19, A = 19) of the interviewed participants reported challenges during this phase of the process mining project.

About half of the participants, 18/41 (P = 8, A = 10) reported difficulties connected to their **"Tool Knowledge" (C11)**. They stated that they *"didn't feel very comfortable with the tool"* (p8) or that they *"had to apply filters and [were] not sure where to find it"* (p10). Participant p15 summarized that the tools *"work all in a very similar way and they basically use the same algorithms. But, remembering where those patterns are and how to click in the right sequence, it's not always easy"*. This leads to the assumption that tools require a certain level of expertise and training to perform an efficient and meaningful analysis. However, when looking at the background questionnaires (cf. Sect. 3) only two of the 18 participants reporting this challenge ranked themselves as 'slightly familiar' with process mining tools, while all the others were moderately, very or extremely familiar with process mining software.

Another important aspect during the analysis phase is the **"Event Log &
Data Model Understanding" (C12)**, for which 15/41 (P = 8, A = 7) participants described challenges. They include difficulties in understanding attributes
of the event log (*"the main challenge was to understand the attributes of this
event log because many of them had a similar name"* [p41]) as well as *"understanding the data model"*, which *"is probably the biggest challenge"* (p14). Indeed,
different process mining tools support different kinds of data structures. While
some participants are used to work with a data model based on several tables,
other tools are designed to load only one table representing the event log.

Challenges related to the available analysis techniques and their combination
are covered in the category **"Process Mining Techniques" (C13)** which was
supported by 14/41 (P = 8, A = 6) of the interviewees. Although techniques continue to evolve and new features are constantly added into tools [9], challenges
related to the technical maturity of root cause analysis based on process data,
the combination of process mining and robotic process automation (RPA), the
"inability of any algorithm to split labels based on context" (p39) and shortcomings in the configuration of the dotted chart in ProM are reported to still exist. Of
this list, dissatisfaction with results based on the integrated root causes analysis
was most frequently mentioned. Participants noted that *"conformance analysis
is extremely complex and resource consuming"* (p3) and pose the question: *"How
can we bring in and integrate process mining, maybe with other tools or improve
its own methodologies in theory to help finding the root causes?"* (p1).

"Access to Additional Information" (C14) was remarked as challenging by 10/41 (P = 7, A = 3) participants. They stated that *"it's often the case
that we need some additional knowledge to really get into an event log"* (p8), but
at the same time do not have access to *"good documentation"* (p34). Access to
stakeholders as a source of information is required, but also perceived as challenging. Participant p17 reported: *"These are all assumptions that we make, so
we need to have like a confirmation from the business that's actually a right,
attribute that you need to have a look into"*. If access to stakeholders is not available during this phase, analysts are limited to *"check what was obvious"* (p7).

The **"Process Visualization" (C15)** covers challenges reported by 8/41
(P = 2, A = 6) participants. Out of the interviewees, especially academics referred
to the directly-follows graph (DFG) representation as an unsolved challenge, but
also practitioners reported that they *"don't trust the maps [...] because of this
slider, we see paths, which already means you don't see variants. You see paths,
the most frequent paths. And that's not the same thing, I mean, that's not something that really happens"* and stated that *"you cannot already tell from seeing
the map, ok, that's how it behaves because there's some paths missing"* (p37).

A completely different aspect, namely the prior **"Analysis Experience"
(C16)** is reported to be a challenge by 7/41 (P = 3, A = 4) participants. Without further elaboration, participants stated that they *"don't have that much
practice, so it [the analysis] was challenging in general"* (p10) and that the
"process mining is very, very easy to learn and I think time consuming to really

master it" (p13). Apparently, learning the *"way of thinking as a process mining analysts"* (p22) requires time and experience.

The last challenge we identified for the "Mining & Analysis" phase is **"Analysis Focus" (C17)**. Statements from 6/41 participants (P = 6, A = 0), all practitioners, are related to this challenge. It is reported that it is difficult to stop the analysis at a certain point because there is always the risk of *"diving deep into one specific [aspect] but actually loosing the big picture"* (p24). Analysts can *"lose themselves too quickly into the details"* (p25) partially because it is *"hard to not deviate from your original aim"* (p26).

4.5   Stakeholder Evaluation

During the "Stakeholder Evaluation" phase, the process mining analyst presents and discusses insights from the analysis and answers the research question. Meanwhile, tangible conclusions and next steps are suggested for improving the process regarding identified shortcomings [5]. The challenges encountered in this phase are supported by 11/41 (P = 7, A = 4) participants of our study.

One important aspect of the stakeholder evaluation is to find causality to answer the research question. However 8/41 (P = 4, A = 4) participants reported that they struggle with **"Conclusions & Question Answering" (C18)**. It was stated that there is a danger of jumping to wrong conclusions (*"you have the data loaded and the data are correct, it's fairly easy to do an analysis, so a major pitfall is that you jump to incorrect conclusions"* [p11]), and the majority of the interviewees agreed that it is generally difficult to *"come to, let's say, hard conclusions or to find let's say, OK, this is really what we should change now"* (p20). One of the interviewed analysts additionally links the problem to C13 ("Process Mining Techniques") and stated that *"process mining cannot answer all the questions you have. You need to combine it with all the approaches to identify all the features that affect your process in order to answer the whys, why something is not working"* (p3).

After analysts have derived conclusions, stakeholders are often interested in next steps. 4/41 (P = 3, A = 1) participants stated challenges connected to **"Recommendations & Next Steps" (C19)**. For example, participant p4 stated: *"I think it's challenging to answer this question with recommendation of what to do afterwards"* and indeed, process mining shows *"where your issues are, but it's not helping you to solve them"* (p17). Although it could be argued that this aspect is outside of the defined scope of process discovery [18], four of the interviewed participants considered this a challenge and expect *"recommendations or proposals to change the process"* (p25) to come out of a process mining project.

4.6   Challenges Ranging Across All Phases

In addition to the challenges that could be mapped to one of the process mining phases [5], four additional challenges emerged, spanning across (parts of) the project. They are supported by 34/41 (P = 19, A = 15) participants.

22/41 (P = 13, A = 9) analysts reported challenges around **"Process Domain Understanding" (C20)**. Both, acquiring domain knowledge as well as performing various activities throughout the project in the absence of domain knowledge are perceived as challenging. This seems to not be surprising considering that *"without domain knowledge, you won't achieve much or nothing at all"* (p38). Even though associated with all phases, participants explicitly pointed out the shortcomings during the analysis of the process: *"Business knowledge is something that one really needs to have when analyzing the process"* (p17) because *"if you have more of the domain knowledge, you would know like which path to check first"* (p14). Thus, domain knowledge supports the analysis process and leads analysts to more relevant, business-related findings.

Another group of statements is tied to the **"Collaboration with Stakeholders" (C21)**. 15/41 (P = 9, A = 6) participants reported problems due to stakeholder expectations regarding the process mining technique, different backgrounds of the parties involved (e.g. IT versus business), little or different levels of understanding of process mining, and reluctance of stakeholders to work together with the process mining analyst. Regarding the latter aspect, participants speculated that stakeholders *"don't want that somebody external of their business puts his eyes on it"* (p34) and stated that they are *"hitting a wall"* (p34) within their organizations. Compared to the challenge of not having access to the stakeholder during the analysis (C14) this challenge rather connects to having the stakeholders, but that *"communicating effectively what process mining can and should do to people from businesses is maybe the biggest challenge"* (p36).

The **"Business Process Complexity" (C22)** covers challenges related to the interplay between departments, complex IT landscapes and the resulting intricacy of organizations and processes executed within them. 10/41 (P = 5, A = 5) participants reported that *"in process mining you have the problem that you have this complex behavior"* and that *"real processes, with several process objects are more complex than, let's say, the standard process coming from the vendors"* (p33). Demonstrated use cases of process mining often fail to address business reality. Some of our participants mentioned this challenges in the context of designing the business questions or in the context of the analysis of 'spaghetti-like' processes with many events and endpoints.

Detached from the actual process analysis itself, 9/41 (P = 6, A = 3) participants addressed problems during or due to the **"Enablement/Training" (C23)**. Analysts, who have been involved in training colleagues or academics who teach process mining, reported that it is challenging to provide the correct level of knowledge and to plan the training in a way that it is appropriate for the target group, e.g., for *"students, which are not computer scientists at all"* (p36) or *"for beginners"* where the problem is *"that there are lots of very different fields that you have to have some kind of basic understanding like how process models look like and, um uh, well, basic algorithms and not to misinterpret the process models that you get at the beginning like directly-follows graphs"* (p15). Additionally, one participant reported that it is challenging to find the courses and pointed out that available trainings and lectures should be better promoted.

Concluding, based on interviews with 41 participants, we identified 23 challenges, each one supported by at least four interviewees. We can observe that especially C3, C6, C7, C17 and C19 are mainly perceived by practitioners, whereas all other challenges are reported across the different sectors the participants were working in at the time the interviews were conducted. Based on the explanations given by the interviewees, we related 19 challenges to process mining project phases [5] and identified four cross-cutting challenges occurring in and affecting all project phases. We couldn't identify any significant correlation between single challenges and the self-rated expertise or experience of the participants reporting the challenge.

5 Discussion

In this section, we will review the identified challenges, link them to related work, and discuss whether technical or methodological approaches exist that can help process analysts to overcome them.

Among our findings, one first major cluster of challenges concerns data-related ones. All of these challenges fall into the data collection and pre-processing phase (C4-C6 and C8-C10) and include availability, access, quality, validation, extraction, and transformation. Such challenges have already been discovered in different fields, for example, considering data as a prerequisite for data science projects. The authors of [8] and [20] identified comparable challenges from their interview studies around the acquisition of data, working with different amounts or forms of data and dealing with concrete data quality issues. However, comparable challenges have also been discovered in process mining, where "data" mainly refers to the special format of event logs. The authors in [11] identified specific data-related challenges, referred to as C.4, C.7–C.9, C.12 and C.14, which they mainly captured in the area of governance on the organizational level. Based on our study, we can confirm that these challenges are not only perceived at the organizational level but also affect the work of individuals. Especially C5 and C10 extend challenges reported in [11] by bringing in an individual perspective.

Several approaches have already been proposed to tackle specific aspects of these data-related challenges. For example, Suriadi et al. [15] proposed a structured approach to deal with quality issues in event logs, while Diba et al. [4] provided an overview of existing methods to extract event log data (C4) and create meaningful abstractions (C8). However, for most existing approaches, major shortcomings are reported [4] and their integration into many of the process mining tools is limited. As a result, their broad application in practice is missing [1]. Our work suggests that further research in this direction is required and that existing techniques will need to be better integrated into commonly used data pre-processing tools to support analysts in overcoming data-related challenges and lower the entry hurdle for creating event logs of good quality.

Another group of challenges that we observed is connected to the adoption of process mining by the analysts themselves but also by project stakeholders with whom the analysts interact (C2–C3, C11, C16, C21 and C23). These challenges span across all process mining project phases apart from the data collection and pre-processing phase and include limited access to process mining tools, non-suitability of process mining for the analysis or problems in the collaboration with stakeholders, who might not be willing to share information or do not trust the results of the process discovery. While some of our challenges overlap with organizational challenges reported in [11] (in particular C.23–C.32 on the cultural level), others seem to be more tight to the individual level (especially C2, C11 and C23 from our work) and go beyond what was reported by [11].

To overcome difficulties regarding the adoption of new technologies, different approaches and methods have been proposed over the last decades in various fields, such as manufacturing or information systems [17,19]. However, in the area of process mining only first attempts exist to better understand the transition of stakeholders from old practices to the usage of process mining [7,16], and aspects such as training and enablement have received little attention. Hence, we conclude that access to comprehensive trainings and a deeper understanding of the required skill set of process mining analysts is still missing.

Further challenges emerged, revolving around the individual understanding of the analysts (C7, C12, and C17–C20), such as understanding the process domain and the event log, or having issues with answering the research question and deriving improvement recommendations. These challenges occur mainly in late project phases, i.e., the mining & analysis and the stakeholder evaluation phases. We observed that these challenges are especially related to the individual level since there is limited support for them in the findings of Martin et al. [11]. While the authors in [11] identify challenges like the insufficient domain expertise (C.20) or incomprehensible outcomes (C.16) and insufficient prescriptive capabilities of process mining tools (C.17) on the organizational level, the angle from which these challenges are covered differs from our findings and cannot be connected to the understanding of individuals. Based on our knowledge, there exists little support to help analysts guide their analysis based on the research question and reduce the risk of losing the analysis focus and there is limited guidance for understanding event logs and data model structures [21]. Besides, the authors in [5] even observed that the thoroughness of reports for the stakeholder evaluation phase is decreasing in published case studies in the area of process mining. Thus, we think that research on the factors determining the understanding of analysts needs to be enhanced to enable the implementation of targeted support.

To summarize, we discovered that although approaches exist to tackle some of the discussed challenges, their application in process mining practice is limited. We observed a mismatch between the solutions provided by existing approaches, which are oftentimes targeting technical problems, and the challenges faced by individual process mining analysts in practice. We encourage future research to take the individual perspective into account by proposing new methodologies and evaluating existing ones based on their effectiveness on the work of individuals.

Limitations. Since the data supporting our findings was gathered during semi-structured interviews, our work comes with some limitations typical of interview studies. First, we only present and discuss challenges that were directly derived from the data, meaning that they were explicitly stated by our participants. Therefore, there is a possibility that our findings are not complete, since our participants might have not been able to recall and describe all the challenges they face in their work practices. Additionally, the perception of what constitutes a challenge may be subjective and can vary across participants. Nevertheless, in order to obtain valid and reproducible results, we selected a sample of more than 40 interviewees and only considered challenges that were reported by at least 4 individuals. Moreover, the interviews directly followed an analysis task and thus, reported challenges may be biased by the recent experience of conducting this specific task. Still, the study was designed to be representative of typical process analysis tasks and the interviewees were also asked to consider general challenges and difficulties. Interviews anchored to other types of tasks or triangulated with behavioral data can help to complement and generalize our findings.

6   Conclusion

In this paper, we focused on process mining challenges from an individual perspective. Based on the analysis of 41 interviews conducted with practitioners and academics working in the field, we identified 23 challenges. All of these challenges hinder the work of individual analysts, preventing them from working efficiently and effectively and, in the worst case, discouraging them from conducting further projects in their organizations. While focusing on the individual perspective, we identified that the discovered challenges also affect the organizational, group and technical levels. Although approaches exist to address these challenges, most of them have not been applied to the field of process mining yet and the assessment of their ability to support individual analysts during a process mining project remains open. In the future, we plan to continue our work to better understand the factors that cause process mining challenges and individual support needs. Besides, we aim to investigate potential approaches and solutions that experienced analysts implement to overcome the challenges, paving the way for easier access and improved use of process mining, especially for novices.

Acknowledgment. We thank participants for taking time to participate in the study and for sharing their experience. *Funding.* This work is part of the ProMiSE project, funded by the Swiss National Science Foundation under Grant No.: 200021_197032.

References

1. Andrews, R., et al.: Leveraging data quality to better prepare for process mining: an approach illustrated through analysing road trauma pre-hospital retrieval and transport processes in Queensland. Int. J. Environ. Res. Public. Health. **16**(7), 1138 (2019)
2. vom Brocke, J., Jans, M., Mendling, J., Reijers, H.A.: A five-level framework for research on process mining. Bus. Inf. Syst. Eng. **63**(5), 483–490 (2021). https://doi.org/10.1007/s12599-021-00718-8

3. De Leoni, M., Mannhardt, F.: Road Traffic Fine Management Process. Eindhoven University of Technology, Dataset (2015)
4. Diba, K., Batoulis, K., Weidlich, M., Weske, M.: Extraction, correlation, and abstraction of event data for process mining. WIREs Data Mining Knowl. Discov. **10**(3), e1346 (2020)
5. Emamjome, F., Andrews, R., ter Hofstede, A.H.M.: A case study lens on process mining in practice. In: Panetto, H., Debruyne, C., Hepp, M., Lewis, D., Ardagna, C.A., Meersman, R. (eds.) OTM 2019. LNCS, vol. 11877, pp. 127–145. Springer, Cham (2019). https://doi.org/10.1007/978-3-030-33246-4_8
6. Goodman, L.A.: Snowball sampling. Ann. math. stat. 148–170 (1961)
7. Grisold, T., Mendling, J., Otto, M., vom Brocke, J.: Adoption, use and management of process mining in practice. Bus. Process Manag. J. (2020)
8. Kandel, S., Paepcke, A., Hellerstein, J.M., Heer, J.: Enterprise data analysis and visualization: an interview study. IEEE Trans. Vis. Comput. Graph. **18**(12), 2917–2926 (2012)
9. Kerremans, M., Searle, S., Srivastava, T., Iijima, K.: Market Guide For Process Mining. Gartner Inc. (2020)
10. Klinkmüller, C., Müller, R., Weber, I.: Mining process mining practices: an exploratory characterization of information needs in process analytics. In: Hildebrandt, T., van Dongen, B.F., Röglinger, M., Mendling, J. (eds.) BPM 2019. LNCS, vol. 11675, pp. 322–337. Springer, Cham (2019). https://doi.org/10.1007/978-3-030-26619-6_21
11. Martin, N., et al.: Opportunities and challenges for process mining in organisations: results of a Delphi study. Bus. Inf. Syst. Eng. **63**, 1–7 (2021)
12. Munoz-Gama, J., et al.: Process mining for healthcare: characteristics and challenges. J. Biomed. Inform. **127**, 103994 (2022)
13. R'Bigui, H., Cho, C.: The state-of-the-art of business process mining challenges. Int. J. Bus. Process. Integr. Manag. **8**(4), 285–303 (2017)
14. Saldaña, J.: The Coding Manual For Qualitative Researchers. Sage, Thousand Oaks (2015)
15. Suriadi, S., Andrews, R., ter Hofstede, A.H., Wynn, M.T.: Event log imperfection patterns for process mining: towards a systematic approach to cleaning event logs. Inf. Syst. **64**, 132–150 (2017)
16. Syed, R., Leemans, S.J.J., Eden, R., Buijs, J.A.C.M.: Process mining adoption. In: Fahland, D., Ghidini, C., Becker, J., Dumas, M. (eds.) BPM 2020. LNBIP, vol. 392, pp. 229–245. Springer, Cham (2020). https://doi.org/10.1007/978-3-030-58638-6_14
17. Taherdoost, H.: A review of technology acceptance and adoption models and theories. Proc. Manuf. **22**, 960–967 (2018)
18. van der Aalst, W., et al.: Process mining manifesto. In: Daniel, F., Barkaoui, K., Dustdar, S. (eds.) BPM 2011. LNBIP, vol. 99, pp. 169–194. Springer, Heidelberg (2012). https://doi.org/10.1007/978-3-642-28108-2_19
19. Venkatesh, V., Thong, J.Y., Xu, X.: Unified theory of acceptance and use of technology: a synthesis and the road ahead. J. Assoc. Inf. Syst. **17**(5), 328–376 (2016)
20. Wongsuphasawat, K., Liu, Y., Heer, J.: Goals, Process, and Challenges of Exploratory Data Analysis: An Interview Study. arXiv:1911.00568 (2019)
21. Zerbato, F., Soffer, P., Weber, B.: Initial insights into exploratory process mining practices. In: Polyvyanyy, A., Wynn, M.T., Van Looy, A., Reichert, M. (eds.) BPM 2021. LNBIP, vol. 427, pp. 145–161. Springer, Cham (2021). https://doi.org/10.1007/978-3-030-85440-9_9

Towards Process-Oriented IIoT Security Management: Perspectives and Challenges

Stefan Schönig[(✉)], Markus Hornsteiner, and Christoph Stoiber

University of Regensburg, Regensburg, Germany
{stefan.schoenig,markus.hornsteiner,christoph.stoiber}@ur.de

Abstract. The Industrial Internet of Things (IIoT) enables the connection of industrial operational technology (OT) with information technology (IT). However, the convergence of IT and OT has the drawback that machines become increasingly vulnerable to cyber attacks. Therefore, security aspects for OT areas require special attention. The integration of Security Operations Centers (SOC) and OT offers a possible solution approach. A SOC is related to the people, processes and technologies that provide awareness through the detection, containment, and remediation of IT threats. The basis for integrating an IIoT-based SOC are well defined processes and their information needs. In this respect, the discipline of Business Process Management (BPM) offers numerous established methods, concepts and technologies for the systematic modeling and system-supported execution and analysis of processes. This paper aims to highlight the opportunities that the application of BPM concepts holds for IIoT security management. Based on the IIoT security management process, we show several exemplary ways how to leverage BPM methods for improving IIoT security.

Keywords: Internet of Things · Process management · IIoT security

1 Introduction

Within the Industry 4.0 paradigm, the aim is to create horizontal or vertical integrations of production systems and classical information systems. In this regard, especially the Industrial Internet of Things (IIoT) offers a compendium of technologies from the Internet of Things (IoT) to automate and network production systems. This networking is achieved by connecting industrial operational technology (OT) with information technology (IT). OT includes the systems needed to control and monitor physical devices such as machines or plants. The convergence of IT and OT stands for the integration of both systems. This convergence leads to more efficient systems and enables new solutions. However, the convergence of IT and OT has an important drawback: machines and plants become vulnerable to external attack due to holistic networking and the renunciation from closed, proprietary systems [1]. It is important to understand

© Springer Nature Switzerland AG 2022
A. Augusto et al. (Eds.): BPMDS 2022/EMMSAD 2022, LNBIP 450, pp. 18–26, 2022.
https://doi.org/10.1007/978-3-031-07475-2_2

that cyber security is a joint and overarching task of IT and OT areas. The convergence of IT and OT increases the extent of damage from cyber attacks in a dramatic way as incidents in one of the two domains can directly affect and damage the other. Therefore, security aspects for IIoT environments require special attention and new solutions for maintaining cyber security are necessary. The integration of *Security Operations Centers (SOC)* and OT offers a possible solution approach [2]. SOC have established themselves as a centralized unit for improving cyber security. A SOC is related to the people, processes and technologies that provide situational awareness through the detection, containment, and remediation of IT threats in order to manage and enhance an organization's security posture [2]. SOCs in IIoT environments can enable a holistic view of cyber security in manufacturing operations to accurately identify attack vectors, avert potential attacks or derive measures to prevent control system failure [2]. The basis for designing and integrating an IIoT-based SOC are well defined processes and their information needs of the corresponding industrial environment. Based thereon risks can be identified, protective measures can be taken and security incidents can be monitored within the SOC. Against this background, the discipline of Business Process Management (BPM) offers numerous established methods, concepts and technologies for the systematic modeling and system-supported execution and analysis of operational processes [3]. We claim that BPM methods represent an unexploited source for improving cyber security in manufacturing companies. This paper aims to highlight the opportunities that the application of BPM concepts and technologies holds for IIoT security management. Based on the latest IIoT security management process of the VDI/VDE [4], we show some exemplary ways how to leverage BPM methods for improving IIoT security. This paper is structured as follows: Sect. 2 briefly presents the phases of the IIoT security management process. Section 3 shows the opportunities where BPM concepts can support. Section 4 discusses open research gaps and challenges, whereas Sect. 5 summarizes the paper and gives an outlook of future research.

2   IIoT Security Management Process

There are regulatory efforts to establish the implementation of security measures like IEC62443 in the EU as a standard [5]. These require an implementation of the security by design paradigm. The latest VDI/VDE standard paper *IT-security for industrial automation* [4] describes how specific measures can be implemented in order to guarantee the IT-security of automated plants. Here, aspects of the automation devices, automation systems, and automation applications used are considered. In addition, a uniform, feasible procedure for ensuring IT-security throughout the entire life cycle of automation devices, systems, and applications is described. The guideline proposes a simple process comprising eight phases for processing and presenting information security (cf. Fig. 1). These phases enable the analysis of the status quo, the assessment of security threats and risks, and the implementation of protective measures that are appropriate

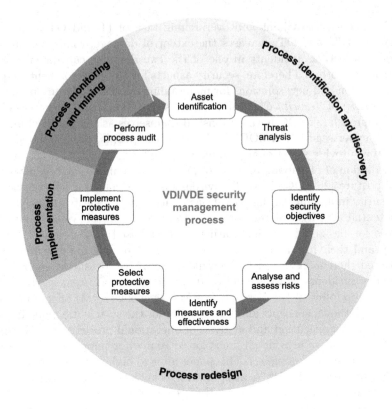

Fig. 1. IIoT security process and potential support of BPM methods

for the specific and individual need for protection. The concrete phases of the lifecycle are as follows: *(i) Asset identification:* The goal of this phase is the definition of a target state as well as the identification of all OT and IT assets and their necessary connections. *(iii) Threat analysis:* The goal of this step is to identify relevant threats for each asset under consideration. When analyzing threat scenarios, the potential organizational, technical and user-related threats must be systematically identified. *(iii) Identify relevant protection objectives:* This step specifies the protection objectives at risk from the identified threats for each asset listed. *(iv) Analyze and assess risks:* In this step, the existing risks arising from threats are analyzed and evaluated. To this end, the probabilities of occurrence of the threats identified in the previous step and thus potential for the object of consideration are to be estimated. *(v) Identify protective measures and evaluate effectiveness:* This step describes protective measures and implementations of protective measures against threats. *(vi) Select protective measures:* The aim of this step is to select from the large number of protective measures listed those that can be combined and that provide an appropriate, economically viable overall solution. *(vii) Implement protective measures:* Once the overall solution to be implemented has been determined, the individual protective measures must be implemented in the overall context. In this context, an operational concept must be designed to ensure the sustainable implementation of the solution. *(viii) Perform process audit:* In the audit, all steps of the described process model that led to the security breach are reviewed. The review is performed according to the following characteristics: Were all process steps performed? Has an assessment of the results been made for each process step? In the following section we outline how principles of the BPM discipline can support the different phases of the security management processes.

3   Perspectives for Process-Driven IIoT Security

Similar to the VDI/VDE IIoT security management process, the BPM lifecycle encompasses a range of methods and tools to identify and manage individual processes. It constitutes an enterprise capability to enable consistently positive outcomes and deliver maximum value to the organization [3]. In this section, we show where concepts and principles of the BPM lifecycle can be applied to support IIoT security management (cf. Fig. 1).

3.1   Process-Oriented Asset Identification and Threat Analysis

To conduct a sustainable security management, it is necessary to know the corporate assets that must be protected, e.g., process know-how in the sense of production parameters or critical control devices. Hence, it is necessary to identify value-adding processes, document the components and information involved, and then derive the need for protection. In addition to the critical assets, relevant communication relationships, components and people involved in them as well as various data streams must be recorded. In production, a complete overview of the existing assets is rarely available. The concepts, principles, and technologies of BPM, in particular the first phase of the BPM cycle "process identification and modeling", can be used here in a promising way. Production processes, involved actors and components as well as the necessary security requirements and technologies can be mapped in process models by means of common modeling notations. The advantage lies in the easily understandable and multidisciplinary language that process models offer. The current situation is modelled in as-is process models (*cf. Asset identification*) that are understandable for both shop floor employees and IT security experts. Based on these models, potentially critical security gaps and threats can be identified (*cf. Threat analysis*). Using appropriate modelling notations, i.e., notations that provide modeling elements for IIoT objects as well as security aspects, to-be process models can then be developed. These include a revised security concept of the modelled production processes (*cf. Identify relevant protection objectives, identify and select protective measures*). Again, the advantage here lies in the multidisciplinary nature of the modeling notations, since both shop-floor processes and communication as well as IT processes can be mapped within one single model.

3.2 Process-Oriented Risk and Measure Assessment

After the identification of assets and potential threats, and the development of revised processes and security concepts, an extensive assessment is required. This does not only include the assessment of risks that emerge from the identified threats, but also the assessment of methods to mitigate these risks. Established principles of "process redesign" and Business Process Improvement have proven to be effective to (1) assess risks and approaches, (2) define requirements, and (3) provide tools for a goal-oriented selection [6]. The goal is to identify changes to the as-is state that would help to address the security risks and to achieve the defined objectives. On the basis of the created as-is process models, existing threats can be translated into risks by including further process and OT as well as IT information. This can be supported by process risk assessment methods, e.g., Failure Mode and Effects Analysis (FMEA). Eventually, potential measures to mitigate risks must be assessed to create a decision-basis for a goal oriented selection. Multiple options must be analyzed and compared while the most promising ones are combined into a redesigned and improved to-be state. Established analysis and redesign methods as well as general principles of process redesign can be adopted for the IIoT security management process.

3.3 Process-Oriented Measure Implementation

After the identification of security gaps and requirements and the development of revised processes and security concepts, these concepts must be implemented (*cf. Implement protective measures*). For this phase of the IIoT security management process, the methods and principles of BPM offer extensive support. For example, read or write access to certain machine and process parameters can be made directly dependent on the current situation or progress within a running process by means of task-based access control mechanisms. Also attribute-based access control mechanisms can control the access to process tasks or IIoT devices based on predefined attributes and their thresholds. In this respect, a mutual access control principle can be defined: IIoT data can grant or prohibit access to specific process tasks, while also data from tasks can grant or prohibit access to associated IIoT devices. This leads to more secure operations within organizations, as a mutual control of authorization can be implemented that includes physical machines and tasks and activities represented as process models. Furthermore, by integrating OT and IT into processes, security response processes can be triggered automatically in the event of security anomalies during operation. This enables a shorter response time and reduces negative outcomes.

3.4 Process-Oriented Monitoring and Security Process Audit

The integration of a SOC into production environments provides the basis for comprehensive security monitoring. The goal is to combine real-time data from a digital twin, i.e., network data, machine data, and executed process models within a SOC. The integration and system-supported monitoring of modelled processes by means of the SOC enables automated compliance with modeled security concepts and security requirements, such that deviations are no longer possible. In addition, BPM methods and technologies provide a broad basis for the audit phase of the security process (*cf. Carry out process audit*). On the one hand, the as-is process models serve directly as documentation of the initial situation. On the other hand, to-be process models serve as a starting point for auditing threat analyses performed and the protective measures implemented. Furthermore, event log analyses during ongoing operation of the SOC offer enormous analysis potential. By applying process mining to event logs of executed and integrated IIoT and security processes in the SOC, compliance with security policies can be verified and traced. In particular, the implementation of key security *requirements such as accountability, auditability, and non-repudiation* can be accomplished through existing process analysis methods. Additional potential is created by the extensive data available in the SOC. For example, event logs can be derived from network communication protocols and analyzed in combination with activity-centric event logs of processes.

4 Challenges and Intersections

However, there are still a number of challenges to the successful and industrially usable implementation of process-driven IIoT security management.

4.1 Modelling Notations for IIoT- and Security-Aware Processes

Process modeling languages must be designed or extended to fully represent security requirements and possible protective measures. On the one hand, new elements for modeling IIoT assets in production processes [7] and their communication are needed and, on the other hand, modeling constructs for OT security concepts. While some language extensions of BPMN already exist for security aspects in the classical IT domain [8], language constructs for OT security are still missing. There is already research about mapping security aspects in BPMN. For example, [9] integrates the security requirements *Confidentiality, Integrity, and Availability (CIA)* in BPMN. However, there is no approach that explicitly considers IIoT security aspects. To represent security and IIoT aspects in business processes, both concepts must be represented accordingly in one single notation. However, such an integrated notation is still missing.

4.2 Process Modelling Guidelines and Procedures

A method for process modeling not only includes a notation, e.g., BPMN, but also a systematic procedure for eliciting the processes under consideration and the entities involved [10]. Guidelines and procedure models for eliciting models already exist for classic business processes [11]. However, the domains of the IIoT and the associated and necessary OT security require new and adapted procedures and modeling guidelines. For example, process discovery and elicitation methods such as workshops and employee surveys must be adapted to the given domain and redesigned. Due to the additional number of modeling elements for IIoT objects and security aspects, the resulting process models become increasingly complex and potentially difficult to understand. Therefore, novel abstraction methods or interactive modeling and visualization concepts need to be conceived, realized and industrially evaluated.

4.3 Executable Process Models

In order to be able to systematically monitor OT processes and ensure compliance with security aspects, the system-supported execution of the modeled processes within the SOC is necessary. To implement executable models, the designed extensions must be defined not only syntactically but also semantically. Furthermore, automated mappings from model attributes to attributes in security description languages must be developed. For example, access rights to IIoT devices and their variables defined in the process model can be transformed to *eXtensible Access Control Markup Language (XACML)* using an automated mapping. This way, system-supported control and monitoring of access to IIoT objects is implemented. Context attributes of wearable process user interfaces [12], such as current location information, could be used to implement task- and attribute-based access control mechanisms. Here, interfaces for location information to process engines need to be implemented and evaluated.

4.4 Process Analytics for IIoT and Security

Process analysis methods can be used to verify compliance with security policies and document security incidents. The implementation of key security requirements such as accountability, auditability, and non-repudiation can be accomplished through existing process analysis methods. For example, process mining techniques can be used to analyze and improve incidence response processes that at best have been recorded in event logs using a process-based SOC. In many cases, however, recorded process data must first be converted into suitable formats and missing but necessary information extracted from additional data sources such as digital twins. For example, network traffic logs can be used as a basis for extracting OT process knowledge. From these logs, the communication between entities involved in the process can be extracted and reconstructed using network analysis techniques such as [13]. To discover actual process models from network traffic logs, however, case identifiers must be derived from additional data. Furthermore, new or adjusted process mining techniques need to be developed that explicitly take into account security aspects in IIoT environments.

5 Conclusion and Outlook

This paper outlines the need for developing new solutions to improve security in IIoT environments. SOC in IIoT environments can enable a holistic view of cyber security in industrial operations. We showed that the BPM discipline offers numerous established principles, methods, concepts, and technologies for the systematic modeling and system-supported execution and analysis of operational processes. We also highlighted the opportunities that BPM holds for IIoT security management and described relevant starting points for further research. Based on the IIoT security management process, we showed some exemplary ways how to leverage BPM methods for improving IIoT security. We see the contents of this paper as a research agenda for underlying field of IIoT security. In future research, we will look in depth at the research gaps raised above. The first step will be the development of a syntactically and semantically well-defined notation for the definition of IIoT and security-aware processes.

Acknowledgement. This work is funded by the "Bavarian Ministry of Economic Affairs, Regional Development and Energy" within the project *INduStrial IoT Security Operations CenTer (INSIST)*.

References

1. Conklin, W.A.: IT vs. OT security: a time to consider a change in CIA to include resilience. In: 49th Hawaii International Conference on System Sciences (HICSS), pp. 2642–2647. IEEE (2016)
2. Vielberth, M., Böhm, F., Fichtinger, I., Pernul, G.: Security operations center: a systematic study and open challenges. IEEE Access **8**, 227756–227779 (2020)
3. Dumas, M., La Rosa, M., Mendling, J., Reijers, H.: Fundamentals of Business Process Management. Springer, Heidelberg (2018). https://doi.org/10.1007/978-3-662-56509-4
4. VDI/VDE: Informationssicherheit in der industriellen Automatisierung - Allgemeines Vorgehensmodell. VDI/VDE 2182 Blatt 1:2011–01 (2020)
5. International Electrotechnical Commission: IEC 62443 Security for Industrial Automation and Control Systems (2018)
6. Stoiber, C., Schönig, S.: Process-aware decision support model for integrating internet of things applications using AHP. In: Proceedings of the 23rd International Conference on Enterprise Information Systems (ICEIS), pp. 869–876 (2021)
7. Erasmus, J., Vanderfeesten, I., Traganos, K., Grefen, P.: Using business process models for the specification of manufacturing operations. Comput. Indust. **123**, 103927 (2020)
8. Zarour, K., Benmerzoug, D., Guermouche, N., Drira, K.: A systematic literature review on BPMN extensions. Bus. Process Manage. J. **26**(6), 1473–1503 (2019)
9. Altuhhova, O., Matulevičius, R., Ahmed, N.: An extension of business process model and notation for security risk management. Int. J. Inf. Syst. Model. Des. **4**(4), 93–113 (2013)
10. Mendling, J., Reijers, H.A., van der Aalst, W.M.: Seven process modeling guidelines. Inf. Softw. Technol. **52**, 127–136 (2010)
11. Avila, D.T., dos Santos, R.I., Mendling, J., Thom, L.H.: A systematic literature review of process modeling guidelines and their empirical support. Bus. Process Manage. J. **27**, 1–23 (2020)

12. Schönig, S., Aires, A.P., Ermer, A., Jablonski, S.: Workflow support in wearable production information systems. In: Mendling, J., Mouratidis, H. (eds.) CAiSE 2018. LNBIP, vol. 317, pp. 235–243. Springer, Cham (2018). https://doi.org/10.1007/978-3-319-92901-9_20
13. Bonchi, F., Castillo, C., Gionis, A., Jaimes, A.: Social network analysis and mining for business applications. Trans. Intell. Syst. Technol. (TIST) 2(3), 1–37 (2011)

Business Process Modeling (BPMDS 2022)

RBPMN - The Power of Roles for Business Process Modeling with BPMN

Tarek Skouti[1]([⊠]) [iD], Frank J. Furrer[2] [iD], and Susanne Strahringer[1] [iD]

[1] Business Informatics, esp. IS in Trade and Industry, TU Dresden, Dresden, Germany
{tarek.skouti,susanne.strahringer}@tu-dresden.de
[2] Software Technology Group, TU Dresden, Dresden, Germany
frank.j.furrer@bluewin.ch

Abstract. Developing a system for an interconnected world presents various challenges, from demanding disrupting technologies to a higher context-sensitivity. To solve these challenges, we researched the application of a modern understanding of roles for business process modeling. Roles are an approach with a long history in business process models and a proven value in other modeling perspectives. They provide multiple benefits, such as unifying structural and behavioral modeling and a rich adaptation of reference models.

Furthermore, as we prove in this paper, a modern understanding of roles can be implemented as a standard conform BPMN extension. Based on these benefits, we chose a design science approach to develop the role-based BPMN extension RBPMN, which we present in this paper. We demonstrate how RBPMN unleashes the power of roles to overcome modern business process modeling challenges and briefly evaluate our approach. The use of roles with a coherent understanding at every abstraction level supports modelers and engineers equally in developing systems for an interconnected ever-changing world.

Keywords: Process modeling · Role modeling · Unification

1 Introduction

Business process (BP) modeling faces many challenges in a modern interconnected world. Processes have a high complexity due to their context-dependent execution [1]. They must be adaptable [2], which requires the model describing the process to reflect the implemented process more accurately [3]. Additionally, with AI technology, BPs are improved continuously by the underlying system [4]. This led to many challenges, of which we specifically look at the challenges concerning BP modeling.

1.1 Challenges of BP Modeling

In their research note, Beverungen et al. [3] present two main challenges for BP modeling: the necessity for additional modeling constructs and tighter integration to the process data generated during the process. For the first challenge, they explain that the

© Springer Nature Switzerland AG 2022
A. Augusto et al. (Eds.): BPMDS 2022/EMMSAD 2022, LNBIP 450, pp. 29–42, 2022.
https://doi.org/10.1007/978-3-031-07475-2_3

current modeling constructs are insufficient to express the diverse data and effects at the right abstraction level. A future-ready BP modeling language should display AI-enhanced devices, which can be sensors or actuators in a process. Furthermore, it should enable stakeholders to communicate over different abstraction levels and integrate activities more tightly with analytics. This would enable a context-dependent adaptation of the process during the execution [3]. For the second challenge, they see BP models less as printable and more as evolving artifacts. When a BP model is created from process mining, it reflects the reality and not the ideal state that BP models currently represent. Furthermore, there is usually an additional difference between the design and implementation of a process, given that software engineers and process analysts have different backgrounds [3].

In their research manifesto for augmented business process management systems, Dumas et al. [4] see the challenges to modeling in automated process adaptation and multi-perspective processes support. There will never be contingencies for every possible outcome at the outset, or much information in a BP model becomes obsolete as soon as the process evolves. Therefore, it is crucial to support adaption for more than ad-hoc manual changes [4]. The process structure itself might even be unclear at design time and only emerge at runtime [4]. Dumas et al. envision that support during process execution can be achieved through an ontological mapping between different perspectives for the second challenge. Additionally, behavioral characteristics of entities should be shared between the different perspectives [4].

Ozkaya and Erata [5] surveyed software engineers for software modeling in general. Their findings can relate to some extent to BP modeling. They found that 45% of the surveyed participants see challenges with language complexity. If we consider that the de facto industry standard for BP modeling BPMN has 90 objects and 143 properties, that comes without surprise (cf. UML activity diagram 9 objects and 6 properties). 62% see problems with model analysis, and 49% see problems with model simulation, both aspects a modeling tool could and should provide. 46% have problems with analyzing the relationships between models of different perspectives.

Most recently, Weber et al. [1] made a study on context-aware BP modeling. They concluded that traditional modeling is suited for low variability processes but insufficient for high variability processes. They propose that future research should find "ways to integrate different stakeholder views during the design phase [1]" and "be approached both at organizational and technical levels [1]". They also state the importance of context-sensitive BP modeling approaches.

In sum, we can derive that traditional modeling approaches are insufficient because they lack context-sensitivity, adaptability, a tighter integration to other modeling perspectives, and modeling constructs for diverse data and AI-enhanced objects.

1.2 Research Approach

We employed a design science approach to solve the challenges and follow the approach suggested by Peffers et al. [6]. It consists of six phases 1. Problem identification 2. Objectives of a solution 3. Design and Development 4. Demonstration 5. Evaluation 6. Communication. We presented the first two phases – the problems and objectives of a solution – above and hence started our research at the design and development phase.

Therefore, the result will be an artifact in the form of a BP modeling language. We investigated approaches that were successfully applied in other modeling perspectives. One approach is using the role concept with a modern understanding of roles. Roles are already an established modeling concept in behavior modeling, whose meaning has evolved. Hence, we use Schön's [7] understanding of roles, who defines a role as: "A contextual modeling construct with state and behavior that is fulfilled by an object or its roles to represent it in the user's context and extend or change its corresponding specifications and interactions [7]". We introduce this modern understanding to the current standard of business process modeling BPMN with a standardized extension. We show how the power of roles can overcome the challenges mentioned above.

The rest of the paper is structured as follows. First, we present the role concept and our understanding of it in detail, followed by the evolution of the role understanding in behavior modeling. Next, Sect. 3 presents how the industry-standard BPMN can be extended, followed by its application for the role-based BPMN extension (RBPMN). We then present an example of an RBPMN model to showcase its benefits. Finally, we evaluate RBPMNs' role-feature coverage and additional expressible workflow patterns compared to the standard BPMN and conclude our paper.

2 Role Modeling

2.1 Roles

Roles are a long-standing concept in behavioral models [8–11], structural models [7, 12], data models [13, 14], security models [15] even in programming languages [16]. Essentially, roles are so fundamental that they are found in every aspect of modeling, engineering, and architecture [17].

Bachman and Daya [13] introduced the role concept for data models. Roles were used to overcome the binary 1:n relationships of the owner (1) and member (n) types in-network data models. Roles were defined as behavior patterns that one or more entities can play, and an entity can play one or more roles concurrently. In Bachman's role data model, entities play roles by becoming members of a relationship and drop these roles by leaving the relationship. Hence, the relationship is between the roles, not the entities [13]. Roles are also part of the EER modeling language and Object-Role Modeling language [18].

In structural models, roles introduce behavior and temporal aspects [18, 19]. Both are aspects for which the concept *class* is too limited to represent them. Furthermore, roles are used in structural models to provide adaptability and context-sensitivity [19]. Schön et al. [19] applied roles to develop the Business Role-Object Specification (BROS), a behavior-aware structural modeling language. BROS introduced behavioral aspects to structural modeling and related it closer to BP modeling.

The importance of roles for modeling was also recognized in the 2020 revision of the ISO 19940 standard for enterprise modeling [20]. It defines roles as the specialization of an entity in a specific context: "The same entity may have different roles in different contexts that may overlap in time and place, and at different times over its life cycle [20]".

Even though roles are found in multiple areas, they do not appear as a coherent concept. This problem comes from the various understandings of roles, which is unclear, as role research suffered from discontinuity [18]. Nevertheless, most role-based approaches share the two main attributes of roles: anti-rigid and context-dependent [16]. The example of Kühn et al. [12] presents this ideally. A Buyer *Role* and as counter-part a Seller *Role* exist in the *Context* of a Shop. The roles would not exist without the *context* Shop and a *Performer* fulfilling the Buyer *Role*, and a *Performer* fulfilling the Seller *Role*. Hence, roles are anti-rigid. The performers fulfilling these roles would exist nevertheless, but not in these roles, making the performer rigid [12].

Besides the two main attributes of roles, Steimann [14] derived 15 role-features, which Kühn [16] extended to 27, that characterize role-based modeling languages. In their respective research, both Steimann and Kühn evaluated role-based modeling languages. They found that rarely all role-features are considered, as there is no single definition of roles [14, 16]. Therefore, a researcher developing a role-based modeling language must first define their understanding of roles [18]. With the publication of the compartment role object model (CROM), a metamodel for role-based modeling languages, researchers can easily define roles for their modeling languages by extending or incorporating CROM [16]. Schön's role definition [7] mentioned above as the one our work builds on relies on CROM in this way. Since we focus on BP modeling, we now examine roles in BP models more closely.

2.2 Roles in Business Process Modeling

Roles have a long history in BP modeling languages. Role Activity Diagram (RAD), Role Interaction Nets (RIN), and the Object-Oriented Role Analysis Method (OORAM) are earlier approaches that used roles. They all see roles as sets of sequentially ordered actions and/or interactions [10]. However, with the introduction of knowledge processes in which actions are performed independently of their sequence, this understanding was no longer sufficient. The understanding of roles evolved to the knowledge of a process participant, which is needed to perform a process action successfully. The sequence is independent [10]. Saidani and Nurcan [9] used roles to introduce flexibility to business processes by assigning activities to roles instead of performers. The approach showed that roles could capture delegation and solve the separation of duty [9]. Thus, the understanding evolved further, as roles and not performers now executed the process activities. Other BP modeling languages focusing on actor-role perspective are the REA (resource, event, agent) language and e^3value [21]. REA stemmed from the accounting domain and was developed to reengineer accounting systems for the digital age. e^3value emphasizes business modeling more strongly than BP modeling. BP modeling languages that aim to provide a behavioral and functional perspective like UML activity diagrams and BPMN also contain some role modeling characteristics [21].

The BPMN, the de-facto standard of BP modeling, specifies two types of roles: *ResourceRole* and *ProcessRole*. *ResourceRole* defines the performer responsible for either the process or the activity. Furthermore, the BPMN 2.0 introduces human roles as a specialization of resource roles [22]. A performer can be "a specific individual, a group, an organization role or position, or an organization" [22]. This definition leaves out the virtual performers (AI-enhanced objects) mentioned in the introduction. The concrete syntax for *ResourceRole* is the use of task types adding an icon to a task. A *ProcessRole* describes an internal organizational (e.g., Manager, Associate) or business (e.g., Buyer, Seller) role that participates in the process. It organizes and categorizes activities within a Pool. The concrete BPMN syntax for a *ProcessRole* is the Lane [22]. ResourceRole and ProcessRole capture only a partial view of roles, limiting modelers [18].

3 The RBPMN Modeling Language

3.1 Developing the RBPMN Modeling Language

We expect a broader introduction of roles with a role-based BPMN extension (which we term RBPMN) to provide multiple benefits. First, it will enable the unification of modeling perspectives, especially with role-based structural models. If roles are used coherently across multiple modeling perspectives, communication between stakeholders will be less ambiguous. Second, it increases expressiveness without a substantial increase in complexity. Third, while we see the advantages of developing a new role-based modeling language from scratch, we see the advantages of remaining in the industry-standard to outweigh them. Tool support is given for a standardized extension of BPMN, and modelers will not have to learn an entirely new language. Fourth, BPMN already has some aspects of roles; hence the modeling method will not change. Fifth, roles are by their nature context-sensitive. Additionally, roles were successfully applied to provide adaptability (e.g., BROS). We expect them to provide the same for BP modeling.

Previous BPMN extensions we want to mention here have focused on integrating the resource perspective [23, 24], context [25], and even roles [26]. The RALph approach introduced multiple new connectors to BPMN to express when a performer (resource) executing an activity should stay the same for the subsequent activity or change [23]. Braun and Esswein developed an additional Resource Diagram to represent resources in BPMN [24]. C-BPMN presented context in an additional context model instead of incorporating it into the BPMN. Both models are linked. Context changes lead to switching the BPMN model [25]. R-BPMN by Kim and Chung [26] was developed for abstract modeling of process patterns for reuse. Their application of roles is powerful and shows their value. However, if applied coherently across multiple modeling perspectives, we surmise that roles can provide even more value.

We base our understanding of roles on the CROM model of Kühn [16] and on Schön's work [7] respectively. Since we decided to extend the BPMN, we could not express all role-features in RBPMN, but that is unnecessary, as some role-features are only for runtime. More critical for unifying multiple modeling perspectives is the coherent understanding of roles, which we ensure by adhering to the CROM model. We then incorporated those aspects of the CROM model of importance to BP modeling.

3.2 Extending the BPMN

With BPMN 2.0, OMG introduced an extension mechanism based on additions to the BPMN metamodel [22]. Nevertheless, extending BPMN is not a trivial task. Moreover, missing guidelines for extending it led to many BPMN extensions that do not conform to the standard [27]. Therefore, Stroppi et al. [27] proposed an approach called BPMN+X to develop standard conform domain-specific extensions. However, since our approach is not domain-specific but of a more overarching nature, the BPMN+X approach is insufficient. Therefore, we opted for the evolved BPMN+X method of Braun and Esswein [24] (Fig. 1), which they used to develop an extension for integrating modeling perspectives for linked modeling. We explain their method by showing our application of it.

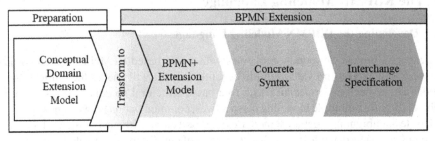

Fig. 1. Adapted picture of the method of Braun and Esswein [24]

It consists of 4 phases. In the first phase, we developed a conceptual domain model extension (CDME) that we present in Fig. 2. RBPMN is for BP models. Our RBPMN incorporates parts of the CROM [16] and of the role-based structural modeling language BROS [7], which we highlighted red in Fig. 2. The BPMN [22] concepts are highlighted green, and additional concepts necessary to tackle the BP modeling challenges listed in the introduction are highlighted orange. We provide the alternative terms in brackets if different terms were used to describe the same concept in other metamodels (BROS or CROM).

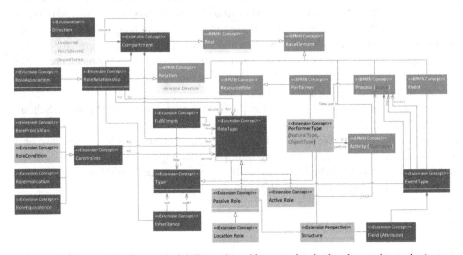

Fig. 2. The RBPMN metamodel (Best viewed by zooming in the electronic version)

To transition from the first phase to the second phase requires the transformation of the RBPMN metamodel by describing the extension in terms of the BPMN extension mechanism. This encompasses the abstract syntax and semantics of the extension elements. However, not every element of the RBPMN metamodel is transformed to the RBPMN extension model, which we show in Fig. 3.

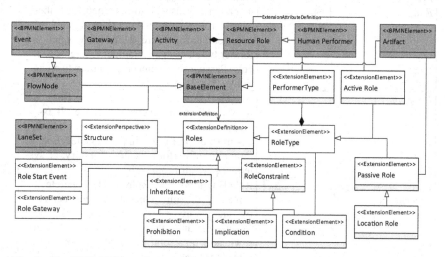

Fig. 3. The RBPMN Extension model (Best viewed by zooming in the electronic version)

The elements we did not transform are not of importance for BP modeling but for unifying RBPMN with other role-based modeling approaches that base their role understanding on CROM. The standard BPMN elements are green, and the extension elements are white for better understanding. BPMN elements not affected by the RBPMN extension are omitted. The third step is the development of the concrete syntax of the RBPMN extension elements, which we present in the next section. The development of a BPMN extension is always finished by specifying it in an interchange format, thus making it useable in existing BPMN modeling tools.

3.3   The Syntax of RBPMN Elements

Table 1 presents the syntax of the RBPMN elements. As a BPMN extension needs to keep a BPMN model's feel, the new elements do not conflict with existing BPMN elements. All roles are depicted as rectangles to maintain ontological clarity. The concrete syntax of a passive role depends on the modeler. The modeler can define the performer type by using icons or stay more general with a rectangle. The symbols of new relations were designed to be distinct from existing BPMN relations. Role Inheritance and Role Condition were inspired by the relations used in UML [28]. Role Implication and Role Prohibition were to some extend inspired by the BROS language [19].

Table 1. Concrete Syntax of RBPMN elements

Element	Concrete syntax	Abstract syntax
Active Role		Same as BPMN
Passive Role		New specification of RoleType. Not every role in a BP performs activities. Nonetheless, these passive roles are crucial to achieving the business goal. Furthermore, it enables new performer types, such as intelligent systems or robots. Passive role connects resources to an activity.
Location Role		A specialization of passive role. Locations can be physical or virtual enclosed spaces. It expresses that roles only exist, and some activities must be performed in the same location. Examples of performers are laboratory, IT system or pure air room.
Role Inheritance		Role B inherits from Role A. The concrete syntax of role inheritance differs between active and passive roles. Active roles make use of subswimlanes. Passive roles use a white arrowhead with a solid line. It also enables deep roles (a role playing a role).
Role Condition		Task 1 must have occurred for Role A to be performable.
Role Implication		Fulfilling Role A leads to fulfilling Role B.
Role Prohibition		Prohibits Role A and Role B from being fulfilled by the same performer.
Role Start Event		A role is fulfilled and therefore starts to exist. The intermediate event can be throwing or catching.
Role Gateway		Splitting: Either Role A or Role B continues the sequence. Merging: Only one role is played by the performer after the gateway.

4 Modeling Case Study

We implemented RBPMN with the ADOxx modeling toolkit[1]. We extended the BPMN implementation in ADOxx to prove that our RBPMN stays true to being a standard conform extension. To present the benefits of RBPMN, we developed a small case study of a fictional simplified recruitment process. This also corresponds to the fourth phase of Peffers et al.'s approach for design science research, which is demonstration [6]. To show how RBPMN supports the unification of multiple modeling perspectives, we

---

[1] https://www.adoxx.org/live/home.

also included the corresponding BROS model in Fig. 4. There are 10 roles, 6 active and 4 passive roles. When the performer *Talent* applies to the *Company* by sending its *Application*, the *Talent* starts fulfilling the *Applicant role*. The *Application* is received by the *Recruitment System* (The *HR Manager* is responsible for the *Recruitment System*) and evaluated by the *HR Manager role*. An *Employee role* fulfills the *HR Manager*. If the *Applicant* is invited, they fulfill the *Candidate role*. *Simultaneously*, the *Candidate information* is established, which inherits from the *Application information*. The *Interviewer role* is fulfilled by another or the same *Employee* that fulfills the *HR Manager*. Suppose the interview is successful for the *Candidate*. In that case, they fulfill the *Future Employee role*, and the *Employee drops the Interviewer role*. The *Candidate Information* is superseded by the *Employee Information*, which inherits qualifications and general information of the *Future Employee* from it. The *Future Employee* eventually becomes an *Employee*, which can then be *HR Manager* or *Interviewer* in another process instance.

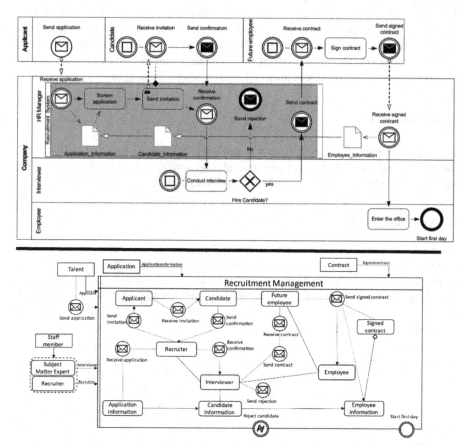

Fig. 4. Exemplary use of an RBPMN and a BROS model of a recruitment process (Attributes and methods are omitted in the BROS model for better readability).

The unified modeling is apparent when both models are analyzed, proving the first benefit. A software engineer who is more akin to structural models and a system analyst who is more akin to the BP models can see where their perspectives are represented in the other models. The overall complexity of our RBPMN is not much higher than BPMN. Nevertheless, we can express more information, such as with the location role that the recruitment system is a subsystem in the overarching employee management system. Additionally, the screening of the application could be automated for matching qualifications by modeling an AI-enhanced object for it. Hence, this proves the second benefit. The data flow from application information to candidate information to employee information is more evident in the RBPMN model than in a BPMN model. With the ADOxx implementation of RBPMN, we proved that tool support is realizable as we expected from our standardized extension. The RBPMN also retains the feel of a BPMN model, proving the fourth benefit. The fifth expected benefit, adaptability and context-sensitivity, is not apparent from our example. Adapting the process at design time is always possible. Other roles can perform the activities, or the activities can be split differently between the roles. In the example process, it could be another location role for conducting the interview as a video call. Additionally, the adaptation by BROS can directly influence the RBPMN model if both models are unified. Showing the context-sensitivity of roles in RBPMN requires a far more complex example.

5 Evaluation

After the demonstration, we also want to present a brief evaluation of our RBPMN. This conforms to the fifth phase of Peffers et al.'s approach, which is evaluation [6]. We evaluated RBPMN's workflow patterns [29] and role-feature coverage [16].

5.1 Workflow Patterns

The workflow pattern initiative, a joint effort of Eindhoven University of Technology and Queensland University of Technology, was established to provide a conceptual basis for process technology [29]. We focus on the control-flow, resource, and data patterns [29]. At a minimum, RBPMN, as an extension of BPMN by addition, can support all of BPMN's workflow patterns. Therefore, we analyze patterns that can be expressed additionally. The strength of BPMN was in the control-flow and the weakness in data and resource patterns [29]. Figure 5 showcases the realization of 2 patterns.

The *Control-Flow* patterns *Milestone* and *Critical Section* are supported. Since roles hold the activities, we can express a milestone with the 'role condition'. The role holding the activity is fulfillable only after the milestone is achieved. Role implication and role prohibition together enable the workflow pattern Critical section. The pattern is supported by expressing that the same performer must fulfill 2+ roles with the critical sections but not simultaneously.

The *Data* patterns *Scope Data* and *Environment Data* are supported. The Scope Data pattern is supported by modeling the data role within a location role (data is only available in the system) or a pool (data is available for all roles in the pool). *Environment Data* is supported by modeling passive roles outside of a pool.

The *Resource* patterns *Authorization, Separation of Duties, Retain familiar, Delegation, Stateful Reallocation, and Additional Resources* are supported. Roles specify priv-ileges of the performer fulfilling it, which is the *Authorization* pattern. A *Separation of Duties* is expressible by role prohibition. Since the performer is not expressed in RBPMN, the *Retain Familiar* requires the role implication to support this pattern. The support of the *Delegation* and *Stateful Reallocation* patterns is realized via multiple performers fulfilling the same role. Finally, the *Additional Resources* pattern is sup-ported by associating passive roles to an activity.

Overall, RBPMN supports 10 workflow patterns in addtion to those supported by BPMN. This was achieved without adding much modeling complexity. As the BPMN extension R-BPMN of Kim & Chung showed, roles can also be used specifically for pattern modeling [26]. An approach that does not fit with our RBPMN but nevertheless highlights the value of roles.

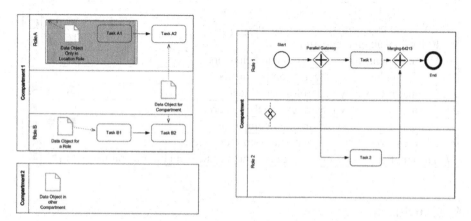

Fig. 5. The data pattern Scope Data (left) and the resource pattern Separation of Duties (right)

5.2 Role Feature Coverage

There are 27 role-features to classify role-based languages [16]. We evaluate and compare BPMN [22], R-BPMN [26], and RBPMN [8] on features of the model level. The term compartment in Table 2 is defined as: "objectified collaboration with a limited number of participating roles and a fixed scope [12]".

RBPMN does not cover all role-features since it is a BPMN extension and not an entirely new modeling language. Nevertheless, it covers more role-features than standard BPMN or the role-based BPMN extension R-BPMN.

Table 2. *Role feature* [16] *coverage* No support: □ Partial support: ◨ Full support: ■

Role Feature	BPMN	R-BPMN	RBPMN
1. Roles have properties and behaviors	■	■	■
2. Roles depend on relationships	■	■	■
3. Objects may play different roles simultaneously	■	■	■
6. The sequence of role acquisition and removal may be restricted	□	□	◨
7. Unrelated objects can play the same role	□	■	■
8. Roles can play roles	◨	■	■
11. Features of an object can be role-specific	□	□	◨
13. Different roles may share structure and behavior	◨	◨	■
16. Relationships between roles can be constrained	□	□	□
17. There may be constraints between relationships	□	□	□
18. Roles can be grouped and constrained together	■	■	■
19. Roles depend on compartments	■	■	■
20. Compartments have properties and behaviors	■	■	■
21. A role can be part of several compartments	□	□	□
22. Compartments may play roles like objects	■	■	■
23. Compartments may play roles which are part of themselves	□	□	◨
24. Compartments can contain other compartments	■	■	■
25. Different compartments may share structure and behavior	□	□	◨
27. The number of roles occurring in a compartment can be constrained	■	■	■

6 Conclusion

If applied at all abstraction levels in the software development process, roles support the design of adaptation and continuous context-sensitive systems. The presented role-based BP modeling language RBPMN contributes to this goal as one step towards unified modeling with a coherent understanding of roles across multiple perspectives.

Looking back at the BP modeling challenges mentioned in the introduction, our RBPMN presents a viable solution to many parts of these challenges. The passive role element of RBPMN can express diverse data roles, AI-enhanced objects, and future technologies. The tighter integration with other modeling perspectives is shown through our example and also by the RBPMN metamodel containing the BROS metamodel. The tighter integration is only achieved when role models with a coherent understanding of roles are used in design and development, but role models are not yet standard. The modeling complexity is not increased significantly, yet the expressiveness of RBPMN is high. The part of reducing modeling complexity remains as a challenge. Roles are context-sensitive by nature, but we could not showcase this thoroughly in this paper. We expect roles to aid in the challenge of increasing and modeling adaptability, as they have proven to be able to do so in other modeling perspectives [7]. Nevertheless, we proved the power of roles for overcoming some of the modern BP modeling challenges while remaining within the industry standard. Our RBPMN, which provides a broader introduction of roles to BPMN, is more expressive than the standard, brings context into the spotlight, and enables unified role-based modeling.

We also want to address some limitations of our research. Other understandings of roles, such as presented in [10, 17, 26], might produce a different solution. A second limitation lies in the tradeoff between keeping an existing language's integrity and representing every aspect of the new concepts. For example, an entirely new role-based modeling language might have addressed more workflow patterns [25] or incorporated more role-features [12]. This could also increase ontological clarity over multiple modeling perspectives by using purely the same symbols.

However, the advantages of developing from scratch reduce the industry acceptance and the support by modeling tools. Since RBPMN is a standardized BPMN extension, it can be implemented in existing BPMN modeling tools.

Future work will address the missing guidelines for model transformation and naming conventions for roles. In addition, the RBPMN modeling tool will support this semi-automated transformation of RBPMN models to BROS models and vice-versa. Furthermore, we will investigate RBPMNs modeling capabilities with a larger case study in a financial institute by modeling a highly flexible and a standard banking process. Eventually, modelers will not have to unlearn their methods to use the power of roles fully.

Acknowledgment. This work is funded by the German Research Foundation (DFG) within the Research Training Group "Role-based Software Infrastructures for continuous-context-sensitive Systems" (GRK 1907).

References

1. Weber, M., Grisold, T., vom Brocke, J., Kamm, M.: Context-aware business process modeling: empirical insights from a project with a globally operating company. In: ECIS 2021 Research-in-Progress Papers. p. 13 (2021)
2. Cognini, R., Corradini, F., Gnesi, S., Polini, A., Re, B.: Research challenges in business process adaptability. In: Proceedings of the 29th Annual ACM Symposium on Applied Computing - SAC 2014. pp. 1049–1054. ACM Press, Gyeongju, Republic of Korea (2014)
3. Beverungen, D., et al.: Seven paradoxes of business process management in a hyper-connected world. Bus. Inf. Syst. Eng. **63**, 145–156 (2021)
4. Dumas, M., et al.: Augmented Business Process Management Systems: A Research Manifesto. ArXiv220112855 Cs. (2022)
5. Ozkaya, M., Erata, F.: Understanding practitioners' challenges on software modeling: a survey. J. Comput. Lang. **58**, 100963 (2020)
6. Peffers, K., Tuunanen, T., Rothenberger, M.A., Chatterjee, S.: A design science research methodology for information systems research. J. Manag. Inf. Syst. **24**, 45–77 (2007)
7. Schön, H.: Role-based Adaptation of Business Reference Models to Application Models (2020). https://nbn-resolving.org/urn:nbn:de:bsz:14-qucosa2-725441
8. Skouti, T.: RBPMN: A Role-based BPMN for integrating structure and behavior models. Dresd. Beitr. Zur Wirtsch. Nr 7321 (2021)

9. Saidani, O., Nurcan, S.: A role-based approach for modelling flexible business processes. In: Proceedings CAISE06 Workshop Business Process Modelling Devlopment and Support, pp. 111–120 (2006)

10. Balabko, P., Wegmann, A., Ruppen, A., Clément, N.: The Value of Roles in Modeling Business Processes. CAiSE Workshop, vol. 9 (2004)

11. Caetano, A., Silva, A.R., Tribolet, J.: Using roles and business objects to model and understand business processes. In: Proceedings of the 2005 ACM Symposium on Applied computing - SAC 2005. p. 1308. ACM Press, Santa Fe, New Mexico (2005)

12. Kühn, T., Leuthäuser, M., Götz, S., Seidl, C., Aßmann, U.: A metamodel family for role-based modeling and programming languages. In: Combemale, B., Pearce, D.J., Barais, O., Vinju, J.J. (eds.) SLE 2014. LNCS, vol. 8706, pp. 141–160. Springer, Cham (2014). https://doi.org/10.1007/978-3-319-11245-9_8

13. Bachman, C.W., Daya, M.: The role concept in data models. In: Proceedings of the 33rd International Conference on Very Large Data Bases, vol. 3, pp. 464–476 (1977)

14. Steimann, F.: The role data model revisited. Appl. Ontol. **2**, 89–103 (2007)

15. Ferraiolo, D.F., Kuhn, D.R.: Role-based access controls. In: 15th National Computer Security Conference, pp. 554–563 (1992)

16. Kühn, T.: A Family of Role-Based Languages (2017). https://nbn-resolving.org/urn:nbn:de:bsz:14-qucosa-228027

17. von Rosing, M., Arzumanyan, M., Zachman, J.A., Sr.: The relationship between ontology and modelling concepts: example role oriented modelling. Int. J. Concept. Struct. Smart Appl. **5**, 25–47 (2017)

18. Bera, P., Burton-Jones, A., Wand, Y.: Improving the representation of roles in conceptual modeling: theory, method, and evidence. Require. Eng. **23**(4), 465–491 (2017). https://doi.org/10.1007/s00766-017-0275-9

19. Schön, H., Strahringer, S., Furrer, F.J., Kühn, T.: Business role-object specification: a language for behavior-aware structural modeling of business objects. In: Ludwig, T., Pipek, V. (eds.) Wirtschaftsinformatik 2019 Proceedings, pp. 244–258 (2019)

20. ISO: ISO 19440:2020 Enterprise modelling and architecture—constructs for enterprise modelling (2020). https://www.iso.org/standard/74491.html

21. Krogstie, J.: Perspectives to process modeling – a historical overview. In: Bider, I., et al. (eds.) BPMDS/EMMSAD -2012. LNBIP, vol. 113, pp. 315–330. Springer, Heidelberg (2012). https://doi.org/10.1007/978-3-642-31072-0_22

22. OMG (ed.): Business Process Model and Notation (BPMN), Version 2.0 (2011) https://www.omg.org/spec/BPMN/2.0

23. Cabanillas, C., Knuplesch, D., Resinas, M., Reichert, M., Mendling, J., Ruiz-Cortés, A.: RALph: a graphical notation for resource assignments in business processes. In: Zdravkovic, J., Kirikova, M., Johannesson, P. (eds.) CAiSE 2015. LNCS, vol. 9097, pp. 53–68. Springer, Cham (2015). https://doi.org/10.1007/978-3-319-19069-3_4

24. Braun, R., Esswein, W.: Towards multi-perspective modeling with BPMN. In: Aveiro, D., Pergl, R., Valenta, M. (eds.) EEWC 2015. LNBIP, vol. 211, pp. 67–81. Springer, Cham (2015). https://doi.org/10.1007/978-3-319-19297-0_5

25. Santra, D., Sankhayan, C.: C-BPMN: A Context Aware BPMN for Modeling Complex Business Process. CoRR. abs/1806.01333 (2018)

26. Kim, D.-K., Chung, Y.K.: R-BPMN for abstract modeling of business process patterns. Bus. Process Manag. J. **27**, 1445–1462 (2021)

27. Stroppi, L.J.R., Chiotti, O., Villarreal, P.D.: Extending BPMN 2.0: method and tool support. In: Dijkman, R., Hofstetter, J., Koehler, J. (eds.) BPMN 2011. LNBIP, vol. 95, pp. 59–73. Springer, Heidelberg (2011). https://doi.org/10.1007/978-3-642-25160-3_5

28. Unified Modeling Language, v2.5.1. Unified Model. Lang. 796

29. Workflow Patterns Home Page. http://www.workflowpatterns.com/. Accessed 12 Feb 2021

A Complementary Analysis of the Behavior of BPMN Tools Regarding Process Modeling Problems

João Vitor de Camargo[1], Nicolas Mauro de Moreira Bohnenberger[1],
Vinicius Stein Dani[2], José Palazzo Moreira de Oliveira[1], Encarna Sosa-Sánchez[3],
Gregor Polančič[4], and Lucineia Heloisa Thom[1(✉)]

[1] Institute of Informatics, Federal University of Rio Grande do Sul, Porto Alegre, Brazil
{jvcamargo,nicolas.bohnenberger,palazzo,lucineia}@inf.ufrgs.br
[2] Department of Information and Computing Sciences, Utrecht University,
Utrecht, The Netherlands
v.steindani@uu.nl
[3] Department of Computer Systems and Telematics Engineering, University of Extremadura,
Badajoz, Spain
esosa@unex.es
[4] Faculty of Electrical Engineering and Computer Science, University of Maribor,
Maribor, Slovenia
gregor.polancic@um.si

Abstract. Business process models are essential for organizations, enabling participants to understand the business processes in which they are involved. These models are mainly designed using process modeling tools, supporting Business Process Model and Notation (BPMN) 2.0, which is widely accepted by the community. However, representation of modeling problems in process models may generate inconsistent interpretations, leading to the implementation of incorrect modeling solutions. As such, BPMN 2.0-based process modeling tools should detect these problems. The literature shows that modeling tools behave differently when facing identical problems. This paper analyzes how BPMN 2.0-based process modeling tools currently react and provide feedback about modeling problems in business process models. Process modeling anti-patterns are used as study cases; they compose a class of commonly recreated modeling bad practices. This paper also reviews and complements experiments from the literature to understand the current state of problem detection by modeling tools. Each of the ten anti-patterns is modeled in ten modeling tools. An analysis of which types of problems are more often detected and how modeling tools react to them is presented. Furthermore, problem feedback should be displayed understandably. So, problematic models are created, and visual feedback about their problems is generated according to recommendations from the literature. These problematic models are then introduced into the modeling tools. The tools' reactions are compared to the literature recommendations to evaluate the current gaps in visual feedback presented by modeling tools.

Keywords: Business Process Management · BPMN · Business process modeling problems · Business process modeling anti-patterns · Visual feedback

© Springer Nature Switzerland AG 2022
A. Augusto et al. (Eds.): BPMDS 2022/EMMSAD 2022, LNBIP 450, pp. 43–59, 2022.
https://doi.org/10.1007/978-3-031-07475-2_4

1   Introduction

A business process is a set of activities performed by an organization to deliver value to its customers. Among the most valuable resources of an organization are its business processes [9]. A business process can be graphically represented by a process model, the output of the process modeling, an essential activity of Business Process Management - BPM [9]. Process models are essential assets while developing software solutions [23] and essential in communicating an organization's processes, enabling participants to understand the processes they are involved in [9]. A widely accepted notation for modeling business processes in the BPM community is the Business Process Model and Notation - BPMN 2.0, specified by the Object Management Group [21] and standardized by ISO[1].

Modeling a business process is a complex, human-intensive, and error-prone task, as ambiguity leads to multiple interpretations and lack of shared understanding of the process [8]. The literature describes modeling patterns for business process models to lessen this complexity [10]. Conversely, process modeling anti-patterns describe common errors detected in business process models [16] and are not only related to syntax errors. Koschmider et al. [16] proposed seven anti-pattern categories, only one of them "syntax errors," and 7 of the 15 most common anti-patterns detected by Rozman et al. [23] in BPMN process models were related to syntax.

In order to comply with notation, BPMN modeling tools must provide feedback to the modeler at least about syntax errors. However, common problems detected in process models are not only related to syntax [10, 16]. Moreover, process modeling tools usually present feedback about problems using non-instructive text messages [7], with the problematic process element often impossible to locate, particularly in larger models [25]. In this paper, we investigate and analyze the behavior of BPMN process modeling tools regarding process modeling problems, using anti-patterns as a study case.

Our research questions are *RQ1)* What is the current state of detection of modeling problems presented by business modeling tools; and *RQ2)* Does the visual feedback about modeling problems present in business process modeling tools follow literature recommendations described in [25]. We propose a three-stage methodology to answer these questions, illustrated in Fig. 1. In stage 1, we analyze and select available process modeling tools to employ in the following stages. In stage 2, we recreate experiments performed by Dias et al. [7] and compare and analyze the differences, also complementing results with a new set of analyzed process modeling tools. In stage 3, we create problematic process models based on anti-patterns to model in each tool, design the recommended feedback for these models based on literature [25], and compare them with the results from the process modeling tools.

This paper is organized as follows. Section 2 provides the necessary background, introducing the BPMN 2.0 and an overview of process modeling anti-patterns. Section 3 discusses related works on the topics approached in this paper. Section 4 displays the selection of the tools used, stage 1 of the methodology. Moreover, in this section, we go through stage 2 of our methodology, producing the results of our analysis on the behavior of process modeling tools and comparing previous and current results for tools

---

[1] ISO/IEC 19510:2013: http://www.omg.org/spec/BPMN/ISO/19510/PDF.

that have documented results in the literature. Section 5 reports on the results for stage 3 of our methodology, related to visual feedback in process modeling tools. Finally, we present conclusions and future works on the topic.

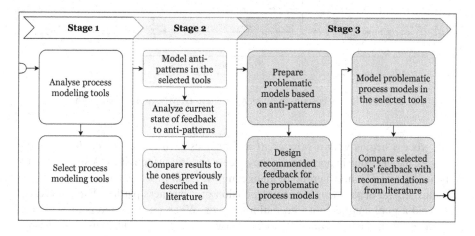

Fig. 1. Methodology for this study. Source: the authors.

2 Background

In this section, we present the associated conceptual background. We quickly show BPMN 2.0 in the context of this paper and then the concept of process modeling anti-patterns.

2.1 Business Process Model and Notation

Models are created using a notation. BPMN is currently the standard for business process models, described as accessible for stakeholders while still presenting a technical aspect that allows the translation into software [21]. It is composed of multiple modeling elements, being able to represent different types of processes. Some of the core elements are tasks, sub-processes, flows (sequence and message), events (start, intermediate, and end), gateways (*AND*, *OR*, and *XOR*), pools, and lanes. Figure 2 illustrates the BPMN model of an issue reporting process in a software provider company.

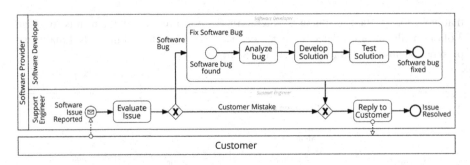

Fig. 2. Example of a business process modeled in BPMN. Source: The authors.

A process begins with a *start event* and finishes with an *end event*. *Intermediate events* are the ones that happen during the process and trigger activities. A single activity is named by a *task*, while a group of them compose a *sub-process*. Participants perform activities, e.g., a department in the organization or a business partner. *Pools* represent them, and a pool can be split into multiple *lanes*. When on the same pool, activities are connected through a *sequence flow*. Otherwise, a *message flow* is used. *Gateways* represent decision points in the process.

2.2 Process Modeling Problems and Anti-patterns

According to notation syntax and semantics, a process modeling problem is generated through the incorrect usage of BPMN elements [23]. However, a process model can be problematic by not matching business requirements [2] or being designed to impair readability [23].

Business process modeling problems can be classified as syntactic, which violate the syntax of the notation employed; semantic, which impair the semantic quality of the model, measured through metrics of validity, completeness and feasibility, that evaluate the ability of a model to be complete and per its domain [17]; and pragmatic, which affect the understandability of the process model by its participants [23].

Widely discussed in the software engineering field, anti-patterns are faulty solutions that are recurrently reinvented [15]. In the context of BPM, a process modeling anti-pattern is the common inadequate usage of BPMN elements during the modeling task [16]. We present, based on Rozman et al. [23], in Fig. 3, three examples of process modeling anti-patterns with BPMN 2.0.

(a) Activities in one pool are not connected

(b) Intermediate events placed on the edge of the pool

(c) Message flow used inside the pool

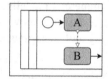

Fig. 3. Three examples of process modeling anti-patterns. Colored modeling elements either cause or are affected by the anti-pattern. Source: Adapted from [23].

The first anti-pattern, Fig. 3a, leads to an unreachable activity due to it not having an incoming flow. The second anti-pattern, Fig. 3b, leads to events not having an incoming flow, thus being unreachable within the process; the incorrect usage of these elements may lead to an incorrect interpretation that events can happen anytime in the process [23]. The third anti-pattern, Fig. 3c, relates to the message flow being specifically for communication between different pools [21], not to be used as sequence flows, which connect elements within a pool. Applying this anti-pattern leads to uncertainty while executing the process [23]. The first of these anti-patterns is categorized as a syntax and pragmatic error, and the others are syntax errors.

3   Related Works

This section presents two categories of related works: business process modeling anti-patterns, related to the work in Sect. 4, and visual feedback about problems in process models, which serves as the basis for Sect. 5.

3.1   Anti-patterns on Business Process Models

The topic of anti-patterns for business process models has been relevant for over a decade now. Rozman et al. [23] list the 15 most common modeling anti-patterns based on a large set of models produced by BPM students. More recently, Koschmider et al. [16] created a taxonomy of 48 articles regarding business process modeling anti-patterns, allotting them into seven categories and stressing that there is broad literature coverage regarding categories *control-flow* (e.g., deadlocks) and *understandability* (e.g., complexity), but not *composition* and *ecological impact* anti-patterns. Fellmann et al. [10] developed a similar study covering modeling patterns.

Koehler et al. [14] studied anti-patterns detection in business process models, analyzing hundreds of "real world" process models to extract anti-patterns and guide modelers on how to detect and avoid modeling them; this guidance is also provided by Rozman et al. [23]. The identification of anti-patterns was also covered by Lehmann et al. [18], in which the authors discuss modeling anti-patterns in Enterprise Architecture (EA) models, proposing 18 anti-patterns based on [16] for this specific class of models.

Dias et al. [7] researched the subject of anti-patterns in modeling tools, selecting ten anti-patterns among the ones described by Rozman et al. [23] and modeling them in four commercial modeling tools to analyze how modeling tools react to these patterns. To the best of our knowledge, no other related works analyze the current behavior of modeling tools regarding anti-patterns, motivating RQ1.

3.2 Visual Feedback About Problems in Business Process Models

Visual feedback about problems in process models has been studied in the last few years by Stein Dani et al. [26], who performed a Systematic Literature Review (SLR) regarding the visualization of business process models. The authors selected 46 papers and classified them into six categories, *visual feedback concerning problems detected in process models* among them, described by the authors as "less explored" and representing "challenges for further exploration."

Based on this SLR [26], Stein Dani et al. [25] performed a survey with 57 participants to understand the demands of process modelers regarding visual feedback about problems in process models. Combining its results with the literature and the behavior of analyzed modeling tools, the authors proposed recommendations on how modeling tools should provide feedback to modelers, covering scenarios with both small and large models [25]. We found no further studies on how modeling tools react visually to business process modeling problems. Therefore, to the best of our knowledge, there is no study more updated than [26] regarding the current state of visualization of problems in business process models.

4 Analysis of Business Process Modeling Tools Behavior Regarding Business Process Modeling Problems

This section presents the application of our methodology's first and second stages. The first stage deals with the analysis and selection of process modeling tools in the paper. In the second stage of the methodology, we recreate the experiments described by Dias et al. [7] with the selected process modeling tools.

4.1 Process Modeling Tools Selection

Our goal is to understand how modeling tools currently react to process modeling errors and compare these findings to recommendations in the literature. Therefore, we established three selection criteria for process modeling tools: *i)* The tool must support the creation (or importing) of BPMN models; *ii)* The tool must support the validation of syntax and correctness of BPMN models; *iii)* The tools must be free or offer a free available version (e.g., trial or academic edition). Table 1 displays the selected tools, each with the edition, availability, and version used in our study.

Table 1. Edition, availability, and version of the selected process modeling tools

Modeling tool	Edition	Availability	Version
Adonis [4]	Community	Web	11
ARIS [1]	Basic	Web	10.0.13.1
Bizagi modeler [3]	Standard	Local	3.8.0.191
Bonita BPM [5]	Community	Local	7.12.1.1
Camunda modeler [6]	Standard	Local	4.6.0
IBM blueworks live [13]	Standard	Web	June 2021
Microsoft visio [20]	Professional	Local	2106
Oracle BPM studio [22]	Standard	Local	12c
QualiBPMN [11]	Standard	Web	-
Signavio process manager [24]	Academic	Web	14.16.0

One of our objectives is to recreate the experiments performed by Dias et al. in [7]. Therefore, all modeling tools in those experiments are included in the initial selection of modeling tools. Also included for initial selection are tools enumerated in [9]. We also included the 6 top modeling tools rated by customers in [12]. Finally, additional research found OracleBPM and QualiBPMN as viable options to be analyzed. From this initial selection of process modeling tools, iGrafx and Mavim were excluded as they did not satisfy selection criteria *iii*.

When the tool had only one available edition, it was labeled *Standard*. We found no official version information for QualiBPMN. We limit our study of these tools to their modeling and validation features, regardless of any others they might have, due to our focus on business process models.

4.2 Experiment Parameters

To review, update and complement the analysis of Dias et al. [7], which contains documented results for four of the ten selected tools, we model the same modeling anti-patterns used in the experiments performed by Dias et al. [7] in every selected tool in order to enable us to understand the current state of problem feedback in modeling tools. These anti-patterns are: (1) *Activities in one pool are not connected*; (2) *Process does not contain an end event*; (3) *Sequence flow crosses sub-process boundary*; (4) *Sequence flow crosses pool boundary*; (5) *Gateway receives, evaluates, or sends a message*; (6) *Intermediate events are placed on the edge of the pool*; (7) *Hanging intermediate events or activities*; (8) *Each lane in the pool contains a start event*; (9) *Exception flow is not connected to the exception*; (10) *Message flow used inside the pool*.

Since QualiBPMN had no modeling feature, we consider that *i)* the tools allowed modeling if the model was successfully imported and the anti-pattern is visually displayed and that *ii)* modeling feedback is the outcome of the validation performed on an imported model. As the other nine tools have native modeling functionalities, we model each anti-pattern from empty models on them.

Modeling tools can respond differently when dealing with anti-patterns. Tools may allow the anti-pattern to be modeled or not, and in either scenario, may provide feedback about the problem or not. For every anti-pattern, in each tool, we inform if the tool *i)* enables modeling the problem and *ii)* provides feedback about it.

4.3   Overall Results

Figure 4 displays the grouped results for each anti-pattern and tool. A dark dot means the tool provided visual feedback about the problem, and a cross within the dot indicates the tool allowed modeling. Signavio is the only tool that provides feedback for all anti-patterns, while Adonis only presented feedback for two of them. Anti-pattern 6 was the only anti-pattern observed in all modeling tools, and anti-pattern 10 had feedback in only three of them, which were the only ones in which the problem could be modeled.

Five of the selected modeling tools were ranked in the top ten business process tools: Visio, ARIS, Adonis, Signavio, and Blueworks [12]. All of those are proprietary and related to large companies [1,4,13,20,24]; we refer to them as "premium" for simplification. The remaining modeling tools all have at least one version permanently available [3,5,6,11,22]. From instances where feedback was observed, 51.6% were in "premium" tools, with the remaining 48.4% being in free tools, as illustrated in Fig. 5(a). Several tools from both groups were not consistent in detecting and providing feedback about problems; therefore, the fact that a tool is paid and maintained by a large vendor does not correlate directly with it providing better feedback about modeling problems.

When analyzing anti-patterns by classification, six of the ten are syntax errors, three are pragmatical, and two are semantic issues (anti-pattern 1 is both syntactically and pragmatically incorrect [23]). The anti-patterns detected with feedback by the selected tools were semantic issues in 40.8% of cases, syntactical in 30.6%, and pragmatical in 28.6%, as illustrated in Fig. 5(b); therefore, although syntax problems are more commonly detected by modeling tools [23], this tendency is not observed in the visual feedback provided by these tools.

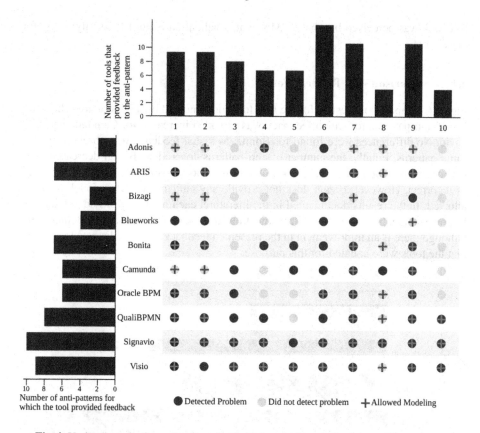

Fig. 4. Updated results for anti-pattern feedback in modeling tools. Source: The authors.

(a) For the instances an anti-pattern was detected with feedback, the modeling tool was

(b) For the instances an anti-pattern was detected with feedback, its error type was

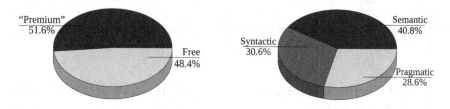

Fig. 5. Results of modeling anti-patterns in business process modeling tools. Source: The authors.

Although better results were observed for semantic issues, the validation of these problems can be complicated, demanding a human expert with business knowledge [27]. Our models have no business context, being less challenging to detect for automated tools; therefore, the observed results do not indicate that good semantic feedback was perceived but that BPMN syntax validation is not necessarily trivial for these tools.

4.4 Comparison with Related Work

Figure 6 compares our results for the four tools documented by the literature. The number of anti-patterns for which feedback was provided increased for Camunda and Signavio. No differences were found for Bonita, as visual feedback was observed for the same patterns. Finally, the number of anti-patterns covered by Bizagi decreased. The tool currently prohibits modeling a problem that was possible to model and detected as incorrect. However, Bizagi does not provide any guidance on why modeling is not allowed. In the results documented in the literature, each modeling provided feedback for, on average, 5 anti-patterns [7]. In our study, this average increased to 6.2; therefore, although there is an improvement in the presented feedback, it is too discrete to confirm that the tools were updated for this purpose.

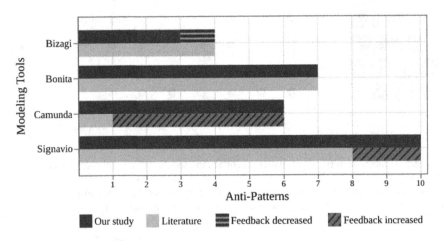

Fig. 6. Comparison of previous and current number of anti-patterns detected per modeling tool. Source: the authors, with literature results from [7].

5 Visual Feedback Implemented by Modeling Tools in Comparison with the Literature

In this section, we review and complement the analysis of how the modeling tools provide visual feedback. We illustrate how literature recommends visual feedback to be presented and then model this in the modeling tools to compare the results to the literature. The results shown in Sect. 4 were highly heterogeneous; no one pair of modeling tools behaved equally for all anti-patterns, and no single anti-pattern was both allowed to be modeled and had feedback provided by the tools. Therefore, we could not use the same group of patterns in all tools.

For each tool, one small and one large model were designed, as visual feedback problems can manifest differently in them [25], with a set of anti-patterns for which detection and feedback were known to happen. The subset of anti-patterns 2, 7, and 9 used to evaluate ARIS, Bonita, Camunda, Oracle BPM, QualiBPMN, and Visio is an example.

After proposing and validating the process models, we design how the literature recommends that feedback should be displayed for problems. Table 2 exhibits the visual feedback recommendations about problems presented in the literature for small and large models [7].

Table 2. Recommendations for visual feedback about problems on small and large business process models, adapted from [25]

Recommendations for small process models
1	Highlight the problem with a visual element (e.g., an icon)
2	Highlight the problem through the coloring of the problematic element
3	Provide explanations when hovering the mouse on the problem
4	Provide a list of all the problems in the model
5	Link the problematic element with the respective entry of the problem list
6	Provide problem documentation or suggestions on how to fix it

Recommendations for large process models
1	When viewing the entire model, without zoom, problems should be grouped into problematic areas, according to their type (error or warning)
2	When zooming in a problematic area, the modeling tool should focus on the problems included in the area, providing details about them
3	When zooming in a problematic area, the problem list should contain the problems included in the area
4	When zooming in a problematic area, the modeling tool should visually show where the other problems are in the model

5.1 Applying Recommendations for Small Process Models

An example of the outcome of applying recommendations to small problems in our models is displayed in Fig. 7. All problems therein are highlighted with icons and colors, fulfilling recommendations 1 and 2. Per recommendation 3, an explanatory floating message is provided when hovering the mouse on the problem. While the list called *Problems Detected* (recommendation 4) presents all problems, the hovered problematic element is highlighted on the list, as described in recommendation 5. Finally, recommendation 6 is implemented by providing access to the problem documentation through the blue icon with an interrogation point in the pop-up and the overall list.

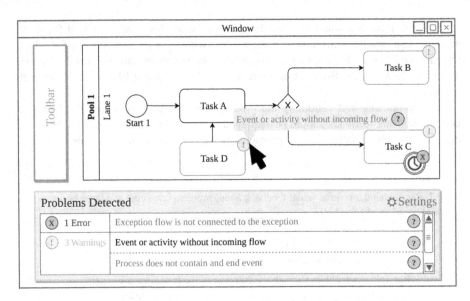

Fig. 7. Recommended feedback applied in a small process model. Source: the authors, following recommendations of [25]

5.2 Applying Recommendations for Large Process Models

A model can be considered large when it cannot be adequately displayed in the modeling area of a modeling tool [25]. The large models used in this paper were tested in the tools analyzed and considered large due to the high impairment of readability in their elements. Moreover, BPMN modeling guidelines a 50 element threshold per model, as larger models are more likely to generate errors [19]. Our models pass this threshold. Examples applying recommendations in a model with anti-patterns are presented in Figs. 8 and 9.

For large process models, two complementary visualizations are recommended. The first one provides a view of the entire model, grouping problems into problematic areas. The second is shown when the user zooms the screen in a problematic area. In the latter, details for each problem are provided through the same visual indicators used for small models (e.g., icons and coloring).

When displaying the entire model, as in Fig. 8, recommendation 1 is implemented through colored circles, grouping problems by type (red for errors, yellow for warnings). The zoomed visualizations, portrayed in Fig. 9, follow the other three recommendations by providing details about the problems in the area in both the model and the list while indicating where other problems are through colored arrows, following the same color-coding. These arrows contain a number, informing how many problems of that type can be found in the pointed directions, and allow the modeler to decide which problem area they want to solve first [25].

None of the ten evaluated modeling tools implement any of the four recommendations for visual feedback about problems in large models. All tools behaved equally

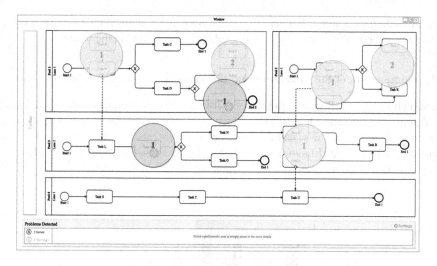

Fig. 8. Recommended feedback applied in a large model when viewing the entire model. Source: The authors, following recommendations of [25].

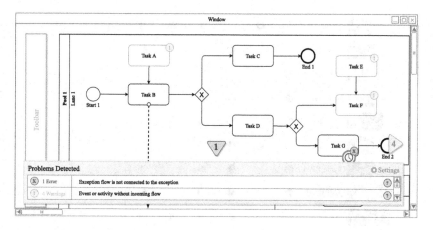

Fig. 9. Recommended feedback when zooming into a part of the model. Source: The authors, following recommendations of [25].

to what they did when facing problems in a small model. When viewing the entire model without zoom, details are still presented about each error individually. The lack of the problematic areas, as suggested by recommendation 1, leads to one visualization with several errors and warning symbols, which makes it difficult to understand the problems.

No visual feedback changes are observed when the zoom is applied to an area in the model. In addition, there is no form of highlight for the problems in the area, and the list of detected problems does not focus on the issues on screen, not following recommendations 2 and 3. Finally, no navigation helpers, defined by recommendation 4, were provided to indicate where other problems are located in the model.

5.3   Comparison of the Literature and the Visual Feedback Provided by Tools

As shown in Fig. 10, Signavio implements five out of ten recommendations, followed by Adonis, Bonita, and QualiBPMN, which implement four out of ten each. Among the ten analyzed tools, the visual feedback behavior observed on these four tools is the most similar to what the literature recommends. On average, each modeling tool follows three out of ten recommendations on visual feedback about problems.

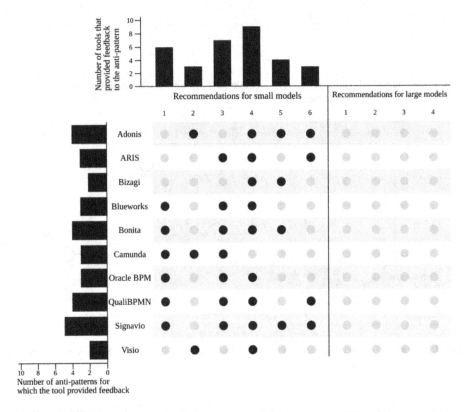

Fig. 10. Visual feedback about problems recommendations implemented by each modeling tool. Source: the authors.

Recommendations 1, 3, and 4 for small models - highlighting issues with icons, displaying floating problem messages, and providing a problem list - are the most recurrent among tools, while recommendation 2, coloring the problematic element, is the least recurrent. Regarding recommendations for large models, no tool implements any of these four recommendations, which implies a major difference between what tools provide and what the literature recommends. Furthermore, apart from the ones covered by the recommendations, the tools offered no other distinct visual feedback. These findings answer our RQ2.

6   Conclusion

In this paper, we presented the current state of visual feedback about modeling problems in process modeling tools. We reviewed and complemented the experiments of Dias et al. [7], confirming there is still no common ground on how process modeling tools react to modeling problems. All tools behaved differently when facing the same set of problems, and only one problem out of ten was detected by all tools, each tool behaving differently towards the problem.

Our analysis shows no significant differences in problem detection and feedback between "premium" and free modeling tools. Furthermore, though literature indicates syntax validation on business process models is less challenging for the automated validation in process modeling tools, our results indicate this class of problems is still not trivial for them.

When analyzing the visual aspects of feedback about problems, we verified that there is still a distance between literature recommendations and what modeling tools actually display to their users. From the recommendations of Dani et al. [25], we identified that process modeling tools are inconsistent in implementing recommendations for small models and implement none of the suggested helpers for visualization of problems in large process models. We believe the presented analysis can be helpful to both process modelers and process modeling tools developers in understanding how process modeling tools currently detect and visually respond to modeling problems.

A possible limitation of our study is the unavailability of some business process modeling tools, such as iGrafx and Mavim. No free or trial versions of these two top-ranked commercial modeling tools were found, limiting our analysis of how they react to problems and provide visual feedback. Additionally, short trial periods, such as 30 days for Blueworks and Visio, hinder the recreation and revalidation of the experiments.

In future work, we aim to investigate the lack of feedback directed at large models in business process modeling tools. A possible reason is that larger models are considered a modeling *smell* in the literature, and keeping models small is a process modeling guideline. However, none of the ten modeling tools studied indicated that the model should be decomposed. Additionally, we intend to develop a process modeling prototype following the visual feedback about problems recommendations in Stein Dani et al. [25], complemented by a survey to more comprehensively evaluate user satisfaction with the recommended visual feedback elements.

Acknowledgments. This study was financed in part by the Coordenação de Aperfeiçoamento de Pessoal de Nível Superior - CAPES, Brazil, Finance Code 001 and by the National Council for Scientific and Technological Development - CNpQ. This study was also funded by the Government of Extremadura (Spain), Council for Economy, Science and Digital Agenda under the grants GR21133 and IB18053, by the European Regional Development Fund (ERDF).

References

1. AG Software: About software AG. https://www.softwareag.com/en_corporate/company. html. Accessed 20 Dec 2021
2. Barjis, J.: The importance of business process modeling in software systems design. Sci. Comput. Programm. **71**(1), 73–87 (2008)
3. Bizagi: About bizagi. https://www.bizagi.com/en/about. Accessed 07 Sep 2021
4. BOC: BOC group (2021). https://boc-group.com/boc-group/. Accessed 07 Sep 2021
5. Bonitasoft: Bonita: Digital process automation for a competitive edge. https://www.bonitasoft.com/bonita-platform. Accessed 07 Sep 2021
6. Camunda: Modeler. https://camunda.com/products/camunda-platform/modeler/. Accessed 09 Sep 2021
7. de Brito Dias, C.L., Stein Dani, V., Mendling, J., Thom, L.H.: Anti-patterns for process modeling problems: an analysis of BPMN 2.0-based tools behavior. In: Di Francescomarino, C., Dijkman, R., Zdun, U. (eds.) BPM 2019. LNBIP, vol. 362, pp. 745–757. Springer, Cham (2019). https://doi.org/10.1007/978-3-030-37453-2_59
8. van Dongen, B.F., van der Aalst, W.M.P., Verbeek, H.M.W.: Verification of EPCs: using reduction rules and petri nets. In: Pastor, O., Falcão e Cunha, J. (eds.) CAiSE 2005. LNCS, vol. 3520, pp. 372–386. Springer, Heidelberg (2005). https://doi.org/10.1007/11431855_26
9. Dumas, M., et al.: Fundamentals of Business Process Management, vol. 1. Springer, Heidelberg (2013). https://doi.org/10.1007/978-3-642-33143-5
10. Fellmann, M., Koschmider, A., Laue, R., Schoknecht, A., Vetter, A.: Business process model patterns: state-of-the-art, research classification and taxonomy. BPMJ (2019)
11. freebpmnquality: QualiBPMN. https://freebpmnquality.github.io/. Accessed 11 Oct 2021
12. Gartner: Enterprise business process analysis (EBPA) reviews and ratings (2021). https://www.gartner.com/reviews/market/enterprise-business-process-analysis. Accessed 20 Oct 2021
13. IBM: Blueworks Live. https://www.ibm.com/products/blueworkslive. Accessed 20 Oct 2021
14. Koehler, J., Vanhatalo, J.: Process anti-patterns: how to avoid the common traps of business process modeling. IBM WebSphere Dev. Tech. J. **10**(2), 4 (2007)
15. Koenig, A.: Patterns and antipatterns. The Patterns Handbook: Techniques, Strategies, and Applications **13**, 383 (1998)
16. Koschmider, A., Laue, R., Fellmann, M.: Business process model anti-patterns: a bibliography and taxonomy of published work. In: European Conference of Information Systems (2019)
17. Krogstie, J., Sindre, G., Jørgensen, H.: Process models representing knowledge for action: a revised quality framework. EJIS **15**(1), 91–102 (2006)
18. Lehmann, B.D., Alexander, P., Lichter, H., Hacks, S.: Towards the identification of process anti-patterns in enterprise architecture models. In: QuASoQ@ APSEC, pp. 47–54 (2020)
19. Mendling, J., Reijers, H.A., van der Aalst, W.M.: Seven process modeling guidelines (7PMG). Inf. Softw. Technol. **52**(2), 127–136 (2010)
20. Microsoft: Visio. https://www.microsoft.com/pt-br/microsoft-365/visio/. Accessed 20 Oct 2021
21. OMG: Business process model and notation (BPMN), version 2.0 (2011). https://www.omg.org/spec/BPMN/2.0/PDF. Accessed 20 Sep 2021
22. Oracle: Oracle BPM. https://www.oracle.com/middleware/technologies/bpm.html. Accessed 20 Oct 2021
23. Rozman, T., Polancic, G., Horvat, R.V.: Analysis of most common process modeling mistakes in BPMN process models. In: Eur SPI 2007 (2008)

24. Signavio: Signavio business transformation suite. https://www.signavio.com/products/business-transformation-suite/. Accessed 09 Sep 2021

25. Stein Dani, V., Freitas, C., Thom, L.: Recommendations for visual feedback about problems within BPMN process models. Softw. Syst. Mod. 1–27 (2022). https://doi.org/10.1007/s10270-021-00972-0

26. Stein Dani, V., Freitas, C.M.D.S., Thom, L.H.: Ten years of visualization of business process models: a systematic literature review. Comput. Stand. Interfaces **66**, 103347 (2019)

27. Weber, I., Hoffmann, J., Mendling, J.: Semantic business process validation. In: SBPM'08, CEUR-WS Proceedings. vol. 472, Citeseer (2008)

Understanding Collaboration: One Issue, Many Perspectives (BPMDS 2022)

A Technique for Collaboration Discovery

Flavio Corradini[1], Barbara Re[1], Lorenzo Rossi[1(✉)], and Francesco Tiezzi[2]

[1] School of Science and Technology, University of Camerino, Camerino, Italy
`lorenzo.rossi@unicam.it`
[2] Dipartimento di Statistica, Informatica, Applicazioni, University of Florence, Florence, Italy

Abstract. In the last years, researchers have contributed to the process mining domain with several techniques and tools supporting the discovery of business processes. Almost all these contributions rely on event logs stored in the information systems of single organizations. In contrast, the discovery of collaborative scenarios where the information systems are distributed among different interacting organizations has been disregarded. In this context, we propose a novel technique for discovering collaboration models from sets of event logs stored in distributed information systems. Given the distributed logs of interacting organizations, the technique discovers each organization's process through one of the available algorithms introduced by the process mining community. It also analyzes the logs to extract information on messages exchange. This information permits automatically combining the discovered processes into a collaboration diagram representing the distributed system's behavior and providing analytics on messages exchange. The technique has been implemented in a tool and evaluated via several experiments.

Keywords: BPMN collaborations · Processes discovery · Messages analysis

1 Introduction

Nowadays, organizations increasingly need to interact to achieve their goals collaboratively and create new forms of business. This requires organizations to form distributed systems, guaranteeing their interoperability. However, this task is made complex by the need to coordinate the interactions of various participants, dealing with requirements, constraints, and regulations coming from different organizations. Effective cooperation among organizations demands the compatibility of their business processes. Such cooperation can be supported by the observations of systems' behavior rather than by sharing documentation that is often incomplete and out of date [6].

In this direction, the most significant contributions come from the process mining community, referring to the automated *discovery of business process models* from data produced by IT systems, i.e., *event logs* [17]. Despite *"there is no foundational reason why"* to not apply process mining in presence of multiple organizations [16], thus using distributed event logs, the techniques already

© Springer Nature Switzerland AG 2022
A. Augusto et al. (Eds.): BPMDS 2022/EMMSAD 2022, LNBIP 450, pp. 63–78, 2022.
https://doi.org/10.1007/978-3-031-07475-2_5

available consider mostly the point of view of a single organization, focusing on (re-)discovery of individual business processes from a single log source [19]. Only a few research lines, i.e., cross-, intra-, and inter-organizational process mining, address, albeit marginally, the problem of discovering on a whole the collaborative behavior of the involved parties and their interactions. This results in a lack of techniques for discovering collaborative models and for detecting issues that typically occur in distributed systems. We refer to problems implied by the interplay among control- and message-flow, e.g., pending messages caused by a lack of synchronization, or a deadlock resulting from activities that are stuck waiting for messages [7, 8].

To fill the gap discussed above, we propose a novel **technique for discovering a collaboration model from a set of event logs of a distributed system**. The technique adopts BPMN [14] *collaborations* as target notation, since they provide a suitable modeling abstraction where different organizations exchange messages. It consists of four phases: (i) *logging*, where each system participant locally logs events related to its process execution; (ii) *processes discovery*, producing a process model for each participant using a given discovery algorithm; (iii) *messages analysis*, extracting information suitable to generate the collaboration diagram and to provide analytics on messages exchange; (iv) *collaboration building*, generating a BPMN collaboration model as a combination of the process models and tailoring it to consider distinctive collaboration aspects related to communication. Notably, the technique is parametric to the algorithm used for processes discovery. This allows exploiting algorithms already validated and their reliable implementations defined by the process mining community.

We call COLLIERY (COLLaboration dIscovERY) the technique described above. To foster its adoption, we propose a tool that supports the COLLIERY's phases. The feasibility of COLLIERY has been evaluated in several experiments via logs we produced using a log generator tool, which is a by-product of this work that we also make available.

The rest of the paper is organized as follows. Section 2 provides a running example and introduces the COLLIERY technique. Section 3 presents the related tool. Section 4 reports on the technique evaluation. Section 5 reviews related works. Finally, Sect. 6 concludes and discusses directions for future work.

2   The COLLIERY Technique

This section introduces the BPMN collaboration representing a collaborative scenario used for better presenting the COLLIERY technique and its phases.

The collaboration model in Fig. 1 illustrates a healthcare scenario combining the activities of a *Patient*, a *Gynecologist*, a *Laboratory*, and a *Hospital* as follows. The *Patient* provides details about his/her health status and waits for information related to the home treatment or to hospitalization. The *Gynecologist* coordinates the activities of the *Laboratory* and *Hospital*, caring of blood analysis and hospitalization respectively. The collaboration starts when the *Patient* sends the information about the disease to the *Gynecologist*. Then, the *Gynecologist*

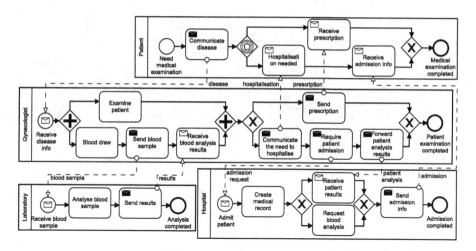

Fig. 1. A healthcare business process collaboration.

examines the *Patient* and, in parallel, draws a blood sample and sends it to the *Laboratory*. The *Laboratory* analyzes the sample and gives back the results to the *Gynecologist*. When both the *Patient* has been examined and the analysis results are received, the *Gynecologist* decides whether to send a medicine prescription or hospitalize the *Patient*, and informs the *Patient* accordingly. Only in the latter case, the *Gynecologist* triggers the *Hospital* by requesting the *Patient* admission and sending the analysis results. When the *Hospital* starts its process, it creates a medical record for the *Patient*, and then decides whether to consider the results of the blood analysis already done or ask for a new analysis; in any case, then it sends the admission information to the *Patient*.

Distributed systems like that can be discovered with the COLLIERY technique we are going to introduce. Figure 2 depicts the structure of the technique, highlighting the phases by which it is composed.

Logging Phase. Process mining relies on the assumption that systems record events about the actual execution of their processes. These events are collected in the so-called *(event) logs*. A log consists of a set of *cases*, each of which refers to a list of events, i.e., a possible run of the system. An *event* refers to the execution of system activity and is described by a set of *attributes*, e.g., the activity name and the timestamp. The sequence of events related to a given case is called *trace*.

The COLLIERY technique relies on logs as well. However, since its goal is to extract information from distributed systems, it has to work on sets of logs. We call *process log* the log of a single participant of a distributed system, and *collaboration log* the set of process logs of all participants of a system. Collaboration logs have the following distinctive features. Firstly, the process logs included in a collaboration log register information about the messages exchanged via communication activities. For example, in our running scenario, an event corresponding to the execution of the activity "Communicate disease" by the *Patient* keeps trace of the sending of a message of type "disease". Secondly, a run of the

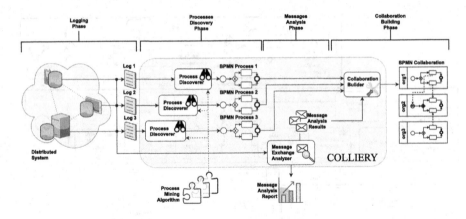

Fig. 2. The COLLIERY technique.

distributed system, namely a *collaboration case*, corresponds to a set of cases one for each involved participant. Figure 3 shows an excerpt of the collaboration log of our running example, where we highlighted the events belonging to two different collaboration cases. In particular, we considered a case of a patient that has been hospitalized (events in blue bounded by a solid line), and a case of a patient that did not need hospitalization and directly received a prescription from the Gynecologist (events in yellow bounded by a dotted line).

The logging activities of participants are kept independent to ensure the loose coupling of system participants, which is a typical requirement of distributed systems. Hence, we do not rely

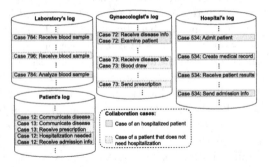

Fig. 3. Example of collaboration cases.

on any identifier for collaboration cases, which would have required an agreement among the participants. Although the content of each process log is independently produced, events stored in different logs belonging to the same collaboration case may have causal dependencies, which are indeed determined by the exchanged messages through their content. Our technique correlates the collaboration cases assuming the presence of the same *message instance identifier* among the attributes of the sending and receiving events as already done in [10]. This is not a limitation of the approach since unique message identifiers are already applied in several communication protocols, e.g., web-service addressing and HTTP cookie.

Like almost all process mining techniques and tools, we consider event logs compliant with the eXtensible Event Stream (XES) format [12], which is the standard for storing and exchanging event logs. To keep track of the additional

```
<event>
  <string key='communicationMode' value='receive'/>
  <string key='concept:name' value='Receive disease info'/>
  <string key='org:group' value='Gynecologist'/>
  <date key='time:timestamp' value='2021/10/30 11:22'/>
  <string key='msgType' value='disease'/>
  <string key='msgInstanceID' value='disease_38'/>
  <string key='eventType' value='start'/>
</event>
```

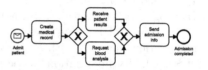

Fig. 4. An event with message in XES format.

Fig. 5. Hospital's process discovered by the Split Miner.

information about messages and event types required by the COLLIERY technique, we have extended the log format by relying on the extensibility mechanism of XES. Figure 4 shows an example of an extended event drawn from the gynecologist's XES log. This is a *receive* event (key `communicationMode`), corresponding to the system activity *Receive disease info* (key `concept:name`) performed by the *Gynecologist* participant (key `org:group`), who has received on October 30, 2021 at 11:22 (key `time:timestamp`) the message of type *disease* (key `msgType`) uniquely identified by *disease_38* (key `msgInstanceID`); the key `eventType` indicates that this event corresponds to the starting event of the enclosing case for the gynecologist's log. Notably, we assume an asynchronous communication model with point-to-point interactions, meaning that the delivered messages are inserted into queues, and for each message, there is exactly one sender and one receiver.

Processes Discovery Phase. This phase has been specifically designed to exploit process discovery algorithms already defined, and possibly implemented, by the research community. It takes as input a collaboration log under consideration, and generates the corresponding BPMN processes. The models' generation can be realized by means of any process discovery algorithm that produces process models in the BPMN notation, or in other notations that can be automatically translated into BPMN [4]. At the time being, we considered the following algorithms as instantiations for this parameter in our experimentation: Alpha [18], Alpha+ [18], Heuristic Miner [20], Inductive Miner [13], and Split Miner [3]. As a matter of example, by applying the Split Miner algorithm to the Hospital's log of our running scenario, we obtain the BPMN process in Fig. 5. The process is similar to the one enclosed on the Hospital pool in Fig. 1, except for the communication aspects that are not dealt with by the Split Miner algorithm.

Messages Analysis Phase. In this phase, the messages exchange analyzer inspects all process logs to correlate the information concerning the sent messages with the received ones. The aim of this phase is twofold. Firstly, it produces information on communication aspects necessary in the next phase to properly build a BPMN collaboration diagram from the discovered processes. Secondly, analytics on messages delivery and consumption, and related time, are produced to help the user to identify potential issues affecting the proper functioning of the distributed system under analysis.

Let us first focus on the information used for building the collaboration. In the following, we will use a, a_1, a_2, ... to denote activity names (which correspond to the values of key `concept:name` within an *event* element in the XES logs), m, m_1, m_2, ... to denote message flow names (which correspond to the values of key `msgType` in the XES logs) and o, o_1, o_2, ... to denote organization names (which correspond to the values of key `org:group` in the XES logs). The information passed to the collaboration builder contains firstly a set M of quintuples of the form (o_1, a_1, m, o_2, a_2), meaning that the send activity a_1 in the pool of organization o_1 has to be linked to the receive activity a_2 in the pool of organization o_2 by means of a message flow labeled by the message name m. In addition, the collaboration builder receives the set L of message flows in which one or more messages have been lost (i.e., messages that are sent but not consumed), the set S of activities corresponding to starting events (identified by the value *start* for the `eventType` key), and the predicate $rc(m_1, m_2)$ that holds if m_1 and m_2 are in race condition. More specifically, $rc(m_1, m_2)$ holds if m_1 and m_2 are both sent in the same trace and only the message sent for first is consumed by a receiving event.

Let us consider now the analysis of message exchanges in the collaboration log performed to obtain analytics for the user. For each type of message (a.k.a. message flow in the BPMN model) we compute the following information: *(i)* number of sent and lost messages; and *(ii)* minimum, average, and maximum stay time in the queue corresponding to the message type. The information *(i)* is simply computed by counting the number of sending and receiving events in the logs for a given value of the `msgType` key. The information *(ii)*, instead, requires taking care of the timestamp of events and properly determining the amount of time elapsed between the sending and the corresponding receiving events. For the sake of simplicity, we assume as irrelevant the transmission time (i.e., the amount of time from inserting the message in the queue), and we do not consider clocks de-synchronization issues, i.e. we assume that logs are generated by systems relying on a clock synchronization solution (see, e.g., [15, Ch. 6]) or working in contexts where the clock drift effects are irrelevant. Even if this analysis is not particularly sophisticated, the produced results may be very effective in identifying communication-related issues in the considered system. The analysis results are visualized in intuitive charts to facilitate both quick interpretation and deep analysis. It is worth noticing that, differently from the message exchange analysis required by the collaboration building, this part of the analysis could be extended or customized according to specific user requirements. The messages analysis for our running example identifies that there are some lost messages. This information would allow the user to intervene in the system to fix the issues causing the loss of messages. We discuss the results of this analysis in Sect. 4.

Collaboration Building Phase. The last phase of the COLLIERY technique concerns the building of the BPMN collaboration from the products of the previous phases. Firstly, we enclose each BPMN process discovered in the second phase within a pool element, whose name corresponds to the system participant that has generated the log (recorded in the key `org:group`). At this point, we have a collaboration with disconnected pools, whose processes only include non-communicating activities. For example, given the processes and the set of

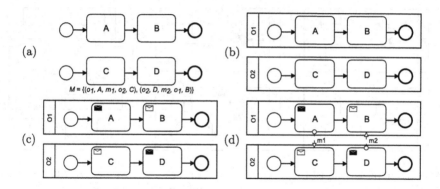

Fig. 6. Collaboration building example.

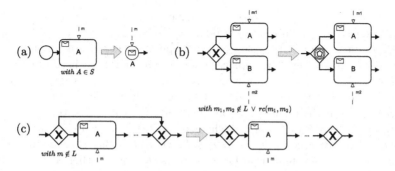

Fig. 7. Fixing communication aspects.

quintuples in Fig. 6(a), the collaboration resulting after these initial operations is the one in Fig. 6(b). Then, send and receive activities in all processes are identified, and hence properly specified in the model. These data can be easily retrieved from the set M of quintuples produced in the third phase: the set of sending activities for an organization o is $\{a \mid (o, a, m, o_2, a_2) \in M\}$, while the set of receiving activities is $\{a \mid (o_1, a_1, m, o, a) \in M\}$. For example, using the quintuples in Fig. 6(a), we obtain the model with specialized activities in Fig. 6(c). Finally, the communicating activities are connected through message flows: for each quintuple (o_1, a_1, m, o_2, a_2) in M, it is inserted in the collaboration model a message flow labeled by m starting from the activity a_1 in the pool o_1 and ending in the activity a_2 in the pool o_2. The final result for the considered simple example is the model in Fig. 6(d).

Since the used process discovery algorithms disregard communication events, the collaboration models obtained so far may present issues. Therefore, a second step in the collaboration building phase is needed to refine the model and properly represent communication aspects. Figure 7 reports the transformation we apply to fix the communication issues. The first transformation, Fig. 7(a), replaces a receive task at the beginning of a process, corresponding to a start event in the log (condition $A \in S$, where S is the set of starting activities computed in the third

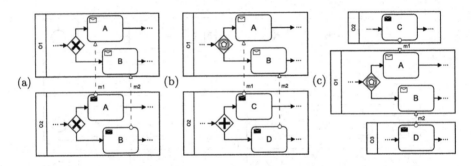

Fig. 8. Examples of model fragments with (a) lost messages, (b) race condition due to parallel gateway, (c) race condition due to multiple sender participants.

phase), by a BPMN message start event element. In this way, in the execution of the resulting BPMN collaboration model, the considered process will be instantiated and started only when a message of type m is actually received. The second transformation, Fig. 7(b), replaces an exclusive choice (realized in BPMN by means of an XOR gateway) between receive activities by a message-driven choice (realized in BPMN by means of an event-based gateway). The figure depicts only two activities, but the transformation works likewise with more than two activities. This transformation is applied when either *(i)* there are no lost messages for the involved receives (condition $m_1, m_2 \notin L$, where L is the set, computed in the third phase, of message flows that have lost messages) or *(ii)* there is a race condition from the messages incoming into the involved receives (condition $rc(m_1, m_2)$, where rc is the race condition predicate computed in the third phase). In fact, the event-based gateway may not be appropriate when the condition *(i)* is not satisfied, because the gateway permits to receive any type of message between m_1 and m_2. Instead, as in the example in Fig. 8(a), the use of an XOR gateway can lead to situations where a participant is waiting for a given message, say m_1, while another is sending another type of message, say m_2; in such a case, the message of type m_1 will be lost ($m_1 \in L$). Notably, this transformation is a heuristic rule; in fact, there may be issues (e.g., a deadlock upstream) causing the loss of messages. Condition *(ii)* permits, instead, to apply the transformation also in some cases of lost messages. In case of a race condition between messages (as in the examples in Fig. 8(b)–(c)), the first arrived message triggers the corresponding receiving activity and disables the others, hence the other messages will be lost. In these situations, the event-based gateway is the appropriate gateway, as it is the BPMN element specifically devoted to dealing with race conditions. Finally, the third transformation, Fig. 7(c), aims at fixing misbehavior concerning the blocking capability of receive activities. Indeed, process mining algorithms do not distinguish between sending, receiving, and internal activities, hence it considers all of them as non-blocking elements. However, when asynchronous communication enters the game, a receive activity has to wait for the corresponding message, possibly forever. Consider, for example, a collaboration log composed of: the process

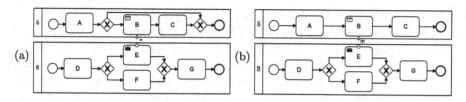

Fig. 9. Examples of discovered collaboration (a) before and (b) after the transformation in Fig. 7(c).

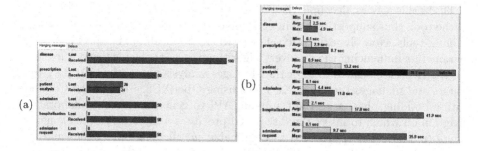

Fig. 10. COLLIERY interfaces for (a) pending messages and (b) message delays.

log of the organization o_1, containing h occurrences of trace $\langle ABC \rangle$ (with B receiving a message m) and k occurrences of trace $\langle A \rangle$, and the process log of the organization o_2, containing h occurrences of trace $\langle DEG \rangle$ (with E sending a message m) and k occurrences of trace $\langle DFG \rangle$. In this case, every mining algorithm properly discovers the process corresponding to the o_2's log, while for the o_1's log the model may differ: the Alpha and the Alpha+ generate a process producing only $\langle ABC \rangle$ traces, the Inductive generates an overfitting model, and only the Heuristic and the Split miners properly discover the process. For instance, the collaboration in Fig. 9(a) has been discovered with the Split Miner. In this case, the coexistence of traces $\langle ABC \rangle$ and $\langle A \rangle$ has been interpreted as the possibility of skipping activities B and C after the execution of A, which would be a correct interpretation if one did not take into account the blocking behavior of the receive activity in a communicative scenario. However, this collaboration model does not faithfully represent the behavior registered in the collaboration log, because it allows execution traces where activity E is performed while activities B and C are skipped, leading to losses of messages of type m that do not occur in the log. Instead, the collaboration in Fig. 9(b), resulting from the application of the transformation in Fig. 7(c), does not exhibit this issue, but it precisely represents the content of the collaboration log.

3   The COLLIERY Tool

We present here the COLLIERY tool implementing three out of the four phases of the technique presented in Fig. 2, since the Logging phase is charged to the distributed system itself. The COLLIERY tool takes as input a set of logs of different organizations and generates a BPMN collaboration model along with a communication analysis report. The tool is developed in *Java*, to guarantee compatibility with any operating system, and exploits external libraries, which helped us to implement the COLLIERY's phases. For the Processes discovery phase we make use of the open-source platform PM4Py (https://pm4py.fit.fraunhofer. de/), as it implements many discovery algorithms, i.e., Alpha, Alpha+, Inductive Miner, and Heuristics Miner, and the transformation algorithm to obtain BPMN models. For the Split Miner we used the Java implementation introduced in [3]. In this way we decouple the process discovery functionalities from the rest of the tool, thus supporting the integration of different discovery algorithms and mining tools. Notably, COLLIERY allows (where applicable) the specification of parameters influencing the discovery algorithms (e.g., the dependency threshold for the Heuristic algorithm). For the Messages analysis phase, the COLLIERY tool parses and manages the input XES files using OpenXES. Finally, the Collaboration building phase uses the Camunda API to generate a fresh collaboration diagram on which to insert the discovered processes and decorate the elements. The COLLIERY tool is provided as a runnable *jar* file; the binary files and the source code, instructions, and examples are available at https://pros.unicam.it/ colliery/. Part of its graphical interface is shown in Fig. 10(a)–(b).

4   Experimental Evaluation

This section presents the technique evaluation carried out with the tool on a set of scenarios, including the running example, to check the quality of the discovered collaborations, and to discuss the outcomes of the communication analysis.

Dataset. The following experiments have been conducted on ten collaboration logs representing the executions of distributed systems. Usually, real(-istic) event logs are made available by open-access repositories (e.g., https://data.4tu.nl), or are synthetically generated by tools (e.g., https://plg.processmining.it). In both cases, the logs that can be obtained represent the executions of single organization processes in which the communication events are missing. Therefore, we developed a new tool for logs generation, which is a by-product of this work that we also make available. It executes BPMN collaborations and records activity and message events into XES files, one for each participant, as discussed in Sect. 2. In addition to the running example, we selected artificial and realistic collaboration models, and we generated collaboration logs from their execution. Notably, the models we selected differ in: the number of participants (from 2 to 4), size (from 16 to 42), and the number of messages (from 2 to 8). Moreover, for making the dataset as heterogeneous as possible, some models are unsound, unsafe, unstructured, or contain loops. The generator of collaboration logs, the models, the event logs, and all the data used and produced in the evaluation are made available at http://pros.unicam.it/colliery/.

Evaluation Approach. Discovery techniques are evaluated through conformance checking [17]: it assesses the quality of a discovered model by comparing

Table 1. Results of the evaluation (f stands for fitness, and p for precision).

	Artificial 1		Artificial 2		Artificial 3		Artificial 4		Artificial 5	
	f	p	f	p	f	p	f	p	f	p
alpha	1	0.7242	0.9261	0.6348	0.9573	0.4565	1	0.6050	0.9149	0.3973
alpha+	1	0.7242	0.9350	0.6378	0.9573	0.4714	1	0.6050	0.9149	0.3973
heu.	1	0.7242	0.9350	0.6378	0.9573	0.4133	1	0.6050	0.9149	0.3973
ind.	1	0.7242	0.9350	0.6378	0.9460	0.4457	1	0.6050	0.9149	0.3973
split	1	0.7242	0.9605	0.6121	0.9563	0.3865	1	0.6050	0.9149	0.3973
	Real 1		Real 2		Real 3		Real 4		Real 5	
	f	p	f	p	f	p	f	p	f	p
alpha	unb.	unb.	unb.	unb.	unb.	unb.	unb.	unb.	unb.	unb.
alpha+	unb.	unb.	unb.	unb.	unb.	unb.	unb.	unb.	unb.	unb.
heu.	unb.	unb.	0.7867	0.6613	unb.	unb.	0.9999	0.7593	unb.	unb.
ind.	0.7913	0.6629	0.8753	0.3832	0.9663	0.2729	0.9945	0.7866	0.7786	0.7043
split	0.7457	0.6176	unb.	unb.	unb.	unb.	0.9220	0.7570	0.7437	0.6863

the behavior observed in an event log with the one described by a process model. Unfortunately, the conformance checking techniques and tools available today compare process models (usually Petri nets) with process logs while lacking approaches that compare collaboration models and collaboration logs.

To apply conformance checking in our context it is necessary to transform each discovered collaboration into a Petri net, and appropriately merge the traces of each participant into a *collective* event log, i.e., a single log file where the traces contain ordered lists of events triggered by any participant. Concerning the collective logs, they are generated by the above-introduced log generator tool we developed. Instead, the translations of the BPMN collaborations into behaviorally equivalent Petri nets have been performed in two steps. The first step consists of using the *Convert BPMN diagram to Petri net (control-flow)* plugin of ProM (www.promtools.org) to produce a set of Petri nets, each of which represents the control-flow of a participant process. In the second step, we combine these Petri net processes to include also the message-flow. This is achieved by connecting through a place each transition that represents a sending action to the transition that represents the corresponding receiving activity. Therefore, with such data and the aid of ProM, we performed conformance checking to measure *fitness*, i.e., the ability of a model to reproduce the behavior contained in a log, and *precision*, i.e., the ability of a model to generate only the behavior discovered in a log, following respectively the approaches proposed in [1] and [2].

Evaluation Results. Hereafter, we present the result of the experiments. For the sake of presentation, we discuss in detail only the results obtained on the running example. Independently from the mining algorithm selected for the discovery phase, the collaboration models obtained using COLLIERY on the collaborative log of the running example report the four pools of the original model

(Fig. 1), correctly labeled with the corresponding organization name. All the message flows, the event-based gateway in the *Patient* pool, and the message start events in the *Hospital, Laboratory* and *Gynecologist* pools are discovered. Moreover, referring to the collaboration discovered by COLLIERY with the Inductive Miner algorithm, also the participant processes are identical in the topology to the original ones, while the other algorithms fail in reproducing properly the block of parallel tasks. For instance, with the Heuristics Miner this block of tasks ends with an exclusive join gateway (instead of a parallel one), and the task *Receive blood analysis results* is placed after the block. This discrepancy changes the behavior of the whole system, introducing unsafeness. This is not due to the Collaboration building phase; it is due to the discovery of the *Gynecologist* process made by the Heuristics Miner. In fact, considering a different discovery algorithm we obtain a different result. In particular, by selecting the Inductive Miner, the *Gynecologist* process results identical to the original model (see the repository we made available online).

About the results of the conformance checking, only the collaborations of the running example discovered using the Inductive and Split Miner can be analyzed, as the others cannot be transformed into bounded Petri nets. The collaboration discovered by means of the Inductive Miner has the higher results (fitness ≈0.79 and precision ≈0.66), strictly followed by the results of the Split Miner (fitness ≈ 0.75 and precision ≈ 0.62). In both cases, the values of the conformance checking show that the collaborations discovered by COLLIERY are good in reproducing the behaviors shown in the logs without overfitting them too much. The values of fitness and precision achieved for the other examples with different discovery algorithms are resumed in Table 1. The first five rows regard the collaborations discovered from event logs of artificial (and structured) models. In this case, we can always calculate fitness and precision values because all the collaborations discovered by COLLIERY are bounded. While the last five rows regard collaboration discovered from real (and often unstructured) models that in fact result very often in unbounded nets for which we cannot apply conformance checking. Overall, the observed values are high, especially for the fitness that reaches in some cases the maximum (i.e., 1).

Regarding the communication analysis performed on the event logs of the running example, Fig. 10(a) reports the number of messages exchanged or lost for each message flow name. From this plot, we can observe a problem with messages of type *patient analysis*. Specifically, 26 messages have been sent but not received, while 24 have been correctly received. This information permits to spot a potential problem in the distributed system under analysis, whose identification is facilitated by the discovered model that provides an abstract view of the system behavior. Indeed, the *Gynecologist* always forwards the patient analysis to the *Hospital* that, in its turn, can skip the receive task *Receive patient analysis*. Figure 10(b) reports the minimum, the maximum, and the average number of seconds elapsed between a send event and a receive event with the same message instance identifier. Notably, in the case of lost messages, the tool depicts a maximum time equal to infinite, together with the maximum time calculated considering only the received messages. This information opens the possibility to monitor and predict the delays related to message exchanges, thus enabling the identification of bottlenecks.

Threats to Validity. Since process mining focuses almost entirely on process logs rather than on collaboration ones, datasets and approaches supporting the evaluation of techniques like COLLIERY are missing, as also reported in [9]. A possible solution would be to transform existing event logs into distributed logs suitable for our technique. However, this would imply manually inserting communication events, thus knowing the system that generates these logs. Another concern regards the absence of conformance checking approaches and related tools supporting the evaluation of discovery techniques for collaborative scenarios. We managed to arrange collaboration logs and BPMN collaborations to work with existing conformance checking approaches, but a conformance technique specific for this collaborative setting would avoid or reduce errors introduced by logs and models transformations. Indeed, despite very often COLLIERY discovers exactly the original model, fitness and precision values are lower than 1.

5 Related Works

Despite almost all process mining approaches being devoted to gathering knowledge on single organization processes, works exploiting process mining in collaborative settings exist in the literature. These techniques come under the umbrella of *cross-*, *intra-*, and *inter-organizational* process mining. Cross-organizational process mining aims at spotting differences between processes of the same or different organizations [17]. Intra-organizational process mining tends to detect resources, roles, and departments involved in single organization processes [23]. While, more in line with our work, inter-organizational process mining deals with logs distributed over different organizations [10,16]. Here we discuss approaches somehow similar to ours.

Zeng et al. present in [22] a framework for the discovery of cross-organizational models, where participants can communicate. The framework relies on distributed logs, each of which permits the discovery of a colored Petri-net enriched with resources and communication. Then, these nets are grouped in a collaborative workflow via coordination patterns. Differently from us, this approach does not allow the selection of the desired discovery algorithm. Moreover, the use of Petri-nets, instead of BPMN collaborations, results in a less intuitive modeling notation, reducing the comprehension of the system behavior significantly. Finally, the approach does not give insights about the message exchange, and no tool support is given. Bernardi et al. define a similar approach in [5] resulting in the discovery of business rules, instead of models. In the same fashion, Zeng et al. provide in [21] an approach for building Petri-nets from distributed event logs. The approach produces a top-level process model enriched with abstract transitions representing coordination models among the participants. Every abstract transition refers to a single participant process given as output using standard Petri-nets. Finally, the participant processes are integrated with the coordination model obtaining the whole collaboration. Even this approach has not been implemented in a tool, and no support to high-level notation, like BPMN, and no insights on the communication are given. Differently, Engel et al. [10] present a framework addressing the inter-organizational process mining of organizations interacting via the Electronic Data Interchange (EDI) messages standard. The framework permits getting insights from EDI data by transforming them into event logs. However, the focus of this work is more on extracting information about the interactions, than on producing collaboration models. Indeed, on the produced logs, the authors apply existing discovery algorithms that cannot produce collaborations. Hernandez-Resendiz et al. present in [11] a methodology to discover choreographies from the logs of distributed organizations. The methodology merges the logs on the basis of a similarity matrix obtained by calculating the distance between the traces of each participant and discovers the choreography by means of the Split Miner. Differently from us, no automatic tool is provided, the possibility to use other discovery algorithms is forbidden, and the number of participants is limited to two. Finally, Elkoumy et al. show in [9] an approach for applying process mining in collaborative scenarios without exposing sensitive data, business secrets, etc. The approach makes the organizations' logs anonymous and extracts from them a directly-follows graph, to which apply the discovery. This work points out the security problems that may arise when we deal with data from different organizations. Despite our technique does not address this problem, we could easily extend it to preserve privacy: the Processes discovery phase could be performed internally to each organization, while the Messages analysis phase can be performed in the same way on logs that have been anonymized.

6   Concluding Remarks

This paper presents COLLIERY: a technique for discovering collaboration models from distributed event logs. COLLIERY exploits existing discovery algorithms to re-create process models of organizations involved in a distributed system, then it merges them into a BPMN collaboration. The resulting model is decorated in order to reproduce the communication aspects extrapolated from the logs. Moreover, COLLIERY provides an analysis of the communication events to get insights about message exchanges. Finally, COLLIERY has been implemented in a tool we used to evaluate the technique against several logs.

Discussion. We were motivated by the increasing adoption of distributed paradigms in IT systems and by a general lack of process mining solutions suitable for these scenarios. In particular, almost all the discovery techniques consider the perspective of single organizations. Driving process mining to deal with distributed scenarios can bring the advantage of gathering information on message exchanges and on their impact on the involved processes. The technique we propose could have practical applicability in many research fields around which the BPM and the process mining communities are spending a lot of efforts such as the Internet of Things, Cyber-physical systems, and microservices, in which the distribution of the information is even more evident.

Future Work. We plan to implement the COLLIERY technique within existing process mining frameworks, e.g., ProM. On the one hand, this would allow increasing the number of supported discovery algorithms. On the other hand, researchers would have the possibility to develop related techniques such as conformance checking or model enhancement suitable for collaborations. Moreover, we plan to support other methods for correlating the collaboration cases to make COLLIERY works also in case message identifiers are not present, for instance, using pattern matching or other heuristics on the attributes contained in the message events.

References

1. Adriansyah, A., van Dongen, B., van der Aalst, W.: Conformance checking using cost-based fitness analysis. In: Enterprise Distributed Object Computing, pp. 55–64. IEEE (2011)
2. Adriansyah, A., Munoz-Gama, J., Carmona, J., van Dongen, B.F., van der Aalst, W.M.P.: Alignment based precision checking. In: La Rosa, M., Soffer, P. (eds.) BPM 2012. LNBIP, vol. 132, pp. 137–149. Springer, Heidelberg (2013). https://doi.org/10.1007/978-3-642-36285-9_15
3. Augusto, A., Conforti, R., Dumas, M., La Rosa, M., Polyvyanyy, A.: Split miner: automated discovery of accurate and simple business process models from event logs. Knowl. Inf. Syst. **59**(2), 251–284 (2018). https://doi.org/10.1007/s10115-018-1214-x
4. Augusto, A., Conforti, R., Dumas, M., La Rosa, M., Bruno, G.: Automated discovery of structured process models from event logs: the discover-and-structure approach. Data Knowl. Eng. **117**, 373–392 (2018)
5. Bernardi, M.L., Cimitile, M., Mercaldo, F.: Cross-organisational process mining in cloud environments. Inf. Knowl. Manag. **17**(02), 1850014 (2018)
6. Beschastnikh, I., Brun, Y., Ernst, M., Krishnamurthy, A.: Inferring models of concurrent systems from logs of their behavior with CSight. In: International Conference on Software Engineering, pp. 468–479. ACM (2014)
7. Corradini, F., Morichetta, A., Polini, A., Re, B., Rossi, L., Tiezzi, F.: Correctness checking for BPMN collaborations with sub-processes. Syst. Softw. **166**, 110594 (2020)
8. Corradini, F., Muzi, C., Re, B., Rossi, L., Tiezzi, F.: Formalising and animating multiple instances in BPMN collaborations. Inf. Syst. **103**, 101459 (2022)
9. Elkoumy, G., Fahrenkrog-Petersen, S.A., Dumas, M., Laud, P., Pankova, A., Weidlich, M.: Secure multi-party computation for inter-organizational process mining. In: Nurcan, S., Reinhartz-Berger, I., Soffer, P., Zdravkovic, J. (eds.) BPMDS/EMMSAD -2020. LNBIP, vol. 387, pp. 166–181. Springer, Cham (2020). https://doi.org/10.1007/978-3-030-49418-6_11
10. Engel, R., et al.: Analyzing inter-organizational business processes. IseB **14**(3), 577–612 (2015). https://doi.org/10.1007/s10257-015-0295-2

11. Hernandez-Resendiz, J.D., Tello-Leal, E., Marin-Castro, H.M., Ramirez-Alcocer, U.M., Mata-Torres, J.A.: Merging event logs for inter-organizational process mining. In: Zapata-Cortes, J.A., Alor-Hernández, G., Sánchez-Ramírez, C., García-Alcaraz, J.L. (eds.) New Perspectives on Enterprise Decision-Making Applying Artificial Intelligence Techniques. SCI, vol. 966, pp. 3–26. Springer, Cham (2021). https://doi.org/10.1007/978-3-030-71115-3_1

12. IEEE: Standard for eXtensible Event Stream (XES) for Achieving Interoperability in Event Logs and Event Streams (2016)

13. Leemans, S.J.J., Fahland, D., van der Aalst, W.M.P.: Discovering block-structured process models from event logs containing infrequent behaviour. In: Lohmann, N., Song, M., Wohed, P. (eds.) BPM 2013. LNBIP, vol. 171, pp. 66–78. Springer, Cham (2014). https://doi.org/10.1007/978-3-319-06257-0_6

14. OMG: Business Process Model and Notation (BPMN) v2.0 (2011)

15. Tanenbaum, A., van Steen, M.: Distributed Systems. Pearson, London (2007)

16. Aalst, W.M.P.: Intra- and inter-organizational process mining: discovering processes within and between organizations. In: Johannesson, P., Krogstie, J., Opdahl, A.L. (eds.) PoEM 2011. LNBIP, vol. 92, pp. 1–11. Springer, Heidelberg (2011). https://doi.org/10.1007/978-3-642-24849-8_1

17. van der Aalst, W.: Process Mining: Data Science in Action. Springer, Heidelberg (2016). https://doi.org/10.1007/978-3-662-49851-4

18. van der Aalst, W., Weijters, T., Maruster, L.: Workflow mining: discovering process models from event logs. IEEE Trans. Knowl. Data Eng. **16**(9), 1128–1142 (2004)

19. Vom Brocke, J., Rosemann, M.: Handbook on Business Process Management 1. Springer, Heidelberg (2014). https://doi.org/10.1007/978-3-642-45100-3

20. Weijters, A., van Der Aalst, W., De Medeiros, A.: Process mining with the heuristics miner-algorithm. TU/e, Technical report, WP 166, pp. 1–34 (2006)

21. Zeng, Q., Duan, H., Liu, C.: Top-down process mining from multi-source running logs based on refinement of petri nets. IEEE Access **8**, 61355–61369 (2020)

22. Zeng, Q., Sun, S.X., Duan, H., Liu, C., Wang, H.: Cross-organizational collaborative workflow mining from a multi-source log. Decis. Support Syst. **54**, 1280–1301 (2013)

23. Zhao, W., Zhao, X.: Process mining from the organizational perspective. In: Wen, Z., Li, T. (eds.) Foundations of Intelligent Systems. AISC, vol. 277, pp. 701–708. Springer, Heidelberg (2014). https://doi.org/10.1007/978-3-642-54924-3_66

Understanding Process Management in Non-profit Organisations Without Formal Business Process Management

Chezre Fredericks and Lisa F. Seymour[⊠]

CITANDA, Department of IS, University of Cape Town, Cape Town, South Africa
lisa.seymour@uct.ac.za

Abstract. Non-Profit Organisations (NPOs) are crucial in society, but many have not adopted systematic Business Process Management (BPM). This qualitative case study explains how and why three South Africa NPOs manage their business processes without adopting BPM. Through inductive thematic analysis of interviews and organisational documents, we describe how NPOs manage processes instinctively and using strategic approaches. Maximising their use of technology was a useful method employed. The main drivers for managing processes were found to come from their governance and external bodies. The influential role of donors and auditors is described. These findings should help NPOs, their managers, donors, auditors, and consultants identify how to improve NPO processes.

Keywords: Non-profit · BPM adoption · Business process management

1 Introduction

Non-Profit Organisations (NPOs) are crucial in society, supporting government in service delivery, social and developmental issues [1]. Yet, many struggle to deliver their outcomes and comply with legislative obligations [2]. Organisational inefficiency reduces funding, highlighting the need for process management [3] and a lack business process management (BPM). BPM is a strategic management approach that improves organisational performance, flexibility, and strengthen competitive advantage through business processes [4]. A growing NPO market and a declining donor constituency, increase the need for competitive advantage [1]. Literature covers why organisations adopt BPM, but not non adoption and how NPOs informally manage processes. The BPM community has called for empirical case studies to understand organisational issues with BPM [5]. Hence, we tried to answer: Why is there a lack of BPM adoption in NPOs and how do NPOs who have not adopted BPM manage their processes? This paper now briefly reviews literature, the method, findings, limitations, and conclusion.

2 Literature Review

Process work is stated to currently be in a lull between hypes, and transforming into digital transformation [6]. While 84% of companies surveyed are committed to business

© Springer Nature Switzerland AG 2022
A. Augusto et al. (Eds.): BPMDS 2022/EMMSAD 2022, LNBIP 450, pp. 79–87, 2022.
https://doi.org/10.1007/978-3-031-07475-2_6

process work, only 23% consider it a strategic commitment and only 15% have an organized BPM group. Process focus has waned to merely improving specific departmental
processes. An organisational innovation is as an idea or behaviour that is new to the
organisation [7]. BPM is considered as an organisational innovation for NPOs, hence
the conceptual framework of organisational innovation adoption (CFOIA) framework
[8] could explain BPM non-adoption. According to CFOIA, the adoption decision goes
through the stages of awareness, consideration, and intention to adopt which are. influenced by the perceived characteristics of the innovation, the adopter characteristics and
environmental influences. The perceived innovation characteristics are influenced by
supplier marketing efforts, the social network and environmental influences [8]. During
awareness, organisations learn about their inefficiencies, obtain the desire to change and
learn about BPM [9]. NPOs using BPM, did recognise their problems and saw BPM as
the solution [2]. A lack of BPM awareness is a general concern [10], in Bosnia, a lack of
BPM awareness across NPOs was noted [11]. If NPOs are aware of BPM they may not
have made a decision to reject BPM. Once an NPO recognises BPM as a solution, it can
consider if it is necessary and what the alternatives are. Issues that negatively affect BPM
adoption can include: a lack of practical guidelines to ensure critical success factors are
achieved [12], a lack of awareness of process-orientation [11], the confusion of BPM
with WFM [2] and the difficulty of affecting process-based work despite considerable
investment into BPM initiatives [13].

3　Research Method

Our purpose was to understand Process Management in NPOs without formal BPM.
The interpretive paradigm followed in this study seeks to understand the way humans
interpret their roles as social actors with emphasis placed on conducting research among
people in their natural environment [14]. In this study, a NPO was considered to be
the case and unit of analysis. Yin [15] suggests that something needs to make the case
special. The distinctive event defining a case in this study, is the non-adoption of BPM.
This study included three South African NPOs who had not adopted BPM. The three
NPOs selected are all classified as Small to Medium Enterprises. The research design
was submitted to the university's ethics committee for approval prior to data collection. The primary data was semi-structured interviews supplemented by secondary data.
Using purposive critical case sampling [16], we selected to interview members of senior
management at NPOs, based on their critical knowledge of their NPO's decisions. All
signed a participant consent form and were given a unique code (P1–P7) to keep their
identities confidential. The three cases are now described. NPO-A, a registered non-profit
company, publishes religious artefacts to make them accessible in suitable formats to all
people in South Africa in all 11 official languages and has a literacy program for school
children. NPO-B, a voluntary association in the sports sector, has as a core focus the
administration of a sport (which is not revealed to protect anonymity) within a province,
spanning grassroots development to the professional provincial team. They are affiliated
to a national body, their primary funder. NPO-C, a religious institution, is a voluntary
association. Their core focus is to train, encourage and coordinate religious workers in
South Africa. The regional office included in this study, reports to the national office,
but is run autonomously.

Table 1 shows the data collected. The data was analysed following the inductive thematic analysis procedure of Thomas [17] and used the Nvivo software package. Firstly, raw data were prepared by transcribing the audio files into text files and importing them into Nvivo. Coding initially revealed seventy-three codes which were iteratively revised to 15 codes and were then categorised into seven theme categories.

Table 1. Data collected

NPO Id	Interviewee data (Years of Experience)	Secondary data
NPO-A	Head of IT (20), Head of Finance (9), CEO (4)	Annual Reports (SD1, SD2)
NPO-B	Company Secretary (10), Services Manager (3)	Annual Report (SD3)
NPO-C	Regional Director (4.5), Staff Worker (1.5)	Minutes (SD4), Website (SD5)

4 Findings and Discussion

Our findings are now discussed. Our first finding was that in all NPOs, there was a distinct lack of BPM awareness and no formal decision, to not adopt BPM was taken.

4.1 There is a Lack of BPM Awareness, BPM Evaluation and BPM Resources

BPM was not clearly understood by NPOs, who assigned their own definitions to BPM. Only one of the respondents had previous BPM experience while employed at a large corporation. Respondents that were aware of BPM, were confused about what BPM was and hence did not think it was necessary. Their awareness of BPM did not make the link between their inefficiencies and adopting BPM as a potential solution. None of the NPOs had considered adopting BPM and hence had not formerly decided to not adopt BPM. This confirms what was found in literature, that NPOs need to know what BPM is before they can accept it [9]. Even if they were aware of BPM, resourcing was a challenge to BPM consideration. When asked what it would take to run processes optimally, respondents in two NPOs referred to resources as a challenge, as funding and capacity are a problem. The number of posts in many cases are restricted and hence many strategic implementation projects can't be implemented. BPM implementations are costly and time-consuming [18] which is a barrier to BPM adoption. When asked about alternatives to BPM most respondents didn't think that there were any, citing BPM as the only way to improve organisational performance. This is not reflected in the data, as there are other ways they manage processes which we now describe. The final list of codes and categories with sample quotes in support are in Table 2.

Table 2. Data coding results

Categories and (Sub-Themes)	Data quote [Data source]
A Lack of BPM Awareness BPM has not been Formerly Considered or Evaluated	I am aware of business process management, we didn't call it that, we called it business optimisation and we used it mainly to review our internal structure [P4]
A Lack of Resources for BPM	In terms of the plan for the next five years, the organization realized that it lacked capacity to fully actualize strategic thrusts [SD3]
NPOs Instinctively Manage Processes	Well I think that it's something instinctively that is part of our leadership approach at the moment. I think it's part of our governance [P3]
(By Maximising the Use of Technology)	I went to visit them in February live.. and people thought I was their best friend because they know me from the Skype and they gave us a very generous gift… but that's amazing what technology can actually do [P5]
(By Maximising Human Resources)	That is why they are appointed.. they get measured against an execution agreement and an internal performance review [P7]
(Through Organisational Learning)	Because this issue has arisen, how do we function not only how do we manage it well, do our policies and procedures, are they up to date enough to manage this incident and inform us of how we operate [P6]
NPOs Employ Strategic Approaches to Manage Processes	We have policies and procedures in place, to manage the efficiencies and make sure that the operational processes are in place [P7]
(Using Structural Re-alignment)	This restructure will allow for a more sharply focused sales division on the one hand, and on the other a marketing division that will focus fully on marketing not only the products but indeed the total brand and mission [SD2]
(Through External Collaboration)	[NPO] is in competition with other sports… but the way to deal with it is by joining forces with them. For example, hosting [two other sports] matches [SD3]
(Through For-profit Revenue Activities)	We did have a team of marketers, but now it was expanded to sales people [P1]
(By Using Audit Controls to Manage Processes)	In our auditing processes and the controls that we have introduced for stock control and stock levels as well, also the cash handling as far as donations is concerned and so on, then it is in terms of standard business practice [P1]

(continued)

Table 2. (*continued*)

Categories and (Sub-Themes)	Data quote [Data source]
NPO Governance Drives Process Change (NPO Boards Ensure Strategic Objectives are Achieved)	Whilst the strategic direction of the organisation is determined by the Board of Directors and institutionalised by its subcommittees, the strategy is operationalised through the Chief Executive and his Executive Management team [SD3]
(Processes are Controlled by Donors)	We took some funding which was around our life skills stuff, but it actually messed up our basic ethos and key functions of what we were doing, so instead of us utilising life skills as another objective, it actually became the tail that wags the dog and a lot of those, what we were known for, got lost [P6]
External Bodies Impact Processes	[NPO] finished fourth on the [mother body] Incentive Scorecard system - that rewards members who exceed in delivering the basic activities and compliance requirements of the [mother body] [SD3]
(Through Advice from Auditors and Consultants)	We had the auditors as well, that came as advice, so we felt if we don't have the knowledge ourselves, we can always call in external guys [P2]
(Through Advice from Sister Companies)	Ongoing consultations with the [sister NPO1] and [sister NPO2], [mother body] and it's peer the [sister NPO3] and any improvements applicable to [NPO] is implemented [P4]
(Through Legislative Compliance)	If we didn't get certification then we wouldn't be able to host matches here, be it domestic or international matches [P4]

4.2 NPOs Instinctively Manage Processes

While they had not adopted BPM, the NPOs were functioning with sufficient efficiency. All NPOs had to report to their governance structures, and management teams had to deliver results and without making performance improvements, this requirement would not be met. Therefore, changes made to processes to improve performance, are seen as instinctive as organisational performance was attained without a formal approach to managing processes. Literature shows that governance is one of the core elements of BPM [19]. In the same way that BPM governance ensures good performance from a business process, governance structures at NPOs ensure good organisational performance. How they instinctively perform process management is now discussed.

All NPOs had seen significant benefits from the use of IT, although most respondents acknowledge that they have can improve their technological state. IT greatly impacted the efficiency of the operational processes at NPOs and helped create a space for new funding and the fulfilment of their social causes. One NPO found direct access to new funding from an international donor using video conferencing. This confirms literature

[20], that when NPOs adopt technology, they are likely to increase their funding. IT use was reported in annual reports presented to donors and, in line with literature [21], that using enterprise systems benefitted NPO's process performance.

Maximising human resources was seen to be instinctive management of their processes. NPOs try to employ talented staff, making sure that the employee's skills and capabilities match roles adequately. Performance of employees is then managed to ensure that the NPO receives maximum return on investment from staff. Employees are also trained to ensure that they remain productive. NPOs realise the importance of their employees as a core element of organisational performance. This is like the importance BPM literature places on people, where business process performance is as a direct result of people capabilities [19], a core BPM capability.

NPOs deal with problems when they arise and often make improvements based on these events. Organisational learning is then used to mitigate future occurrences of the event. Two of the NPOs referred to this for dealing with problems. Organisational learning is defined as process where organisations learn from their understanding and consequent management of their experiences [22].

4.3 NPOs Employ Strategic Approaches to Manage Processes

While process management was instinctive, strategic approaches, other than BPM, were also employed. NPOs confirmed that they have strategic plans in place to achieve improved efficiency through four strategic approaches. Firstly, NPOs realign their structure to achieve their efficiency strategic goals. Commitment to process-orientation often leads to structural redesign in BPM [23]. It is interesting to note the similarity between re-aligning for process-orientation in comparison to NPOs re-aligning for strategic ends. Secondly, to achieve improved efficiency, NPOs collaborate with like-minded competitors as an alternative to gaining a competitive advantage on them. All NPOs acknowledged the existence of competition within their respective sectors and surprisingly identified a preference for collaboration as opposed to gaining competitive advantage over them. As NPOs seek to benefit society rather than make profit, they choose to work together, mitigating the risk of unnecessary competition. Thirdly, while NPOs are not competing for profits, they sometimes employ for-profit activities to fund their social causes and gain a competitive advantage [24]. All three NPOs had for-profit activities as an alternate source of funding to donations. One NPO found that they could rent the unutilised sections of their property and one NPO adapted roles to suit for-profit activities. A final strategy employed by all NPOs, is to follow audit controls within their processes. This puts stakeholders at ease, as compliance with audit requirements reduces mismanagement of NPO resources. Data found in annual reports stress the importance of audited financial statements, defining them as imperative to fiduciary responsibility. Audit controls drive the sustainability of NPO's performance and process change. There is related to the growing understanding that BPM is needed ensure a connection between strategy and compliance [6].

4.4 NPO Governance and External Bodies Drive Process Change

The respondents described drivers of process management. The dominant driver category was NPO governance that can sustain and improve organisational performance. All NPOs have good governance structures, where their executive management teams are accountable to their respective boards. This accountability strengthens the performance of the NPO, as strategic objectives get implemented operationally. Two NPOs demonstrated a clear boundary between the board and the executive management team which reduces the risk of board members influencing operational decisions and allows the management team to freely decide on the operational activities needed to deliver strategic objectives. Two NPOs found that their processes were controlled by funding which had both positive and negative implications for the NPOs. This can either erode or improve organisational performance, having positive and negative implications for the NPO's business processes. This finding confirms literature that NPOs often relinquish some decision-making to secure a donor's financial support [1, 24]. Most participants could identify at least one source of external advice, such as auditors or consultants, that used to improve their processes. NPOs also look to their sister organisations to share solutions and then adopt solutions that have been found to have some success. Literature speaks of the degree of interconnectedness between NPOs having an influence on the decision of NPOs to adopt BPM [8]. If BPM is discussed within the social circles, it is likely to be adopted. This is somewhat confirmed by the findings of this study, NPOs do adopt innovations shared within their social circles, but they have not found BPM yet. Government often has a role to play in the environment of an NPO, as legislative requirements set by government often force an NPO to adapt its processes. Two of the NPOs expressed concern about legislative compliance affecting their processes. Literature case studies exist demonstrating the successful implementation of BPM and the benefits of legislative compliance as a direct result [9, 25]. In this study NPOs were adapting processes to ensure legislative compliance.

5 Conclusion

While NPOs play a crucial role in society, there is evidence that many could benefit from BPM. This research aimed to understand how and why NPOs manage their business processes when not using a formal BPM method. The findings are modelled in Fig. 1. The three South African NPOs studied, had not made a formal decision to not adopt BPM, were unaware of or misunderstood BPM, did not have the relevant resources for it, and hence had not evaluated it. Yet they instinctively managed processes and employed strategic approaches to manage processes. The dominant approaches were using relevant technology and skilled staff and through structural alignment. The main drivers for managing processes were from their governance and external bodies. From a research perspective we have provided a description of process management dynamics in NPOs. Yet this study has limitations. Firstly, the context is restricted to NPOs in South Africa who had not adopted systematic process management. It would be useful to study NPOs who have adopted BPM and NPOs in other regions. Secondly, while the interpretive method gives richness of understanding, it has limitations. Another method, such as critical realism, could give a richer understanding of the mechanisms driving process management and why they are not always successful.

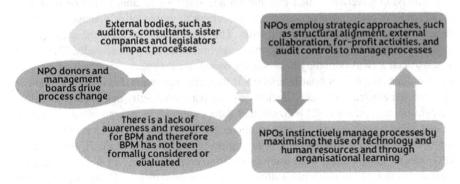

Fig. 1. Model of NPO process management

References

1. Wiggill, M.N.: Donor relationship management practices in the South African non-profit sector. Public Relations Rev. **40**, 278–285 (2014). https://doi.org/10.1016/j.pubrev.2013.10.005
2. Haddad, C.R., Ayala, D.H.F., Uriona, M.M., Forcellini, F.A., Lezana, Á.G.R.: Process improvement for professionalizing non-profit organizations: BPM approach. Bus. Process Manage. J. **22**, 634–658 (2016). https://doi.org/10.1108/BPMJ-08-2015-0114
3. Jacobs, F.A., Marudas, N.P.: The combined effect of donation price and administrative inefficiency on donations to US nonprofit organisations. Finan. Account. Manage. **25**, 33–53 (2009). https://doi.org/10.1111/j.1468-0408.2008.00464.x
4. Singer, R.: Business process management in small-and medium-sized enterprises: an empirical study. In: Proceedings of the 7th International Conference on Subject-Oriented Business Process Management, p. 9. ACM (2015)
5. Recker, J., Reijers, H.A.: The panel discussion at BPM 2019. Lect. Notes Bus. Inf. Proces. **362**, vii–x (2019). https://doi.org/10.1007/978-3-030-37453-2
6. Harmon, P., Garcia, J., The State of Business Process Management 2020 (2020). https://www.bptrends.com/bptrends-surveys/
7. Swanson, E.B.: Information systems innovation among organizations. Manage. Sci. **40**, 1069–1092 (1994)
8. Frambach, R.T., Schillewaert, N.: Organizational innovation adoption: a multi-level framework of determinants and opportunities for future research. J. Bus. Res. **55**, 163–176 (2002). https://doi.org/10.1016/s0148-2963(00)00152-1
9. Buh, B., Kovačič, A., Indihar Štemberger, M.: Critical success factors for different stages of business process management adoption–a case study. Econ. Res.-Ekonomska istraživanja **28**, 243–258 (2015)
10. Hammer, M.: What is business process management? In: vom Brocke, J., Rosemann, M. (eds.) Handbook on Business Process Management 1. IHIS, pp. 3–16. Springer, Heidelberg (2015). https://doi.org/10.1007/978-3-642-45100-3_1
11. Kasim, T., Haracic, M., Haracic, M.: The improvement of business efficiency through business process management. Econ. Rev. J. Econ. Bus. **16**, 31–43 (2018)

12. vom Brocke, J., Schmiedel, T., Recker, J., Trkman, P., Mertens, W., Viaene, S.: Ten principles of good business process management. Bus. Process Manage. J. **20**, 530–548 (2014). https://doi.org/ https://doi-org.ezproxy.uct.ac.za/https://doi.org/10.1108/BPMJ-06-2013-0074

13. Trkman, P.: The critical success factors of business process management. Int. J. Inf. Manage. **30**, 125–134 (2010)

14. Saunders, M., Lewis, P., Thornhill, A.: Research Methods for Business Students, 7th edn. Pearson Education Limited (2016)

15. Yin, R.K.: A (very) brief refresher on the case study method. In: Knight, V., Habib, L., Koscielak, K., Virding, A., Speer, M. (eds.): Application of Case Study Research, pp. 3–20. Sage (2012)

16. Marshall, M.N.: Sampling for qualitative research. Fam. Pract. **13**, 522–525 (1996). https://doi.org/10.1093/fampra/13.6.522

17. Thomas, D.R.: A general inductive approach for analyzing qualitative evaluation data. Am. J. Eval. **27**, 237–246 (2006). https://doi.org/10.1177/1098214005283748

18. Sadiq, S., Indulska, M., Bandara, W., Chong, S., Major issues in business process management: a vendor perspective. In: Tan, F.B., Thong, J., Janczewski, L.J.: Proceedings 11th Pacific Asia Conference on Information Systems (PACIS 2007): Managing Diversity in Digital Enterprises, pp. 40–47. Auckland, New Zealand (2007)

19. Rosemann, M., vom Brocke, J.: The six core elements of business process management. In: vom Brocke, J., Rosemann, M. (eds.) Handbook on Business Process Management 1. IHIS, pp. 105–122. Springer, Heidelberg (2015). https://doi.org/10.1007/978-3-642-45100-3_5

20. Wraikat, H., Bellamy, A., Tang, H.: Exploring organizational readiness factors for new technology implementation within non-profit organizations. Open J. Soc. Sci. **5**, 1 (2017)

21. Mukwasi, C.M., Seymour, L.F.: Enterprise resource planning business case considerations: a review for small and medium-sized enterprises. J. Innov. Manage. Small Medium Enterp. **2012**, 1 (2012)

22. Wang, C.L., Ahmed, P.K.: Organisational learning: a critical review. Learn. Organ. **10**, 8–17 (2003). https://doi.org/10.1108/09696470310457469

23. Pritchard, J.P., Armistead, C.: Business process management – lessons from European business. Bus. Process Manage. J. **5**, 10–35 (1999).https://doi.org/10.1108/146371599102 49144

24. Véricourt, F.d., Lobo, M.S.: Resource and revenue management in nonprofit operations. Oper. Res. **57**, 1114–1128 (2009). https://doi.org/10.1287/opre.1080.0682

25. Bider, I., Jalali, A.: Agile business process development: why, how and when—applying Nonaka's theory of knowledge transformation to business process development. ISEB **14**(4), 693–731 (2014). https://doi.org/10.1007/s10257-014-0256-1

Event Logs - Why it Deviates? (BPMDS 2022)

Deviance Analysis by Means of Redescription Mining

Martin Käppel[✉], Engjëll Ahmeti, and Stefan Jablonski

Institute for Computer Science, University of Bayreuth, Bayreuth, Germany
{martin.kaeppel,engjell.ahmeti,stefan.jablonski}@uni-bayreuth.de

Abstract. Often business processes deviate in a positive or negative way from their expected or desired behavior. Deviance mining aims at detecting deviant process executions and at revealing their causes. In this paper we propose a novel approach for identifying the causes of a deviant process execution based on redescription mining, which extracts knowledge in form of logical rules. By analyzing, combining, and filtering these rules we identify the reasons for the deviating behavior of a business process in general as well as of particular process instances. Afterwards the results of this analysis are transformed into an understandable and well-readable natural language text that can be taken by business analysts and process owners to optimize processes in a reasoned manner.

Keywords: Deviance mining · Redescription mining · Process mining · Natural language generation

1 Introduction

Process Mining aims to extract knowledge of business processes from process event logs [2]. It encompasses, among others, techniques for automated process model discovery, techniques for checking the conformance between a process model and an event log, as well as several techniques for enhancing the execution of business processes [2]. One of these enhancement techniques is *deviance mining* that deals with identifying process executions which deviates from its expected or desired behavior and uncovering the causes of the deviations by analyzing a given event log [13]. Such deviations can be either of positive or negative nature, depending on whether this deviance leads to a better process performance or not. Depending on a particular application such process performance measures can be, for instance, execution times, resource usage, costs or compliance.

Often deviance mining approaches only classify process instances as deviant or not and the causes for the deviance initially remain unclear and must be eventually explored by business analysts. Other approaches, which extract the causes of deviance, suffer from the fact that their output is not easily interpretable due to their size (often these sets encompass several hundreds of rules) and very formal structure (e.g. in form of logical rules). In this paper, we propose a novel approach that takes process executions that were classified as deviant as starting point and reveals the causes for the deviant behavior of a process in general as

© Springer Nature Switzerland AG 2022
A. Augusto et al. (Eds.): BPMDS 2022/EMMSAD 2022, LNBIP 450, pp. 91–107, 2022.
https://doi.org/10.1007/978-3-031-07475-2_7

well as for particular process instances. Therefore we use an unsupervised data mining technique called *redescription mining*, which extracts knowledge in form of logical rules (so called redescriptions) from a given dataset. We apply this technique to process event logs with desired and deviant process executions to extract rules for both, desired and deviant process executions. Analyzing these sets of rules enables to explain the causes for the deviations. Additionally, we deal with the problem of difficult understandable output by analyzing, combining, and filtering those rules and generate concise and well-readable statements in natural language that explain the reasons why a process deviates in general as well as the reasons for particular deviant executions.

The paper is structured as follows: Sect. 2 recalls basic terminology. Section 3 discusses existing work in the field of deviance mining and delimits our approach from existing ones. Section 4 introduces the redescription mining technique. In Sect. 5 we propose our approach. Section 6 evaluates our approach. Finally, Sect. 7 gives an outlook on future work.

2   Background

2.1   Event Logs

The main input of a process mining technique is a *process event log* (*event log* for short). An event log consists of a set of records of already completed process executions that are related to the same business process (model) [2]. These records, so called *traces* (or *cases*), are temporally ordered sequences of events that belong to the same process instance. An *event* encapsulates the execution of a process activity, i.e. a single step in a business process. Events are described by various *properties* (so called *event attributes*) such as the time of execution (timestamp), the name of the corresponding activity or further event attributes (e.g., the executing resource or further data elements). The set of attributes of an event is called its *payload*.

2.2   Deviance Mining

Deviance mining aims to identify process executions which deviates from their expected or desired behavior and tries to reveal the reasons why a business process deviates by analyzing and comparing records of deviant and non-deviant process executions [13]. These analyses are carried out on single process instances as well as across multiple instances and often take the underlying process model into account. Deviant process executions are often called *negative process executions* (regardless whether they deviate in a positive or negative way), while non-deviant ones are called *positive process executions*. For investigating causes of deviance, they are stored in separated event logs: *positive log* and *deviant log* (also called *negative log*). This separation is most of the time done manually, by heuristic rules or by approaches that were trained to identify deviant process executions. The results of a deviance mining can help business analysts and process owners to optimize their processes and helps to avoid mistakes in process execution in a reasoned manner.

2.3 Declare

Declare is a single-perspective declarative process modelling language originally introduced in [1]. Instead of defining all valid execution paths in a process model, Declare defines a set of constraints applied to activities that must be satisfied throughout the whole process execution. All executions that do not violate these constraints are allowed. Hence, the control-flow is implicitly specified by these constraints, which makes Declare well-suited for modelling processes with a large number of execution paths. The constraints are described in linear temporal logic (LTL) over finite traces (LTL$_f$). Declare offers a broad repertoire of pre-defined templates that can be instantiated for defining a constraint, so that the process modeler must need not to be aware to the underlying logic formalism [3]. Table 1 summarizes the most common Declare templates. For a better understanding, we exemplary consider the response constraint $\mathbf{G}(A \rightarrow \mathbf{F}B)$. This template means that if A occurs, B must eventually follow sometimes in the future. We consider for example the following traces: $t_1 = \langle A, A, B \rangle$, $t_2 = \langle B, B, D \rangle$, $t_3 = \langle A, B, B \rangle$ and $t_4 = \langle A, B, A \rangle$. In t_1, t_2 and t_3 the response template is satisfied. In t_2 this constraint is trivially fulfilled since A does not occur. However, t_4 violates the constraint, because after the second occurrence of A no execution of B follows. We say that an event activates a constraint in a trace if its occurrence imposes some obligations on other events in the same trace. Such an activation either leads to a fulfillment or to a violation of a constraint.

3 Related Work

Redescription mining is used in a plethora of different application areas, such as biological, social, political, and economic sciences [7]. In the context of process mining this technique was recently applied in [9] to extract data-aware constraints from event logs to enrich Declare constraints with data conditions. The authors evaluated two redescription mining algorithms (ReReMi and SplitT) for this issue and compare their performance with a combined approach of clustering and rule mining. They investigated that the clustering approach outperforms redescription mining with regard to rediscover constraints. However, they state that this technique could be used to discover outlier behavior, since constraints with high confidence but low support are predominately detected. Hence, this technique seems promising for deviance mining. In [13] a systematic review and evaluation of deviance mining techniques in business process management is conducted and reveals that existing deviance mining techniques are based mostly on the extraction of frequent or discriminative patterns or sequence classification techniques. In [4] the suitability of sequence classification for analyzing deviant process executions are evaluated. Also deviance mining was subject of a multitude of case studies. For example, in [20] a technique called delta-analysis, which compares process models of deviant and non-deviant traces, was applied in context of an insurance company to identify reasons for long processing times of claims. In [21] association rule mining is applied to extract frequent patterns for normal and deviant cases to identify reasons for non-compliant cases in a

Table 1. Semantics for declare constraints in LTL$_f$

Template	LTL$_f$ semantics	Activation	Target
Responded existence	$\mathbf{G}(A \rightarrow (\mathbf{OB} \vee \mathbf{FB}))$	A	B
Response	$\mathbf{G}(A \rightarrow \mathbf{FB})$	A	B
Alternate response	$\mathbf{G}(A \rightarrow \mathbf{X}(\neg A\mathbf{UB}))$	A	B
Chain response	$\mathbf{G}(A \rightarrow \mathbf{XB})$	A	B
Precedence	$\mathbf{G}(B \rightarrow \mathbf{OA})$	B	A
Alternate precedence	$\mathbf{G}(B \rightarrow \mathbf{Y}(\neg B\mathbf{SA}))$	B	A
Chain precedence	$\mathbf{G}(B \rightarrow \mathbf{YA})$	B	A
Not responded existence	$\mathbf{G}(A \rightarrow \neg(\mathbf{OB} \vee \mathbf{FB}))$	A	B
Not response	$\mathbf{G}(A \rightarrow \neg\mathbf{FB})$	A	B
Not precedence	$\mathbf{G}(B \rightarrow \neg\mathbf{OA})$	B	A
Not chain response	$\mathbf{G}(A \rightarrow \neg\mathbf{XB})$	A	B
Not chain precedence	$\mathbf{G}(B \rightarrow \neg\mathbf{YA})$	B	A

procurement process. However most of such studies are focusing on the control-flow perspective and neglect other perspectives. The general idea and aim of deviance analysis is comparable with the emerging field of explainable artificial intelligence (AI), which deals with the question, how decision of AI models can be made transparent and comprehensible. This is why we also consider work in that research domain as related to our research. Pioneer work in the intersection of explainable AI and process mining was done, for instance, in [16]. Also deviance mining can be considered as partially related to predictive business process monitoring, e.g. [11,12] where the authors try to predict business rule violations. The same aim is pursued in [22] were an outcome-oriented predictive business process monitoring method was proposed, that can predict business process deviations with high accuracy, especially in case of processes with less variants. Hence, this work differs from ours, since we are focusing on processes with a large number of paths and are more interested in determining the reasons for deviance rather than predicting them.

4   Redescription Mining

Redescription mining is a family of unsupervised techniques that aims at finding correlations between subsets of elements in a dataset by providing two or more different views on the same entities [7]. The data model for a redescription mining task is a triple $\mathcal{D} = (\mathcal{E}, \mathcal{A}, \mathcal{V})$, consisting of sets of entities $\mathcal{E}$, attributes $\mathcal{A}$, and views $\mathcal{V}$. An entity $e \in \mathcal{E}$ is described by attributes $\mathcal{A}$. Let $a \in \mathcal{A}$ be an attribute, then the function $\pi_a : \mathcal{E} \rightarrow \text{dom}(a)$ assigns a value of the domain of attribute a to an entity. Redescriptions provide different views on the data [7]. Therefore, the set of attributes $\mathcal{A}$ is partitioned into a disjoint set of at least two views, i.e.

$$\mathcal{A} = \bigcup_{i=1}^{k} \mathcal{V}_i,$$

with $\mathcal{V}_i \cap \mathcal{V}_j = \emptyset$ for all $i, j \in \mathbb{N}_{\leq k}$ with $i \neq j$ and $2 \leq k \leq |\mathcal{A}|$. Note, that in the finest partition, i.e. $k = |\mathcal{A}|$ each view corresponds to a single attribute. We denote the corresponding view of an attribute a with $\mathcal{V}_a$.

According to [7] this data model can be simplified to a *table-based data model*. Here the data model consists of one or more tables. A *table* $\mathcal{T}$ over a set of attributes is a subset of the cartesian product of the attributes domain, i.e. $\mathcal{T} \subseteq \text{dom}(a_1) \times \cdots \times \text{dom}(a_n)$. Then the columns of the table represent the attributes and the rows the entities in form of tuples. Hence, each view corresponds to exactly one table.

Since, descriptions are logical rules, each attribute value of an entity must be mapped to a boolean value. Hence, we define for each attribute $a \in \mathcal{A}$ a predicate $p_a : \mathcal{E} \rightarrow \{\text{true}, \text{false}\}, e \mapsto [P_a(e)]$ that assigns a truth value to attribute a of an entity based on a logical proposition $[P_a(e)]$ [7]. Since the attributes possess different domains (numeric, boolean, categorical, etc.) their values must be transformed into a boolean value. Hence, we must define for each attribute an appropriate logical proposition $[P_a(e)]$. In case of an attribute that is already of boolean type we return its value directly. In case of categorical attributes the proposition is defined as $[\pi_a(e) = X]$, where X defines some constant. For further transformation of different domains we would like to refer to [7]. Based on this transformation we can define a *description* as a boolean query $q : \mathcal{E} \rightarrow \{\text{true}, \text{false}\}$ over the predicates and their negations, by concatenating the different predicates via conjunctions and disjunctions. We denote with $attr(q)$ the set of attributes that appear in this query and with $views(q)$ the union of all views of attributes in q, i.e. $views(q) = \cup_{a \in attr(q)} \mathcal{V}_a$. We can evaluate this description by determining the support of q,

$$\text{supp}(q) = \{e \in \mathcal{E} \mid q(e) = \text{true}\}$$

that returns all entities for which the description is true.

A redescription is now a pair (p, q) of descriptions p and q which forms a logical formula of the form $p \implies q$, with disjoint views and with similar support. Hence, we can think of a redescription as a way of characterizing the same entities in two different ways by providing different views (p and q) on the data. The requirement of disjoint views ensure that we get descriptions from different angles, while the similarity prevents a redescription of different entities. The similarity of the support sets is calculated by the Jaccard distance:

$$d(p, q) = 1 - \frac{|\text{supp}(p) \cap \text{supp}(q)|}{|\text{supp}(p) \cup \text{supp}(q)|}.$$

Note, that the Jaccard distance requires that either $\text{supp}(p) \neq \emptyset$ or $\text{supp}(q) \neq \emptyset$. If $d(q, p) = 0$ then the support sets are identical. In case of a distance of 1 the support sets are completely different. In most cases we cannot expect that the redescription matches exactly, so we must define a threshold $\tau \in [0, 1]$ until which we accept q as a description of p, i.e. $p \sim q$ if and only if $d(p, q) \leq \tau$.

The goal of a redescription algorithm is now to find all valid redescription (p_i, q_i) in a data model $\mathcal{D}$ which satisfy the a priori defined threshold τ.

5   Deviance Mining Approach

In this section we describe our redescription based deviance mining pipeline. We first give an overview on the total structure of the pipeline and afterwards explain all steps in depth.

5.1   Overall Structure of the Pipeline

In summary our proposed approach comprises five successive steps. This pipeline is depicted in Fig. 1. For our approach we need three artifacts as input: a positive event log, a deviant event log, and a (Declare) process model. We limit ourselves to Declare as modelling language, since our feature extraction relies on Declare and Declare is a well accepted language for descriptive process modelling. Since in practice a process model is often missing, our pipeline contains an optional step (Fig. 1, step 1) for mining a process model from the positive event log. If all the required inputs are available, we build two data models representing a positive and a deviant event log, respectively (Fig. 1, step 2). Afterwards we apply two redescription mining algorithms (ReReMi and SplitT algorithm) to the data models to discover rule sets for positive and deviant cases (Fig. 1, step 3). In the fourth step we compare and analyze those sets of rules to get a detailed explanation of why deviance is occurring. The results of this analysis are then passed into a natural language generation component that produces a human-readable natural language text explaining the causes for deviance of the event logs in general as well as their process executions (Fig. 1, step 5).

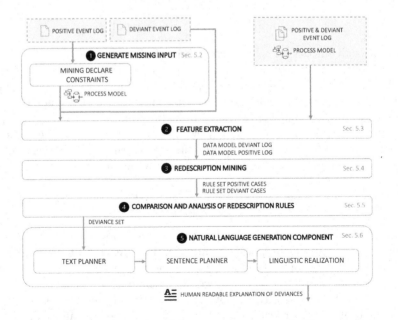

Fig. 1. Overview of the deviance mining pipeline

5.2 Generate Missing Input

Often only records of historical process executions are given in form of two process event logs depending on whether they are classified as deviant or not. However, the underlying process model is unknown. In this case we extract a Declare process model from the positive event log by applying the approach proposed in [17], which applies SQL queries to an event log to discover declarative constraints. This technique requires event logs in the *relational XES format (RXES)* [6], why we must convert the positive event log to RXES format. Note that this approach of mining can be replaced by any declarative mining approach.

5.3 Declare Constraint Based Feature Extraction

Before we can carry out the redescription mining, we have to build a data model for each of the two event logs. Therefore, we extract features for representing the event logs. Since, we are interested in detecting deviances, these features must link the event logs and the process model. For this issue, we use the same strategy as proposed in [9]: The idea for linking an event log with a process model is to build pairs of activation events and corresponding target events for all of its Declare constraints. Therefore, we apply the following steps to each trace in the event log: For each constraint in the process model we create two vectors: a vector id_a for representing the position of the activation occurrences and a vector id_t for representing the position of the target occurrences in the trace. For example, for trace $t = \langle A, A, A, B, A, B, A, B \rangle$ and a response(A, B), we get $id_a = (1, 2, 3, 5, 7)$ and $id_t = (4, 6, 8)$. Based on id_a and id_t we can build pairs of activation and target by combining the elements of the vectors in an adequate way. In case of the response template, we combine each element i of id_a with the first element of id_t that is greater than i. In our example this leads to the following set of pairs: $\{(1, 4), (2, 4), (3, 4), (5, 6), (7, 8)\}$. Note, that the way how to combine the elements of id_a and id_t depends on the particular Declare template. We use this set of pairs now to build up our data model. Each data model consists of two views: a view $\mathcal{V}_a$ for the activation component in the pairs and a view $\mathcal{V}_t$ for the target component. We insert into them the payload of the events (attributes $\mathcal{A}_a$ and $\mathcal{A}_t$). Hence, we get data models $\mathcal{D}_p = \left(\mathcal{E}_p, \{\mathcal{A}_{a_p}, \mathcal{A}_{t_p}\}, \{\mathcal{V}_{a_p}, \mathcal{V}_{t_p}\} \right)$ and $\mathcal{D}_d = \left(\mathcal{E}_d, \{\mathcal{A}_{a_d}, \mathcal{A}_{t_d}\}, \{\mathcal{V}_{a_d}, \mathcal{V}_{t_d}\} \right)$ that describe positive and deviant event log.

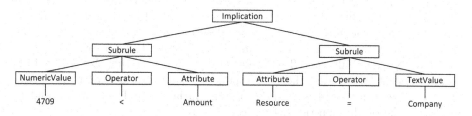

Fig. 2. Syntax tree for the redescription $4709 < Amount \implies Resource = Company$

5.4   Redescription Mining

In the redescription step we apply redescription algorithms to both $\mathcal{D}_p$ and $\mathcal{D}_d$. These algorithms discover for each of $\mathcal{D}_p$ and $\mathcal{D}_d$ a set of redescriptions ($\mathcal{R}_p$ and $\mathcal{R}_d$ respectively). A redescription (p, q) is a logical formula, of the form $p \implies q$ with $p \sim q$ and $d(p, q) \leq \tau$. For example: 4709 < **Amount** $\implies$ **Resource** = *Company*. This redescription states that in traces where a product is bought more than 4709 times, the buyer of that product is mostly a company. In this redescription 4709 < **Amount** represents p and **Resource** = *Company*, represents q. Note, that p and q contain literals from $\mathcal{A}_a$ and $\mathcal{A}_t$ respectively. For extracting those redescriptions, we apply redescription algorithms. In general there are two classes of redescription algorithms: greedy-based and tree-based algorithms. For our approach we select the most popular representative of each class. The decision tree-based *SplitT* algorithm and the greedy algorithm *ReReMi*.

SplitT Algorithm: The idea of this algorithm is to grow for each view a decision tree with the aim that they will be joined in their leaves. Therefore, the expansion of each tree goes through the attribute sets of both views, until no more attributes are available. After the trees are fully grown, the corresponding leave nodes of the trees are melted together. Finally, the rules are extracted by following all paths from the root of one tree to the root of the other tree [23].

ReReMi Algorithm: This algorithm starts from the redescription with the highest confidence, that has only one variable on each side. Then, the algorithm extends this rule by appending attributes, which are not already included in the rule using conjunctions and disjunctions. The appending stops when the maximum length of the rule is reached or when further appending does not improve the performance of the rule anymore [7].

5.5   Comparisons and Analysis of Discovered Redescription Rules

For giving detailed explanations why a process deviates from the desired behavior, we must compare and analyze the extracted sets of redescription rules. We base the comparison algorithm on a tree structure, that allows us to compare entire redescription rules as well as their subrules. We map the redescription rules into a tree structure by deriving a syntax tree from a context-free grammar $G = (V, \Sigma, R, S)$ which describes any possible redescription rule. In this grammar, V contains the non-terminals, which describe the different types (Implication, Subrule, Rule, Conjunction, Disjunction, Negation, Parentheses, Attribute, Operator, NumericValue and TextValue) of a clause in the rule, Σ the set of all names of events attributes, their corresponding domain values, and the operators $(=, <)$ used in the rules, S is the starting variable (i.e. Implication), and R represents the production rules of the grammar:

Implication → Subrule Subrule | Subrule Rule | Rule Subrule | Rule Rule

Rule → Conjunction | Disjunction | Negation | Parentheses | Subrule

Conjunction → Subrule Subrule | Subrule Rule | Rule Subrule | Rule Rule

Disjunction → Subrule Subrule | Subrule Rule | Rule Subrule | Rule Rule

Negation → Subrule

Parentheses → Rule

Subrule → Attribute Operator NumericValue | NumericValue Operator
Attribute | NumericValue Operator Attribute Operator
NumericValue | Attribute Operator TextValue | Attribute

Operator → =|<

In the derived syntax tree the terminals are mapped to the leaf nodes, while the inner nodes contain the non-terminal symbols, which describe the type of a clause. Subrules are then represented as subtrees. Note, the production rules enforce that a subrule contains exactly one attribute. An example of such a syntax tree is depicted in Fig. 2. After converting each redescription rule to a syntax tree, we associate positive rules and deviant rules that deal with the same attributes. These *corresponding rules* are then analyzed with regard to differences in their attribute values. This process is described in Algorithm 1. The algorithm iterates over the syntax trees of the redescriptions extracted from the deviant event log and compares each deviant rule with each positive rule. Therefore, the algorithm first extracts the subrules of a deviant rule (line 3). For each positive rule the algorithm checks whether the attribute set of the deviant rule is a subset of the positive rule (line 6). If that is true all subrules of the positive rule are extracted (line 7) and compared to each subrule of the deviant rule (line 10–21). In case that the subrules of a positive and a deviant rule deal with the same attribute, it is analyzed whether their attribute values differ (line 13). If the attribute values are identical this subrule does not provide insights for the deviance and is neglected, otherwise the difference is stored.

Besides of explaining the deviance of a process in general, we also analyze the causes for deviance of a particular process instance. Therefore we analyze for each deviant trace, which positive redescription rules are violated (cf. Algorithm 2). For each deviant trace, we check whether it fulfills a positive redescription rule. Therefore, the activation and target event to which a redescription rule applies is identified (line 3), afterwards we replace the attribute names on the left side in the redescription rule by the corresponding attribute values of the extracted activation event. The attribute values of the target event replace the attribute names of the right side. For example, for rule 4709 < **Amount** $\implies$ **Resource** = Company and events $e_a(Activity = OrderProduct, Amount = 4972)$ and $e_t(Activity = PayOrder, Resource = Customer)$ we get as expression 4709 < 4972 $\implies$ Customer = Company. Afterwards we evaluate this logical expression

---

Algorithm 1: Comparing positive and deviant redescriptions

Input: Deviant redescription tree $\mathbf{N}$ and positive redescription trees $\mathbf{P}$
Output: Set of tuples of comparisons between positive and deviant rules $\mathcal{C}$.

```
 1  C ← {}
 2  for n ∈ N do
 3  │   deviantSubrules ← extractSubrules(n)
 4  │   positiveSubrules ← []
 5  │   for p ∈ P do
 6  │   │   if n.attributes ⊆ p.attributes then
 7  │   │   │   positiveSubrules ← extractSubrules(p)
 8  │   │   │   for deviantSubrule ∈ deviantSubrules do
 9  │   │   │   │   for positiveSubrule ∈ positiveSubrules do
10  │   │   │   │   │   aₙ ← deviantSubrule.attribute
11  │   │   │   │   │   aₚ ← positiveSubrule.attribute
12  │   │   │   │   │   if aₙ == aₚ then
13  │   │   │   │   │   │   if aₙ.value != aₚ.value then
14  │   │   │   │   │   │   │   listOfDifferences.append((aₚ, aₙ))
15  │   │   │   │   │   │   end
16  │   │   │   │   │   end
17  │   │   │   │   end
18  │   │   │   end
19  │   │   │   C[n, p] ← listOfDifferences
20  │   │   end
21  │   end
22  end
23  return C
```

Algorithm 2: Analyse the causes for deviance of particular traces

---

Input: Set of deviant traces $\mathbf{T}$ and set of positive redescription rules $\mathbf{P}$.
Output: Set of tuples of deviant traces with their violated positive rules $\mathcal{D}$.

```
 1  for t ∈ T do
 2  │   for p ∈ P do
 3  │   │   eₐ, eₜ ← findEventsWithSameAttributeAsP(t, p.attributes)
 4  │   │   expression ← replaceValuesInRule(p, eₐ, eₜ)
 5  │   │   if ! evaluateBooleanExpression(expression) then
 6  │   │   │   rulesViolated ← rulesViolated ∪ p
 7  │   │   end
 8  │   end
 9  │   D ← D ∪ {(t, rulesViolated)}
10  end
11  return D
```

(line 5). In case of a violation we store the information that this rule is violated by the considered trace. The results of redescription mining are put together to a so called *deviance set* $DS = (\mathcal{R}_p, \mathcal{R}_d, \mathcal{C}, \mathcal{D})$.

5.6   Natural Language Generation

Finally, the deviance set is translated into a well-understandable natural language text. Hereby, the structure of the natural language generation (NLG) component follows the common architecture for NLG pipelines proposed in [15], consisting of three subsequent stages: *(i)* text planning, *(ii)* sentence planning, and *(iii)* linguistic realization. Since the elements of the deviance sets possess a clear structure and there are only a limited number of subrule types that can appear throughout the redescription mining, we use a template based approach, i.e. the information are represented as boilerplate text and parameters that must be inserted into the boilerplate [15].

Text Planning: The text planning stage handles the non-linguistic input (i.e. the deviance set) and process them into a formal format that enables the generation of a linguistic result. In our pipeline this task is trivial, since the previously generated syntax trees are already well-suited.

Sentence Planning: Sentence planning describes the process of refining and reorganizing content before the syntactic realization of phrases [19]. This encompasses the definition of templates that can be used for text generation. We define these templates in two different ways: *(i)* as simple parameterizable text modules, and *(ii)* as sentence planning trees. In both cases we define a template for each type of subrule. For example, a subrule of form [Attribute Operator TextValue], is represented by the text module "the [Domain Entity] [Attribute] is equal to[TextValue]". In the second way we use the Sentence Planning Language (SPL) proposed by [8] to specify a template for each type of subrule. In SPL a sentence is described by a fixed set of attributes and values, and allows values themselves again to contain attributes and their values [15]. Also it allows to specify for the replacement of the parameters which word type, tense, and role must be fulfilled. For a more sophisticated text we apply a domain entity generation to the activity name. This step extracts the proper noun (if available) from the activity name to extract objects that are processed in an activity. For example, the activity *OrderProduct* is mapped to the domain entity *Product*.

Linguistic Realization: Finally, we instantiate the templates with the information of the deviance set, to generate a syntactically, morphologically, and orthographically correct text. In our approach we used for this task two linguistic realizer: *(i)* the Komet-Penman Multilingual realizer (KPML)[1], *(ii)* and an own simple customized realizer. While our custom realizer instantiates the text modules, the KPML realizer instantiates the sentence planning trees.

---

[1] http://www.fb10.uni-bremen.de/anglistik/langpro/kpml/README.html.

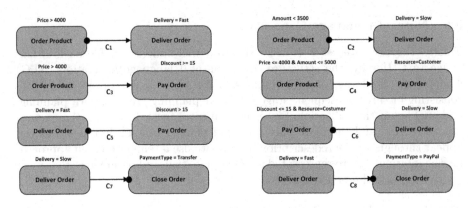

Fig. 3. Sample process order-to-cash

Table 2. Descriptive statistics for the generated process event logs.

	Positive event log		Deviant event log	
	No. of cases	No. of activities	No. of cases	No. of activities
Order-to-Cash	325	4	200	4
Repair Example	804	3	1000	3
Road Traffic Fines	612	4	1000	4
Credit Application Subset	766	3	1000	3

6   Implementation and Evaluation

We have implemented our pipeline as an open-source prototype tool[2]. For performing the redescription mining step we include the SIREN[3] framework. We conducted different experiments to show the feasibility of our approach. Accordingly, we investigated the following research questions: Which redescription mining algorithm meets the requirements for deviance mining better? Which NLG approach performs better with regard to text quality and understandability?

6.1   Datasets

A common problem in conducting an evaluation of deviance mining approaches is that there are barely datasets of real-life event logs available that provide both positive and deviant process executions. Hence, we decided to use artificial event logs generated via the MP-Declare generator tool [18]. MP-Declare is an extension of Declare that also incorporates further process perspectives, like data-oriented or organizational perspective. It is necessary to use a MP-Declare model, because otherwise the event logs would be limited to the control-flow perspective. The generator tool allows both the generation of traces that satisfy

---

[2] The source code can be accessed at https://github.com/engjellahmeti.

[3] http://cs.uef.fi/siren/main/intro.html.

Table 3. Evaluation metrics (ReReMi algorithm is denoted as Re and SplitT as ST).

	# Pos. rules		# Dev. rules		BLEU		ROUGE		TER	
	Re	ST	Re	ST	Re	ST	Re	ST	Re	ST
Order-to-Cash	7	10	3	6	0.98	0.98	0.99	0.91	0.08	0.01
Repair Example	3	3	2	3	0.83	0.83	0.94	0.95	0.3	0.28
Road Traffic Fines	4	4	2	3	0.98	0.92	0.99	0.98	0.17	0.19
Credit Application	5	10	3	4	0.99	0.94	1	0.85	0.14	0.03

the process model (positive traces) as well as of traces that violate the process specification (deviant traces). We evaluate our approach on four handcrafted process models with diverse characteristics that are summarized in Table 2. Due to the limited space we explain the experiment setup in general, but discuss only one process model in detail and go directly over to discuss our total findings. All further evaluation files are provided in a GitHub repository [See footnote 2].

For detailed discussion we use a fictive order-to-cash process (cf. Fig. 3). When a product with a price higher than 4,000 euros is ordered, then eventually a fast delivery of that product is carried out (*response constraint* C_1). When less than 3,500 products are ordered, then eventually a slow delivery of that amount of product is carried out (C_2). If a product with price higher than 4,000 euros is ordered, eventually a payment of that order with a discount higher or equal to 15% is performed (C_3). If less or equal to 5,000 products with price lower or equal than 4,000 euros are ordered, a payment of that order from a non-company customer is carried out (*response constraint* C_4). A fast delivery of an order should be provided in order to gain a discount more than 15% (*responded existence constraint* C_5). A product bought by a customer (not company) with a discount smaller or equal to 15% is required in order to have a slow delivery (*responded existence constraint* C_6). If an order is closed and paid through a bank transfer, then this event is always preceded by a slow delivery (*precedence constraint* C_7). If an order is closed and paid through PayPal, then this event is always preceded by a fast delivery (*precedence constraint* C_8).

6.2   Evaluation Setup

We applied the ReReMi and SplitT algorithm with the SIRENs default threshold and processed the output with both realizers. For each run of the experiment we analyzed the discovered redescription rules and the textual output. Due to the synthetical data it is ensured that there are no contradictions between the both event logs. Hence, the detected deviances are always correct, which is why we can neglect the evaluation of the correctness and usefulness of the redescription rules. To measure the quality of the generated text, we manually corrected grammar errors of the generated text and compared the generated one with the edited one calculating the following common metrics: *(i)* Bilingual Evaluation Understudy (BLEU Score) [14], *(ii)* Recall-Oriented Understudy for

Table 4. Mined redescription rules from deviant event log (above) and of positive event log using ReReMi algorithm

ID	C	A/T	A/T rule	NLG
r_2	C_2	Order Product	$7344 <$ Amount < 9642	If the product amount stretches from
		Deliver Order	Delivery = Slow	7344 to 9642 that implicates that the order delivery is Slow
r_{10}	C_3	Order Product	$18022 <$ Price < 19671 |	If the product price varies between
			$3941 <$ Amount < 6237	18022 and 19671 or the product amount
		Pay Order	$13 <$ Discount < 15	ranges from 3941 to 6237 that implies the order discount ranges from 13 to 15
r_{23}	C_8	Close Order	PaymentType = PayPal	If the order payment type is equal to
		Deliver Order	Delivery = Slow	PayPal that implicates that the order delivery is equal to Slow
ID	C	A/T	A/T Rule	NLG
r_2	C_1	Order Product	$3697 <$ Price	If the product price is above 3697 that
		Deliver Order	Delivery = Fast	implies that the order delivery is Fast
r_5	–	Order Product	$4709 <$ Amount	If the product amount is higher than
		Pay Order	Resource = Company	4709 that implicates that the order resource is Company
r_7	C_4	Order Product	Amount < 4704	If the product amount is below 4704
		Pay Order	Resource = Customer	that implicates that the process is executed by Customer
r_9	C_5	Deliver Order	Delivery = Fast	If the order delivery is equal to Fast
		Pay Order	$17 <$ Discount < 47	that implicates that the order discount stretches from 17 to 47
r_{11}	–	Pay Order	$17 <$ Discount < 47	If the order discount stretches from 17
		Deliver Order	Delivery = Fast	to 47 that implicates that the order delivery is equal to Fast
r_{12}	C_7	Close Order	PaymentType = Transfer	If the order payment type is Transfer
		Deliver Order	Delivery = Slow	that implies the order delivery is Slow
r_{13}	C_8	Close Order	PaymentType = PayPal	If the order payment type is PayPal
		Deliver Order	Delivery = Fast	that implies the order delivery is Fast

Gisting Evaluation (ROUGE) [10] and *(iii)* the Translation Error Rate (TER) (cf. Table 3). While the first two metrics measure how much the words in the generated text appeared in the manual edited one and vice versa, the TER metric determines the number of required post-editing. Especially, the BLEU-Score is known for correlating well with human judgement [5]. Since it is the first NLG approach for describing deviances of event logs, we cannot compare with other approaches.

6.3   Discussion of the Order-to-Cash Process

For the order-to-cash sample process we observed the positive and deviant redescriptions presented in Table 4. Note, that the number of redescriptions rules and the length of the natural output depend in general on the size of the event log and the complexity of the rules. Within this table each mined redescription is enumerated with a unique ID. Furthermore, we stored, whether a redescription is a rediscovery of a constraint of the process model (column C), activation and target activity (column A/T), and the discovered redescription rule (where the

Table 5. Excerpt of the deviance report in natural language text

---

Deviances of the event logs in general:

The first mined negative rule is *'If the order payment type is equal to PayPal that implicates that the order delivery is Slow.* (r_{23}) and its subrules comparisons to the positive subrules are below:

- The payment type for the event 'Close Order' is equal to PayPal in the negative rule, while in the positive rule r_{12}, it is Transfer.
- The delivery for the event 'Deliver Order' is Slow in the negative rule, while in the positive rule r_{13}, it is Fast.

Analysing traces in detail:

- The process execution with 'Case No. 103' is deviant because the order delivery differs from Fast (r_6).
- The process execution with 'Case No. 198' is deviant because the product price goes lower than 3697 (r_6) and the product amount is not bigger than 4709 (r_{13}).

---

first line represents the left side (p) and the second line the right side of the rule (q)). In the last column the representation as natural text is given. In Table 5 the created report as natural language text that describes the deviance of the process in general as well as the causes for deviance of single traces is shown. For example, if we take rules r_{12}, r_{13}, and r_{23} from Table 4, we can see that the ReReMi algorithm has discovered opposite behaviours of the order-to-cash business process. For example, it shows that in a normal execution of the process paying with PayPal leads to fast payment, and therefore it is succeeded by a fast delivery. However, in deviant execution paying with PayPal was succeeded by a slow delivery. Also some redescriptions are refinements or descriptions of the behavior from different perspectives (e.g. r_5 and r_7 in Table 4).

6.4   Overall Results and Conclusion

Our overall analysis shows that the performance of our approach is similar on all datasets used for evaluation. The natural language output can be judged to be of high quality (cf. Table 3) and confirms that a template-based approach is a good choice for translating redescription rules. Note, that the used realizer does not affect the text quality, since they use the same templates and data. However, a manual review of the natural text reveals, that the ReReMi algorithm is better suited, since it extracts rules with less clauses. This is caused by the fact, that the ReReMi algorithm guarantees by design that a rule contains an attribute at most one time, while in the SplitT algorithm a attribute can occur arbitrarily often within a rule. Hence, the SplitT algorithms leads to very long sentences which hampers the understanding drastically. However, this fact is not reflected in the used metrics, since they do not take the sentence length into account.

7 Future Work

In this paper we proposed a novel approach for deviance mining based on redescription mining. Given event logs with normal and deviant process executions the reasons for the deviance are investigated and outputted in form of a human-readable natural text. We evaluated the approach on four handcrafted process models. Our evaluation shows that the ReReMi algorithm is well-suited for this task, while the SplitT algorithm leads to long and complex rules that cannot be processed into well-readable natural output. In future work we plan to extend the evaluation to real-life event logs and to improve the analysis step to draw more general conclusions for process optimization. Also, the generation of the natural text should be improved to deliver more fluent explanations by replacing the template based approach by deep learning techniques.

References

1. Aalst, W., Pesic, M., Schonenberg, H.: Declarative workflows: balancing between flexibility and support. Comput. Sci. Res. Dev. **23**, 99–113 (2009)
2. Aalst, W.M.P.V.d.: Process Mining - Discovery, Conformance and Enhancement of Business Processes. Springer, Wiesbaden (2011)
3. Burattin, A., Maggi, F.M., Sperduti, A.: Conformance checking based on multi-perspective declarative process models. Expert Syst. Appl. **65**(C), 194–211 (2016)
4. Cuzzocrea, A., Folino, F., Guarascio, M., Pontieri, L.: Experimenting and assessing a probabilistic business process deviance mining framework based on ensemble learning. In: Hammoudi, S., Śmiałek, M., Camp, O., Filipe, J. (eds.) ICEIS 2017. LNBIP, vol. 321, pp. 96–124. Springer, Cham (2018). https://doi.org/10.1007/978-3-319-93375-7_6
5. Denoual, E., Lepage, Y.: BLEU in characters: Towards automatic MT evaluation in languages without word delimiters. In: Proceedings of Conference Including Posters/Demos and Tutorial Abstracts (2005)
6. van Dongen, B.F., Shabani, S.: Relational XES: Data management for process mining. In: CAiSE Forum (2015)
7. Galbrun, E., Miettinen, P.: Redescription Mining. Springer, Heidelberg (2018)
8. Kasper, R.T.: A flexible interface for linking applications to penman's sentence generator. In: Proceedings of Workshop on Speech and NL. HLT 1989, ACL (1989)
9. Leno, V., Dumas, M., Maggi, F.M., La Rosa, M., Polyvyanyy, A.: Automated discovery of declarative process models with correlated data conditions. Inf. Syst. **89**, 101482 (2020)
10. Lin, C.Y.: ROUGE: a package for automatic evaluation of summaries. In: Text Summarization Branches Out. ACL, Barcelona (2004)
11. Maggi, F.M., Di Francescomarino, C., Dumas, M., Ghidini, C.: Predictive monitoring of business processes. In: Jarke, M., et al. (eds.) CAiSE 2014. LNCS, vol. 8484, pp. 457–472. Springer, Cham (2014). https://doi.org/10.1007/978-3-319-07881-6_31
12. Metzger, A., et al.: Comparing and combining predictive business process monitoring techniques. IEEE Trans. Sys. Man Cybern. **45**(2) (2015)
13. Nguyen, H., Dumas, M., Rosa, M.L., Maggi, F.M., Suriadi, S.: Business process deviance mining: review and evaluation (2016)

14. Papineni, K., Roukos, S., Ward, T., Zhu, W.J.: Bleu: a method for automatic evaluation of machine translation. In: ACL (2002)
15. Reiter, E., Dale, R.: Building Natural Language Generation Systems. Cambridge University Press, Cambridge (2000)
16. Rizzi, W., Francescomarino, C.D., Maggi, F.M.: Explainability in predictive process monitoring: when understanding helps improving. In: BPM (2020)
17. Schönig, S., Ciccio, C.D., Maggi, F.M., Mendling, J.: Discovery of multi-perspective declarative process models. In: ICSOC (2016)
18. Skydanienko, V., Francescomarino, C.D., Ghidini, C., Maggi, F.M.: A tool for generating event logs from multi-perspective declare models. In: BPM (2018)
19. Stone, M., Doran, C.: Sentence planning as description using tree adjoining grammar. In: Proceedings of 35th Annual Meeting of ACL. ACL, Madrid (1997)
20. Suriadi, S., Wynn, M.T., Ouyang, C., ter Hofstede, A.H.M., van Dijk, N.J.: Understanding process behaviours in a large insurance company in Australia: a case study. In: Salinesi, C., Norrie, M.C., Pastor, Ó. (eds.) CAiSE 2013. LNCS, vol. 7908, pp. 449–464. Springer, Heidelberg (2013). https://doi.org/10.1007/978-3-642-38709-8_29
21. Swinnen, J., Depaire, B., Jans, M., Vanhoof, K.: A process deviation analysis - a case study, vol. 99, pp. 87–98 (2011)
22. Weinzierl, S., Dunzer, S., Tenschert, J.C., Zilker, S., Matzner, M.: Predictive business process deviation monitoring. In: ECIS 2020 (2021)
23. Zinchenko, T., Galbrun, E., Miettinen, P.: Mining predictive redescriptions with trees, pp. 1672–1675 (2015)

Detecting Context Activities
in Event Logs

Yang Lu[✉][iD], Qifan Chen[iD], and Simon K. Poon[iD]

School of Computer Science, The University of Sydney, Sydney, NSW 2006, Australia
{yalu8986,qche8411}@uni.sydney.edu.au, simon.poon@sydney.edu.au

Abstract. One of the most important goals for process models is to enable users to visualise the control-flow information of a process. Because some activities can happen at anytime during the execution of a process, the execution of these activities are not necessarily dependent on the control-flow information of the process. Such activities are called context activities. Acknowledging that context activities can affect the performance of any process discovery algorithms, such potentially useful information will be lost once they are discarded from the event logs. In this paper, we propose a method with the goal to automatically detect context activities in event logs. The detected context activities can then be further analysed to get deeper insights about the process after the process discovery stage. Both synthetic and real-life datasets are used for evaluation to show the capabilities of our proposed method.

Keywords: Process science · Data science · Complex behaviours detection · Context activities

1   Introduction

One of the most important goals of process discovery algorithms is to capture the order of activities being executed in given traces as control-flow information [2]. The construction of process models is to present the control-flow information of event logs.

In some processes, there can be some activities which do not have strict causal relations with others [9,21]. Some activities can execute at any time during the execution of a process, and the execution of these activities may be dependent on other factors other than the control-flow information. For example, lab tests can be taken at anytime during a healthcare process [9]. It could be important for us to investigate how these lab tests are triggered to avoid the waste of medical resources. In a goods transportation process, the routes can be frequently recalculated due to various complex road and weather conditions [19]. Studying the relationship between the route recalculation and transportation could help improving the efficiency of the delivery process. Besides, some activities can be triggered by a specific temporal event (e.g. every hour, every Friday, every month, etc.) [10]. In this paper, we refer to such activities as context activities. Different from outliers, context activities frequently execute and are part of the process.

© Springer Nature Switzerland AG 2022
A. Augusto et al. (Eds.): BPMDS 2022/EMMSAD 2022, LNBIP 450, pp. 108–122, 2022.
https://doi.org/10.1007/978-3-031-07475-2_8

The performance of existing process discovery algorithms can be heavily affected when context activities exist in event logs [21]. In some cases, "spaghetti models" (i.e. process models which are too complex to be understood) or "flower models" (i.e. process models with high fitness but low precision) are examples resulting from the situation when there are context activities in event logs. Various methods have been proposed in order to filter out outliers from event logs [20]. Context activities would be treated as noises and dismissed to satisfy quality measures like fitness, precision and generalization. In these occasions, important knowledge captured in context activities are ignored.

A method proposed in [21] applies information theory concepts to filter out "chaotic activities" from event logs. Although it could identify context activities as "chaotic activities", context activities are mixed with outliers and are removed from event logs. In addition, it cannot show that the identified activities can execute under various contexts in the event log (i.e. it cannot show the identified activity can happen at anytime during the execution of the process).

According to Breunig et al. [6], a data object is considered as an outlier if there is typically a large distance between the data object and its most similar neighbour. As shown in Fig. 1, when considering each event as a data point, although context activities can happen at any time during the execution of the process, the distances between its points are small (blue points). However, if an activity is considered as outlier, its events will be far away from their neighbors (red points).

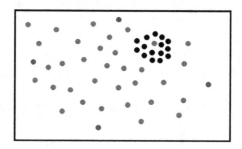

Fig. 1. An example 2-D dataset representing an event log, each point represents an event. The black points represent an activity in the control-flow of the process, blue points represent a context activity and red points represent an outlier activity (Color figure online)

In this paper, we propose a novel method to detect context activities from event logs. Our proposed method can accurately detect context activities from event logs and distinguish context activities from outliers. The detected activities can then be used for further analysis of the process behaviours. The rest of the paper is structured as follows: Sect. 2 is a motivation example to demonstrate the concept of context activities. Section 3 is a literature review of related work.

Section 4 introduces some preliminary concepts. Our method is presented in Sect. 5 and is evaluated in Sect. 6 and Sect. 7. Finally, Sect. 8 concludes our paper.

2 Motivation Example

To illustrate the definition of context activities, a motivation example is provided in this section. Suppose there is an event log L_1, and M_1 (Fig. 2) is the process model mined from L_1 using the inductive miner [15]. M_1 can accurately describe the process described in L_1 since it has a precision of 0.96 and a fitness of 1. Now, assume there is a context activity X. Events of X are randomly inserted into L_1, and the number of inserted events is 10% of the number of total events in L_1. A new event log L_2 is obtained after insertion. M_2 (Fig. 3) is the process model discovered from L_2 using the inductive miner. It only has a precision of 0.5 and is a so-called "flower model" allowing too many behaviours which are not described in L_2. As around 10% of events are the execution records of X, it cannot be simply filtered out and ignored from the event log. The context activities may be removed during the process discovery stage in order to get a more comprehensive process model, but should be preserved and used for further analysis to get deeper insights about the process.

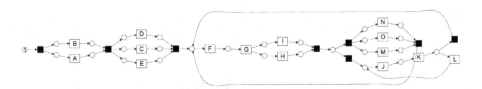

Fig. 2. Process model M_1 without context activities

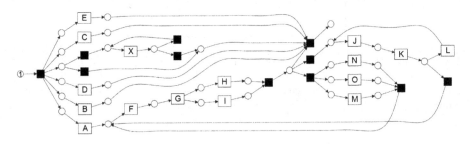

Fig. 3. Process model M_2 with context activity X

3 Background

Although various process discovery algorithms have been proposed, comprehensive process models often cannot be discovered when event logs contain complex behaviours [2,4]. In order to translate from event logs with complex behaviours into process models, some algorithms are proposed to improve current process discovery algorithms. For example, the alpha algorithm [1] is extended to handle short loops [8], invisible tasks [12,22] and non-free-choice behaviours [12]. The inductive miner [15] is also extended to handle infrequent behaviours [16], switch behaviours [18] and cancellation behaviours [14]. Besides improving existing process discovery algorithms to handle complex behaviours, some methods focus on filtering out information in the event log which can affect the performance of process discovery algorithms [20], others cluster the event log and use multiple process models to describe the process behaviours in the event log [23]. However, algorithms to handle context activities need to be further investigated and developed.

Due to the representation bias of process modeling languages [3], traditional process modeling languages like Petri nets and BPMNs are often unable to adequately present context activities in the process model. Dees et al. [9] propose a method using colors to visualize context activities on the edges of process models. It relies on users to select the set of context activities from event logs.

Tax et al. [21] propose a method based on information theory concepts to filter out activities which can happen at arbitrary points in time, and these filtered activities are called "chaotic activities". The goal is to remove "chaotic activities" from event logs so that the f-scores of discovered process models can be improved. Each activity is given an entropy value, and an activity is considered as a "chaotic activity" if it has a high entropy value (i.e. if an activity can follow or be followed by many different activities). Although context activities can be classified as "chaotic activities", Tax et al. [21] is unable to distinguish outliers from context activities. For example, if an activity only randomly happens a few times in a small number of traces, although it has complex directly-follows relations, and removing it from the event log can increase the f-scores of discovered models, it is insufficient enough to conclude that the activity is a context activity which can happen at anytime.

In this paper, we propose a method to automatically discover context activities in event logs. The discovered context activities can be used as input for other tools to do further analysis of the processes.

4 Preliminaries

Definition 1 (Event log, Trace, Activity, Event). *An event log L is a multiset of traces. A trace t, $t \in L$, is an ordered sequence of events. Assuming A is the set of all possible activities, an event e is an execution record of an activity $a \in A$. $\#_n(e)$ denotes the value of attribute n for event e. For example, $\#_{activity}(e)$ refers to the activity label associated with e, and $\#_{timestamp}(e)$ refers to the timestamp of event e.*

Definition 2 (k-Prefix and k-Suffix of an Event). *Given a trace $t \in L$ where $t = <e_1, e_2, e_3, ..., e_n>$. The k-prefix of event e_i where $e_i \in t$ is the ordered sequence $<e_{i-k}, e_{i-k+1}, ..., e_{i-1}>$, and the k-Suffix of event e_i is the ordered sequence $<e_{i+1}, e_{i+2}, ..., e_{i+k}>$. In this paper, when talking about the prefix and suffix sequences, we refer to the activity sequences. For example, the k-suffix of event e_i refers to the ordered sequence $<\#_{activity}(e_{i+1}), \#_{activity}(e_{i+2}), ..., \#_{activity}(e_{i+k})>$.*

5   The Proposed Method

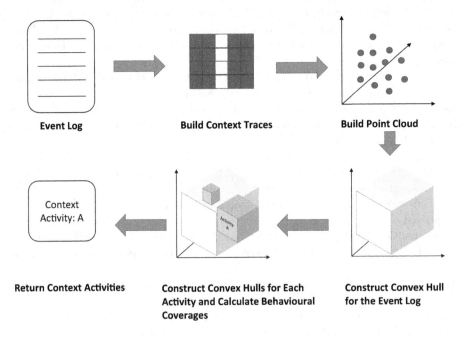

Event Log   **Build Context Traces**   **Build Point Cloud**

Return Context Activities   **Construct Convex Hulls for Each Activity and Calculate Behavioural Coverages**   **Construct Convex Hull for the Event Log**

Context Activity: A

Fig. 4. Overview of our proposed method

The goal of our proposed method is to detect context activities which are parts of the process but cannot be described by process models. These activities may frequently happen during the execution of the process, and they should not be treated as outliers. Although the existence of such activities can heavily impact the performance of process discovery algorithms, we should not simply filter out the context activities and ignore them.

Figure 4 shows an overview of our proposed method. Our algorithm converts the behaviours of the event log into a n-dimensional container, and the behaviours of each activity are then represented by sub-containers within it. Ideally, the container of each activity only takes a small amount of place of the event log's container. However, if there is a context activity, its container will take a large amount of space since it can execute at anytime during the execution of the process.

5.1   Build Context Traces

Firstly, we convert each event into a k-context trace. Each k-context trace is an ordered sequence which concatenates the k-prefix and k-suffix of an event. The context trace represents the behaviour of an event. Two events may have similar context traces if they are the execution records of the same activity or their activities are close in the process model (e.g. they have similar neighbors and locations). The formal definition of a context trace is given below.

Definition 3 (k-Context Trace). *Given a trace $t \in L$ where $t = <e_1, e_2, ...,$ $e_n>$. The k-context trace of event e_i where $e_i \in t$ is the concatenation of the activity sequences of its k-prefix and k-suffix (i.e. $<\#_{activity}$ $(e_{i-k}), \#_{activity}(e_{i-k+1}), ..., \#_{activity}(e_{i-1}), \#_{activity}(e_{i+1}), \#_{activity}(e_{i+2}), ...,$ $\#_{activity}(e_{i+k})>$). Zero padding will be added to the context trace if $i - k < 1$ or $i + k > n$.*

For example, assume an event log $L = [<A, B, C, D>^{10}, <E, F, G, H>^{10}, <I, J, K, L>^{10}]$. The 3-context traces of activity A's context traces are all $<0, 0, 0, B, C, D>$, and the 3-context traces of Activity G's events are $<0, E, F, H, 0, 0>$.

5.2   Build a Point Cloud

In this step, we convert the context traces of all events into a set of data points in a n-dimensional space so that each single data point can represent the behaviour of a single event. The data points of two events will be close if they have similar behaviours, and they will be far away from each other if their behaviours are different. To achieve this goal, we applied the Trace2Vec [7] algorithm. Trace2Vec is an extension to the Doc2Vec [13] algorithm which is an unsupervised algorithm that learns vector representations of sentences and text documents. Trace2Vec treats each trace in the event log as a sentence, and each activity label as a word. By applying the Trace2Vec algorithm, each context trace can be represented by a vector in a n-dimensional space.

At this point, the event log is translated into a point cloud in a n-dimensional space where each data point represents the behaviour of an event. Figure 5 (left) shows the 3-D point cloud built from L_2 described in Sect. 2.

5.3   Construct Convex Hulls for the Event Log

Once the point cloud has been built, a container is supposed to be constructed which can just fit all the data points. In other words, the container can be seen as an upper approximation of the event log's behaviours. To build the container,

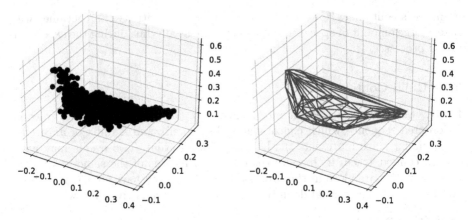

Fig. 5. Point cloud of L_2 (left) and its convex hull (right). outliers have been detected by DBSCAN (eps = 0.1, minPts = 5) and removed from the point cloud

a convex hull is learnt for the point cloud. A convex hull is the smallest shape that encloses all the data points without concavity.

However, if the event log contains outliers (i.e. data points which are far away from their neighbors), or if the data points can be divided into multiple clusters, and the clusters are far away from each other, using one convex hull to accommodate all data points may not give an accurate approximation of the process behaviours.

To solve the problem, DBSCAN [11] is firstly applied to cluster the data points and filter out outliers. DBSCAN is a density-based clustering algorithm which requires two parameters: the maximum radius of a neighborhood (eps) and the minimum amount of points required to form a dense region (minPts). DBSCAN does not require the number of clusters as a user input. In addition, data points which do not belong to any clusters are classified as outliers.

Instead of building one convex hull to accommodate all the data points in the point cloud, we build a convex hull for each cluster separately. Finally, the sum of all convex hulls' volumes are calculated, which will be used as input for the next step. Figure 5 (right) shows the convex hull built for event log L_2. As only one cluster is discovered by DBSCAN, one convex hull is used to represent L_2. outliers are removed from the point cloud before building the convex hull.

The pipeline of this step is presented in Algorithm 1. The point cloud is firstly clustered by the DBSCAN algorithm, and outliers are removed (lines 1–2). Then for the data points in each cluster, a convex hull is learnt and its volume is calculated (lines 4–11). Both the set of filtered data points and the sum of all convex hulls' volumes are returned by the algorithm.

Algorithm 1: Calculating Total Volume and Filtered Points

   Input: Points, minPts, eps

1   Clusters, Outliers ← DBSCAN (Points, minPts, eps)

2   FilteredPoints ← Points \ Outliers

   // Remove outlier points

3   TotalVolume ← 0

4   **for** *cluster in Clusters* **do**

5   clusterPoints ← getPointsInCluster(cluster, FilteredPoints)

6   **if** *A convex hull cannot be built* **then**

7 | continue

8   **end**

9   C ← getConvexHull(clusterPoints)

10   V ← getVolume(C)

11   TotalVolume ← TotalVolume + V

12 **end**

   Output: FilteredPoints, TotalVolume

5.4   Construct Convex Hulls for Each Activity and Calculate Behavioural Coverages

In Sect. 5.2, the event log is converted into a set of data points where each point represents the behaviour of a single event. Since each event is an execution record of an activity, the set of data points representing the behaviours of an activity should be a subset of the point cloud which represents the behaviours of the whole event log. As a result, the convex hulls to accommodate the data points of a single activity should be within the convex hulls which accommodate the behaviours of the whole event log.

For the data points to represent the behaviours of single events, two points are close if their corresponding events share similar behaviours, and they are far away from each other if the behaviours of the events are different. As context activities can happen at any time during the execution of the process, their corresponding data points should span over the whole point cloud of the event log. As a result, their corresponding convex hulls have larger volumes.

In this section, a point cloud of each activity is firstly built. Then similar to Sect. 5.3, DBSCAN is applied to cluster the data points and filter out outliers. A set of convex hulls are then built to represent the behaviours of each activity, and the sum of their volumes are then calculated. We propose a concept called behavioural coverage to measure the complexity of an activity's behaviours. The definition of behavioural coverage is presented in Definition 4. The behavioural coverages for context activities should be much larger than normal activities in the control flow of a process.

Definition 4 (Behavioural Coverage). *Assume $a \in A$ is an activity of event log L, P_L is the set of convex hulls to represent the behaviours of L, and P_a is the set of convex hulls to represent the behaviours of a. If V_L is the sum of volumes of convex hulls in P_L (i.e. $V_L = \sum_{p \in P_L} Volume(p)$), V_a is the sum of volumes* of convex hulls in P_a (i.e. $V_a = \sum_{p \in P_a} Volume(p)$), the behavioural coverage of activity a is the proportion of V_a to V_L (i.e. $Coverage(a) = V_a/V_L$).

It is important to notice that by applying the DBSCAN clustering algorithm, normal activities (activities belong to the normal control-flow of the process) which can execute under different contexts will not be incorrectly classified as context activities (e.g. when the process model has duplicate activities (Fig. 6, right) or if an activity is in the middle of two exclusive choice structures (Fig. 6, left)).

The pipeline of this step is presented in Algorithm 2. For event log L_2, the behavioural coverage for activity X is 0.82, while the behavioural coverages for all other activities are below 0.4. Figure 7 shows the convex hulls for activity A and X. It is clear to see that the convex hull of activity X takes a large amount of space of the convex hull for L_2 while the convex hull for activity A is much smaller, which indicates that activity X can happen at anytime during the execution of the process.

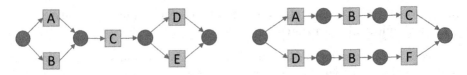

Fig. 6. Artificial process model M_3 (left) and M_4 (right). Activity C in M_3 and B in M_4 can execute under different contexts

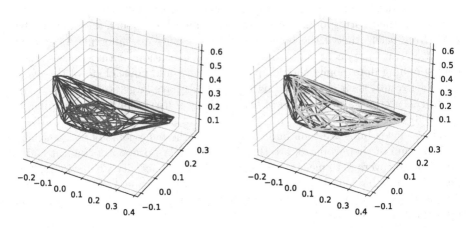

Fig. 7. Convex hulls for event Log L_2 (blue), activity A (red), and activity X (yellow) (Color figure online)

Algorithm 2: Calculating Behavioural Coverage for Each Activity

---

Input: Activities, FilteredPoints, TotalVolume, minPts, eps

```
1  for act in Activities do
2  │   actPoints ← getPoints(FilteredPoints, act)
   │   // Get all data points of act's events from FilteredPoints
3  │   BehaviouralCoverage ← {}
   │   // A dictionary containing all activities and their corresponding
   │      behavioural coverages
4  │   Clusters, Outliers ← DBSCAN (actPoints, minPts, eps)
5  │   actPoints ← actPoints \ Outliers
6  │   actVolume ← 0
7  │   for cluster in Clusters do
8  │   │   clusterPoints ← getPointsInCluster(cluster, actPoints)
9  │   │   if A convex hull cannot be built then
10 │   │   │   continue
11 │   │   end
12 │   │   C ← getConvexHull(clusterPoints)
13 │   │   V ← getVolume(C)
14 │   │   actVolume ← actVolume + V
15 │   end
16 │   actCoverage ← actVolume / TotalVolume
17 │   BehaviouralCoverage.add({act, actCoverage})
18 end
```

Output: BehaviouralCoverage

5.5 Identify Context Activities

Once the behavioural coverage for each activity has been calculated, a threshold can be set so that an activity will be classified as a context activity if its behavioural coverage is larger than the threshold. Besides, we can also rank the behavioural coverages for all activities in descending order and investigate the activities with highest behavioural coverages separately.

6 Evaluation on Synthetic Data

Our method is implemented as a stand-alone python program based on the PM4PY [5] framework. All our code, data and results are publicly-available[1].

To evaluate our proposed method, we firstly collect 2637 synthetic event logs[2] from [17]. The logs are generated from 2637 synthetic process models[3] containing various different behaviours (e.g. loops, invisible tasks, parallel tasks, etc.). Each artificial process model contains 10, 15 or 20 activities, and each generated event

---

[1] https://github.com/bearlu1996/context_activities.

[2] https://doi.org/10.4121/uuid:ea90c4be-64b6-4f4b-b27c-10ede28da6b6.

[3] Only the original event logs generated from artificial process models are used.

log contains 1000 traces. An example artificial model in the dataset is presented in Fig. 2.

As shown in Fig. 8, for each artificial event log, we randomly insert 1, 3, 5 context activities. The number of events inserted for each activity ranges from 10% to 20% of the total number of events in the event log. In addition, for each log with context activities, we insert the same number of noisy activities, each takes 1% of the total number of events. For example, an event log with 3 context activities will also contain 3 noisy activities, each takes 1% of the total number of events.

Fig. 8. Artificial Process Model M_3 (left) and M_4 (right). Activity C in M_3 and B in M_4 can execute under different contexts

For our proposed method, we use 3-context traces to represent the context of each event, and each context trace is represented by a 3 dimensional vector. We keep all other default settings for the Trace2Vec algorithm. For the DBSCAN algorithm, minPts is set to 5, and eps is set to 0.1.

To demonstrate the effectiveness of the proposed method, the direct entropy-based activity filtering method proposed in [21] is also implemented as a baseline. As the goal of [21] is to filter out activities with undesired behaviours, we slightly modify it in order to detect context activities. For each activity $a \in L$, an entropy $H(a, L) = H(dfr(a, L) + dpr(a, L))$ is calculated. $H(X) = -\sum_{x \in P_X} x log_2(x)$, $dfr(a, L)$ (or $dpr(a, L)$) is a vector which measures the probability that activity a is followed by (or follows) other activities (including artificial end or start activities). For example, for event log $L = [<a, b, c, x>^{10}, <a, b, x, c>^{10}, <a, x, b, c>^{10}]$, $dfr(a, L) = <0, \frac{20}{30}, 0, \frac{10}{30}, 0>$, $dpr(a, L) = <0, 0, 0, 0, 1>$.

Suppose the number of inserted context activities is n, for our method, we report the n activities with the highest behavioural coverages as context activities, For the baseline, we report the n activities with the highest entropy as context activities. As the number of reported activities is always the same as the number of actual context activities, we use accuracy to measure the performance of both methods. The accuracy is the proportion of the number of detected context activities to the number of all context activities.

Table 1 reports the average accuracy values for our method and the baseline when noises are not added into the event logs. Each accuracy is the average of 2637 results. The accuracy values for both our method and the baseline are very high, indicating that almost all inserted context activities can be successfully identified. Table 2 reports the accuracy values when noisy activities are inserted into the event logs. When noisy activities are inserted into the event logs, our method can still successfully detect most of the context activities. However, the baseline can only successfully detect 50% of the context activities on average.

It has to be noted that although our method performs better than the baseline when noises are added into the event log, the original aim of the baseline method is not to differentiate context activities from noises.

Table 1. Average accuracy of our method and the baseline when no noises are added into the event logs. For example, "5 context activities, 10%" means 5 context activities are inserted into the event log, and the number of events for each inserted activity is 10% of the number of total events

	Our Method	Baseline
5 Context Activities, 10%	0.96	**0.99**
5 Context Activities, 20%	**0.98**	**0.98**
3 Context Activities, 10%	0.95	**0.99**
3 Context Activities, 20%	**0.98**	0.97
1 Context Activity, 10%	0.95	**0.99**
1 Context Activity, 20%	**0.99**	**0.99**

Table 2. Average accuracy of our method and the baseline when adding noisy activities into event logs. The number of inserted noisy activities is the same as context activities. Each takes 1% of the total number of events

	Our Method	Baseline
5 Context Activities, 10%	**0.90**	0.73
5 Context Activities, 20%	**0.98**	0.61
3 Context Activities, 10%	**0.88**	0.59
3 Context Activities, 20%	**0.98**	0.45
1 Context Activity, 10%	**0.91**	0.40
1 Context Activity, 20%	**0.98**	0.23

7   Evaluation on Real-Life Data

We evaluate our method on a publicly-available event log which describes processes to deal with sepsis patients in a hospital[4]. The event log contains 16 activities, 15214 events and 1050 traces, of which 846 are distinct traces. According to [9], three activities in the event log are related to lab tests (i.e. CRP, Lactic Acid and Leucocytes), and they can execute at anytime during the execution of the process. We apply our method on the event log. Similar to the previous section, the event log is converted into a 3-dimensional convex hull, and for the DBSCAN algorithm, we set minPts to 5, and eps to 0.5.

---

[4] https://doi.org/10.4121/uuid:915d2bfb-7e84-49ad-a286-dc35f063a460.

The behavioural coverage for each activity is then calculated by our proposed method. The three activities with highest behavioural coverages are Leucocytes (Coverage = 0.9), CRP (Coverage = 0.86) and LaticAcid (Coverage = 0.71) respectively, which conform to the domain knowledge provided in [9]. In addition, the behavioural coverage for Admission NC is 0.60, and the behavioural coverages for all other activities are below 0.4. Figure 9 shows the convex hulls for the Sepsis event log, a context activity (CRP) and a normal activity (Release C). It is clear to see that the behavioural coverage for CRP is much larger than it for Release C.

Finally, we remove the three context activities from the event log. While the event log still has 1050 traces, the number of distinct traces drops from 846 to 182, which indicates a simpler model can be discovered to represent the main control-flow of the process. Further analysis can then be conducted on the three context activities (lab tests).

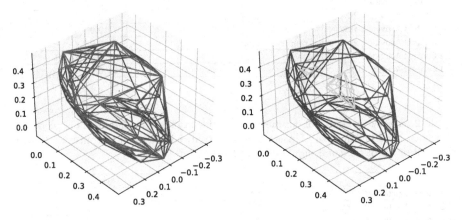

Fig. 9. Convex hulls for the Sepsis event Log (1 blue convex hull), activity CRP (1 red convex hull), and activity Release C (2 yellow convex hulls) (Color figure online)

8   Conclusion

In this paper, we propose a novel method to detect context activities which can happen at anytime during the execution of the process. Different from outliers, context activities are a part of the process and should not be ignored when studying the process behaviours. Comparing to the baseline, both methods can successfully detect activities which do not belong to the control flow of the process. In addition, our method can distinguish context activities from outliers. After context activities are detected, they can be removed from the event log when discovering process models, but further attention needs to be attracted to analysis the roles of these context activities in the process (e.g. if the detected context activity is triggered by other external factors such as the weather condition, etc.). Besides, the output of our method can also be used as input for tools such as [9] to visualise context activities.

A drawback of our method is that when there are many context activities in event logs, the context for all other activities may also become more complex, which could lead to a higher behavioural coverage for all other activities. It has to be noted that in this paper, we only use 3-dimensional vectors to represent the behaviours of events, and 3-context traces are used to represent all events. Although evaluation results show that the current settings are capable of detecting context activities, it would be interesting to investigate how the number of dimensions and the number of events in context traces can affect the performance of the method and the behavioural coverages in the future.

References

1. Van der Aalst, W., Weijters, T., Maruster, L.: Workflow mining: discovering process models from event logs. IEEE Trans. Knowl. Data Eng. **16**(9), 1128–1142 (2004)
2. Van der Aalst, W.M.: Process Mining: Data Science in Action. Springer, Heidelberg (2016). https://doi.org/10.1007/978-3-662-49851-4
3. Van der Aalst, W.: On the representational bias in process mining. In: 2011 IEEE 20th International Workshops on Enabling Technologies: Infrastructure for Collaborative Enterprises, pp. 2–7 (2011). https://doi.org/10.1109/WETICE.2011.64
4. Augusto, A., et al.: Automated discovery of process models from event logs: review and benchmark. IEEE Trans. Knowl. Data Eng. **31**(4), 686–705 (2019). https://doi.org/10.1109/TKDE.2018.2841877
5. Berti, A., Van Zelst, S.J., van der Aalst, W.: Process mining for python (PM4Py): bridging the gap between process-and data science. arXiv preprint arXiv:1905.06169 (2019)
6. Breunig, M.M., Kriegel, H.P., Ng, R.T., Sander, J.: LOF: identifying density-based local outliers. In: Proceedings of the 2000 ACM SIGMOD International Conference on Management of Data - SIGMOD 2000, Dallas, Texas, United States, pp. 93–104. ACM Press (2000). https://doi.org/10.1145/342009.335388
7. De Koninck, P., vanden Broucke, S., De Weerdt, J.: act2vec, trace2vec, log2vec, and model2vec: representation learning for business processes. In: Weske, M., Montali, M., Weber, I., vom Brocke, J. (eds.) BPM 2018. LNCS, vol. 11080, pp. 305–321. Springer, Cham (2018). https://doi.org/10.1007/978-3-319-98648-7_18
8. De Medeiros, A.A., van Dongen, B.F., Van der Aalst, W.M., Weijters, A.: Process mining: extending the α-algorithm to mine short loops (2004)
9. Dees, M., Hompes, B., van der Aalst, W.M.: Events put into context (EPiC). In: 2020 2nd International Conference on Process Mining (ICPM), pp. 65–72. IEEE (2020)
10. Dumas, M., La Rosa, M., Mendling, J., Reijers, H.A., et al.: Fundamentals of Business Process Management, vol. 1. Springer, Heidelberg (2013). https://doi.org/10.1007/978-3-642-33143-5
11. Ester, M., Kriegel, H.P., Sander, J., Xu, X., et al.: A density-based algorithm for discovering clusters in large spatial databases with noise. In: KDD, vol. 96, pp. 226–231 (1996)
12. Guo, Q., Wen, L., Wang, J., Yan, Z., Yu, P.S.: Mining invisible tasks in non-free-choice constructs. In: Motahari-Nezhad, H.R., Recker, J., Weidlich, M. (eds.) BPM 2015. LNCS, vol. 9253, pp. 109–125. Springer, Cham (2015). https://doi.org/10.1007/978-3-319-23063-4_7

13. Le, Q., Mikolov, T.: Distributed representations of sentences and documents. In: Xing, E.P., Jebara, T. (eds.) Proceedings of the 31st International Conference on Machine Learning. Proceedings of Machine Learning Research, Bejing, China, vol. 32, pp. 1188–1196. PMLR (2014)

14. Leemans, M., van der Aalst, W.M.P.: Modeling and discovering cancelation behavior. In: Panetto, H., et al. (eds.) OTM 2017. LNCS, vol. 10573, pp. 93–113. Springer, Cham (2017). https://doi.org/10.1007/978-3-319-69462-7_8

15. Leemans, S.J.J., Fahland, D., van der Aalst, W.M.P.: Discovering block-structured process models from event logs - a constructive approach. In: Colom, J.-M., Desel, J. (eds.) PETRI NETS 2013. LNCS, vol. 7927, pp. 311–329. Springer, Heidelberg (2013). https://doi.org/10.1007/978-3-642-38697-8_17

16. Leemans, S.J.J., Fahland, D., van der Aalst, W.M.P.: Discovering block-structured process models from event logs containing infrequent behaviour. In: Lohmann, N., Song, M., Wohed, P. (eds.) BPM 2013. LNBIP, vol. 171, pp. 66–78. Springer, Cham (2014). https://doi.org/10.1007/978-3-319-06257-0_6

17. Lu, X., Fahland, D., van den Biggelaar, F.J.H.M., van der Aalst, W.M.P.: Handling duplicated tasks in process discovery by refining event labels. In: La Rosa, M., Loos, P., Pastor, O. (eds.) BPM 2016. LNCS, vol. 9850, pp. 90–107. Springer, Cham (2016). https://doi.org/10.1007/978-3-319-45348-4_6

18. Lu, Y., Chen, Q., Poon, S.: A novel approach to discover switch behaviours in process mining. In: Leemans, S., Leopold, H. (eds.) ICPM 2020. LNBIP, vol. 406, pp. 57–68. Springer, Cham (2021). https://doi.org/10.1007/978-3-030-72693-5_5

19. Mandal, S., Hewelt, M., Weske, M.: A framework for integrating real-world events and business processes in an IoT environment. In: Panetto, H., et al. (eds.) OTM 2017. LNCS, vol. 10573, pp. 194–212. Springer, Cham (2017). https://doi.org/10.1007/978-3-319-69462-7_13

20. Marin-Castro, H.M., Tello-Leal, E.: Event log preprocessing for process mining: a review. Appl. Sci. **11**(22), 10556 (2021). https://doi.org/10.3390/app112210556

21. Tax, N., Sidorova, N., van der Aalst, W.M.P.: Discovering more precise process models from event logs by filtering out chaotic activities. J. Intell. Inf. Syst. **52**(1), 107–139 (2018). https://doi.org/10.1007/s10844-018-0507-6

22. Wen, L., Wang, J., van der Aalst, W.M., Huang, B., Sun, J.: Mining process models with prime invisible tasks. Data Knowl. Eng. **69**(10), 999–1021 (2010)

23. Zandkarimi, F., Rehse, J.R., Soudmand, P., Hoehle, H.: A generic framework for trace clustering in process mining. In: 2020 2nd International Conference on Process Mining (ICPM), pp. 177–184 (2020). https://doi.org/10.1109/ICPM49681.2020.00034

Event Log Generation: An Industry Perspective

Timotheus Kampik[1](✉)(iD) and Mathias Weske[2](iD)

[1] SAP Signavio, Berlin, Germany
timotheus.kampik@sap.com
[2] Hasso Plattner Institute, University of Potsdam, Potsdam, Germany
mathias.weske@hpi.de

Abstract. This paper presents the results of an industry expert survey about event log generation in process mining. It takes academic assumptions as a starting point and elicits practitioner's assessments of statements about process execution, process scoping, process discovery, and process analysis. The results of the survey shed some light on challenges and perspectives around event log generation, as well as on the relationship between process models and process execution, and derive challenges for event log generation from it. The responses indicate that particularly relevant challenges exist around data integration and quality, and that process mining can benefit from a systematic integration with more traditional and wide-spread business intelligence approaches.

Keywords: Process mining · Event logs · Business process management

1 Introduction

Started as an academic discipline, the focus of process mining has mostly been on concepts and algorithms that analyze observed process behavior and compare it to behavior that has been defined in process models. Process mining is based on event logs, which represent real-world business process executions. More concretely, an event log consists of a sequence of events, each of which includes at least a case identifier and an activity reference. Until recently, the assumption has been that event logs of this structure are readily available [5]. With the industrial uptake of process mining, this assumption has been challenged, and the importance of event log generation has become evident. Practical experiences indicate that the generation of event logs incurs substantial efforts [4,7].

In order to better understand the practical challenges of event log generation in process mining, the authors have conducted a survey with different stakeholders ranging from domain experts to systems designers and software engineers. This paper describes the structure of the survey as well as the main results of

M. Weske—Work by this author supported by the SAP Academic Fellowship program.

A. Augusto et al. (Eds.): BPMDS 2022/EMMSAD 2022, LNBIP 450, pp. 123–136, 2022.
https://doi.org/10.1007/978-3-031-07475-2_9

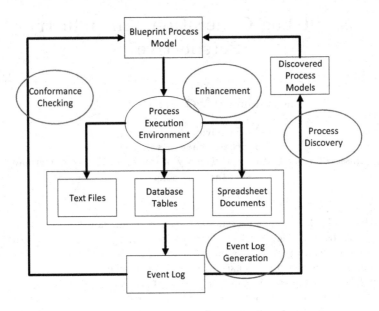

Fig. 1. Overview of process mining concepts and tasks.

the empirical study, and it derives focal areas for industrially relevant research in event log generation, and – more broadly – in process mining.

The remainder of this paper is organized as follows. After introducing the main concepts in process mining, we motivate the survey and provide the research questions that we aim to answer. The survey is presented and its results are discussed, before concluding remarks complete the paper.

2   Process Mining Overview

For more than a decade, the academic process mining community has developed an impressive arsenal of process mining methods, techniques, and tools. Several of those have recently found their way to industrial practice. In this section, the main tasks that can be performed in process mining projects are categorized and the role of event log generation is highlighted. In Fig. 1 important concepts in process mining are presented, and the different process mining tasks are shown.

Business process management is based on process models that provide an abstract representation of the business processes of an organization. These process models are used in different ways. So-called *as-is* process models describe the current state of the business processes. They are analyzed and improved, leading to *to-be* process models, which represent new and improved business processes that will be implemented in the organization. Since they acts as blueprints for business processes, we refer to them as "blueprint process model(s)" in Fig. 1.

A blueprint process model is used to implement the corresponding business process, configuring a process execution environment as specified in the process model. It is worth noting that processes are not always implemented exactly as specified by the blueprint process model. In fact, finding and quantifying deviations of the blueprint process model and the executed process instances is one important challenge in process mining. Blueprint process models can even be missing, so that the process is implemented based on a traditional requirements engineering effort, or merely based on the understanding that the systems engineers have of the process.

During process execution, process execution data is generated. This data is located in different data stores. It can be of an arbitrary structure, ranging from well-structured data stored in relational databases to spreadsheets and text files. Event log generation is facing the challenge of integrating those data sources and to provide an appropriate basis for the main process mining tasks *process discovery, conformance checking* (and other analyses), and *process enhancement.*

In process discovery, the event log is used to "re-engineer" a process model whose instances have been observed in the event log. Ideally, the generated process model matches the blueprint process model. As experience shows, this is hardly ever the case. Conformance checking provides techniques and tools to compare an event log with the blueprint process model. Valuable insights can be inferred from conformance checking, for instance about missing activities or activities that have been observed in the event log and that cannot be found in the blueprint process model. Obviously, conformance checking can only be performed if a blueprint process model is available. In process enhancement, we analyze the discovered process model and draw conclusions on how to improve – or, enhance – the blueprint process model. This task is typically performed by domain experts that are knowledgeable about the process and can interpret the discovered process model properly.

3   Motivation, Research Questions, and Survey Structure

While at first sight event log generation seems like a straightforward task, in practice, it turns out that it is not. The complicating factors are manifold, ranging from heterogeneous data sources and data quality issues to challenges that are related to the goal of the process mining task at hand.

To motivate challenges in process mining and their effect on event log generation, we consider a process mining project in a hospital setting that looks at medication aspects of patients with lower back pain syndrome. An important aspect of event log generation is the definition of a case identifier. In the hospital example, we might choose the patient identifier as case identifier. This is convenient, since the data entries that we find always have a patient identifier associated. However, selecting the patient identifier as case identifier might lead to undesired outcomes during process analysis. This is due to the fact that a case does not only contain activities that are related to lower back pain, the disease we are interested in. Instead, other diseases that the patient has suffered from are also part of the process that we mine (and its instances). If a patient suffered from an arm fracture, she might have been administered painkillers already, which would be falsely associated with her lower back pain condition that we are interested in. This example illustrates that the selection of the case identifier has severe implications on event log generation.

Based on these considerations, the survey aims at answering the following research questions.

RQ1: How do process models impact process executions and how are process mining opportunities affected?

RQ2: What are the main conceptual challenges in event log generation?

RQ3: What are the main technical challenges in event log generation?

To provide a holistic view on the different challenges of event log generation and to address the research questions, the following areas are covered by the survey.

- Process Execution: Since event logs are based on data that is generated during business process execution, it is essential to investigate how business processes are actually executed. This area of questions involves the role of process models as well, because those are required for specific process mining tasks, for instance for conformance checking [2].
- Process Scoping: If events in an event log belong to different business processes and we use that log in process discovery, the resulting process model becomes complex and does not reflect the desired process properly. One reason is improper scoping of the process, which is another important aspect that needs to be covered when generating event logs [1].
- Data Sources and Event Logs: Event logs use data that might be stored in different, heterogeneous data sources [5]. The questions in this area address the quality and number of data sources used in process mining projects as well as the effort that is incurred by event log generation.
- Process Discovery: In process discovery, we are interested in discovering process models from event logs. We can compare those discovered process models with process models that have served as blueprints of the process execution. To find out more about these aspects, the survey contains questions related to issues in process discovery that might point to problems related to the event log that was used as input to process discovery.
- Process Analysis: Even though process discovery can be regarded as a subset of process analysis, we have decided to separate these two areas. In process analysis, we ask questions related to performance indicators of the process. The questions are important for event log generation, since we have to make sure that the relevant data attributes actually find their way to the events in the generated event log.

In each area mentioned, the survey asked for the assessment of several statements, such as "It is straightforward to find the correct scope of a process, from start to end.". The survey invited answers based on a 5-point Likert scale (*Strongly disagree/SD*, *Disagree/D*, *Neutral/N*, *Agree/A*, and *Strongly Agree/SA*). The area *Data Sources and Event Logs* was augmented by two additional questions about the typical number of data sources of an event log and common types of data sources. Broader open text feedback could be provided as well, but is subject to organizational nondisclosure requirements[1].

4   Survey Results

The authors have conducted the survey from December 2021 through January 2022. Employees of a large enterprise systems vendor have been asked to participate, and respondents were sampled from teams of process mining and business process intelligence experts. Subjects have different educational and professional backgrounds, from technical and engineering to business and management. They also serve in different roles in the company, including solutions, engineering, and product innovation. In the remainder of this section, we focus on the demographics of subjects, before considering the responses to the survey questions.

Prior to the survey, a pilot survey was conducted to gather feedback from five selected experts; the refinement based on the feedback resulted in the presented survey. For each Likert-scale assessment, a bar chart with the responses is provided, alongside a table that provides (for the overall group of respondents, as well as for demographic groups) the median, mode, and a simplified mode (*Sim. Mode*) that aggregates "strongly disagree" (SD) and "disagree" (D) to "disagree" (D), as well as "strongly agree" (SA) and "agree" (A) to "agree" (A). One question asked for an approximate quantification (as a categorical answer/selection). The content of one free-text answer is aggregated and summarized.

Because the differences between demographic groups are not the main focus of the study, and because it was not possible to control for confounding features like team-level organizational assignment or role changes over time, no analysis of the statistical significance of the assessment differences between demographic groups is made. We merely observe that general alignment with respect to the assessment direction typically brings with it alignment between demographic groups. In contrast, investigating the demographic impact on the lack of alignment as observed in the assessments of some statements is out of the scope of this paper and would require further research.

To comply with page limitations, diagrams that visualize the results have – with one exception – not been included in the paper. An extended version of this paper that features an appendix with diagrams, as well as with tables that give an overview of the medians and modes of responses for different demographic groups, is available at https://arxiv.org/abs/2202.02539.

4.1   Demographics

Overall, the survey was answered by 32 subjects. Demographic information can be summarized as follows.

---

[1] Let us highlight that no open feedback that contradicts the other survey results was received.

Years of industry work experience: 2 subjects (6.3%) reported 0–1 years; 4 (12.5%) 1–3 years; 11 (34.4%) 3–5 years; 2 (6.3%) 5–10 years; 13 (40.6%) more than 10 years.

Years of process mining work experience: 3 subjects (9.4%) reported 0–1 years; 15 (46.9%) 1–3 years; 13 (40.6%) 3–5 years; 1 (3.1%) 5–10 years.

Educational background: The survey offered a range of options, as well as an open text field to specify the educational background. Aggregated, the categories *Science/Engineering*: 23 (71.9%) and *Mixed/other*: 9 (28.1%) were obtained.

Role in the organization: the survey provided a selection of prevalent internal roles, as well as an open text field. The results were then aggregated into the categories *Product/Engineering* (abbreviated as Pro./eng.): 15 (46.9%) and *Solutions/Consulting* (Sol./cons.): 17 (53.1%).

One respondent reported more process mining work experience than industry work experience, which can potentially be explained by work experience in a non-industry context, such as in academia. As another aggregated category, the experience levels are aggregated to *Experienced* (Exp) (14, 43.8%) and *Newcomers* (New) (18, 56.2%), where falling into the former category requires at least three years of process mining experience, as well as at least five years of industry experience.

4.2 Process Execution

The to-be-assessed statements regarding process execution aimed at eliciting a broader, nuanced perspective on the roles that (formal) process models play in business process execution. Assessments of the following statements were requested.

1. *Business processes are executed exactly as specified in process models.* This statement reflects the traditional academic assumption that process models are executable specifications. Not surprisingly, most respondents disagreed (14) or strongly disagreed (12) with this statement, while merely two respondents agreed (one of the two strongly agreed)[2]. No substantial differences between demographic groups seem to exist.

2. *Process models are used as requirements specifications that are then implemented in IT systems.* This statement can be considered a relaxation of the previous one: if process models are not 'directly' executed, they at least inform the specification of systems that execute business processes. There is no consensus about this statement, but a simple majority (14: 10 *A*, 4 *SA*) of the respondents agreed with the statement, while relatively few (7) disagreed (no one strongly disagreed). Consultants reported to agree more with this statement than product managers and engineers; the same applies to respondents with technical education vs. 'other/mixed' education and experienced practitioners vs. newcomers.

---

[2] Here and henceforth, the number of *neutral* responses can – if not explicitly stated – be determined by subtracting the number of all other respondents from 32.

3. *Process models are not used to implement processes.* This statement can be considered a contradiction of the former statement. Indeed, no respondent expressed agreement with this statement *and* with the former statement. Most respondents disagreed (6) or strongly disagreed (15), whereas only two respondents agreed (no one strongly agreed). The assessment is consistent across demographic groups.

The responses suggest that process models are rarely directly executed, but still relevant for execution in that they inform business process implementation in IT systems in some ways. While this conclusion is not particularly surprising from an industry perspective, it allows for the conclusion that academically it is important to acknowledge that many process models are primarily for humans to understand and discuss and not necessarily for machines to automatically execute.

4.3   Process Scoping and Data Sources

The statements regarding process scoping aimed at eliciting an assessment of how challenging the identification of events and the data sources that provide them actually is. Assessments of the following statements were requested.

1. *It is straightforward to find the correct scope of a process, from start to end.* This statement challenges the assumption that identifying the scope of a process, from start to end, is indeed challenging. Most respondents strongly disagreed (7) or disagreed (15) with this statement; a small minority of respondents (3) agreed with the statement (no one strongly agreed). Disagreement is consistent across demographic groups.
2. *It is straightforward to group events to process instances (finding the case ID, group by case ID).* This statement challenges the assumption that event correlation is challenging. Respondents broadly disagreed (15) or strongly disagreed (5) with the statement; however there is some misalignment among respondents, with seven respondents reporting agreement and two strong agreement. Still, disagreement is dominant across demographic groups.
3. *It is straightforward to locate the data sources that we need for generating an event log.* The statement claims that locating data sources for event log generation is trivial. While most respondents strongly disagreed (3) or disagreed (13) with this claim, there are also some who agreed (7) or strongly agreed (1). Overall, the median is between disagreement and a neutral attitude. We find differences among the demographic groups. The median is 'disagree' for respondents who work in product development, as well as for respondents who have a not exclusively technical education and respondents who are relatively new to process mining or industry work. It is 'neutral' for respondents with technical education, respondents who work in solutions/consulting, and respondents who are generally more experienced. While some form of disagreement is the most common response type across all demographic groups, the responses are largely inconclusive: locating data sources may be a challenge, but is not necessarily so.

4. *Typically, data quality issues do not affect event log generation.* The statement challenges the practical assumption that a key problem in process mining is obtaining high-quality data and mitigating data quality issues. Most respondents strongly disagreed (13) or disagreed (12) with this statement, while there was little agreement (3) and strong agreement (1). Disagreement dominates across demographic groups, suggesting that addressing issues around data quality is in fact a challenge when generating event logs.

The responses suggest that scoping business processes regarding their temporal scope (from start to end), as well as correlating events to cases (identifying case IDs) is challenging. Also, data quality issues are prone to affect event log generation. It could not be confirmed that the identification of data sources poses a substantial challenge.

4.4   Event Logs

The requests for assessment were augmented with additional questions about data sources for event logs. Assessments of the following statements/answers to the following questions were requested.

1. *Event log generation incurs significant efforts in process mining projects.* This statement reflects the assumption that a substantial part of overall efforts in process mining are spent on event log generation. Most respondents strongly agreed (13) or agreed (13) with this statement. Merely 2 respondents disagreed (and no one strongly disagreed). Agreement is largely consistent across demographic groups.
2. *Extract-Transform-Load (ETL) pipelines provide all information needed in an event log.* The statement asks for an assessment of the extract-transform-load pipeline architecture for event log generation. A simple majority of respondents assessed the statement as neutral (13), whereas eight respondents agreed, ten disagreed and one strongly disagreed (no one strongly agreed). Disagreement is somewhat stronger among respondents with a product/engineering background, as well as among respondents with a non-technical or hybrid education. Overall, no clear signal of support or opposition to the statement could be elicited.
3. *How many backend systems are typically providing the data for a single event log?* The statement challenges the assumption that event logs are typically generated from the data provided by a single system. Generally, there is no agreement on how many systems are typically used; six respondents stated that one system is used (6/"one"); otherwise the responses are: (8/"two"), (1/"three"), (9/"more than three"), and (8,"I don't know"). The relatively large proportion of participants that answered "I don't know" can potentially be explained by the fact that some respondents wanted to indicate that there is no simple answer, i.e., the number of systems varies between projects. Interestingly, respondents who work as consultants most frequently stated that typically, one backend system is used, whereas respondents with

an exclusively technical education equally frequently reported the use of one and of two backend systems; respondents with substantial industry and process mining experience most frequently selected "two" (however, equally many selected "I don't know"); these modes are lower than the overall mode, and the modes provided by other demographic groups. The responses allow drawing the conclusion that event logs are not necessarily generated from a single backend system.

4. *In a given system, the information needed for an event log is stored in a single relational table.* This statement somewhat naively asserts that event log data can be extracted from exactly one relational database table but does not directly contradict the previous statement (as it is possible that the data can be provided by several systems, but by exactly one table in each system). Most respondents strongly disagreed (17) or disagreed (10) with this statement; merely one respondent agreed with the statement (no one strongly agreed). Disagreement is largely consistent across demographic groups. The results suggest that typically, event logs cannot straightforwardly be extracted by reading out data from one specific database table.

5. *What are typical data sources of event logs? (E.g., relational database tables, document collections, CSVs, ...).* The question aims at getting an overview of typical data sources. After manually clustering the responses (considering that one participant can provide multiple responses as part of the free-text answer), the following categories are obtained and populated. i) relational databases and tables thereof (RDB): 16 respondents; ii) API access or similar to enterprise systems (API): 8; iii) CSVs files (CSVs): 8; iv) Database (generic, DBG): 5; v) no SQL/big data storages/data lakes (NoSQL/DL): 5; vi) Message queues/event-based (MQS): 3; viii) JSON content (JSON): 2; XES or XML files, or logs: 1 each. Figure 2 displays the categories and the number of responses that reflects each category.

The responses confirm the assumption that event log generation efforts are substantial and that sources for event logs are often relational databases of enterprise systems or CSVs, whereas data lakes and event-based systems seem to be emerging as alternatives. In contrast, XES is – apparently – typically not used (and possibly not available), which raises questions about the practical importance of the XES XML standard[3]. Additionally, the responses suggest that event logs are typically not extracted from a single database table and not necessarily from a single backend system.

4.5   Process Discovery

The statements regarding process discovery aimed at gauging the relevance of mining complex control flows from an industry perspective. Assessments of the following statements were requested.

---

[3] This finding is to some extent confirmed by the results of another recent expert survey [8].

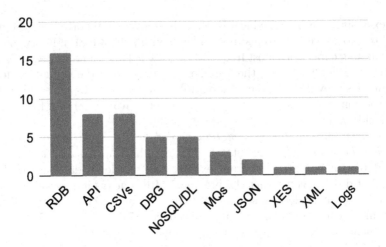

Fig. 2. Data sources for event log generation.

1. *In process discovery, we encounter complex process models.* The statement asserts that process complexity plays a role in process discovery. Almost all respondents strongly agreed (18) or agreed (13) with this statement (no one disagreed or strongly disagreed). Agreement is largely consistent across demographic groups, with respondents working in product or engineering roles expressing slightly less strong agreement. This lets us conclude that managing complexity plays a relevant role in process discovery.

2. *In process discovery, the ordering of activities is important to me (e.g., it is important to know that "activity A always precedes activity B").* This statement asserts that the notion of a process as an ordered sequence of activities is practically relevant when discovering processes. Almost all respondents strongly agreed (14) or agreed (15) with this statement (no one strongly disagreed or disagreed). Across demographic groups, agreement strength varies, but there is generally clear agreement, which supports the conclusion that activity ordering is indeed important.

3. *Most discovered processes are sequential (no branching or concurrency).* This statement challenges the assumption that process complexity in terms of variance and concurrency matters and stands in contrast to the first statement in this group. Most respondents strongly disagreed (8) or disagreed (14), whereas relatively few agreed (3) or strongly agreed (2). Disagreement is somewhat consistent across demographic groups, although respondents working in consulting exhibit a more neutral attitude. Disagreement is relatively strong among respondents with substantial experience or with a not exclusively technical background. The results allow us to carefully draw the conclusion that discovered processes tend to be not sequential. Interestingly, the signal we get from these responses is weaker than the signal that we get from the responses to the first statement, indicating that branching and concurrency may not account for all complexity that we encounter in process discovery.

The responses suggest that managing complexity, activity ordering and (to a slightly lesser extent) variants, are indeed practically relevant challenges.

4.6   Process Analysis

The statements regarding process analysis aimed at eliciting an assessment of the relevance of Key Performance Indicators (KPIs), conformance checking, and traditional Business Intelligence (BI) in the context of process analysis. Assessments of the following statements were requested.

1. *An important goal of process mining is the calculation of KPIs.* The statement asserts that Key Performance Indicators (KIPs, or, in the context of business process management: Process Performance Indicators, PPIs) play an important role in process mining. Most respondents strongly agreed (10) or agreed (17) with this statement. Merely two respondents disagreed (no one strongly disagreed). Agreement is consistent across demographic groups, which lets us conclude that KPI calculation is indeed important.

2. *In process mining, it is difficult to identify meaningful KPIs.* The statement asserts that identifying meaningful KPIs is a challenge, which is a widely accepted premise for performance measures in general. There is broad disagreement among the respondents with respect to this statement. While no respondent strongly agreed, many (12) agreed, and many strongly disagreed (3) or disagreed (11). Respondents that work as consultants or have an exclusively technical background expressed more agreement than other demographic groups. The results merely allow for the conclusion that it is not clear whether identifying meaningful KPIs is difficult; it may be difficult in some scenarios and straightforward in others.

3. *Comparing the event log with a process model is important in process analysis.* This statement reflects the notion of conformance checking, which is a key aspect of academic research on process mining. Most respondents strongly agreed (9) or agreed (13), while few strongly disagreed (1) or disagreed (4). Agreement is largely consistent across demographic groups, which lets us conclude that comparing event logs with blueprint process models is indeed important.

4. *A better integration of Business Intelligence (BI) and process mining would be valuable.* This statement reflects the practical intuition that process mining and related analyses is related to business intelligence and hence should be integrated with it. Most respondents strongly agreed (11) or agreed (17) with the statement, whereas merely one disagreed (no one strongly disagreed). Agreement is largely consistent across demographic groups. The results conclude that the integration of BI and process mining is indeed a relevant frontier for research and innovation.

The responses suggest that KPIs play an important role in process mining, and that the integration of business intelligence and process mining is a practically relevant research direction, but also that comparing event logs with manually created process models (which relates to the academic research field of confor-mance checking) appears to be an important aspect. Whether it is difficult or not to identify KPIs cannot be answered by our study.

5 Discussion

It is important to highlight that the survey's findings need to be seen in the light of its limitations. In particular, the survey was conducted among employees of a single enterprise software system vendor with strong expertise in process man-agement and process mining. Our 'insider' access allowed for a precise targeting of potential respondents. Considering that respondents are i) from different parts of an organizational unit that has been recently (prior to the survey) created as the result of an acquisition and ii) relatively diverse given their experience levels and roles in the organization, the strong alignment of results across demo-graphics suggests that many of the findings can potentially (but not necessarily) be generalized by broader follow-up studies. Such studies are relevant future research, considering the specific population that the survey sampled from, as well as the relatively small sample size. The remainder of this section discusses the key findings of the survey.

5.1 Questioning Academic Assumptions

The academic business process management and process mining community has traditionally close contacts to industry, which is evident given the many uni-versity spin-offs (startups) in the area and many collaboration projects between academia and industry. Still, the focus of academia and research is, by nature, dif-ferent from the main objectives of industry organizations. While industry focuses on practical challenges that provide value to customers, academia's main interest is well-scoped, intellectually challenging problems that look for elegant solutions. To come up with those solutions, academic assumptions have to be made.

With this survey we could confirm some of those assumptions, while rejecting others. Traditionally, academia has frequently assumed that process models are interpreted by process engines that would enact the process exactly as speci-fied. More recently, academia is increasingly critical about this assumption, even challenging the value of process models. The survey provides interesting findings in this regard. It rejects the idea that business process models are exact specifi-cations of processes that run in the real-world. At the same time, process models provide significant value by their role in defining requirements during systems development.

It is worth noting that the finding questions the direct link between model and execution, as depicted by Fig. 1. We have to read this link as information flow, being used in a translation from model to executable process. This translation requires human interpretation, typically with the help of dedicated systems for enterprise system configuration. More broadly speaking, because process models may be useful in ways that diverge from academic assumptions, approaches to assessing their correctness need to be re-thought as well[4].

5.2 Relevance of Academic Research

The results indicate that well-established research directions that are concerned with the mining of process control flow and variants therein, as well as with the comparison of expected (modeled) and factual (mined) flow are important from an industry perspective. These findings are to be interpreted carefully, i.e., there are process mining practitioners who believe in the importance, but industry experts that focus on traditional business intelligence or machine learning-based analytics may assess the corresponding statements differently – or are not aware of their potential. Process complexity is regarded as an important problem, which might hint at the challenges in process scoping, discussed above. If processes are not well scoped, this means that events of different processes are used in process discovery. Since these processes might run independently from each other, events occur concurrently, leading to complex process structures.

5.3 Emerging Research Directions

The findings suggest that questions of particular importance evolve around data quality, event correlation, and the integration of event log-based process mining with traditional business intelligence. While recent research starts to address some of these challenges, in particular around data on-boarding and integration [4,6,7], as well as event correlation and object-centered process mining [3], the free text feedback gathered from the survey points to largely unexplored questions, e.g., to the aforementioned integration of business intelligence approaches into process mining and to the use of models as tools for event log generation and process scoping.

6 Conclusion

The survey results presented in this paper shed some light onto challenges around event log generation. In particular, the results allow drawing the following conclusions: i) process models are typically not directly executed, but rather serve as input for enterprise software system specification and configuration, which is obvious from an industry perspective, but is potentially a useful insight for academia; ii) identifying process start and end, as well as event correlation is a challenge; iii) data quality issues have an impact on event log generation; iv) classical academic questions in process discovery about process complexity, activity ordering and process variants are practically relevant; v) event log generation incurs indeed substantial effort and event logs are usually generated based on

---

[4] To allude to the famous quote that "[e]ssentially all models are wrong, but some of them are useful", as commonly attributed to George Box.

several relational database tables, and frequently based on data from several backend systems; vi) data sources for event log generation are most commonly traditional relational databases of enterprise systems whose content is sometimes transferred into CSV format as a 'low tech' export/import procedure, but event-based systems and data lakes are emerging as sources as well; vii) the mining of control flow is practically relevant, and so is the generation of KPIs and the integration of process intelligence and business intelligence. As a broader conclusion, the survey results suggest that the role of process models in process mining and event log generation, but also generally in architectural perspective on the process management life-cycle, needs to be re-assessed. In particular, the results indicate that while the connection between designed blueprint process models and executed process instances is rather indirect than direct. Models i) play a role in process implementation, but not as strong of a role as often assumed by academia; ii) can be used to better inform process scoping and event correlation; iii) can ideally combine knowledge-based and data-driven process insights.

References

1. van der Aalst, W.M.P.: Extracting event data from databases to unleash process mining. In: vom Brocke, J., Schmiedel, T. (eds.) BPM - Driving Innovation in a Digital World. MP, pp. 105–128. Springer, Cham (2015). https://doi.org/10.1007/978-3-319-14430-6_8

2. van der Aalst, W.M.P.: Process Mining - Data Science in Action, 2nd edn. Springer, Heidelberg (2016). https://doi.org/10.1007/978-3-662-49851-4

3. van der Aalst, W.M.P.: Object-centric process mining: dealing with divergence and convergence in event data. In: Ölveczky, P.C., Salaün, G. (eds.) SEFM 2019. LNCS, vol. 11724, pp. 3–25. Springer, Cham (2019). https://doi.org/10.1007/978-3-030-30446-1_1

4. Andrews, R., van Dun, C., Wynn, M., Kratsch, W., Röglinger, M., ter Hofstede, A.: Quality-informed semi-automated event log generation for process mining. Decis. Support Syst. **132**, 113265 (2020). https://doi.org/10.1016/j.dss.2020.113265. https://www.sciencedirect.com/science/article/pii/S0167923620300208

5. Diba, K., Batoulis, K., Weidlich, M., Weske, M.: Extraction, correlation, and abstraction of event data for process mining. Wiley Interdiscip. Rev. Data Min. Knowl. Discov. **10**(3), e1346 (2020). https://doi.org/10.1002/widm.1346

6. Dijkman, R., Gao, J., Syamsiyah, A., van Dongen, B., Grefen, P., ter Hofstede, A.: Enabling efficient process mining on large data sets: realizing an in-database process mining operator. Distrib. Parallel Databases **38**(1), 227–253 (2020). https://doi.org/10.1007/s10619-019-07270-1

7. González López de Murillas, E., Reijers, H.A., van der Aalst, W.M.P.: Connecting databases with process mining: a meta model and toolset. Softw. Syst. Model. **18**(2), 1209–1247 (2019). https://doi.org/10.1007/s10270-018-0664-7

8. Wynn, M.T., et al.: Rethinking the input for process mining: insights from the XES survey and workshop. In: Munoz-Gama, J., Lu, X. (eds.) Process Mining Workshops, pp. 3–16. Springer, Cham (2022). https://doi.org/10.1007/978-3-030-98581-3_1

Foundations of Modeling and Method Engineering (EMMSAD 2022)

Towards a Systematic Method for Developing Meta Attack Language Instances

Simon Hacks[1,3(✉)], Sotirios Katsikeas[1], Engla Rencelj Ling[1], Wenjun Xiong[1], Jérôme Pfeiffer[2], and Andreas Wortmann[2]

[1] KTH Royal Institute of Technology, Stockholm, Sweden
{shacks,sotkat,englal,wenjx}@kth.se
[2] University of Stuttgart, Stuttgart, Germany
{jerome.pfeiffer,andreas.wortmann}@isw.uni-stuttgart.de
[3] University of Southern Denmark, Odense, Denmark
shacks@mmmi.sdu.dk

Abstract. Successfully developing domain-specific languages (DSLs) demands language engineers to consider their organizational context, which is challenging. Action design research (ADR) provides a conceptual framework to address this challenge. Since ADR's application to the engineering of DSLs has not yet been examined, we investigate applying it to the development of threat modeling DSLs based on the Meta Attack Language (MAL), a metamodeling language for the specification of domain-specific threat modeling languages. To this end, we conducted a survey with experienced MAL developers on their development activities. We extract guidelines and align these, together with established DSL design guidelines, to the conceptual model of ADR. The research presented, aims to be the first step to investigate whether ADR can be used to systematically engineer DSLs.

Keywords: Domain specific language (DSL) · Language engineering · Action design research (ADR)

1 Introduction

Cybersecurity is a key concern and fundamental aspect of information technology (IT) and operational technology (OT). Cyberattacks on these systems can have severe consequences [9]. At the same time, it is difficult to assess the security of IT systems, which demands identifying system assets, their weaknesses, and mitigations. To proactively address security concerns, threat modeling [45,54] and attack simulations [22] can be used to assess the cybersecurity and make it more difficult for attackers. Threat models serve as inputs for attack simulations to simulate cyberattacks, identify weaknesses, and provide quantitative security measurements [12,20]. The required concepts are highly domain-specific (i.e., modeling automotive threats vs. Industry 4.0 threats). Hence, the employed threat modeling languages need to be domain-specific as well.

© Springer Nature Switzerland AG 2022
A. Augusto et al. (Eds.): BPMDS 2022/EMMSAD 2022, LNBIP 450, pp. 139–154, 2022.
https://doi.org/10.1007/978-3-031-07475-2_10

Previously, the Meta Attack Language (MAL) [22] was proposed, which serves as a basis to develop domain-specific languages (DSLs) for specific attack modeling contexts. MAL is a meta-language featuring generic concepts that are needed for modeling systems, threats, and attacks in different domains. The resulting instances of MAL are DSLs for threat modeling. To date, several MAL DSLs have been devised [16,27,28,40,55]. However, the development process of these MAL DSLs varies. To unify the development of MAL DSLs, we propose a software language engineering (SLE) approach to develop MAL instances (i.e., MAL DSLs) using action design research (ADR). This approach aims to systematically collect guidelines and structure them to obtain a comprehensive overview for MAL DSLs' development. To this end, we conducted a survey with eleven experienced MAL developers to understand their developing methods. From these surveys, we extract guidelines and align these, together with established DSL design guidelines, with the conceptual model of ADR. Our approach is a novel application of ADR to develop DSLs through the lens of MAL DSLs with the intention of generalizing the method for other DSLs in the future. Hence, the contributions of this paper are threefold: (1) We provide the first ADR-based approach towards the systematic development of MAL DSLs and maybe DSLs in general; (2) We provide a comprehensive overview of how DSL guidelines can be used for developing MAL DSLs; and (3) We retroactively demonstrate our approach on three existing and documented MAL DSLs.

2   Background

2.1   Design Science Research

In information systems research, DSR is a popular approach to develop and evaluate designed artifacts [18]. As the initial proposal seemed to be too abstract to effectively steer research, alternatives have been proposed. One of the most popular alternatives proposes an iterative six-step process [38]: (1) The researcher defines the problem. (2) The objectives of a suitable artifact are determined. (3) The actual artifact is designed. (4) It is demonstrated that the designed artifact solves the given problem. (5) An evaluation is conducted, in which the researcher shows that the new artifact is performing better than existing solutions. (6) The outcomes are communicated. This process, however, has been criticized for not involving stakeholders sufficiently. To address this action design research (ADR) was devised [43]. ADR is characterized by a much closer exchange between researchers and stakeholders and mimics the development from the waterfall process to agile methods in software engineering.

2.2   Meta Attack Language

A MAL DSL contains the main elements that are encountered on the domain under study, called `assets` (cf. MAL metamodel in Fig. 1). The assets contain `attack steps`, which represent the actual attacks that can happen to them.

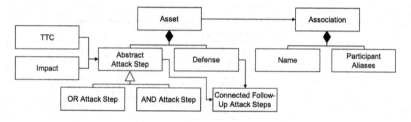

Fig. 1. The metamodel of MAL

An `attack step` can be connected with creating an attack path. These are combined to create attack graphs on which the attack simulation is run. An `attack step` can be of type OR or AND, respectively indicating that performing any individual parental `attack step` is required (OR) or performing all parental `attack steps` is required (AND) for the current step to be performed. Additionally, each `attack step` can be related to any combination of impact types (i.e., confidentiality, integrity, and availability) to specify the risks. A `defense` is an entity that prohibits connected `attack steps` to be performed if they are enabled. Finally, `probability distributions` can be assigned to `attack steps` to represent the effort needed to complete the related `attack step` and which is expressed on the time to compromise (TTC) in the simulation results. `Assets` have `associations` and related cardinalities between them. Inheritance between `assets` is allowed and each child `asset` inherits all the `attack steps`.

3   Method

To design our approach, we follow a four-step process: First, we opt for an established guiding approach. Our approach relies on the principle of DSR [18] since we are creating a concrete artifact that will be used in an information systems environment. Various interpretations of DSR as well as decision support to choose the best approach [50] have been developed. Therefore, research differentiates between objectivist, positivist and subjectivist, interpretive methodologies: if one expects the designed artifact to be the best solution for a generalized target group that behaves the same, then the objectivist, positivist methodologies are best. As we expect that each created DSL will serve a purpose and might not be completely generalizable [15], we opt for the latter. Those methodologies are distinguished by the domains they address. As most of the MAL DSLs are developed for a single organization, we decide to adapt ADR [43].

Second, we investigate how other research addresses the stages of ADR. For the stages "Problem Formulation", "Reflection and Learning", and "Formalization of Learning", we consider articles citing the original ADR description [43] explicitly addressing these stages. While these stages are similar for all artifacts, the second stage "Building, Intervention, and Evaluation" is dependent on the artifact(s) to be developed. Consequently, we consider for this stage research on building threat models [31,42,47,56] and creating DSLs [5,19]. Next, we follow

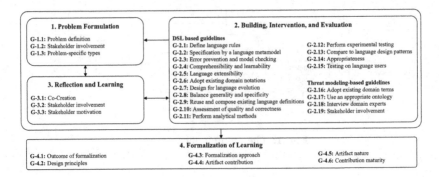

Fig. 2. ADR method: stages and guidelines (adapted from Sein et al. [43])

the conceptual-to-empirical approach [35] based on the identified literature and create categories and labels to classify the different tasks in the creation of MAL DSLs. This is independently performed by all authors, who subsequently discuss their results to come to one set of categories and labels and to reduce the subjective influence. We used deductive coding [33], i.e., the labels are defined before the coding, and the survey responses do not influence the labels (Fig.2).

Third, we perform a survey among experienced MAL DSL developers to gather information on their language development. We received eleven fully answered questionnaires. Considering 19 MAL DSLs [15], this corresponds to a return rate of 63%, which is satisfying for an online survey [10]. Moreover, we check if the survey is answered for all published MAL DSLs, which is the case.

The questionnaire[1] consists of 41 questions. The first section comprises questions about the MAL developer's educational and professional background. The second section asks questions regarding which MAL DSL is referred to. The third section inquiries about the purpose of the MAL DSL, the fourth section asks about the language engineering approach, and the fifth section about the language artifact. Finally, the last two sections comprise validation and maintenance questions. To analyze the open-ended questions, we employed coding to identify recurring themes [39]. This method is suitable as we aim to find and categorize common or contradicting methods of developing MAL DSLs.

We work with two independent groups to codify the findings and align it with the stages of ADR. Given the categories and labels from the second step, the answers are classified. Following [35], we complement the categories and labels if an aspect is not covered yet. Afterward, the groups discuss their results to come to a unified understanding of the actions in the single stages and reflect our approach on the documented development processes of three MAL DSLs.

---

[1] MAL Survey https://forms.gle/Wuv5sJgqZSctgP4LA (Accessed 2021-06-01).

4 The Approach: Applying ADR to Create MAL DSLs

4.1 Stage 1 - Problem Formulation

The first stage of ADR is about the formulation of the problem to be solved, which can be typically identified either by practitioners or by researchers. In this step, the initial scope of the problem, the roles and scope of each stakeholder, and the initial research questions are defined. The problems formulated in this stage can be assigned to one of the following two problem principles: i) practice-inspired research and ii) theory-ingrained artifact. For the first principle, the problem that is perceived by practitioners should be induced to a class of problem(s), a process that creates an opportunity for new knowledge to be generated. The problem identified will then be used to exemplify that knowledge. For the second principle, it is suggested that all the artifacts created to solve a problem are based on some previous theory to: (1) to structure the problem, (2) to identify solution possibilities, or (3) to guide the design of the artifact.

The labels that were detected from the reviewed literature and correspond to the formulation of the problem can be categorized into three discrete categories:

G-1.1: Problem Definition. Performing a systematic literature review (SLR) is a way of detecting a problem [1,23,36]. Alternatively, systematic empirical investigations, focus groups meetings, or expert interviews work [32,36]. A problem can also be encountered during the organizations' operations [32] or cause-effect diagram modeling can detect a problem [1].

G-1.2: Stakeholder Involvement. The possible involved stakeholder types are: 1) researchers, 2) end-users, and 3) practitioners [14,32]. Then, the involvement of the stakeholders can be achieved via the following detected dimensions: 1) expert interviews [32,36], 2) focus groups [32,36], 3) surveys [36], and 4) status seminars [36].

G-1.3: Problem-Specific Types. The problem itself can either be categorized as an abstract problem or an instantiated problem [1]. Further, we can differentiate two types of gaps: theoretical or design [1]. For a theoretical gap, theoretical knowledge is missing to justify the artifact's design. The design gap refers to knowledge that is missing regarding the created artifact rather than the theoretical foundations.

Application on MAL DSLs: The survey performed with MAL DSLs developers showed that in most cases, the definition of the problem was identified through interviews with experts and by performing an SLR. The stakeholders usually came from the industry, while researchers came second. In some other cases, sponsors were mentioned with small influence in the design process. The stakeholder's involvement in the design process was commonly achieved through focus group meetings and surveys. Finally, the problem originated from a design gap, while the percentage of the instantiated problems is larger than abstract.

4.2 Stage 2 - Building, Intervention, and Evaluation

Stage 2 employs an iterative design cycle with three steps to achieve the realized design of the artifact: 1) building of the IT artifact, 2) intervention in the organization, and 3) evaluation (BIE). The initial design of the artifact is based on the problem statement. After the first BIE cycle, the artifact is refined and build upon the feedback. By deploying the artifact to the organization early, practitioners get to experience and test the design. They can influence it by giving feedback on how well the design performs. This feedback is evaluated and in case the organization adopts or rejects the artifact, a new BIE cycle starts. The labels identified from the literature related to the second stage can be classified into two parts: 1) DSL guidelines and 2) threat modeling guidelines.

DSL Guidelines: To achieve a better quality of the language design and improve acceptance among language users, DSL guidelines guide language designers in the process of DSL development. We gathered DSL design guidelines from literature and selected the ones that apply to the development of MAL languages as well as to DSL development in general.

G-2.1: Define Language Rules [30]. Models often have to adhere to rules derived from the domain they are applied to, the language itself, or usage conventions. Language rules or well-formedness rules enable early error detection and prevent invalid or unwanted models. The language rules for a MAL DSLs, are defined by the MAL.

G-2.2: The Modeling Language is Specified by a Language Metamodel [21]. Specifying the modeling language in a language metamodel includes defining the abstract syntax, concrete syntax, well-formedness rules, and semantics. This metamodel facilitates easy understanding of the scope and elements of the language and provides a standardized way for further changes and adaptions. In the case of a MAL DSLs, the language metamodel is dictated by the MAL.

G-2.3: DSL's Support for Error Prevention and Model Checking [24]. Error prevention and model checking are important for producing reliable programs. Because often the inspection of all relevant parts of a model for errors and completeness are either missing or incomplete, DSLs need improvement in this area.

G-2.4: Comprehensibility and Learnability [24]. For DSLs to be comprehensible, language elements have to be understandable to be able to design programs with it.

G-2.5: Provide for Language Extensibility [44]. Software languages are software too [6] and, hence, often subject to evolution beyond the conceptions leading to its first release(s). This especially holds where languages are relatively generic and will be specialized by future users, such as the UML with MechatronicUML [4] or UML/P [41].

G-2.6: Adopt Existing Domain Notations [26,51]. For the language to be suitable, its concrete syntax should reflect concepts known by the modeler. These concepts, generally, originate from related domains, that flatten the learning curve by providing an intuitive understanding of notations. For MAL DSLs, such notations can be used as part of the asset or attack step names.

G-2.7: Design for Language Evolution [29,51]. As languages will evolve, they should be designed accordingly. This includes the modularization of concepts.

G-2.8: Balance Generality and Specificity [26,51]. Modeling languages should abstract from implementation details. However, at the same time, they have to offer appropriate expressive modeling techniques for their use case. Because these requirements often contradict each other, finding a balance between both is crucial.

G-2.9: Reuse and Compose Existing Language Definitions [26, 29, 51]. Modeling languages often are composed of and reuse existing concepts of other languages to reduce the implementation and maintenance effort and to increase sustainability in developing new languages. For MAL DSLs, parts of other DSL that share common assets and/or attack vectors can be re-used, via inheritance, to achieve this.

G-2.10: The Language is Assessable Regarding its Quality and correctness [21]. To ensure a certain quality and correctness of the language, the DSL should be evaluated and refined constantly throughout the development process.

G-2.11: Perform Analytical Methods [49]. To ensure that the modeling language fulfills certain functional requirements it is important to perform analytical methods, e.g., static analysis, architecture analysis, optimization, and dynamic analysis.

G-2.12: Perform Experimental Testing, and Descriptive Methods [49]. To measure and to ensure that the language in development fits functional and nonfunctional requirements, experimental and descriptive methods should be applied. One example of testing MAL-based DSLs is via unit and integration tests.

G-2.13: Compare to Language Design Patterns [2]. Research already published a multitude of language design guidelines, patterns, and best practices. During the development process of DSLs, they should be constantly compared to these guidelines to further improve the DSL in the next development iteration.

G-2.14: Users Can Recognize Whether the DSL is Appropriate for Their Needs [24]. For the DSL to be successful it needs to fulfill the requirements stated by its users. To achieve this, the users should be enabled to recognize whether or not the DSL is appropriate for their needs.

G-2.15: Testing: Test the Language Design on Language Users [53]. For the DSL to meet the language user's needs, it is important to constantly involve the intended users in the development process by letting them test the language design. Example methodologies of testing MAL DSLs on real users, are hands-on evaluation sessions with domain experts, as well as the Feigenbaum methodology.

Application of DSL Guidelines to MAL DSLs: The survey that was performed with MAL DSL developers showed that some of the guidelines presented above were already included in the MAL development process. The survey indicates that most of the language developers defined language rules for their languages. The presented DSL guidelines are taken into account at different stages of stage 2. When designing or building their DSL, they reused existing documentation or reused already existing language definitions to define the rules for their language. 75% of the survey participants explicitly stated that they designed their DSL for language evolution. For instance, they used abstract assets to be easily extendable in future versions. Regarding balancing specialty and generality, some participants answered that they wanted their DSL to be specialized enough to cover the security aspects of their application, but also wanted it to be general enough for it to be applied to other domains. In the intervention, often, adopting the existing domain notation was a requirement for the design of the developed DSL, e.g., the DSL should enable to model the security aspects of AWS as close as possible. This was ensured by involving stakeholders of the language and users that can recognize whether the DSL is appropriate for their application. For the evaluation, the language developers performed a static analysis of their languages and models by constructing attack paths as well as unit tests. By using their language to model-real world attack scenarios for cloud environments, e.g., AWS, and model known security issues, they performed experimental testing. Only a few of the participants evaluated their DSL by comparing it to existing language design patterns.

Threat Modeling Guidelines: In addition to the DSL guidelines addressed above, the labels identified from the reviewed literature that correspond to threat modeling guidelines are presented as follows.

G-2.16: Adopt Existing Domain Terms. In the building stage, using easy-to-understand icons (symbols) associated with the elements of a threat modeling language can support the communication among participants. Thus, the threat modeling language can be easily understandable and support in-depth risk analysis [52].

G-2.17: Use an Appropriate Ontology. Because an appropriate ontology can provide a formal and comprehensive knowledge base, it can be used to address the lack of domain knowledge issue in modeling threats to a system [42].

G-2.18: Interview Domain Experts. Interviewing domain experts helps to propose a valuable threat model, and the interview results can help to refine the initial threat identification and as a knowledge base for identifying countermeasures [42].

G-2.19: Stakeholder Involvement. Stakeholders shall be involved in identifying the assets of the system [31], who can potentially validate the threat modeling results.

Application of Threat Modeling Guidelines to MAL DSLs: According to all the answers to the questionnaire, all the four categories above are addressed. Regarding the requirement of building a DSL, 81.8% of the respondents require to reuse a threat library/existing artifacts/standards [11,47], and 27.3% of them require to use an appropriate ontology [42]. To customize the DSL, 72.7% of the respondents require to use easy-to-understand icons (symbols) [52]. In terms of validating the DSL, 90.9% of the DSLs are validated through test cases, while only 9% of the DSLs are validated through industry/security experts or Turing tests. However, some dimensions are missing from the answers, e.g., validating the modeling language by the Delphi method [8]. Specifically, threat modeling work can lack semantics making it difficult for both humans and systems to understand the architecture deception exactly and commonly, and ontology-based approaches can be applied to solve this issue [25]. Also, the Delphi method has not been addressed by the answers or at least fully used when evaluating the built DSLs, which is a forecasting process framework based on the results of multiple rounds of questionnaires sent to a panel of experts. While security experts, domain experts are found to be involved in the intervention and evaluation steps of several DSLs, e.g., sclLang [40], powerLang [16], and coreLang [27].

4.3 Stage 3 - Reflection and Learning

The two previous stages focus on a problem and its solution for a single instance in stage 3, the solution is conceptualized to address a broader class of problems [43]. Stage 3 parallels the previous stages and fosters a conscious reflection on the problem, the applied theories, and the emerging artifact. Moreover, the researchers should alter the research process based on evaluation results if necessary. To reflect on the developed artifact, the MAL DSL developers mentioned different approaches that were also highlighted in the literature.

G-3.1: Co-Creation. For learning activities, the co-creation of artifacts [17] between MAL developers and stakeholders were reported. However, for successful learning a tight coupling between researchers and stakeholders is necessary as well as a continuous exchange between these two groups [17]. The latter is also observable in the questionnaires, as some of the participants acknowledge a continuous evaluation of the artifact in close exchange with the stakeholders. Complementary, Haj-Bolouri et al. [17] name also prototypes, the direct implementation in an organization, and continuous documentation of the artifact as means for reflection.

G-3.2: Stakeholder Involvement. According to our participants, the exchange between the developers and the stakeholders takes place in workshop formats, in which the artifacts are presented and discussed. Additionally to these workshops, scientific literature [17] mentions training sessions to foster teach the stakeholders about the artifact. Such training sessions can be a useful supplement to the existing approaches to communicate MAL DSLs.

G-3.3: Stakeholder Motivation. There are two drivers for the stakeholders to participate in the aforementioned workshops. On the one hand, the stakeholders are interested in assessing the security of their systems. On the other hand, the interest is on automating the existing assessment. Hence, we can see a maturation of the stakeholders' interest in MAL related to their actual application of security measures.

4.4 Stage 4 - Formalization of Learning

Finally, in stage 4, the objective is to formalize the findings by providing a general solution to a class of problems [43]. Therefore, the researcher is supposed to reflect on the accomplishments realized in the artifact and characterize the organizational impact.

G-4.1: Outcome of Formalization. Research related to the formalization differentiates between two different artifact types in the realm of ADR [17,32]: either the solution is focused on an information system or on changing the organization. As expected, we found in all answers of the questionnaire that the research was related to information systems. We could not generate deeper insights for the formalization with the questionnaires. Most likely, this is caused by the fact that MAL DSLs are usually designed to solve a certain problem and the efforts to generalize these languages to a broader corpus of problems are omitted. Exceptions can be found [15], where an ecosystem of MAL DSLs to foster reuse among the languages is proposed. To enable future formalization, the development of MAL DSLs can benefit from the existing DSR.

G-4.2: Design Principles. One approach to formalize the outcomes of the research is to distill design principles. These design principles can relate to the artifact itself and its properties [7,13,14], the purpose and context of the artifact [3,7,14,48], the design process of the artifact [3,7], and the evaluation process of the artifact [7,14].

G-4.3: Formalization Approach. The formalization can also be guided by different approaches such as problem structuring [14,48], utility theory [48], hypothesis building [48], grounded theory [14,32], heuristic theorizing [14], or engaged scholarship [14,36].

G-4.4: Artifact Contribution. Depending on the abstraction level of the solution, we can differentiate between three classes of solutions [13,48]: a well-developed design theory, a nascent design theory, and a situated implementation. For classical MAL DSLs (e.g., [16,28]), the contribution is expected to be a situated implementation, while for some approaches (e.g., [15,27]) one can also argue for a nascent design theory.

G-4.5: Artifact Nature. The resulting artifact can either be of descriptive or prescriptive nature [1,13]. The MAL DSLs describe classically known vulnerabilities related to certain assets and their relations. Hence, the contribution is descriptive. However, those descriptive languages can be used to describe possible future configurations and, thus, the contribution can be prescriptive.

G-4.6: Contribution Maturity. The contribution can be classified to its maturity [13]. If a known solution is applied to a known problem (Routine Design), there is no significant contribution to the work. If an existing solution is extended to a new problem (Exaptation), there is a research opportunity and a knowledge contribution. The same contribution holds for the cases if there is a new solution for a known problem (Improvement) or if there is a new solution for a new problem (Invention). As MAL DSLs are relying on an existing solution (i.e., MAL) and are developing for a new domain that is not covered yet, the contribution is expected to be an exaptation. If a language is redesigned, an improvement is also possible.

5   Demonstration

To demonstrate the applicability of our findings, we retroactively detect their use on three existing MAL instances and reflect how the rules could improve their quality. We observe that not all guidelines from all stages were actively used in the languages. This could be an early indicator of a possible problem in the languages, but it might as well not cause a true problem. For example, missing out stage 3 guidelines, threatens the practical applicability of the language due to missing involvement of stakeholders. However, it is still possible that the language is sufficiently designed.

The vehicleLang [28] is a DSL for the automotive domain, and the problem that tries to solve is how to perform cyber-attack simulation on vehicular infrastructures. In the process followed for the development of this language and by following the four stages of the ADR we can identify the following labels.

Stage 1. Regarding the first stage, the main method for information gathering and defining the problem was an SLR of the domain (G-1.1) and some limited input from experts. Then the problem that this language tries to solve can be categorized as an instantiated problem (G-1.3).

Stage 2. The building of the language was heavily based on existing literature and therefore clear language rules were set (G-2.1). Additionally, since MAL was used as the development framework, a metamodel frames the structure of the language (G-2.2). When it comes to stakeholder intervention/involvement, this was minimal, since only a few interviews with one domain expert were conducted during the development phase (G-2.18). Then, regarding validation, again one interview with a domain expert was used together with unit tests (G-2.15).

Stage 3. A reflection on the created artifact was done both by writing a scientific paper but also on presenting it in both a conference but also a workshop. Finally, a formalization and generalization of the created artifact was not done, since an attempt to solve a very specific problem was the main goal of it. To improve vehicleLang, stakeholders should have been involved more, because this would also allow a higher level of validation of the artifact in stage 2.

Stage 4. Finally, the final stage of the ADR process is completely missing. To improve here, the language should be built with future extensions in mind. Additionally, one could elaborate on the generalization of the designed artifact.

The coreLang [27] was designed as basis for other MAL DSLs.

Stage 1. Although the problem identification is not clearly stated, the language reduces redundant work for developing new MAL DSLs, which can be characterized as an instantiated problem that addresses an implementation gap (G-1.3).

Stage 2. coreLang adopts a common terminology (G-2.6) found on all IT infrastructures. Stakeholder were highly involved, since weekly meetings with domain experts were conducted for both brainstorming (G-2.19) but also for providing feedback and improvements. Finally, test cases and unit tests (G-2.15) were used.

Stage 3. Due to the high involvement of the stakeholders, coreLang covers most of the processes found on this stage (G-3.2 and G-3.3). Additionally, a generalization comes as a natural consequence. This was supported by evaluating coreLang against the MITRE ATT&CK matrix.

Stage 4. coreLang was built with future extensions in mind, and a MAL DSL ecosystem was proposed [15] (G-4.1).

The powerLang [16] was designed to enable organizations in the power domain to assess the security of their IT and OT environments. Therefore, it reuses two existing languages (coreLang [27] and sclLang [40]) to provide assets for office and for substation environments. To bridge the gap between these two worlds, icsLang was proposed to represent the environment controlling the substation.

Stage 1. The problem identification is not explicitly elaborated. However, we can deduce that stakeholders have been involved (G-1.2). The problem itself can be categorized as instantiated addressing a design gap (G-1.3).

Stage 2. A main characteristic of powerLang is that it reuses and composes existing language definitions (G-2.9). To ease the use of powerLang by practitioners, it further adopts their terminology (G-2.6, G-2.16). However, to find a balance between generality and specificity (G-2.8), icsLang –as a subset of powerLang– uses the terminology of industrial control systems but is not further tailored to the power domain. The development process of powerLang is not further detailed. It is solely stated that icsLang is build using MITRE ATT&CK for Industrial Control Systems[2] (G-2.1). Concerning evaluating the language (G-2.15) unit tests have been developed and it is demonstrated on a real-world attack.

Stage 3. There are no activities to involve stakeholders and, thus, no joint learning activities. Consequently, stage 3 has not been addressed.

Stage 4. There are two contributions to formalization. Firstly, icsLang is designed to cover also other domains (G-4.3). Secondly, design principles are suggested to ease the linking of different MAL DSLs (G-4.2).
Reflecting on the development process of powerLang, we can presume that there is an opportunity for improvement. Especially, it is recommended to involve stakeholders to a greater extend. This includes the problem definition, but also the development of the language and the paralleling learning activities.

6   Related Work

We provide guidelines for developing MAL DSLs. Since MAL is both a domain-specific and a threat modeling language framework, we consider both as related. There are guidelines for framing the design of DSLs, e.g., by describing patterns in the phases of DSL development [34]: decision, analysis, design and implementation. Comparing their patterns to our approach, they describe implementation in detail, which we do not since the method we have developed is for MAL instances and therefore these patterns are already decided by the MAL framework. Two of their patterns from the design phase have been adapted in our work. Other researchers propose guidelines regarding purpose, implementation, contents, syntax of a DSL [26]. Three of their guidelines have been adapted in our work. Compared to our guidelines, they do not provide any guidelines regarding reflection and learning but focus on the development itself. Since some of these guidelines are implementation and syntax specific, and are already inherited from the MAL framework, they are not included in our method.

Torr divides the threat modeling process into determining scope, gathering background information, describing the component, and recording any weaknesses [46]. Finally, the author outlines how to gather threats for the model by brainstorming. This is similar to how we base our approach on previous MAL developer's experience, but we fit this into the ADR framework. Other research identifies a process of four steps [11]: create a Dataflow Diagram (DFD), gathering attacks with the help of a threat library, assessing the risks, and mitigating

---

[2] https://collaborate.mitre.org/attackics/index.php/Main_Page.

the risks. The stages are identification of assets, architectural overview, fragmentation of the system, identification of threats, documentation of these threats, and lastly rating them. Overall, these guidelines, are similar to those in stage 2 of the ADR but do not focus on insights into the other three stages.

7   Discussion and Conclusion

We have investigated whether ADR, a form of DSR tailored to creating IT artifacts that are shaped by their organizational context during development and use, can be used to create DSLs based on of the Meta Attack Language. Even though the focus in this paper is on MAL, our intention is to generalize the method to other DSLs in the future. To this end, we have surveyed experienced developers of such languages. From their answers and literature on DSL development, we extracted guidelines for the development of MAL DSLs using ADR.

Our approach is subject to various threats to validity. First, the few participants, which is due the small population of MAL developers so far. Among these, a response rate of 63% was achieved, which is above average for online surveys [10]. However, the participants were only from two closely linked to each other organizations, which leads to a similar socialization of the participants. Accordingly, there is a risk for uniform answers from the participants. To mitigate this, we could have taught MAL to other DSL developers to gather their experiences, but this could introduce other biases to the survery. Instead, we consider conducting a similar survey on other families of modeling languages (such as UML or SysML) to better understand how our findings generalize.

Second, we opted for open-ended questions to gather a wide spectrum of answers and to prevent steering the answers of the participants. The formalization of these answers then becomes more challenging and subjective. Yet, we opted against closed questions, which would ease the formalization, and prioritized the opportunity to gather unexpected results over more objective results, which we will address in our future work. In the future, we plan to experiment with more objective methods that rely on numerical measures [37].

Moreover, our research cannot argue for prioritizing the guidelines in any way. Which guidelines are considered necessary to follow for a 'proper' DSL strongly depends on the shape of the DSL as well as on its context. Similarly, different guidelines might conflict with another. Engineering DSLs always is an optimization problem and where guidelines conflict, developers must adjust to the context of the DSL accordingly.

Acknowledgements. This project has received funding from the European Union's H2020 research and innovation program under the Grant Agreement No. 832907, the Swedish Centre for Smart Grids and Energy Storage (SweGRIDS), and the Deutsche Forschungsgemeinschaft (DFG) under Grant Agreement No. 441207927.

References

1. Avdiji, H., Winter, R.: Knowledge gaps in design science research. In: ICIS 2019 (2019)

2. Barišić, A., Amaral, V., Goulão, M.: Usability evaluation of domain-specific languages. In: QUATIC 2012, pp. 342–347. IEEE (2012)
3. vom Brocke, J., Maedche, A.: The DSR grid: six core dimensions for effectively planning and communicating design science research projects. Electr. Mark. **29**(3), 379–385 (2019)
4. Burmester, S., Giese, H., Tichy, M.: Model-driven development of reconfigurable mechatronic systems with MECHATRONIC UML. In: Aßmann, U., Aksit, M., Rensink, A. (eds.) MDAFA 2003-2004. LNCS, vol. 3599, pp. 47–61. Springer, Heidelberg (2005). https://doi.org/10.1007/11538097_4
5. Clark, T., van den Brand, M., Combemale, B., Rumpe, B.: Conceptual model of the globalization for domain-specific languages. In: Combemale, B., Cheng, B., France, R., Quel, JM., Rumpe, B. (eds.) Globalizing Domain-Specific Languages. LNCS, vol. 9400, pp. 7–20. Springer, Cham (2015). https://doi.org/10.1007/978-3-319-26172-0_2
6. Combemale, B., France, R., Jézéquel, J.M., Rumpe, B., Steel, J., Vojtisek, D.: Engineering Modeling Languages: Turning Domain Knowledge into Tools. Chapman & Hall , November 2016
7. Cronholm, S., Göbel, H.: Guidelines supporting the formulation of design principles. In: ACIS 2018 (2018)
8. Dalkey, N., Helmer, O.: An experimental application of the Delphi method to the use of experts. Manag. Sci. **9**, 351–515 (1963)
9. Defense Use Case: Analysis of the cyber attack on the ukrainian power grid (2016). https://ics.sans.org/media/E-ISAC_SANS_Ukraine_DUC_5.pdf
10. Deutskens, E., De Ruyter, K., Wetzels, M., Oosterveld, P.: Response rate and response quality of internet-based surveys: an experimental study. Mark. Lett. **15**(1), 21–36 (2004)
11. Dhillon, D.: Developer-driven threat modeling: lessons learned in the trenches. IEEE Secu. Privacy **9**(4), 41–47 (2011)
12. Ekstedt, M., Johnson, P., Lagerström, R., Gorton, D., Nydrén, J., Shahzad, K.: Securi CAD by Foreseeti: A CAD tool for enterprise cyber security management. In: EDOCW 2015, pp. 152–155. IEEE (2015)
13. Gregor, S., Hevner, A.R.: Positioning and presenting design science research for maximum impact. MIS Q. **37**, 337–355 (2013)
14. Gregory, R.W., Muntermann, J.: Research note -heuristic theorizing: proactively generating design theories. Inf. Syst. Res. **25**(3), 639–653 (2014)
15. Hacks, S., Katsikeas, S.: Towards an ecosystem of domain specific languages for threat modeling. In: CAiSE 2021, pp. 3–18 (2021)
16. Hacks, S., Katsikeas, S., Ling, E., Lagerström, R., Ekstedt, M.: powerLang: a probabilistic attack simulation language for the power domain. Energy Informat. **3**(1) (2020)
17. Haj-Bolouri, A., Bernhardsson, L., Rossi, M.: PADRE: a method for participatory action design research. In: Parsons, J., Tuunanen, T., Venable, J., Donnellan, B., Helfert, M., Kenneally, J. (eds.) DESRIST 2016. LNCS, vol. 9661, pp. 19–36. Springer, Cham (2016). https://doi.org/10.1007/978-3-319-39294-3_2
18. Bichler, M.: Design science in information systems research. MIS Q **48**(2), 133–135 (2006). https://doi.org/10.1007/s11576-006-0028-8
19. Hölldobler, K., Rumpe, B., Wortmann, A.: Software language engineering in the large: towards composing and deriving languages. Comput. Lang. Syst. Struct. **54**, 386–405 (2018)
20. Holm, H., Shahzad, K., Buschle, M., Ekstedt, M.: P^2CySeMoL predictive, probabilistic cyber security modeling language. IEEE TDSC **12**(6), 626–639 (2015)

21. Jannaber, S., Riehle, D.M., Delfmann, P., Thomas, O., Becker, J.: Designing a framework for the development of domain-specific process modelling languages. In: Maedche, A., vom Brocke, J., Hevner, A. (eds.) DESRIST 2017. LNCS, vol. 10243, pp. 39–54. Springer, Cham (2017). https://doi.org/10.1007/978-3-319-59144-5_3
22. Johnson, P., Lagerström, R., Ekstedt, M.: A meta language for threat modeling and attack simulations. In: ARES 2018, p. 38. ACM (2018)
23. Jones, C., Venable, J.R.: Integrating CCM4DSR into ADR to improve problem formulation. In: Hofmann, S., Müller, O., Rossi, M. (eds.) DESRIST 2020. LNCS, vol. 12388, pp. 247–258. Springer, Cham (2020). https://doi.org/10.1007/978-3-030-64823-7_23
24. Kahraman, G., Bilgen, S.: A framework for qualitative assessment of domain-specific languages. Softw. Syst. Model. **14**(4), 1505–1526 (2013). https://doi.org/10.1007/s10270-013-0387-8
25. Kang, D., Lee, J., Choi, S., Kim, K.: An ontology-based enterprise architecture. Exp. Syst. Appl. **37**(2), 1456–1464 (2010)
26. Karsai, G., Krahn, H., Pinkernell, C., Rumpe, B., Schindler, M., Völkel, S.: Design guidelines for domain specific languages. In: DSM'09, pp. 7–13 (2009)
27. Katsikeas, S., Hacks, S., Johnson, P., Ekstedt, M., Lagerström, R., Jacobsson, J., Wällstedt, M., Eliasson, P.: An attack simulation language for the IT domain. In: Eades III, H., Gadyatskaya, O. (eds.) GraMSec 2020. LNCS, vol. 12419, pp. 67–86. Springer, Cham (2020). https://doi.org/10.1007/978-3-030-62230-5_4
28. Katsikeas, S., Johnson, P., Hacks, S., Lagerström, R.: Probabilistic modeling and simulation of vehicular cyber attacks: an application of the meta attack language. In: ICISSP 2019 (2019)
29. Kelly, S., Pohjonen, R.: Worst practices for domain-specific modeling. IEEE Softw. **26**(4), 22–29 (2009)
30. Kelly, S., Tolvanen, J.P.: Domain-Specific Modeling: Enabling Full Code Generation. John Wiley & Sons, New York (2008)
31. Ling, E., Lagerström, R., Ekstedt, M.: A systematic literature review of information sources for threat modeling in the power systems domain. In: Rashid, A., Popov, P. (eds.) CRITIS 2020. LNCS, vol. 12332, pp. 47–58. Springer, Cham (2020). https://doi.org/10.1007/978-3-030-58295-1_4
32. Maccani, G., Donnellan, B., Helfert, M.: Systematic problem formulation in action design research: the case of smart cities. In: ECIS 2014, January 2014
33. Medelyan, A.: Coding qualitative data: how to code qualitative research (2020). https://getthematic.com/insights/coding-qualitative-data/
34. Mernik, M., Heering, J., Sloane, A.M.: When and how to develop domain-specific languages. ACM Comput. Surv. **37**(4), 316–344 (2005)
35. Nickerson, R.C., Varshney, U., Muntermann, J.: A method for taxonomy development and its application in information systems. Euro. J. Inf. Syst. **22**(3), 336–359 (2013)
36. Nielsen, P., Persson, J.: Engaged problem formulation in is research. Commun. Assoc. Inf. Syst. **38**, 720–737 (2016)
37. O'Connor, C., Joffe, H.: Intercoder reliability in qualitative research: debates and practical guidelines. Int. J. Qual. Methods **19** (2020)
38. Peffers, K., Tuunanen, T., Rothenberger, M.A., Chatterjee, S.: A design science research methodology for information systems research. J. Manag. Inf. Syst. **24**(3), 45–77 (2007)
39. Popping, R.: Analyzing open-ended questions by means of text analysis procedures. Bull. Sociol. Methodol. **128**(1), 23–39 (2015)

40. Rencelj Ling, E., Ekstedt, M.: Generating threat models and attack graphs based on the IEC 61850 system configuration description language. In: AT-CPS 20'21, pp. 98–103. ACM (2021)
41. Rumpe, B.: Modeling with UML: Language, Concepts, Methods. Springer, Cham, July 2016. https://doi.org/10.1007/978-3-319-33933-7
42. Sabbagh, B.A., Kowalski, S.: A socio-technical framework for threat modeling a software supply chain. IEEE Secur. Privacy **13**(4), 30–39 (2015)
43. Sein, M.K., Henfridsson, O., Purao, S., Rossi, M., Lindgren, R.: Action design research. MIS Q **35**, 37–56 (2011)
44. Selic, B.: The theory and practice of modeling language design for model-based software engineering—a personal perspective. In: Fernandes, J.M., Lämmel, R., Visser, J., Saraiva, J. (eds.) GTTSE 2009. LNCS, vol. 6491, pp. 290–321. Springer, Heidelberg (2011). https://doi.org/10.1007/978-3-642-18023-1_7
45. Shostack, A.: Threat Modeling : Designing for Security. Wiley, Hoboken (2014)
46. Torr, P.: Demystifying the threat modeling process. Secur Priv **3**(5), 66–70 (2005)
47. Uzunov, A., Fernandez, E.: An extensible pattern-based library and taxonomy of security threats for distributed systems. Comput. Stand. Int. **36**(4), 734–747 (2014)
48. Venable, J.: The role of theory and theorising in design science research. In: DESRIST 2006, pp. 1–18. Citeseer (2006)
49. Venable, J., Pries-Heje, J., Baskerville, R.: A comprehensive framework for evaluation in design science research. In: Peffers, K., Rothenberger, M., Kuechler, B. (eds.) DESRIST 2012. LNCS, vol. 7286, pp. 423–438. Springer, Heidelberg (2012). https://doi.org/10.1007/978-3-642-29863-9_31
50. Venable, J.R., Pries-Heje, J., Baskerville, R.: Choosing a design science research methodology. In: ACIS 2017 (2017)
51. Völter, M.: Best practices for DSLs and model-driven development. J. Object Technol. **8**(6), 79–102 (2009)
52. Vraalsen, F., Lund, M.S., Mahler, T., Parent, X., Stølen, K.: Specifying legal risk scenarios using the CORAS threat modelling language. In: Herrmann, P., Issarny, V., Shiu, S. (eds.) iTrust 2005. LNCS, vol. 3477, pp. 45–60. Springer, Heidelberg (2005). https://doi.org/10.1007/11429760_4
53. Walter, R., Masuch, M.: How to integrate domain-specific languages into the game development process. In: ACE 2011, pp. 1–8 (2011)
54. Xiong, W., Lagerström, R.: Threat modeling - a systematic literature review. Comput. Secur. **84**, 53–69 (2019)
55. Xiong, W., Legrand, E., Åberg, O., Lagerström, R.: Cyber security threat modeling based on the MITRE Enterprise ATT&CK Matrix. SoSyM (2021)
56. Yskout, K., Heyman, T., Van Landuyt, D., Sion, L., Wuyts, K., Joosen, W.: Threat modeling: from infancy to maturity. In: ICSE 2020, pp. 9–12. ACM (2020)

Enterprise, Business Process, and Capability Modeling (EMMSAD 2022)

Enterprise Modeling in Support Of Transparency in the Design and Use of Software Systems

Mario Nolte[(✉)] and Monika Kaczmarek-Heß

University of Duisburg-Essen, Essen, Germany
{mario.nolte,monika.kaczmarek-hess}@uni-due.de

Abstract. Transparency is increasingly perceived as a relevant requirement for the design and use of software in general, and for systems using machine learning (ML) algorithms in particular. The existing approaches to ensuring software transparency however, among others, often follow only a one-sided perspective on transparency and, at the same time, neglect the organizational context of software design and use. Since enterprise modeling (EM) allows to analyse enterprise information systems (EIS) and organizational aspects in tandem, in this paper we focus on how EM can support transparency while designing and using software. To this aim, we propose an interactive understanding of transparency, which has the collaboration of different stakeholders at its core. Based on this understanding, we derive a set of requirements, and use them to extend a selected EM approach. We evaluate the extended approach two-fold: against requirements and using an exemplary scenario.

Keywords: Transparency · Enterprise modeling · Machine learning

1 Introduction

In recent years, the demand for transparency has become central part of many debates. On the one hand, it seems to be caused by striving for democracy and equality, which may be put at risk by information asymmetries [38,58]. On the other hand, it seems to be raised by the increasing usage of software systems in private and professional contexts. For instance, as software systems support business processes, those systems determine the processes execution paths and the decisions being made, however, at the same time, they often remain black boxes to involved stakeholders [58,75]. Considering it, many (legal) institutions and organizations have become aware of the importance of transparency with respect to software systems [1,37,55], leading to transparency of some systems, e.g., those relying on machine learning (ML), being required by law [19,20]. Here the transparency of algorithms [1,31], models [23], and data [19], is called for.

Subsequently, various initiatives emerged that focus on transparency of software systems. Examples include the provision of source code or pseudo code [40], using transparency audits [11,33,52], or, with respect to ML, explainable artificial intelligence (XAI) [32]. While existing approaches relate to domain-specific

© Springer Nature Switzerland AG 2022
A. Augusto et al. (Eds.): BPMDS 2022/EMMSAD 2022, LNBIP 450, pp. 157–172, 2022.
https://doi.org/10.1007/978-3-031-07475-2_11

views and come with specific strengths, the practical implementation of transparency of software systems causes several challenges. Aside from harmonizing partly juxtaposing notions of transparency, different, rather simplistic conceptions, e.g., considering transparency only as a provision of (one-sided) information that relates to specific views, can be dysfunctional to each other, and result in unintended effects like information overload or resignation [3,44,75].

Therefore, based on our analysis of different understandings of transparency, cf. Sect. 2, we argue for an *interactive understanding*, which allows to align transparency-demands and corresponding activities. Specifically, we argue that an instrument to support transparency of software should not only be understood as a mere form of information disclosure in one-way communication to interested parties, but should also account for: (1) different perspectives of involved stakeholders, (2) their views on individual and shared objects, (3) organizational context, and (4) enabling critical analysis and interactions among stakeholders. Consider, e.g., usage of ML: not only there is a diverse understanding of artifacts that are subject of related discourses [6,67], but also, a broad knowledge of the application domain and usage context seems to be of relevance to evaluate and challenge the results of ML to avoid domain-specific pitfalls [17,63].

Considering different facets of transparency of software systems, an instrument is needed that would reduce complexity, increase understanding, and enable multi-perspective analyses. A promising instrument seems to be the application of conceptual modeling (CM), which can be roughly defined as "the activity of formally describing some aspects of the physical and social world around us for purposes of understanding and communication" [53]. We deem it as a promising since (1) different modeling languages applied together may offer a multi-perspective view of a software system, and the way it is used by an organization, (2) application of a modeling language forces one to be concrete, which seems to be beneficial with a contested term such as transparency, and (3) application of CM fosters communication among stakeholders, thus promoting a shared understanding of features of software systems used. From the vast field of CM, especially enterprise modeling (EM) seems to be a promising instrument to support our interactive understanding of transparency, by accounting for EIS and an organizational action system in tandem, cf. [25]. Such a multi-perspective model may not only enable a cross-disciplinary exchange and collaboration (e.g., by outlining differences and similarities between conceptual notions of different software artifacts), but also models of usage context of software systems (e.g., process or goal models) support the corresponding evaluation and reflection.

Although EM has been already explicitly [66,72] or implicitly related to transparency, e.g., by referring to related terms like clarity [76, p. 277], or comprehensibility and understandability of models [53, p. 52]; elaborated or more explicit conceptions of transparency are not considered. Particularly, while some works focus on transparency of EM and related activities [10,22], others are focusing on conceptual models only, ignoring the demand for cross-disciplinary analysis and collaboration, resulting in more one-sided representations [36,45].

Further contributions like, e.g., [16], acknowledge the need for different kinds of models to foster transparency, but focus on specific stakeholders only.

Against this background, we follow two interrelated aims: (1) to propose a broader conception of transparency while designing and using software systems that (i) comprises different conceptions of transparency, and (ii) supports different activities and collaboration; and based on it, (2) to investigate how enterprise modeling can be used in order to support it. This contribution follows the design-oriented research paradigm [56]. Furthermore, we adopt the paradigm of constructivism. Thus, in line with, among others [65], we essentially understand models as means of representation of socially constructed knowledge. The modeling process is understood as the process of constructing, representing and sharing this knowledge between the involved participants.

To reach our aims, first, based on the review of the current use of the term, we derive an interactive understanding of transparency (Sect. 2). Then, by analyzing its main features and contemplating a use scenario, we derive a set of requirements that an EM approach should fulfill (Sect. 3). As none of the existing approaches addresses the identified requirements to the full extent, we select an enterprise modeling approach Multi-Perspective Enterprise Modeling (MEMO) [25], and extend an already existing domain-specific modeling language (DSML) focusing on modeling IT infrastructures, called ITML [27,34], with additional concepts and properties (Sect. 4). To perform the desired extensions, we follow the language development method proposed by [24]. We evaluate the proposed artifact twofold: (1) against the identified requirements to check consistency and comprehensibility, and (2) using an exemplary case scenario (Sect. 5).

2   Towards an Interactive Understanding of Transparency

As already indicated, transparency is a contested term, especially when it comes to the use of software and ML [41,49,71]. In this section, we first discuss the term transparency in general, and then in the context of software design and use. Finally, we propose the *interactive understanding of transparency.*

Transparency in Organizations. Originally coined in a physical context [54, 62], the term was adopted in a figurative manner to social contexts to, e.g., hold members of governments and other organizations legitimate, accountable, or to derive an inter-subjective truth and knowledge about their behavior and actions [35]. Considering it, the term today is widely recognized for its ameliorating potential [7]. Although the early conceptions of transparency were based on the direct observability of actors, inline with the physical sense, the intended motives mentioned above presumed a critical public, e.g., in form of a public-opinion tribunal, to challenge deceptive self-representations [8, p. 158].

While this classical form of transparency still can be found in grassroots democratic initiatives, nowadays the term is widely brought down to information-disclosure, e.g., on financial or social affairs of organisations [48,71]. Even if this understanding seems to be intuitive and widely accepted [2,74], it causes several problems. E.g., as information does not equal facts and often results in self-interested representation, this might lead rather to obfuscation than legitimate knowledge or accountability [15,40,70]. In a similar vein, it is argued that transparency reduced to information disclosure might result in an information overload, hindering a proper assessment [3,44], or that the skills and legibility of a transparency-requester have to be considered, so that information is understood in the intended way [21,49]. As a remedy some propose to view *transparency as a process*, where stakeholders look actively into an organization by evaluating, if the information provided meets their needs and seems relevant [2,44,70].

In-/Transparency of Software. Even if software and related terms, such as algorithms or models, seem to be easy to grasp, a closer look reveals that software can be represented in several ways, e.g., code, documentation, or metrics, as used especially by data scientists to evaluate ML software [14,47,75]. While these views often correspond to transparency-demands in intra-disciplinary settings, such narrow technical understanding of software is of little use, when it comes to transparency-demands of other stakeholders [6,67]. As stated above, also in case of software, provision of narrow and one-sided information might not be sufficient to satisfy related goals of transparency, or even worse, might be dysfunctional to the intended motives of transparency-demands [43,75].

For example, [28] argues that transparency as proposed by the *General Data Protection Regulation* (GDPR) [19] will more likely result in self-interested representations, than in what was intended by the regulation, namely gaining insights and knowledge about the use of personal data for the data-subject. Similarly, but related to Algorithmic-Decision Making (ADM) Systems, [4] argue that "[t]o ask to 'look inside the black box' is perhaps too limited demand and ultimately an ill-fitting metaphor" (p. 982) to gain knowledge. By referring to [50, p. 6], [4] stress that the creation of knowledge as well as individual understanding, both need many views, especially when it comes to such complex systems as ADM. In particular, when transparency should improve accountability, narrow-technical views might intentionally occlude [4, p. 980][18, p. 1830] therefore, to foster accountability, it is demanded to consider responsible persons as well.

With respect to ML systems, apart from the problem that the access to software might not be possible for good reasons (e.g., intellectual property rights, security reasons), or require specialist knowledge [12], in some cases (e.g., artificial neural networks) parts of the software are rather complex and are difficult to be interpreted and explained also by experts [12, p. 4][63, p. 206]. While for data scientists several metrics are proposed to estimate the behavior of the model [32], for (potential) users of such a software system they are of little help, since they are hard to interpret and do not at all explain reasons for decisions [63]. Therefore, to give potential users at least a chance to gain knowledge about a system, other notions of transparency have been proposed. For instance, under the label of *practical transparency*, it is demanded to inform users about assumptions and potential risks, and to enable their interactions with a system to learn how it behaves [59,61]. Furthermore, several questionnaires have been proposed to help users evaluate, if a system is appropriate for the intended context [29,51].

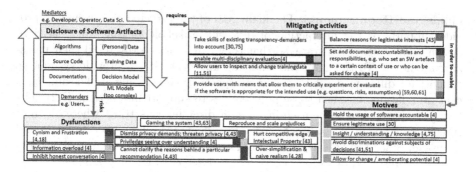

Fig. 1. Interactive understanding of transparency in the design&use of software

Interactive Understanding. Based on the conducted analysis, we propose to consider transparency in the design and use of software in organizations not as a state, but as an interactive process, that comprises various activities between stakeholders, and that depends on the motives of transparency-demand, which often will go beyond the ordinary provision of information, cf. Fig. 1. While in intra-disciplinary settings the provision of a view demanded might satisfy the transparency-demand (e.g., source code for programmers or algorithms and hyperparameters for data scientists), especially in those settings where different stakeholders with different professions strive for transparency, other activities might be of relevance too. In particular, if the demand for transparency is related to social ambiguous concepts like accountability or legitimacy, other activities get relevant to capture the ameliorating potential of transparency. We term these activities *mitigating activities* and present them in Fig. 1, where they are related to potential motives of transparency by colored squares. In addition, we also list dysfunctions that are discussed in literature when transparency is understood as a pure disclosure. Please note that due to space limitations, neither is the list of motives comprehensive, nor is the list of mitigating activities complete. Nevertheless, this selection allows us to show in following sections, how EM can be used to support this conception, while avoiding dysfunctional effects.

3   Goals, Requirements and Existing Approaches

We argue that CM can foster the introduced interactive understanding of transparency in various ways, e.g., by capturing domain-specific knowledge [46], or by documenting information exchanges [36]. In line with the proposed understanding of transparency on the one hand, and the specifics of software design and use on the other hand, we focus here on those scenarios and requirements (denoted 'Rx') that facilitate the interaction between stakeholders of software systems, e.g., user, programmer, data scientists, while providing support for specific views, and related analysis. The requirements have been systematically derived in line with [24]. Due to space restrictions we introduce the identified requirements on a high-level only.

Goals and Requirements. The main goal of the targeted approach is to provide support for the interaction of different stakeholders that are related to design and/or use of software, so that they can satisfactorily fulfill their transparency needs. To this aim, the modeling approach should provide systematic support for different domain-specific perspectives (R1), while at the same time capture relations between those perspectives to support interactions (R2). The targeted approach is to be used in an inter-disciplinary setting, where different stakeholders assign and assess transparency-demands related to a software and its usage. Since software (i) can be quite complex, and (ii) is amorphous and may be represented in various views (e.g., source code for programmers or user interface for users), the approach should provide means to relate these various representations to abstract notions that matter in relevant discourses, i.e., on a language level. With respect to complexity, it should also provide (i) means for decomposition, and (ii) differentiated information on its parts (R3). At the same time, the approach should relate different views to a view-independent, rather abstract software concept, that is subject of the overarching discussion (R4).

To align views on a software with corresponding competencies, e.g., code-literacy, of stakeholders, the following questions should be considered: (Q1) What stakeholders are related to a software and its usage? (Q2) What are the competences of a stakeholder and what domain-specific views are related to them? (Q3) Which views on a software artifact are available? (Q4) Does a stakeholder have access to the available views? (Q5) Who can grant access, if a view is already available? (Q6) Who is responsible for a software artifact and might support the construction of a view? In line with these questions, the approach should support the representation of stakeholders and their competencies, as well as views onto a software that fits those competencies (R5). Additionally, stakeholders with transparency-demands can be manifold, and range from specific individuals to specific types, e.g., programmers. Similarly, also transparency-demands can be assigned to individuals, or types of stakeholder. Therefore, the approach should provide dedicated abstractions differentiating among stakeholder groups and accounting for individual stakeholders (R6).

In line with the proposed interactive understanding, it is important to not only provide information, e.g., in the form of certain views, but also to consider the purpose(s) of transparency demands, e.g., to avoid unintended or dysfunctional effects. While these purposes can be manifold and need specific considerations that cannot be discussed here in detail, e.g., for transparency and accountability, cf. [4,43], we point here to the purpose of legitimacy due to its specific relevance. Namely, acknowledging that stakeholders may reject to work with an organization due to a perceived lack of legitimacy [30], it is of central relevance to strive for legitimacy that can be understood as "a generalized perception or assumption that the actions of an entity are desirable, proper, or appropriate within some socially constructed system of norms, values, beliefs and definitions" [68, p. 574]. For the software itself and its use, this means that even if access to information is granted and well-understood by a stakeholder, they might consider the circumstances that information expresses as illegitimate, risking frustration [18] and turning away. To support the discussion of a legitimate use of a software, the approach should provide concepts that document reasons, e.g., for decisions made, or for rejecting transparency-demands (R7), as well as the state of legitimacy perceived by stakeholders (R8). In addition, it is necessary to document the purpose of a transparency-demand to provide a basis for discussions of unintended or dysfunctional effects (R9).

With respect to the development and use of, e.g., ML, the modeling approach can support what was introduced as *practical transparency* (cf. Sect. 2). Apart from providing diagrams that allow to answer different questions, by capturing assumptions and (not-)intended use cases of (ML) software, the approach might help potential users evaluate, if the software is appropriate for their use (R10). In addition, questionnaires already included in diagrams and directly associated with specific software artifacts might be of help (R11). Even if the different questionnaires are already in use and provide a good orientation for users [60], we propose that CM might foster reuse, if questions and assumptions can be collected during implementation (R12), while being evaluated in diagrams of their context of use (R13). Finally, considering the risk of inappropriate and deflective diagrams or models [13, p. 164][42, p. 2], the information on software provided should be linked to its actual implementation (or its model). It should be indicated whenever the information might be outdated (R14).

Existing Approaches. Various (standalone) modeling approaches exist that support understanding of selected business-related and IT aspects. However, as these standalone modeling approaches focus on selected aspects of an enterprise only, they do not allow for a comprehensive, integrated analysis accounting for multiple perspectives (cf. R1&R2). Such an integrated perspective is offered, as already mentioned, by enterprise modeling approaches. Several EM approaches exist that support modeling of IT infrastructure (cf. R3) in the context of an enterprise action system, e.g., ArchiMate [69], Architecture of Integrated Information Systems (ARIS) [64], and Multi-Perspective Enterprise Modeling (MEMO) [25] with the IT Modeling Language (ITML) [27,34]. Each of these approaches has been designed with a set of intended scenarios in mind [9], supporting transparency analyses, as discussed in this paper, not being one of them. Therefore, to support our vision some extensions to those approaches would be required. Although these approaches exhibit similarities, cf. [9], they also differ substantially in terms of the domain coverage and semantic richness of offered concepts, which is necessary to address the identified requirements (cf. e.g., R3). While ArchiMate and ARIS favor a concise language design by focusing on a small set of essential enterprise (architecture) concepts, MEMO provides domain stakeholders with elaborate reconstructions of the (technical) concepts. Particularly, while ArchiMate, ARIS and MEMO offer means to describe IT infrastructure, they do so at different levels of granularity. And so, ArchiMate provides a set of generic concepts where attributes can only be specified per instance, but not on a language level, which would be however required to differentiate various software artifacts (cf. R3). Similarly, although ARIS offers an extensive set of diagram types, its individual diagram types offer generic concepts with few attributes and relations only. In contrast, MEMO ITML offers a set of more fine-grained concepts with a rich set of attributes (cf. R3&R4). Considering the above, MEMO seems to be a promising approach to support our aims. However, it lacks the ability to, among others, express different views on software and relate them to different competencies of stakeholders, support stating transparency demands or documenting results of analysis, cf. R7 and R8. It also falls short, when it comes to supporting analysis of suitability of a system to certain scenarios (R10), transparency questionnaires (R11–R13), or linking the information to software implementation (R14). Therefore, we take MEMO as point of departure and propose corresponding extensions.

4   Extensions to MEMO in Support of Transparency

Several means of defining a modeling language exist. However, the one frequently used, also in case of MEMO, is by specifying a meta model. As we extend already existing DSMLs, we use the MEMO method's common Meta Modeling Language (MML) [25], and thus, integrate the extensions made into the MEMO method's language architecture. Compared to 'traditional' meta modeling languages, MML provides additional language constructs for expressing: (a) intrinsic attributes and relations, and (b) language-level types. Intrinsic attributes and relations are instantiated only on the instance level, but not on the type level. They are visualized with a white letter 'i' on a black background. In turn, language-level types are instantiated on the type level only, but not further. They are visualized with a grey-background of the concept's name [25].

In terms of the employed language design method, cf. [24], it is notable that: (1) we consider the use scenarios as the first class citizens that drive the design of the language, cf. previous section; and (2) we employ the guidelines for concept inclusion from [24]. Extensions as well as new concepts are shown in Fig. 2. Please note that due to space restriction only selected concepts, attributes, relations and Object Constraint Language (OCL) constraints are shown.

The core concept of interest is `Software`, cf. Fig. 2, originally defined in the ITML, characterized through a rich set of attributes (e.g., version, documentation, source code) and associated with other concepts as, e.g., programming language implementing it, libraries used, functions provided and used, or `UseCases` it is supposed to support (R10). A software may be represented and stored as a `File`. A software can be used in various usage contexts (`UseContext`), e.g., in processes (`AnyProcess`, defined in OrgML [25]), or to satisfy certain goals (`AbstractGoal`, part of MEMO GoalML [57]). In a given usage context, a software provides a `SpecificSupport` with such attributes as IT artifact relevance or support quality. This allows for instance to express, whether a given process type can be also realized without the support of a given type of software artifact.

A `Software` can be decomposed (R3) via a part-of relation. Thus, it is possible to model, e.g., an ERP System (as `ApplicationAndSystemSoftware`), and to decompose it into its different modules (e.g., HR management, financial management) down to the level of sub-routines, if of relevance for transparency

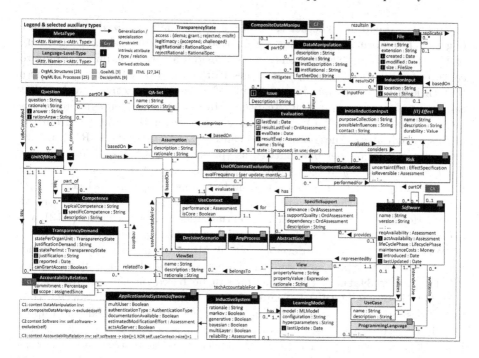

Fig. 2. Meta model excerpt: extended ITML & integration with other DSMLs.

discussions. The software and corresponding modules can be represented by different Views (R4) encompassing a property of interest and a way it should be derived/calculated. Those views can belong to a ViewSet, which considers the TransparencyDemand of different stakeholders. In addition, each ViewSet requires some Competency to be understood.

The meta class TransparencyDemand is central, as it allows to capture the current view of a stakeholder on a software, which helps derive the specific state of transparency in an interactive setting where various users participate (cf. also R7). For example, if a particular user demands on a certain date access to the source code (view) (R4) of a software, e.g., (R9, via justification) to learn about its behavior, e.g., in form of if-else statements, then this demand can be expressed with the attributes on the instance level and the auxiliary type TransparencyState in this case is 'demanded'. If all users, e.g., in the position of HR recruiters, demand this access, this can be expressed on the type level.

To account for different stakeholders and their groups, we use the abstract meta class UnitOfWork from MEMO OrgML [25], specialized into other organizational concepts (e.g., Organizational Unit), to express information on the type level, and through intrinsic attributes and relations, on the instance level (R6). The UnitOfWork can be related to Competences, which allows to analyze, if the access onto views, if granted, can be of use for the stakeholders (R5).

In order to capture whether the state of social affairs realized by a software (e.g., a hetero-normative view in a registration software) is considered legitimate by the stakeholders, `TransparencyState` provides a corresponding attribute to capture it (R8). However, when it comes to the use of a software, we propose that (il)legitimacy can be also the result of a `UseOfContextEvaluation` that can be conducted several times (captured by intrinsic attributes), but where most relevant seems to be the result of the last evaluation (derived from the intrinsic attributes). These evaluations can be based on *QA-Sets* (R11), i.e., to guide the evaluation per `UseContext` as specific as possible, and also support *practical transparency* in the case of ML systems. Even if those `QA-Sets` can be independently defined, they can also stem from a `DevelopmentEvaluation` that is performed during the design phase of a software, independent from its context of use. Here also assumptions and potential risks can be collected (R12), via dedicated concepts, that developers have in mind when publishing a software.

When it comes to the development of ML systems, we consider induction from a `DataInput` as a central characteristic of class of software using ML (`InductiveSystem`). The induction can be based on various ML Models (e.g. CART/C 4.5, Artificial Neural Networks) that come with specific configurations and hyper-parameters an `InductiveSystem` is based on. Important is however, that the process of building such a model depends on various activities, among others, e.g., data cleansing or preparation. We capture such activities with the meta class `DataManipulation` that can be part of `CompositeDataManipulation`. Since these activities can be used to mitigate `Issues` that stem from evaluation of `InductionInput`, a relation to `DevelopmentEvaluation` has been defined.

5   Exemplary Application

As we have pointed to the fulfillment of identified requirements already while describing the extended meta model, here we illustrate how the extended approach may be used in support of transparency analysis.

Figure 3 shows three integrated diagrams supporting interactive transparency. At the very bottom, we present a *ML Development diagram* that is used to document activities, assumptions and rationale during the development of a specific (inductive) software system. The content of the diagram is inspired by a dataset provided in Kaggle [39], a platform for data scientists. It shows the development of a software called *leaveCompPrediction* (LCP), which should support the `UseCase` of predicting the probability of a job change. Developers can use this diagram for an intra-disciplinary form of transparency, i.e., to document what data is taken as `InductionInput`, and how it is processed (`DataManipulation` steps). In addition, inline with the discussion about the kaggle dataset [39,46], several `issues`, activities and `rationales` are documented, which allows developers of the software not only to provide information about narrow technical software artifacts, but also, e.g., to behave responsibly (in the sense of the capacity to respond [73]) towards users of the software. Next, this

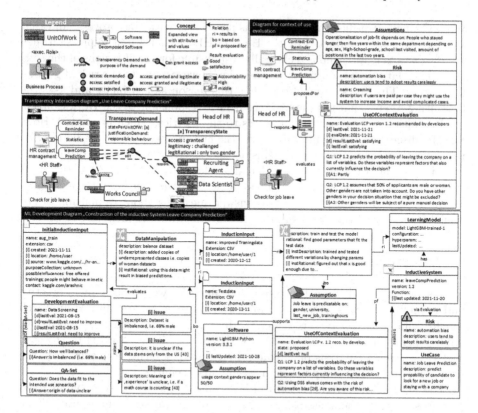

Fig. 3. Diagrams in support of an interactive transparency

diagram captures also `assumptions`, potential `risks` and questions, which should be considered during the use of the LCP. For instance, the LCP is based on the `assumption` that the risk of a job leave can be predicted only via the variables such as gender, university, duration of last job and hours of training within the current company. All assumptions, risks and potential questions can be bundled by the developers as a `UseOfContextEvaluation` with a state `proposed`, and provide a basis for a critical reflection of the software in support of a *practical transparency*. This critical reflection can be supported via the *Diagram for the Context of use evaluation*, where a `Software` and its related `Risks`, `Assumptions` are presented. Answers to the `UseOfContextEvaluation` can be captured per use case, and engage a discussion on the appropriateness of the specific software in this `UseContext`. In this case the LCP is used as part of an *HR contract management* `Software` for a business process in a specific company. Answers to the `UseOfContextEvaluation` are provided by various stakeholders (not shown here), and the `Head of HR` as responsible `UnitOfWork` that seems at least to be satisfied. However, during the use of the LCP the *Work Council* of our case company has a `TransparencyDemand` to clarify complaints about discrimination during contract renewals. Via a *business process model* (not shown here) the

Work Council identifies that the LCP is associated with this process, and that an evaluation was conducted by the Head of HR. To get a first impression they ask the Data Scientist who is technically responsible for specifications of the software. The Data Scientist rejects this decision however, due to the risk of gaming the system. The Work Council considers this reason as legitimate and asks the Recruiting Agents that use the LCP. To behave responsible to the Work Council, the Recruiting Agents ask for an access to the metrics, which is granted. However, by discussing the assumptions, i.e., the factors used for the prediction, the Recruiting Agents come to the conclusion that the software is not legitimate. By considering that the transparency demand relates to discrimination, the Head of HR starts a discussion about fairness. The *Transparency Interaction diagram* captures this situation, and allows to answer questions about responsibilities or available views and their accessibility, and whether stakeholders might make.

6   Conclusions

In this paper, based upon the conducted analysis, we propose an interactive understanding of transparency and identify requirements that an EM approach should fulfill to support this understanding. As none of existing approaches fulfills all requirements, we extend MEMO, in particular the ITML, to support transparency analysis of software design and use. Then, we show how the *extended* ITML can be applied to an exemplary scenario.

The extensions introduced into ITML enhance the set of available analysis scenarios, among others, assessing legitimacy of software design and use. Please note however, that while most of the requirements are being fulfilled through dedicated concepts and relations, some of the aspects have been only superficially addressed, e.g., the concept of competencies and cognitive skills of involved stakeholders related to ideas of views and perspectivity, or not at all, e.g., linking the information on a software artifact to its actual implementation (R14). In addition, due to space limitations, we have focused here on a selected class of software systems only, namely induction-based systems by taking more pragmatic considerations into account. We acknowledge also that a process model guiding the use and adoption of the extended MEMO might be needed. Currently, its usage requires specific skills, and the judgment of transparency measures is dependent on those involved. Finally, while the application of MML allowed us to take advantage of the intrinsic features and relations, and thus, to refer to the instance level, we have faced numerous challenges pertaining to the restrictions given by the type/instance dichotomy or the semantic differences between instantiation and specialization, cf. [26]. As in conventional meta modeling, there is no 'perfect' solution to the mentioned challenges, cf. [5,26], for our future research the application of multi-level modeling [5,26], seems promising. In addition, as some multi-level modeling approaches support integrated modeling and programming [26], also R14 could be in this way fulfilled.

References

1. ACM Public Policy Council: Statement on algorithmic transparency and accountability (2017. https://www.acm.org/. Accessed 1 July 2021
2. Albu, O.B., Flyverbom, M.: Organizational transparency: conceptualizations, conditions, and consequences. Bus. Soc. **58**(2), 268–297 (2019)
3. Alloa, E.: Transparency: a magic concept of modernity. In: Alloa, E., Thomä, D. (eds.) Transparency, Society and Subjectivity, pp. 21–55. Springer, Cham (2018). https://doi.org/10.1007/978-3-319-77161-8_3
4. Ananny, M., Crawford, K.: Seeing without knowing: limitations of the transparency ideal. New Med. Soc. **20**(3), 973–989 (2016)
5. Atkinson, C., Kühne, T.: Reducing accidental complexity in domain models. SOSYM **7**(3), 345–359 (2008). https://doi.org/10.1007/s10270-007-0061-0
6. Barocas, S., Hood, S., Ziewitz, M.: Governing algorithms: provocation piece, SRRN (2013). http://dx.doi.org/10.2139/ssrn.2245322
7. Baume, S.: Publicity and transparency: the itinerary of a subtle distinction. In: Alloa, E., Thomä, D. (eds.) Transparency, Society and Subjectivity, pp. 203–224. Springer, Cham (2018). https://doi.org/10.1007/978-3-319-77161-8_10
8. Bentham, J.: Constitutive authority. In: Bowring, J. (ed.) The Works of Jeremy Bentham, pp. 155–160. Russell and Russell, New York (1962)
9. Bock, A., Kaczmarek, M., Overbeek, S., Heß, M.: A comparative analysis of selected enterprise modeling approaches. In: Frank, U., Loucopoulos, P., Pastor, Ó., Petrounias, I. (eds.) PoEM 2014. LNBIP, vol. 197, pp. 148–163. Springer, Heidelberg (2014). https://doi.org/10.1007/978-3-662-45501-2_11
10. Bork, D., Roelens, B.: A technique for evaluating and improving the semantic transparency of modeling language notations. Softw. Syst. Model. **20**(4), 939–963 (2021). https://doi.org/10.1007/s10270-021-00895-w
11. Brown, S., Davidovic, J., Hasan, A.: The algorithm audit: scoring the algorithms that score us. Big Data Soc. **8**(1) (2021). https://doi.org/10.1177/2053951720983865
12. Burrell, J.: How the machine 'thinks': understanding opacity in machine learning algorithms. Big Data Soc. **3**(1) (2016). https://doi.org/10.1177%2F2053951715622512
13. Christensen, L.T.: Corporate communication: the challenge of transparency. Corp. Commun. Int. J. **7**(3), 162–168 (2002)
14. Chun, W.H.K.: Programmed Visions: Software and Memory. MIT Press, Cambridge (2011)
15. Deetz, S., Mumby, D.: Metaphors, information, and power. In: Ruben, B.D. (ed.) Information and Behavior, pp. 369–385. Transaction Inc., New Brunswick (1985)
16. do Prado Leite, J., Cappelli, C.: Software transparency. BISE **2**(3), 127–139 (2010)
17. Dobbe, R., Dean, S., Gilbert, T., Kohli, N.: A broader view on bias in automated decision-making. FATML, Stockholm (2018). https://doi.org/10.48550/arXiv.1807.00553
18. Draper, N.A., Turow, J.: The corporate cultivation of digital resignation. New Med. Soc. **21**(8), 1824–1839 (2019)
19. European Parliament and the Council of European Union: Regulation (EU) no 679/2016 (GDPR) (2016). https://eur-lex.europa.eu. Accessed 1 July 2021
20. European Parliament and the Council of European Union: Regulation (EU) no 1150/2019 (2019). https://ec.europa.eu. Accessed 1 July 2021
21. Fenster, M.: The opacity of transparency. Iowa L. Rev. **91**, 885 (2005)

22. Fill, H.G.: Abstraction and transparency in meta modeling. In: Schweighofer, E., Kummer, F., Hötzendorfer, W., (ed.) Transparency, pp. 435–442. Österreichische Computer Gesellschaft, Salzburg (2014)
23. Fleischmann, K.R., Wallace, W.A.: Ensuring transparency in computational modeling. Commun. ACM **52**(3), 131–134 (2009)
24. Frank, U.: Outline of a Method for Designing Domain-Specific Modelling Languages. ICB Research Report 42, University of Duisburg-Essen, Essen (2010)
25. Frank, U.: Multi-perspective enterprise modeling: foundational concepts, prospects and future research challenges. Softw. Syst. Model. **13**(3), 941–962 (2012). https://doi.org/10.1007/s10270-012-0273-9
26. Frank, U.: Multilevel modeling - toward a new paradigm of conceptual modeling and information systems design. BISE **6**(6), 319–337 (2014)
27. Frank, U., Kaczmarek-Heß, M., de Kinderen, S.: IT infrastructure modeling language. ICB Research Report 72, Essen (2021)
28. Fuster, G.G.: Transparency as translation in data protection. In: BEING PROFILED, pp. 52–55. Amsterdam University Press (2018)
29. Gebru, T., et al.: Datasheets for datasets. CACM **64**(12), 86–92 (2021)
30. Goad, D., Gal, U.: Understanding the impact of transparency on algorithmic decision making legitimacy. In: Schultze, U., Aanestad, M., Mähring, M., Østerlund, C., Riemer, K. (eds.) IS&O 2018. IAICT, vol. 543, pp. 64–79. Springer, Cham (2018). https://doi.org/10.1007/978-3-030-04091-8_6
31. Goldenfein, J.: Algorithmic transparency and decision-making accountability. In: Closer to The Machine: Technical, Social and Legal Aspects of AI, pp. 41–61 (2019)
32. Guidotti, R., Monreale, A., Ruggieri, S., Turini, F., Giannotti, F., Pedreschi, D.: A survey of methods for explaining black box models. CSUR **51**(5), 1–42 (2018)
33. Guszcza, J., Rahwan, I., Bible, W., Cebrian, M., Katyal, V.: Why we need to audit algorithms. HBR (2018)
34. Heise, D.: Unternehmensmodell-basiertes IT-Kostenmanagement als Bestandteil eines integrativen IT-Controllings. Logos, Berlin (2013)
35. Hood, C., Heald, D.: Transparency in historical perspective. In: Hood, C., Heald, D. (ed.) Transparency: the Key to Better Governance? Oxford University Press (2006)
36. Hosseini, M., Shahri, A., Phalp, K., Ali, R.: Engineering transparency requirements: a modelling and analysis framework. Inf. Syst. **74**, 3–22 (2018)
37. IEEE - Institute of Electrical and Electronics Engineers Inc: IEEEP7001 - Transparency of autonomous systems (draft) (2020)
38. Jobin, A., Ienca, M., Vayena, E.: The global landscape of AI ethics guidelines. Nat. Mach. Intell. **1**(9), 389–399 (2019)
39. Kaggle: HR analytics: Job change of data scientists (2020). https://www.kaggle.com/arashnic/hr-analytics-job-change-of-data-scientists
40. Kitchin, R.: Thinking critically about algorithms. Inf. Comm. Soc. **20**(1), 14–29 (2017). https://doi.org/10.1080/1369118X.2016.1154087
41. Kohli, N., Barreto, R., Kroll, J.A.: Translation tutorial: a shared lexicon for research and practice in human-centered software systems. In: 1st Conference on Fairness, Accountability, and Transparency, New York, NY, USA, vol. 7 (2018)
42. Krogstie, J.: Model-Based Development and Evolution of Information Systems: A Quality Approach. Springer Science & Business Media, London (2012). https://doi.org/10.1007/978-1-4471-2936-3
43. de Laat, P.B.: Algorithmic decision making based on ML from big data. Philos. Technol. **31**(4), 525–541 (2018)

44. Lee, T.H., Boynton, L.A.: Conceptualizing transparency: propositions for the integration of situational factors and stakeholders' perspectives. Public Relat. In. **6**(3), 233–251 (2017)

45. Lukyanenko, R., Castellanos, A., Parsons, J., Tremblay, M.C., Storey, V.C.: Using conceptual modeling to support machine learning. In: Cappiello, C., Ruiz, M. (eds) Information Systems Engineering in Responsible Information Systems. CAiSE 2019. Lecture Notes in Business Information Processing, vol. 350, pp. 170–181. Springer, Cham (2019). https://doi.org/10.1007/978-3-030-21297-1_15

46. Maass, W., Storey, V.C., Lukyanenko, R.: From mental models to machine learning models via conceptual models. In: Augusto, A., Gill, A., Nurcan, S., Reinhartz-Berger, I., Schmidt, R., Zdravkovic, J. (eds.) BPMDS/EMMSAD -2021. LNBIP, vol. 421, pp. 293–300. Springer, Cham (2021). https://doi.org/10.1007/978-3-030-79186-5_19

47. Margetts, H.: The internet and transparency. Political Art. **82**(4), 518–521 (2011)

48. Meijer, A.: Understanding modern transparency. Int. Rev. Admin. Sci. **75**(2), 255–269 (2009)

49. Michener, G., Bersch, K.: Conceptualizing the quality of transparency. Polit. Concepts **49**, 1–27 (2011)

50. Minsky, M.: The Emotion Machine: Commonsense Thinking, Artificial Intelligence, and the Future of the Human Mind. Simon and Schuster, New York (2007)

51. Mitchell, M., et al.: Model cards for model reporting. In: Proceedings of the Conference on Fairness, Accountability, and Transparency, pp. 220–229 (2019)

52. Mittelstadt, B.: Automation, algorithms, and politics— auditing for transparency in content personalization systems. Intl. J. Commun. **10**, 12 (2016)

53. Mylopoulos, J.: Conceptual Modelling and TELOS. Conceptual Modelling, Databases, and CASE: An Integrated View of is Development, pp. 49–68 (1992)

54. Newton, I.: Opticks, or, A Treatise Of The Reflections, Refractions, Inflections & Colours of Light. Courier Corporation (1952)

55. Organisation for Economic Co-operation and Development: Recommendation of the council on artificial intelligence (2021)

56. Österle, H., et al.: Memorandum zur gestaltungsorientierten Wirtschaftsinformatik. ZfBF **62**(6), 664–672 (2010)

57. Overbeek, S., Frank, U., Köhling, C.: A language for multi-perspective goal modelling: challenges, requirements and solutions. CSI **38**, 1–16 (2015)

58. Pasquale, F.: The Black Box Society. Harvard University Press, Cambridge (2015)

59. Paßmann, J., Boersma, A.: Unknowing algorithms: on transparency of unopenable black boxes. In: Schäfer, M., van Es, K. (eds.) The Datafied Society, pp. 139–146 (2017)

60. Raji, I.D., et al.: Closing the AI accountability gap: defining an end-to-end framework for internal algorithmic auditing. In: Proceedings of the 2020 Conference on Fairness, Accountability, and Transparency, pp. 33–44 (2020)

61. Resnick, M., Berg, R., Eisenberg, M.: Beyond black boxes: bringing transparency and aesthetics back to scientific investigation. J. Learn. Sci. **9**(1), 7–30 (2000)

62. Rey, A. (ed.): Dictionnaire historique de la langue française. Le Robert, Dictionnaires Le Robert, Paris, nouv. éd edn. (1995)

63. Rudin, C.: Stop explaining black box ML models for high stakes decisions and use interpretable models instead. Nat. Mach. Intell. **1**(5), 206–215 (2019)

64. Scheer, A.W.: ARIS - Modellierungsmethoden, Metamodelle, Anwendungen, 4th edn. Springer, Heidelberg (2001). https://doi.org/10.1007/978-3-642-97731-2

65. Schuette, R., Rotthowe, T.: The guidelines of modeling – an approach to enhance the quality in information models. In: Ling, T.-W., Ram, S., Li Lee, M. (eds.) ER 1998. LNCS, vol. 1507, pp. 240–254. Springer, Heidelberg (1998). https://doi.org/10.1007/978-3-540-49524-6_20

66. Schwarzer, B., Krcmar, H.: Wirtschaftsinformatik?: Grundlagen betrieblicher Informationssysteme, 4th edn. Schäffer-Poeschel, Stuttgart (2010)

67. Seaver, N., Vertesi, J., Ribes, D.: Knowing algorithms. In: digitalSTS, pp. 412–422. Princeton University Press (2019)

68. Suchman, M.C.: Managing legitimacy: strategic and institutional approaches. Acad. MGM Rev. **20**(3), 571–610 (1995)

69. The Open Group: ArchiMate 2.1 Specification: Open Group Standard. The Open Group Series, Van Haren, Zaltbommel (2013)

70. Timothy Coombs, W., Holladay, S.J.: The pseudo-panopticon. Corp. Commun. Int. J. **18**(2), 212–227 (2013)

71. Turilli, M., Floridi, L.: The ethics of information transparency. Ethics Inf. Technol. **11**(2), 105–112 (2009)

72. Voß, S.: Informationsmanagement : mit 25 Tabellen. Springer, London (2001)

73. Waldenfels, B.: The Question of the Other. Chinese University Press, Hong Kong (2007)

74. Wehmeier, S., Raaz, O.: Transparency matters: the concept of organizational transparency in the academic discourse. PR In. **1**(3), 337–366 (2012)

75. Weller, A.: Transparency: motivations and challenges. In: Samek, W., Montavon, G., Vedaldi, A., Hansen, L.K., Müller, K.-R. (eds.) Explainable AI: Interpreting, Explaining and Visualizing Deep Learning. LNCS (LNAI), vol. 11700, pp. 23–40. Springer, Cham (2019). https://doi.org/10.1007/978-3-030-28954-6_2

76. Zachman, J.A.: A framework for information systems architecture. IBM Syst. J. **26**(3), 276–292 (1987)

Uncertain Case Identifiers in Process Mining: A User Study of the Event-Case Correlation Problem on Click Data

Marco Pegoraro$^{(\boxtimes)}$ ⓘ, Merih Seran Uysal ⓘ, Tom-Hendrik Hülsmann ⓘ,
and Wil M. P. van der Aalst ⓘ

Department of Computer Science, RWTH Aachen, Aachen, Germany
{pegoraro,uysal,wvdaalst}@pads.rwth-aachen.de,
tom.huelsmann@rwth-aachen.de
http://www.pads.rwth-aachen.de/

Abstract. Among the many sources of event data available today, a prominent one is user interaction data. User activity may be recorded during the use of an application or website, resulting in a type of user interaction data often called click data. An obstacle to the analysis of click data using process mining is the lack of a case identifier in the data. In this paper, we show a case and user study for event-case correlation on click data, in the context of user interaction events from a mobility sharing company. To reconstruct the case notion of the process, we apply a novel method to aggregate user interaction data in separate user sessions—interpreted as cases—based on neural networks. To validate our findings, we qualitatively discuss the impact of process mining analyses on the resulting well-formed event log through interviews with process experts.

Keywords: Process mining · Uncertain event data · Event-case correlation · Case notion discovery · Unlabeled event logs · Machine learning · Neural networks · word2vec · UI design · UX design

1 Introduction

In the last decades, the dramatic rise of both performance and portability of computing devices has enabled developers to design software with an ever-increasing level of sophistication. Such escalation in functionalities caused a subsequent increase in the complexity of software, making it harder to access for users. The shift from large screens of desktop computers to small displays of smartphones, tablets, and other handheld devices has strongly contributed to this increase in the intricacy of software interfaces. User interface (UI) design and user experience (UX) design aim to address the challenge of managing complexity, to enable users to interact easily and effectively with the software.

We thank the Alexander von Humboldt (AvH) Stiftung for supporting our research interactions.

© Springer Nature Switzerland AG 2022
A. Augusto et al. (Eds.): BPMDS 2022/EMMSAD 2022, LNBIP 450, pp. 173–187, 2022.
https://doi.org/10.1007/978-3-031-07475-2_12

In designing and improving user interfaces, important sources of guidance are the records of user interaction data. Many websites and apps track the actions of users, such as pageviews, clicks, and searches. Such type of information is often called *click data*, of which an example is given in Table 1. These can then be analyzed to identify parts of the interface which need to be simplified, through, e.g., pattern mining, or performance measures such as time spent performing a certain action or visualizing a certain page.

Table 1. A sample of click data from the user interactions with the smartphone app of a German mobility sharing company. This dataset is the basis for the qualitative evaluation of the method presented in this paper.

Timestamp	Screen	User	Team	OS
2021-01-25 23:00:00.939	`pre_booking`	b0b00	2070b	iOS
2021-01-25 23:00:03.435	`tariffs`	b0b00	2070b	iOS
2021-01-25 23:00:04.683	`menu`	3fc0c	02d1f	Android
2021-01-25 23:00:05.507	`my_bookings`	3fc0c	02d1f	Android
⋮	⋮	⋮	⋮	⋮

In the context of novel click data analysis techniques, a particularly promising subfield of data science is *process mining*. Process mining is a discipline that aims to analyze event data generated by process executions, to e.g. obtain a model of the process, measure its conformance with normative behavior, or analyze the performance of process instances with respect to time.

Towards the analysis of click data with process mining, a foundational challenge remains: the association of event data (here, user interactions) with a *process case identifier*. While each interaction logged in a database is associated with a user identifier, which is read from the current active session in the software, there is a lack of an attribute to isolate events corresponding to one single utilization of the software from beginning to end. Aggregating user interactions into cases is of crucial importance, since the case identifier—together with the *activity label* and the *timestamp*—is a fundamental attribute to reconstruct a process instance as a sequence of activities (*trace*), also known as *control-flow perspective* of a process instance. A vast majority of the process mining techniques available require the control-flow perspective of a process to be known.

In this paper, we propose a novel case attribution approach for click data. Our method allows us to effectively segment the sequence of interactions from a user into separate cases on the basis of normative behavior. We then verify the effectiveness of our method by applying it to a real-life use case scenario related to a mobility sharing smartphone app. Then, we perform common process mining analyses such as process discovery on the resulting segmented log, and we conduct a user study among business owners by presenting the result of such analyses to process experts from the company. Through interviews with such experts, we assess the impact of process mining analysis techniques enabled by our event-case correlation method.

The remainder of the paper is organized as follows. Section 2 discusses existing event-case correlation methods and other related work. Section 3 illustrates a novel event-case correlation method. Section 4 describes the results of our method on a real-life use case scenario related to a mobility sharing app, together with a discussion of interviews of process experts from the company about the impact of process mining techniques enabled by our method. Finally, Sect. 5 concludes the paper.

2   Related Work

The problem of assigning a case identifier to events in a log is a long-standing challenge in the process mining community [5], and is known by multiple names in literature, including *event-case correlation* problem [3] and *case notion discovery* problem [13]. Event logs where events are missing the case identifier attribute are usually referred to as *unlabeled event logs* [5]. Several of the attempts to solve this problem, such as an early one by Ferreira et al. based on first order Markov models [5] or the *Correlation Miner* by Pourmiza et al., based on quadratic programming [17] are very limited in the presence of loops in the process. Other approaches, such as the one by Bayomie et al. [2] can indeed work in the presence of loops, by relying on heuristics based on activities duration which lead to a set of candidate segmented logs. This comes at the cost of a slow computing time. An improvement of the aforementioned method [3] employs simulated annealing to select an optimal case notion; while still very computationally heavy, this method delivers high-quality case attribution results.

The problem of event-case correlation can be positioned in the broader context of *uncertain event data* [15,16]. This research direction aims to analyze event data with imprecise attributes, where single traces might correspond to an array of possible real-life scenarios. Akin to the method proposed in this paper, some techniques allow to obtain probability distributions over such scenarios [14].

A notable and rapidly-growing field where the problem of event-case correlation is crucial is *Robotic Process Automation* (RPA), the automation of process activities through software bots. Similar to many approaches related to the problem at large, existing approaches to event-case correlation in the RPA field often heavily rely on unique start and end events in order to segment the log, either explicitly or implicitly [9,10,18].

The problem of event-case attribution is different when considered on click data—particularly from mobile apps. Normally, the goal is to learn a function that receives an event as an independent variable and produces a case identifier as an output. In the scenario studied in this paper, however, the user is tracked by the open session in the app during the interaction, and recorded events with different user identifier cannot belong to the same process case. The goal is then to subdivide the sequence of interactions from one user into one or more sessions (cases). Marrella et al. [11] examined the challenge of obtaining case identifiers for unsegmented user interaction logs in the context of learnability of software systems, by segmenting event sequences with a predefined set of start and end activities as normative information. They find that this approach cannot discover all types of cases, which limits its flexibility and applicability. Jlailaty et al. [7] encounter the segmentation problem in the context of email logs. They segment cases by designing an ad-hoc metric that combines event attributes such as timestamp, sender, and receiver. Their results however show that this method is eluded by edge cases. Other prominent sources of sequential event data without case attribution are IoT sensors: Janssen et al. [6] address the problem of obtaining process cases from sequential sensor event data by splitting the long traces according to an application-dependent fixed length, to find the optimal sub-trace length such that, after splitting, each case contains only a single activity. One major limitation of this approach that the authors mention is the use of only a single constant length for all of the different activities, which may have varying lengths. More recently, Burattin et al. [4] tackled a segmentation problem for user interactions with a modeling software; in their approach, the segmentation is obtained exploiting eye tracking data.

The goal of the study reported in this paper is to present a method able to rapidly and efficiently segment a user interaction log in a setting where no sample of ground truth cases are available, and the only normative information at disposal is in the form of a link graph relatively easy to extract from a UI. Section 3 shows the segmentation technique we propose.

3   Method

In this section, we illustrate our proposed method for event-case correlation on click data. As mentioned earlier, the goal is to segment the sequence of events corresponding to the interactions of every user in the database into complete process executions (cases). In fact, the click data we consider in this study have a property that we need to account for while designing our method: all events belonging to one case are contiguous in time. Thus, our goal is to determine split points for different cases in a sequence of interactions related to the same user. More concretely, if a user of the app produces the sequence of events $\langle e_1, e_2, e_3, e_4, e_5, e_6, e_7, e_8, e_9 \rangle$, our goal is to section such sequence in contiguous subsequences that represent a complete interaction—for instance, $\langle e_1, e_2, e_3, e_4 \rangle$, $\langle e_5, e_6 \rangle$, and $\langle e_7, e_8, e_9 \rangle$. We refer to this as the *log segmentation* problem, which can be considered a special case of the event-case correlation problem. In this context, "*unsegmented* log" is synonym with "unlabeled log".

Rather than being based on a collection of known complete process instances as training set, the creation of our segmentation model is based on behavior described by a model of the system. A type of model particularly suited to the problem of segmentation of user interaction data—and especially click data—is the *link graph*. In fact, since the activities in our process correspond to screens in the app, a graph of the links in the app is relatively easy to obtain, since it can be constructed in an automatic way by following the links between views in the software. This link graph will be the basis for our training data generation procedure.

We will use as running example the link graph of Fig. 1. The resulting normative traces will then be used to train a neural network model based on the word2vec architecture [12], which will be able to split contiguous user interaction sequences into cases.

3.1 Training Log Generation

To generate the training data, we will begin by exploiting the fact that each process case will only contain events associated with one and only one user. Let L be our unsegmented log and $u \in U$ be a user in L; then, we indicate with L_u the sub-log of L where all events are associated with the user u.

Our training data will be generated by simulating a transition system annotated with probabilities. The construction of a transition system based on event data is a well-known procedure in process mining [1], which requires to choose an event representation abstraction and a window size (or horizon), which are process-specific. In the context of this section, we will show our method using a sequence abstraction with window size 2. Initially, for each user $u \in U$ we create a transition system $TS_u = (S_u, E_u, T_u, i)$ based on the sequence of user interactions in the sub-log L_u. $S_u^{\mathrm{end}} \in S_u$ denotes the final states of TS_u. All such transition systems TS_u share the same initial state i. To identify the end of sequences, we add a special symbol to the states $f \in S'$ to which we connect any state $s \in S$ if it appears at the end of a user interaction sequence. To traverse the transitions to the final state f we utilize as placeholder the empty label τ.

We then obtain a transition system $TS' = (S', A, T', i)$ corresponding to the entire log L, where A is the set of activity labels appearing in L, $S' = \bigcup_{u \in U} S_u$, and $T' = \bigcup_{u \in U} T_u$. Moreover, $S'^{\mathrm{end}} = \bigcup_{u \in U} S_u^{\mathrm{end}}$. We also collect information about the frequency of each transition in the log: we define a weighting function ω for the transitions $t \in T$ where $\omega(t) = \#\,of\,occurrences\,of\,t\,in\,L$. If $t \notin T$, $\omega(t) = 0$. Through ω, it is optionally possible to filter out rare behavior by deleting transitions with $\omega(t) < \epsilon$, for a small threshold ϵ. Figure 2 shows a transition system with the chosen abstraction and window size, annotated with both frequencies and transition labels, for the user interactions $L_{u_1} = \langle M, A, M, B, C \rangle$, $L_{u_2} = \langle M, B, C, M \rangle$, and $L_{u_3} = \langle M, A, B, C \rangle$.

In contrast to transition systems that are created based on logs that are segmented, the obtained transition system might contain states that are not reachable and transitions that are not possible according to the real process. Normally, the transition system abstraction is applied on a case-by-case basis. In our case, however, we applied the abstraction to the whole sequence of interactions that is associated with a specific user, consecutive interactions that belong to different cases will be included as undesired transitions in the transition system. In order to prune undesired transitions from the transition system, we exploit the link graph of the system: a transition in the transition system is only valid if it appears in the link graph. Unreachable states are also pruned.

We will assume a sequence abstraction in TS. Given a link graph $G = (V, E)$, we define the reduced transition system $TS = (S, A, T, i)$, where $T = \{((\langle \ldots, a_1 \rangle, a_2, \langle \ldots, a_1, a_2 \rangle) \in T' \mid (a_1, a_2) \in E\}$ and $S = \bigcup_{(s_1, a, s_2) \in t} \{s_1, s_2\}$.

Figure 1 shows a link graph for our running example, and Fig. 2 shows how this is used to reduce TS' into TS.

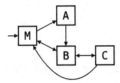

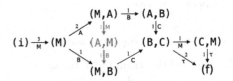

Fig. 1. The link graph of a simple, fictional system that we are going to use as running example. From this process, we aim to segment the three unsegmented user interactions $\langle M, A, M, B, C \rangle$, $\langle M, B, C, M \rangle$, and $\langle M, A, B, C \rangle$.

Fig. 2. The transition system TS' obtained by the user interaction data of the example (Fig. 1). During the reduction phase, the transition (M, A) to (A, M) is removed, since it is not supported by the link graph (M does not follow A). The state (A, M) is not reachable and is removed entirely (in red). Consequently, the reduced transition system TS is obtained. (Color figure online)

Next, we define probabilities for transitions and states based on the values for $\omega(t)$. Let $T_{\text{out}}: S \to \mathcal{P}(T)$ be $T_{\text{out}}(s) = \{(s_1, a, s_2) \in T \mid s_1 = s\}$; this function returns all outgoing transitions from a given state. The likelihood of a transition $(s_1, a, s_2) \in T$ is then computed with $l_{\text{trans}}: T \to [0, 1]$:

$$l_{\text{trans}}(s_1, a, s_2) = \frac{\omega(s_1, a, s_2)}{\sum\limits_{t_* \in T_{\text{out}}(s_1)} \omega(t_*)}$$

Note that if s_1 has no outgoing transition and $T_{\text{out}}(s_1) = \varnothing$, by definition $l_{\text{trans}}(s_1, a, s_2) = 0$ for any $a \in A$ and $s_2 \in S$. We will need two more supporting functions. We define $l_{\text{start}}: S \to [0, 1]$ and $l_{\text{end}}: S \to [0, 1]$ as the probabilities that a state $s \in S$ is, respectively, the initial and final state of a sequence:

$$l_{\text{start}}(s) = \frac{\sum\limits_{a \in A} \omega(i, a, s)}{\sum\limits_{\substack{s_* \in S \\ a \in A}} \omega(s_*, a, s)} \qquad l_{\text{end}}(s) = \frac{\omega(s, \tau, f)}{\sum\limits_{\substack{s_* \in S \\ a \in A}} \omega(s, a, s_*)}$$

In our running example of Fig. 2, $l_{\text{start}}((M)) = \frac{3}{3} = 1$, and $l_{\text{end}}((C, M)) = \frac{1}{3}$. Given a path of states $\langle s_1, s_2, \ldots, s_n \rangle$ transitioning through the sequence $\langle (i, a_1, s_1), (s_1, a_2, s_2), \ldots, (s_{n-1}, a_n, s_n), (s_n, \tau, f) \rangle$, we now have the means to compute its probability with the function $l: S^* \to [0, 1]$:

$$l(\langle s_1, s_2, \ldots, s_n \rangle) = l_{\text{start}}(s_1) \cdot \prod_{i=2}^{n} l_{\text{trans}}(s_{i-1}, a_i, s_i) \cdot l_{\text{end}}(s_n)$$

This enables us to obtain an arbitrary number of well-formed process cases as sequences of activities $\langle a_1, a_2, \ldots, a_n \rangle$, utilizing a Monte Carlo procedure. We can sample a random starting state for the case, through the probability distribution given by l_{start}; then, we compose a path with the probabilities provided by l_{trans} and l_{end}. The traces sampled in this way will reflect the available user interaction data in terms of initial and final activities, and internal structure, although the procedure still allows for generalization. Such generalization is, however, controlled thanks to the pruning provided by the link graph of the system. We will refer to the set of generated traces as the training log L_T.

3.2 Model Training

The training log L_T obtained in Sect. 3.1 is now used in order to train the segmentation models. The core component of the proposed method consists one or more word2vec models to detect the boundaries between cases in the input log. When applied for natural language processing, the input of a word2vec model is a corpus of sentences which consist of words. Instead of sentences built as sequences of words, we consider traces $\langle a_1, a_2, \ldots, a_n \rangle$ as sequences of activities.

The training log L_T needs an additional processing step to be used as training set for word2vec. Given two traces $\sigma_1 \in L_T$ and $\sigma_2 \in L_T$, we build a training instance by joining them in a single sequence, concatenating them with a placeholder activity ■. So, for instance, the traces $\sigma_1 = \langle a_1, a_2, a_4, a_5 \rangle \in L_T$ and $\sigma_2 = \langle a_6, a_7, a_8 \rangle \in L_T$ are combined in the training sample $\langle a_1, a_2, a_4, a_5, ■, a_6, a_7, a_8 \rangle$. This is done repeatedly, shuffling the order of the traces. Figure 3 shows this processing step on the running example.

The word2vec model [12] consists of three layers: an input layer, a single hidden layer, and the output layer. This model has already been successfully employed in process mining to solve the problem of missing events [8]. During training, the network reads the input sequences with a sliding window. The activity occupying the center of the sliding window is called the *center action*, while the surrounding activities are called *context actions*. The proposed method uses the *Continuous Bag-Of-Words* (CBOW) variant of word2vec, where the context actions are introduced as input in the neural network in order to predict the center action. The error measured in the output layer is used for training in order to adjust the weights in the neural network, using the backpropagation algorithm. These forward and backward steps of the training procedure are repeated for all the positions of the sliding window and all the sequences in the training set; when fully trained, the network will output a probability distribution for the center action given the context actions. Figure 4 shows an example of likelihood estimation for a center action in our running example, with a sliding window of size 3.

3.3 Segmentation

Through the word2vec model we trained in Sect. 3.2, we can now estimate the likelihood of a case boundary ■ at any position of a sequence of user interactions. Figure 5 shows these estimates on one user interaction sequence from the running example. Note that this method of computing likelihoods is easy to extend to

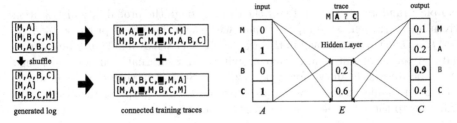

Fig. 3. Construction of the training instances. Traces are shuffled and concatenated with a placeholder end activity.

Fig. 4. The word2vec neural network. Given the sequence $\langle A, ?, C \rangle$, the network produces a probability distribution over the possible activity labels for ?.

an ensemble of predictive models: the different predicted values can be then aggregated, e.g., with the mean or the median.

Next, we use these score to determine case boundaries, which will correspond to prominent peaks in the graph. Let $\langle p_1, p_2, \ldots, p_n \rangle$ be the sequence of likelihoods of a case boundary obtained on a user interaction sequence. We consider p_i a boundary if it satisfies the following conditions: first, $p_i > b_1 \cdot p_{i-1}$; then, $p_i > b_2 \cdot p_{i+1}$; finally, $p_i > b_3 \cdot \frac{\sum_{j=i-k-1}^{i-1} p_j}{k}$, where $b_1, b_2, b_3 \in [1, \infty)$ and $k \in \mathbb{N}$ are hyperparameters that influence the sensitivity of the segmentation. The first two inequalities use b_1 and b_2 to ensure that the score is sufficiently higher than the immediate predecessor and successor. The third inequality uses b_3 to make sure that the likelihood is also significantly higher than a neighborhood defined by the parameter k.

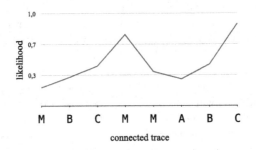

Fig. 5. A plot indicating the chances of having a case segment for each position of the user interaction data (second and third trace from the example in Fig. 1).

These three conditions allow us to select valid case boundaries within user interaction sequences. Splitting the sequences on such boundaries yields traces of complete process executions, whose events will be assigned a unique case identifier. The set of such traces then constitutes a traditional event log, ready to be analyzed with established process mining techniques.

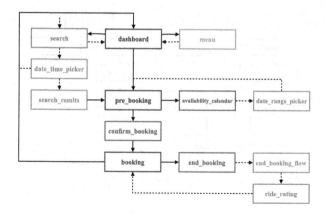

Fig. 6. DFG automatically discovered from the log segmented by our method.

4   User Study

In order to validate the utility of process mining workflows in the area of user behavior analysis, a case study was conducted. Such study also aims at assessing the quality of the segmentation produced by the proposed method in a real-life setting, in an area where the ground truth is not available (i.e., there are no normative well-formed cases). We applied the proposed method to a dataset which contains real user interaction data collected from the mobile applications of a German vehicle sharing company. We then utilized the resulting segmented log to analyze user behavior with an array of process mining techniques. Then, the results were presented to process experts from the company, who utilized such results to identify critical areas of the process and suggest improvements.

In the data, the abstraction for recorded user interactions is the screen (or page) in the app. For each interaction, the system recorded five attributes: timestamp, screen, user, team, and os. The timestamp marks the point in time when the user visited the screen, which is identified by the screen attribute, our activity label. The user attribute identifies who performed the interaction, and the team attribute is an additional field referring to the vehicle provider associated with the interaction. Upon filtering out pre-login screens (not associated with a user), the log consists of about 990,000 events originating from about 12,200 users. A snippet of these click data was shown in Table 1, in Sect. 1.

We applied the segmentation method presented in Sect. 3 to this click data. We then analyzed the resulting log with well-known process mining techniques. Lastly, the findings were presented to and discussed with four experts from the company, consisting of one UX expert, two mobile developers and one manager from a technical area. All of the participants are working directly on the application and are therefore highly familiar with it. We will report here the topics of discussion in the form of questions; for reasons of space, we will only document a selection of the most insightful questions.

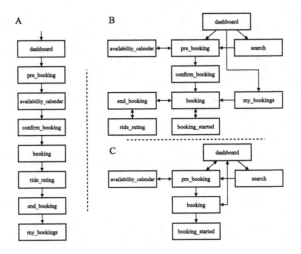

Fig. 7. DFGs created by three of the process experts as part of Q1.

Q1: Draw your own process model of the user interactions

The participants were asked to draw a *Directly-Follows Graph* (DFG) describing the most common user interactions with the app. A DFG is a simple process model consisting in a graph where activities A and B are connected by an arc if B is executed immediately after A. The concept of this type of graph was explained to the participants beforehand. The experts were given five minutes in order to create their models. A cleaned up representation of the resulting models can be seen in Figs. 7 and 8.

For comparison, we created a DFG of the segmented log (Fig. 6). Such model was configured to contain a similar amount of different screens as the expert models. The colors indicate the agreement between the model and the expert models. Darker colors signify that a screen was included in more expert models. The dashed edges between the screens signify edges that were identified by the generated model, but are not present in the participant's models.

The mobile developers (models A and B) tend to describe the interactions in a more precise way that follows the different screens more closely, while the technical manager and UX expert (C and D) provided models that capture the usage of the application in a more abstract way. The fact that the computed model and the expert models are overall very similar to each other suggests that our proposed method is able to create a segmentation that contains cases that are able to accurately describe the real user behavior.

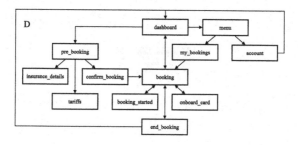

Fig. 8. DFG created by one of the process experts as part of Q1.

Q2: Given this process model that is based on interactions ending on the booking screen, what are your observations?

Given the process model shown in Fig. 9, the participants were surprised by the fact that the map-based dashboard type is used significantly more frequently than the basic dashboard is surprising to them. Additionally, two of the experts were surprised by the number of users that are accessing their bookings through the list of all bookings (my_bookings). This latter observation was also made during the analysis of the segmented log and is the reason that this process model was presented to the experts. In general, a user that has created a booking for a vehicle can access this booking directly from all of the different types of dashboards. The fact that a large fraction of the users take a detour through the menu and booking list in order to reach the booking screen is therefore surprising. This circumstance was actually already identified by one of the mobile developers some time before this evaluation, while they were manually analyzing the raw interaction recordings data. They noticed this behavior because they repeatedly encountered the underlying pattern while working with the data for other unrelated reasons. Using the segmented user interaction log, the behavior was however much more discoverable and supported by concrete data rather than just a vague feeling. Another observation that was not made by the participants is that the path through the booking list is more frequently taken by users that originate from the map-based dashboard rather than the basic dashboard. The UX expert suspected that this may have been the case, because the card that can be used to access a booking from the dashboard is significantly smaller on the map-based dashboard and may therefore be missed more frequently by the users. This is a concrete actionable finding of the analysis that was only made possible by the use of process mining techniques in conjunction with the proposed method.

Q3: What is the median time a user takes to book a vehicle?

The correct answer to this question is 66 s. This was calculated based on the median time of all cases in which a vehicle booking was confirmed. Three participants gave the answers 420 s, 120 s and 120 s. The fourth participants argued that this time may depend on the type of dashboard that the user is using and answered 300 s for the basic dashboard and 120 s for the map-based dashboard. When asked to

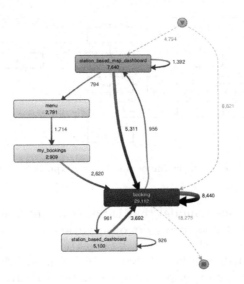

Fig. 9. A process model created using Disco, with the `booking` screen as endpoint of the process.

settle on only one time, the participant gave an answer of 180 s. Overall this means that the experts estimated a median duration for this task of 3 min and 30 s. This again is a significant overestimation compared to the value that was obtained by analyzing the real user behavior. Again, a mismatch between the perception of the experts and the real behavior of the users was revealed.

Q4: Given this process model that is based on interactions ending on the `confirm booking` screen (Fig. 10), what are your observations?
Several of the experts observed that the screens that show details about the vehicles and the service, such as `tariffs`, `insurance_details` and `car_features`, are seemingly used much less frequently than expected. In only about 2–10% of cases, the user visits these screens before booking a vehicle. When considering the concrete numbers, the `availability_calendar` screen (which is used to choose a timeframe for the booking) and the `tariffs` screen (which displays pricing information) are used most frequently before a booking confirmation. This suggests that time and pricing information are significantly more important to the users than information about the vehicle or about the included insurance. These findings sparked a detailed discussion between the experts about the possible reasons for the observed behavior. Nonetheless, this shows that models obtained from segmented user interaction logs are an important tool for the analysis of user behavior and that these models provide a valuable foundation for a more detailed analysis by the process experts. Another observation regarding this model was, that a majority of the users seem to choose a vehicle directly from the dashboard cards present on the app rather than using the search functionality. This suggests that the users are more interested in the vehicle itself, rather than looking for any available vehicle at a certain point in time.

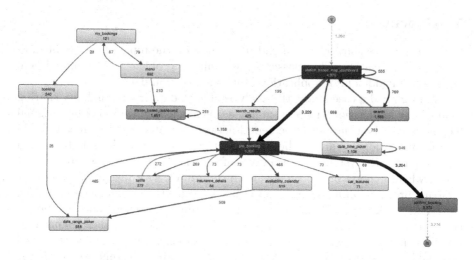

Fig. 10. A process model based on cases that begin in any dashboard and end on the confirm_booking screen.

Q5: Discuss the fact that 2% of users activate the intermediate lock before ending the booking

The smartphone application offers the functionality to lock certain kinds of vehicles during an active booking. This is for example possible for bicycles, which can be locked by the users during the booking whenever they are leaving the bicycle alone. To do so, the intermediate_lock and intermediate_action screens are used. During the analysis, it was found that 2% of users use this functionality in order to lock the vehicle directly before ending the booking. This is noteworthy, as it is not necessary to manually lock the vehicle before returning it. All vehicles are automatically locked by the system at the end of each booking. One expert argued that this may introduce additional technical difficulties during the vehicle return, because the system will try to lock the vehicle again. These redundant lock operations, discovered analyzing the segmented log, may introduce errors in the return process.

Q6: Discuss the fact that only 5% of users visit damages and cleanliness

The application allows users to report damages to the vehicles and rate their cleanliness, through the homonymous pages. It was possible to observe that only a small percentage of the users seem to follow this routine, which was surprising to the experts. For the vehicle providers it is generally important that the users are reporting problems with the vehicles; optimally, every user should do this for all of their bookings. According to the data, this is however not the case, as only a small percentage of the users are actually using both of the functionalities. The experts, therefore, concluded that a better communication of these functionalities is required.

5 Conclusion

In this paper, we showed a case and user study on the topic of the problem of event-case correlation. This classic process mining problem was presented here in the specific domain of application of user interaction data.

We examined a case study, the analysis of click data from a mobility sharing smartphone application. To perform log segmentation, we proposed an original technique based on the word2vec neural network architecture, which can obtain case identification for an unlabeled user interaction log on the sole basis of a link graph of the system as normative information. We then presented a user study, where experts of the process were confronted with insights obtained by applying process mining techniques to the log segmented using our method. The interviews with experts confirm that our technique helped to uncover hidden characteristics of the process, including inefficiencies and anomalies unknown to the domain knowledge of the business owners. Importantly, the analyses yielded actionable suggestions for UI/UX improvements. This substantiates both the scientific value of event-log correlation techniques for user interaction data, and the validity of the segmentation method presented in this paper.

Many avenues for future work are possible. The most prominent one is the need to further validate our technique by lifting it from the scope of a user study by means of a quantitative evaluation, to complement the qualitative one showed in this paper. Our segmentation technique has several points of improvement, including the relatively high number of hyperparameters: thus, it would benefit from a heuristic procedure to determine the (starting) value for such hyperparameters. Lastly, it is important to consider additional event data perspectives: one possibility, in this regard, is to add the data perspective to the technique, by encoding additional attributes to train the neural network model.

References

1. van der Aalst, W.M.P., Rubin, V.A., Verbeek, H.M.W., van Dongen, B.F., Kindler, E., Günther, C.W.: Process mining: a two-step approach to balance between underfitting and overfitting. Softw. Syst. Model. **9**(1), 87–111 (2010)
2. Bayomie, D., Awad, A., Ezat, E.: Correlating unlabeled events from cyclic business processes execution. In: Nurcan, S., Soffer, P., Bajec, M., Eder, J. (eds.) CAiSE 2016. LNCS, vol. 9694, pp. 274–289. Springer, Cham (2016). https://doi.org/10.1007/978-3-319-39696-5_17
3. Bayomie, D., Di Ciccio, C., La Rosa, M., Mendling, J.: A probabilistic approach to event-case correlation for process mining. In: Laender, A.H.F., Pernici, B., Lim, E.-P., de Oliveira, J.P.M. (eds.) ER 2019. LNCS, vol. 11788, pp. 136–152. Springer, Cham (2019). https://doi.org/10.1007/978-3-030-33223-5_12
4. Burattin, A., Kaiser, M., Neurauter, M., Weber, B.: Learning process modeling phases from modeling interactions and eye tracking data. Data Knowl. Eng. **121**, 1–17 (2019)
5. Ferreira, D.R., Gillblad, D.: Discovering process models from unlabelled event logs. In: Dayal, U., Eder, J., Koehler, J., Reijers, H.A. (eds.) BPM 2009. LNCS, vol. 5701, pp. 143–158. Springer, Heidelberg (2009). https://doi.org/10.1007/978-3-642-03848-8_11

6. Janssen, D., Mannhardt, F., Koschmider, A., van Zelst, S.J.: Process model discovery from sensor event data. In: Leemans, S., Leopold, H. (eds.) ICPM 2020. LNBIP, vol. 406, pp. 69–81. Springer, Cham (2021). https://doi.org/10.1007/978-3-030-72693-5_6

7. Jlailaty, D., Grigori, D., Belhajjame, K.: Business process instances discovery from email logs. In: 2017 IEEE International Conference on Services Computing, SCC 2017, June 25–30, 2017, pp. 19–26. IEEE Computer Society (2017)

8. Lakhani, K., Narayan, A.: A neural word embedding approach to system trace reconstruction. In: 2019 IEEE International Conference on Systems, Man and Cybernetics, SMC, October 6–9, 2019, pp. 285–291. IEEE (2019)

9. Leno, V., Augusto, A., Dumas, M., Rosa, M.L., Maggi, F.M., Polyvyanyy, A.: Identifying candidate routines for robotic process automation from unsegmented UI logs. In: 2nd International Conference on Process Mining, ICPM 2020, October 4–9, 2020, pp. 153–160. IEEE (2020)

10. Linn, C., Zimmermann, P., Werth, D.: Desktop activity mining - a new level of detail in mining business processes. In: 48. Jahrestagung der Gesellschaft für Informatik, Architekturen, Prozesse, Sicherheit und Nachhaltigkeit, INFORMATIK 2018 - Workshops, 26–27 September 2018. LNI, vol. P-285, pp. 245–258. GI (2018)

11. Marrella, A., Catarci, T.: Measuring the learnability of interactive systems using a Petri Net based approach. In: Proceedings of the 2018 on Designing Interactive Systems Conference, DIS, 09–13 June 2018, pp. 1309–1319. ACM (2018)

12. Mikolov, T., Sutskever, I., Chen, K., Corrado, G.S., Dean, J.: Distributed representations of words and phrases and their compositionality. In: Advances in Neural Information Processing Systems 26: 27th Annual Conference on Neural Information Processing Systems. Proceedings of a meeting held 5–8 December 2013 (2013)

13. de Murillas, E.G.L., Reijers, H.A., van der Aalst, W.M.P.: Case notion discovery and recommendation: automated event log building on databases. Knowl. Inf. Syst. **62**(7), 2539–2575 (2019). https://doi.org/10.1007/s10115-019-01430-6

14. Pegoraro, M., Bakullari, B., Uysal, M.S., van der Aalst, W.M.P.: Probability estimation of uncertain process trace realizations. In: Munoz-Gama, J., Lu, X. (eds.) Process Mining Workshops - ICPM 2021 International Workshops, 31 October–4 November 2021, Revised Selected Papers. Lecture Notes in Business Information Processing, vol. 433, pp. 21–33. Springer, Cham (2021). https://doi.org/10.1007/978-3-030-98581-3_2

15. Pegoraro, M., Uysal, M.S., van der Aalst, W.M.P.: Conformance checking over uncertain event data. Inf. Syst. **102**, 101810 (2021)

16. Pegoraro, Marco, Uysal, Merih Seran, van der Aalst, W.M.P.: PROVED: a tool for graph representation and analysis of uncertain event data. In: Buchs, Didier, Carmona, Josep (eds.) PETRI NETS 2021. LNCS, vol. 12734, pp. 476–486. Springer, Cham (2021). https://doi.org/10.1007/978-3-030-76983-3_24

17. Pourmirza, S., Dijkman, R.M., Grefen, P.: Correlation miner: mining business process models and event correlations without case identifiers. Int. J. Cooper. Inf. Syst. **26**(2), 1742002:1–1742002:32 (2017)

18. Jimenez-Ramirez, A., Reijers, H.A., Barba, I., Del Valle, C.: A method to improve the early stages of the robotic process automation lifecycle. In: Giorgini, P., Weber, B. (eds.) CAiSE 2019. LNCS, vol. 11483, pp. 446–461. Springer, Cham (2019). https://doi.org/10.1007/978-3-030-21290-2_28

The Integration of Process Simulation Within the Business Architecture

Ben Roelens[1,2]([⊠]) [iD] and Louise Tierens[2]

[1] Open Universiteit, Valkenburgerweg 177, 6419 AT Heerlen, The Netherlands
`ben.roelens@ou.nl`
[2] Ghent University, Tweekerkenstraat 2, 9000 Ghent, Belgium
`ben.roelens@ugent.be`

Abstract. To deal with increased competition and technological change, organizations need to strive for a continuous improvement of their business processes. To realize this, simulation models offer a suitable approach to test different process alternatives. In particular, discrete-event simulation employs stochastic models to support operational decision-making inside the organization. However, this operational focus might cause sub-optimization with respect to higher-level organizational goals. Therefore, an integrative view on the business architecture might align strategic, organizational and process perspectives. This has resulted in the expansion of the Process-Goal Alignment modeling technique with a simulation mechanism. This paper augments the previous research efforts by including simulation results expressed by confidence intervals, such that the results of process simulations can be accurately integrated with the overall business performance. The design of the business architecture simulation technique is guided by the Design Science Research methodology. This paper communicates about both the design and the demonstration of the simulation technique, while the evaluation of this artifact is subject to future research.

Keywords: Discrete-event simulation · Business architecture · Design science research

1 Introduction

Over the years, businesses have been facing intensified competition and an accelerated pace of technological change [1]. To keep a competitive advantage in this dynamic environment, they are continuously looking for ways to improve their business operations. During improvement processes, different alternative process designs need to be explored and the impact of strategic decisions needs to be evaluated with accuracy and speed [2]. However, it is often complicated to adjust business processes in practice as multiple adjustment rounds are needed to fine-tune the operational design and unforeseen circumstances can occur. This brings high risks and costs, which might endanger the business operations.

Simulation is used as a cost effective, accurate and rapid approach to analyze business processes and to evaluate different redesign alternatives by comparing

ⓒ Springer Nature Switzerland AG 2022
A. Augusto et al. (Eds.): BPMDS 2022/EMMSAD 2022, LNBIP 450, pp. 188–202, 2022.
https://doi.org/10.1007/978-3-031-07475-2_13

their performance [2]. In particular, discrete-event simulation (DES) is an analytical approach that is useful to support decision-making activities [3] by making use of stochastic models that consider processes as queues of activities, where state changes occur at discrete points of time [4]. Although this DES application can result in process optimization on an operational level, the impact on the overall business performance is overlooked [5]. Consequently, it is not possible to realize the simultaneous optimization of operational performance and profitability [6]. This causes suboptimization when making business decisions.

To tackle this problem, the PGA (i.e. Process-Goal Alignment) modeling technique [7] offers an integrative representation of the business architecture by combining the strategic, infrastructural and process perspectives. In [8], a PGA simulation technique was developed to support the analysis of possible business process improvements. However, this technique assumes that process simulation results are expressed by a single value. As simulation results expressed by confidence intervals give more accurate information [2], the PGA simulation technique proposed in [8] needs further development such that accurate operational performance results obtained by process simulations can be integrated with the overall business performance (i.e. objective 1). The further development of the simulation technique must also enable to evaluate different process designs at an overall business performance level, such that decision-making within organizations can be improved [3,5] (i.e. objective 2).

To address the solution objectives, the proposed business architecture simulation technique extends the work in [8] by a refinement of the following mechanisms: (i) obtaining process simulation results with a confidence interval that allows to make a univocal statement about the performance, (ii) propagating process simulation results throughout the business architecture hierarchy and (iii) analyzing the impact of operational changes on the realization of the organizational goals.

The proposed business architecture simulation technique is developed according to the Design Science Research (DSR) methodology. Besides the background literature in Sect. 2, this paper presents work-in-progress that includes the following DSR activities [9]: problem identification and motivation (Sect. 1), definition of the objectives for a solution (Sect. 1), design and development of the business architecture simulation model (Sect. 3) and the demonstration by means of an illustrative case example of a company operating in the industry of beauty products (Sect. 3). The evaluation of the artifact is not yet performed and is subject to future research. In this respect, Sect. 4 discusses what is needed to evaluate the functionality and effectiveness of the proposed artifact, such that further improvement opportunities can be detected [10].

2 Background

2.1 Related Work

Related research has attempted to link process simulation with goal modeling approaches. In [11], the i* modeling language is extended to represent the dynamic interactions between goals and dependencies, which establishes a link with the action language ConGolog and allows for process simulation. A similar idea is adopted in [12], which proposes a methodology to map an i* Strategic Rationale diagram to ConGolog by process specification annotations. Kushnareva et al. [13] introduce an approach to design a process from intentions to executable scenarios. This approach makes use of the MAP formalism to capture the intentions behind a crisis management process, while statecharts are employed at the operational level. This allows to analyze how process goals can be achieved by various scenarios. In [14], an approach is presented that employs the User Requirements Notation to model goals and processes and to build Key Performance Indicator models. This is combined with a Business Intelligence tool to monitor and measure business processes, with the aim of an iterative improvement of the business goals and processes.

The presented business architecture simulation technique adopts a different perspective as it considers the infrastructure perspective as the key intermediate layer to align the organizational goals and processes [15]. This is important, as it considers the business architecture as a multi-perspective blueprint of the enterprise that provides a common understanding of the formulation of the organizational objectives (i.e. the strategy perspective), the implementation of the strategy (i.e. the infrastructure perspective) and operational process decisions (i.e. the process perspective) [16].

The work in [17] executes attack simulations based on system architecture models. This is realized by the integration of the Meta Attack Language with an approach to visually model security domains in ArchiMate. Although this approach specifically focuses on cybersecurity, it shows the benefit of integrating simulation results with a multi-perspective view on the problem domain.

2.2 PGA Modeling Technique

The PGA technique [7] is an enterprise modeling language that aims at realizing strategic fit by providing a coherent view on the business architecture. Strategic fit means the alignment of the company's strategy with the organizational activities or processes [18]. Within the business architecture, the infrastructure perspective covers the implementation of the enterprise strategy and therefore acts as an intermediate layer to align the strategy and process perspective of an organization [15]. Hence, the PGA modeling technique consists of the different elements that are part of the strategy, infrastructure or operational perspectives. The strategy perspective contains the organizational goals that describe the vision and strategy of the company. The infrastructure perspective represents strategy implementation, that describes which processes a company needs to perform and what is needed (i.e. capabilities and resources) to create and deliver value. The organizational processes and activities that create or deliver this value are embedded in the operational perspective. To ensure strategic fit between the different business architecture elements, the PGA modeling technique combines the following features: (i) alignment is realized by a modeling language including the different perspectives in the business architecture, (ii) a performance measurement mechanism that serves as a guideline for organizational operations to support the intended strategic business objectives and (iii) a heat mapping visualization that it is comprehensible for different types of business stakeholders. More specifically, a color code (i.e. red, orange or green) is used to express the performance and importance of different business architecture elements. For more background information, we refer the reader to [7].

2.3   PGA Simulation Technique

The PGA simulation technique [8] combines the PGA modeling technique with a simulation mechanism to assess the impact of process simulation results on the overall business performance. This is realized in four steps: (i) building a business architecture hierarchy by means of the PGA modeling technique, (ii) simulating the operational performance measures, (iii) propagating the simulated performance throughout the business architecture hierarchy and (iv) performing a strategic fit improvement analysis to assess whether the simulated process change sustains a better realization of the organizational goals. The previously developed simulation technique only considered a single mean as simulation result. However, when considering simulation results, it is important to assess the reliability of that estimate. Compared to a single mean, confidence intervals give a better idea on the true performance measure value as they capture both the sample mean and variance of a simulation result.

3   Business Architecture Simulation Technique

The procedure of the simulation technique contains four steps: building a business architecture hierarchy (Sect. 3.1), performing a process simulation that generates simulation performance results in the form of a confidence interval (Sect. 3.2), the propagation of the confidence interval for the performance measure throughout the business architecture hierarchy (Sect. 3.3), analyzing if the simulation of a process alternative provides the expected improvements (Sect. 3.4). In the description, PGA meta-model elements are capitalized and model content of the running example is indicated by single quotation marks.

3.1   Building a Business Architecture Hierarchy

Design. When representing the business architecture by making use of the PGA modeling technique, there is a clear and coherent view on how different processes and activities are related to other elements in the business architecture. Roelens and Poels [8] highlight that a particular constraint is needed in the context of simulation. As the simulation technique aims to evaluate the impact of operational changes upon the overall business performance, it is important that the operational elements are also explicitly included in the business architecture. Therefore, one needs to make sure that each chain of valueStream relations in the PGA business architecture ends at least at a Process or Activity element.

An improvement analysis can reveal where operational enhancements are possible within the business architecture. In case of unachieved business objectives, this allows to determine where the cause of the problem is situated. This is done by the identification of a critical path, which is a chain of valueStream relations that mostly have a high or medium importance and that connect business architecture elements on different hierarchical levels of which the performance can be improved [7]. For problematic operational elements, different alternative designs can be evaluated by applying the remaining steps of the business architecture simulation technique.

Demonstration. The company operates in the industry of beauty products and adopts a vertically integrated value chain as it manufactures products as well as sells them in the company's own stores. Currently, the company is looking for ways to increase both profit and customer satisfaction as competition is entering the market. Figure 1 visualizes the business architecture of the company.

Starting from the two goals, 'increase customer satisfaction' represents a Customer Goal and 'increase profit' is a Financial Goal set by the company. To support the Financial Goal, a Financial Structure layer is added, structuring the costs and the revenues by making use of the components 'increase sales volume' and 'decrease costs' in the business architecture.

Next, the Value Proposition layer contains the different products and services that are offered by the company. Firstly, the company offers 'quality beauty products at a competitive price'. By offering these high-quality products, both an 'increase in sales volume' and 'customer satisfaction' can be realized. Additionally, the efficiency within the company's production to offer 'quality products at a competitive price' supports the 'decrease of costs'. The company also sells 'additional innovative products' that are not manufactured in-house, but are purchased from various start-up businesses. As the company's industry is sensitive to trends and innovation of products, 'offering additional innovative products' will 'increase the sales volume' and the 'customer satisfaction'. Besides its highly qualitative and innovative products, the company also 'offers services to the products', such as workshops and classes on how to use the products and on how to keep up with the latest beauty trends. By 'offering extra services', 'sales volume' and 'customer satisfaction' will be increased as hosting workshops on product usage and trends supports the company's image of high quality and innovation. Also, 'additional services offered' will guarantee more direct contact with the customers. This will result in a decrease of the number of complaints that needs to be handled by the customer service department and thus will have a positive impact on the 'decrease of costs'.

The Competences of the company represent the strengths of the company that are needed to offer its products and services. One of the three Competences of the company under study is the practice of 'high quality and effective operations'. This is an important Competence that addresses the in-house production department of the company and ensures that 'quality products can be offered at a competitive price'. This Competence is supported by three Processes, the 'purchasing process', the 'production process' and the 'distribution process', that consequently make up the lowest level in the business architecture. Another Competence of the business is the offering of 'exceptional customer service' to its customers, which focuses more on the end of the value chain and is supported by the 'sales process', 'complaint handling' and 'customer training programs'. 'Exceptional customer service' is important to all the components in the Value Proposition layer. It is clear that customer service is crucial when 'offering services to the products', but also to guarantee total product quality. A third Competence is the involvement of the company in 'innovative partnerships'. Without the partnering with innovative start-ups, it is not possible for the company to 'offer additional innovative products' that are

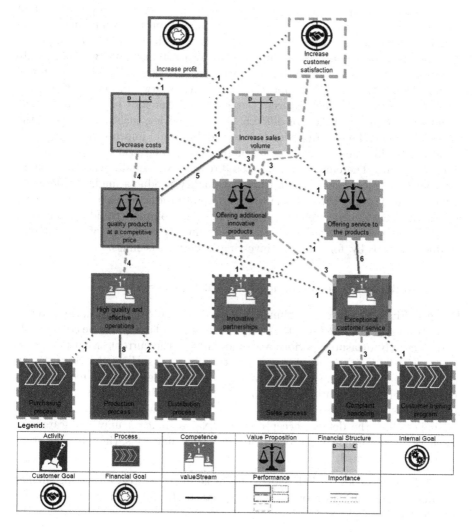

Fig. 1. Business architecture heat map of the current company situation.

not made in-house. Moreover, some of the workshops hosted are focusing on those innovative products and consequently also require the support of the partners.

As can be seen in Fig. 1, the performance of the company's Financial Goal, 'increase profit', is 'bad' and calls for improvement. The performance of the Customer Goal, 'increase customer satisfaction', on the other hand is 'as expected'. However, as the company is experiencing increased competition they would like to further improve this goal by increasing the satisfaction and perception of their customers. When following the critical path starting from the Financial Goal, it is clear that improvements are needed within the 'production process'. To improve the Customer Goal, the critical path indicates the need for improvements in the 'sales process'. In this case example, alternative 'production' and 'sales process' designs are simulated and their impact on the overall business performance is evaluated. Regarding the 'sales process', the company has employed two warehouse pickers and stores are able to reorder items every two weeks, only on Fridays. After analyzing the current situation, it seemed that often too many restock orders arrive at the same time and that the two pickers in the warehouse are not able to timely process these orders. Therefore, alternative designs with more warehouse pickers or different reorder policies, such that orders of the stores to the warehouse are divided more equally, could improve the company's situation. Within the current 'production process', it seems that the product lead time is too long. Therefore, it was proposed to add extra quality checks throughout the production line. In that way, bad quality products might be detected earlier, without going through the whole chain of production steps before being filtered and sent back for remake. Additionally, the company could also improve the performance (i.e. lower the percentage of quality violation) of the different production steps by, for example, investing in better machines.

3.2   Simulate the Performance Level of Process Elements

Design. First, processes are simulated based on the current situation. When accurate simulations are used, the results of these simulations will be comparable to the actually measured performance measures of the current situation. These process simulations require different key components, such as the control-flow, simulation environment, activity durations, decision rules, resource requirements and probability distributions. Thereafter, alternative designs of these processes are evaluated. It is important that the simulated performance confidence interval is smaller than the defined acceptance interval to make a univocal statement about the performance of a process element. To achieve this, the following steps need to be performed:

Step 1. Define the desired half width h of the confidence interval as being smaller or equal to the half width of the 'as expected' performance interval, which can be calculated as follows:

$$h \leqslant PerformanceGoal \cdot AllowedDeviation\%. \tag{1}$$

Step 2. Run the model for a small number of replications n_0 and determine the confidence interval. Depending on the size of the model and the time it takes to execute it, the number of replications might be 5, 10 or 15 [19].

Step 3. If the half width of the confidence interval based on the n_0 replications is smaller than h, one can stop the procedure. In this case, the generated confidence interval is smaller than the acceptance interval and a performance statement can be made. Proceed with the propagation of the performance measures (see Sect. 3.3).

   If the half width based on the preliminary run is bigger than h, the confidence interval will be too big to make a univocal statement about the performance level. In this case, proceed to step 4.

Step 4. One needs to calculate the minimum number of replications needed to obtain a half width smaller than the 'as expected' performance half width as in (2). In this equation, $S(n_0)$ is the variance computed based on the simulation with n_0 replications and z is the statistical z-score associated with the confidence interval.

$$n = \lceil (\frac{zS(n_0)}{h})^2 \rceil. \tag{2}$$

Step 5. Rerun the process simulation with n subruns and determine the confidence interval for the performance measure.

Demonstration. In the case example, the 'sales' and the 'production process' of the company must be simulated. Given the page limit, the description is restricted to the simulation results of the 'production process', which was implemented in CPN tools [20][1]

   The 'production process' is oriented towards how the company's high-quality products are manufactured. In this case example, the 'production process' is represented by one production line, which exists of multiple production steps and produces exactly 500 products with an approved quality. The performance of the 'production process' is expressed by the product lead time. The product lead time is calculated based on the time (in s) that it takes to collect production materials and the duration of the different production steps. Independent subruns are generated by performing five replications, which each contain 500 observations. As the subruns are independent and identically distributed, it allows to calculate a sample mean $= 82.757s$, variance $= 2.757s^2$ and 95% confidence interval $=$ [79.303s, 86.149s] for the simulation.

Step 1. Based on formula (1), a desired half width h of the confidence interval for the product lead time can be determined based on a performance goal of 65s and an allowed deviation of 2%.

$$h = 65s \cdot 2\% = 1.3s. \tag{3}$$

---

[1] The basic CPN models can be found via https://doi.org/10.13140/RG.2.2.30599.68006.

Step 2. The 95% confidence interval based on the simulation with $n_0 = 5$ replications is [79.303s, 86.149s] with half width:

$$\frac{86.149s - 79.303s}{2} = 3.423s. \tag{4}$$

Step 3. The half width of the 95% confidence interval based on five simulation runs 3.423s is larger than 1.3s, so additional simulation runs are needed to obtain meaningful results.

Step 4. The minimum number of simulation replications is calculated as

$$n = \lceil (\frac{2.776 \cdot 2.757}{1.3})^2 \rceil = 35 \tag{5}$$

Step 5. After rerunning 35 replications of the simulation, the 95% confidence interval for the product lead time is [81.361s, 82.931s]. Now, the half width of the 95% confidence interval (i.e. 0.785s) is smaller than h (i.e. 1.3s) and a univocal statement about the performance level is possible.

3.3 Propagation of Performance Measures

Design. In the third step, the simulated performance is propagated throughout the business architecture hierarchy to assess the impact on the performance of the overall business objectives. This step consists of three substeps [8]: (i) rescaling the performance, (ii) aggregating the rescaled performance to higher levels in the business architecture hierarchy and (iii) adapting the border color of the business architecture elements based on the resulting performance levels.

Rescaling the Performance. It is first needed to rescale the simulated performance levels such that they can be interpreted independently of specific measurement details (i.e. measure type, performance goal and allowed deviation %). The formulas proposed in [8] need to be adjusted as the technique considers confidence intervals for the simulated performance. Four rescaled indicators are needed: upper performance upper acceptance level (UPUAL), lower performance upper acceptance level (LPUAL), upper performance lower acceptance level (UPLAL), lower performance lower acceptance level (LPLAL).

When considering a positive performance measure, formulas (6)–(9) are relevant:

$$UPUAL_p = \frac{UpperBoundConfidenceInterval}{PerformanceGoal \cdot (1 + AllowedDeviation\%)} \tag{6}$$

$$LPUAL_p = \frac{LowerBoundConfidenceInterval}{PerformanceGoal \cdot (1 + AllowedDeviation\%)} \tag{7}$$

$$UPLAL_p = \frac{UpperBoundConfidenceInterval}{PerformanceGoal \cdot (1 - AllowedDeviation\%)} \tag{8}$$

$$LPLAL_p = \frac{LowerBoundConfidenceInterval}{PerformanceGoal \cdot (1 - AllowedDeviation\%)} \tag{9}$$

To cope with negative performance measures, formulas (10)–(13) are needed:

$$UPUAL_n = \frac{PerformanceGoal \cdot (1 - AllowedDeviation\%)}{LowerBoundConfidenceInterval} \tag{10}$$

$$LPUAL_n = \frac{PerformanceGoal \cdot (1 - AllowedDeviation\%)}{UpperBoundConfidenceInterval} \tag{11}$$

$$UPLAL_n = \frac{PerformanceGoal \cdot (1 + AllowedDeviation\%)}{LowerBoundConfidenceInterval} \tag{12}$$

$$LPLAL_n = \frac{PerformanceGoal \cdot (1 + AllowedDeviation\%)}{UpperBoundConfidenceInterval} \tag{13}$$

Based on the values of the rescaled indicators, the performance level of an element can be determined. Based on the above formulas, the upper performance score is mathematically higher than the lower performance (i.e. $UPUAL \geqslant LPUAL$ and $UPLAL \geqslant LPLAL$) and the lower acceptance score is higher than the upper acceptance (i.e. $UPLAL \geqslant UPUAL$ and $LPLAL \geqslant LPUAL$). Consequently, five performance levels can be distinguished (i.e. 'excellent', 'positive ambiguous', 'as expected', 'negative ambiguous' or 'bad'). Table 1 indicates how to interpret the rescaled performance values.

Table 1. Performance level based on the rescaled indicators.

UPUAL	LPUAL	UPLAL	LPLAL	Performance level	Visualization
$\geqslant 1$	$\geqslant 1$	$\geqslant 1$	$\geqslant 1$	Excellent	
$\geqslant 1$	<1	$\geqslant 1$	$\geqslant 1$	Positive ambiguous	
<1	<1	$\geqslant 1$	$\geqslant 1$	As expected	
<1	<1	$\geqslant 1$	<1	Negative ambiguous	
<1	<1	<1	<1	Bad	

Aggregation to Higher-Level Business Architecture Elements. The rescaled indicators are used to aggregate the performance of lower-level elements to the appropriate higher-level element. For each of the rescaled indicators, the aggregation value must be calculated. Afterwards, the analysis of Table 1 can be used to determine the performance level of the higher-level element.

When a clear mathematical relation exist between the performance measures of the lower- and higher-level elements in the business architecture, business formulas (e.g. financial ratios) can be used to calculate the aggregated performance.

If there is no mathematical relation between the performance measures of two related elements in the business architecture, the Analytic Hierarchy Process (AHP) [21] can be used. As can be seen in Fig. 1, each valueStream relation between two hierarchical elements in the business architecture is characterized by an importance value (i.e. indicated by a number and corresponding color). These values express how important each lower-level element is to support the value of the higher-level element in the hierarchy. To calculate the rescaled performance of higher-level elements, the weighted average of the rescaled lower-level performances can be calculated by incorporating the appropriate importance values as weights.

As the goal is to obtain the impact on the overall business goals, this aggregation will be repeated in the business architecture until the simulated performance is propagated to all higher levels in the hierarchy.

Adapt Border Color in Business Architecture. After propagating the operational simulation results throughout the business architecture, each element will be characterized by a simulated performance level. Based on the results, the visualization of the element border can be adapted (see Table 1). As we define two new performance levels, the original PGA color-coding is extended.

Demonstration: Production Process

Rescaling the Performance. The product lead time is a negative performance measure, such that the simulated performance of the product lead time [81.361s, 82.931s] can be rescaled as follows:

$$UPUAL_{production} = \frac{65s \cdot (1 - 2\%)}{81.361s} = 0.783 \tag{14}$$

$$LPUAL_{production} = \frac{65s \cdot (1 - 2\%)}{82.931s} = 0.768 \tag{15}$$

$$UPLAL_{production} = \frac{65s \cdot (1 + 2\%)}{81.361s} = 0.815 \tag{16}$$

$$LPLAL_{production} = \frac{65s \cdot (1 + 2\%)}{82.931s} = 0.799 \tag{17}$$

Based on the values in (14)–(17), the performance level of the 'production process' can be determined. As all the values are smaller than one, it can be concluded that the performance level is 'bad'.

Aggregation to Higher-Level Business Architecture Elements. In the case example, the AHP mechanism is applied to aggregate the performance to the higher-level elements in the company's business architecture. As an example, the UPUAL of the Competence 'high quality and effective operations' is calculated as the following weighted average, see (18):

$$\frac{1 \cdot UPUAL_{purchasing} + 8 \cdot UPUAL_{production} + 2 \cdot UPUAL_{distribution}}{1 + 8 + 2} = 0.816 \tag{18}$$

The remaining rescaled performance values for 'high quality and effective operations' are: LPUAL = 0.805, UPLAL = 0.879 and LPLAL = 0.868. Based on these values, it can be concluded that the performance level is 'bad'.

Adapt Border Color in Business Architecture. Based on the performance levels, the visualization of the border of 'production process' and 'high quality and effective operations' can be adapted accordingly. Figure 1 shows the current heat map of the company after the simulated performance is aggregated through the complete business architecture.

3.4   Improvement Analysis

Design. This step is oriented towards the analysis of the impact of the operational changes on the different business architecture elements. Based on the visualized performance levels, it can be determined whether an operational change leads to a better realization of the organizational objectives and which of the improving designs are most preferable for the company to implement. For this purpose, the simulated performance of each design combination is studied, while taking into account the investment in time and costs, as indicated by the number of required changes.

Demonstration. To improve the current situation, the company identified two possible alternative designs for each process. Table 2 shows the different combinations of the alternative production and 'sales process' designs with their simulated impact on the goals of the business. The last column indicates how many operational changes are made compared to the processes in the current business situation (i.e. scenario #0).

Scenario #0 represents the current situation, in which the 'production process' contains only one quality check (i.e. 1QC) and the replenishment of stores in the 'sales process' occurs biweekly on Fridays by two warehouse pickers (i.e. 2P, 2W, Fri). A first alternative design for the 'sales process' is to adjust the current reorder policy of the company's stores (i.e. biweekly on Fridays) to weekly and to keep the current number of warehouse pickers (i.e. two pickers) intact (i.e. 2P, 1W). A second, more drastic and therefore costly adjustment to the 'sales process' is to both change the number of pickers to three and the reorder policy to a weekly reorder (i.e. 3P, 1W). For the 'production process', a first possible alternative design for the company is to introduce three quality checks into the production line instead of only one (i.e. 3 QC). When this alternative design does not suffice, additionally quality improvement can be made to the first, fifth and sixth production step (i.e. 3 QC + QI). The underlying reason is that the time between these production steps and the subsequent quality check is longer compared to other production steps, which implies that it takes longer to detect products with a bad quality.

The results in Table 2 show that design combinations #3 and #6 do not have a positive impact on the performance of the business goals and are therefore not worth pursuing. As design combinations #1, #2, #4, #5 and #7 all have the same impact on the business performance (i.e. both goals are 'as expected'),

Table 2. Impact of different operational changes upon the business goals.

#	Process design: Sales	Process design: Production	Goal performance: Increase profit	Goal performance: Increase customer satisfaction	# changes required
0	2P, 2W, Fri	1QC	Bad	As expected	0
1	2P, 2W, Fri	3QC	As expected	As expected	1
2	2P, 2W, Fri	3QC+Q1	As expected	As expected	2
3	2P, 1W	1QC	Bad	As expected	1
4	2P, 1W	3QC	As expected	As expected	2
5	2P, 1W	3QC+Q1	As expected	As expected	3
6	3P, 1W	1QC	Bad	As expected	2
7	3P, 1W	3QC	As expected	As expected	3
8	3P, 1W	3QC+Q1	As expected	Excellent	4

design combination #1 is preferred because it requires the least operational changes. Finally, design combination #8 improves both business goals compared to the current situation, but has a high implementation cost with four operational changes. It is advisable for the company to gradually make improvements in its business. In the short term, the company should implement three quality checks in the 'production process' to improve short-term profit (i.e. design #1). In the long term, when more resources and time are available, additional quality improvements need to be made to the 'production process' and also the 'sales process' needs to be revised (i.e. design #8), such that customer satisfaction further increases.

4   Conclusion

This paper presents and demonstrates the design of a business architecture simulation technique that allows to evaluate the impact of alternative process designs on the overall business performance. The simulation technique is based on an integrative business view and therefore provides a solution to the problem of suboptimization of existing process simulation techniques. More specifically, the business architecture can be defined by using the PGA technique, which visualizes the different business architecture elements and their valueStream relations. The proposed technique defines how to integrate the output of process simulations with other elements in the business architecture. The design extends the work in [8] to express simulated operational performance by means of a confidence interval. This enables a more accurate analysis of the impact of process performance on the overall business performance.

Several mechanisms are extended to realize this. First, the performance of different strategic decisions needs to be determined by performing process simulations. To obtain accurate and meaningful information on the performance of processes, the results are expressed by performance confidence intervals, which are based on multiple observations of multiple simulation runs. Next, the simulated processes need to be embedded into the overall business architecture. Based on the rescaled performance indicators (i.e. UPUAL, LPUAL, UPLAL and LPLAL), that can be propagated them to higher-level elements in the business architecture (i.e. by business formulas or the AHP mechanism), the elements can be labeled with a performance level (i.e. 'bad', 'negative ambiguous', 'as expected', 'positive ambiguous' or 'excellent') and an according visualization. Finally, the overall impact of alternative process designs can be analyzed, which offers a tool for organizational decision-making.

Important for future research is to evaluate the functionality and relevance of the proposed simulation technique by applying it in a real-life case study. This offers the possibility to evaluate the effectiveness and accuracy of the model as results can be compared to reality. More specifically, it is interesting to check for the accuracy of the performance measure aggregation mechanism, by comparing the performance results obtained by aggregation with the real performances measured in the business architecture. Also, a real-life case study allows to set up more complex simulation models. This is particularly useful to analyze the scalability of the new mechanisms, such as the feasibility of specifying the confidence interval width upfront. Additionally, an opportunity for future research is to automate the calculations for the rescaled performance indicators and the propagation through the business architecture. Therefore, it would be interesting to extend the existing PGA tool support[2] with the concept of confidence intervals and to include the propagation mechanism. Finally, it is worth examining how an automated link could be provided between the results of process simulation tools and the PGA tool, such that simulated process performances can be automatically introduced into the PGA business architecture.

References

1. Veit, D., et al.: Business models. Bus. Inf. Syst. Eng. **6**(1), 45–53 (2014). https://doi.org/10.1007/s12599-013-0308-y
2. Tumay, K.: Business process simulation. In: Charnes, J.M., Morrice, D.J., Brunner, D.T., Swain, J.J. (eds.) Proceedings Winter Simulation Conference, pp. 93–98. IEEE (1996). https://doi.org/10.1109/WSC.1996.873265
3. Tako, A., Robinson, S.: The application of discrete event simulation and system dynamics in the logistics and supply chain context. Decis. Support Syst. **52**(4), 802–815 (2012). https://doi.org/10.1016/j.dss.2011.11.015
4. Brailsford, S., Hilton, N.: A Comparison of Discrete Event Simulation and System Dynamics for Modelling Health Care Systems (2001)
5. Laurier, W., Poels, G.: Invariant conditions in value system simulation models. Decis. Support Syst. **56**, 275–287 (2013). https://doi.org/10.1016/j.dss.2013.06.009
6. Bassett, M., Gardner, L.: Optimizing the design of global supply chains at dow AgroSciences. Comput. Chem. Eng. **34**(2), 254–265 (2010). https://doi.org/10.1016/j.compchemeng.2009.08.002

---

[2] PGA tool support [online], https://austria.omilab.org/psm/content/PGA/info, last visited: 18 Apr 2022.

7. Roelens, B., Steenacker, W., Poels, G.: Realizing strategic fit within the business architecture: the design of a Process-Goal Alignment modeling and analysis technique. Softw. Syst. Model. **18**(1), 631–662 (2017). https://doi.org/10.1007/s10270-016-0574-5

8. Roelens, B., Poels, G.: The design of a modeling technique to analyze the impact of process simulation throughout the business architecture. In: Pergl, R., Lock, R., Babkin, E., Molhanec, M. (eds.) EOMAS 2017. LNBIP, vol. 298, pp. 37–52. Springer, Cham (2017). https://doi.org/10.1007/978-3-319-68185-6_3

9. Peffers, K., Tuunanen, T., Rothenberger, M., Chatterjee, S.: A design science research methodology for information systems research. J. Manag. Inf. Syst. **24**(3), 45–77 (2007). https://doi.org/10.2753/MIS0742-1222240302

10. Hevner, A.R., March, S.T., Park, J., Ram, S.: Design science in information systems research. MIS Q. **28**(1), 75–105 (2004). https://doi.org/10.2307/25148625

11. Gans, G., Jarke, M., Lakemeyer, G., Schmitz, D.: Deliberation in a metadata-based modeling and simulation environment for inter-organizational networks. Inf. Syst. **30**(7), 587–607 (2005). https://doi.org/10.1016/j.is.2004.11.006

12. Wang, X., Lespérance, Y.: Agent-oriented requirements engineering using ConGolog and i*. In: Wagner, G., Karlapalem, K., Lespérance, Y., Yu, E. (eds.) Agent-Oriented Information Systems Workshop (AOIS 2001), pp. 59–78. iCue Publishing, Berlin (2001)

13. Kushnareva, E., Rychkova, I., Deneckére, R., Grand, B.L.: Modeling crisis management process from goals to scenarios. In: Reichert, M., Reijers, H.A. (eds.) BPM 2015. LNBIP, vol. 256, pp. 55–64. Springer, Cham (2016). https://doi.org/10.1007/978-3-319-42887-1_5

14. Chen, P.: Goal-oriented Business Process Monitoring - an Approach Based on User Requirement Notation Combined with Business Intelligence and Web Services. Carleton University, Ottawa, Canada (2007)

15. Maes, R.: A Generic Framework for Information Management. PrimaVera Working Paper 99-02 (1999)

16. Object Management Group: Business Architecture Body of Knowledge Handbook 2.0. (2012)

17. Hacks, S., Hacks, A., Katsikeas, S., Klaer, B., Lagerström R.: Creating meta attack language instances using ArchiMate: applied to electric power and energy system cases. In: IEEE 23rd International Enterprise Distributed Object Computing Conference (EDOC 2019), pp. 88–97 (2019). https://doi.org/10.1109/EDOC.2019.00020

18. Henderson, J.C., Venkatraman, N.: Strategic alignment: leveraging information technology for transforming organizations. IBM Syst. J. **32**(1), 4–16 (1993). https://doi.org/10.1147/sj.382.0472

19. Centeno, M. A., Reyes, M. F.: So you have your model: what to do next. A tutorial on simulation output analysis. In: Proceedings of the 1998 Winter Simulation Conference (Cat. No. 98CH36274), Washington, DC, USA, pp. 23–29. IEEE (1998). https://doi.org/10.1109/WSC.1998.744894

20. CPN tools. http://cpntools.org. Accessed 18 Apr 2022

21. Saaty, T.: Decision making with the analytic hierarchy process. Int. J. Serv. Sci. **1**(1), 83–98 (2008). https://doi.org/10.1504/IJSSci.2008.01759

Information Systems and Requirements Modeling (EMMSAD 2022)

Blockchain Application Development Using Model-Driven Engineering and Low-Code Platforms: A Survey

Simon Curty$^{(\boxtimes)}$, Felix Härer , and Hans-Georg Fill

Digitalization and Information Systems Group, University of Fribourg,
Fribourg, CH, Switzerland
{simon.curty,felix.haerer,hans-georg.fill}@unifr.ch
https://www.unifr.ch/inf/digits/

Abstract. The creation of blockchain-based software applications requires today considerable technical knowledge, particularly in software design and programming. This is regarded as a major barrier in adopting this technology in business and making it accessible to a wider audience. As a solution, no-code and low-code approaches have been proposed that require only little or no programming knowledge for creating full-fledged software applications. In this paper we review academic approaches from the discipline of model-driven engineering as well as industrial no-code and low-code development platforms for blockchains. We further present a case study for an integrated no-code blockchain environment for demonstrating the state-of-the-art in this area. Based on the gained insights we derive requirements for the future development of no-code and low-code approaches that are dedicated to the field of blockchains.

Keywords: Blockchain · Low-code · No-code · Model-driven engineering · Software development

1 Introduction

With the further maturing of blockchain technologies and the soon expected transition to more energy-efficient and faster protocols with higher transaction volumes [11,13,24], a more widespread adoption of these technologies seems within reach. However, one considerable barrier limiting the adoption is the technical and organizational complexity that users are confronted with when creating blockchain-based applications [18]. This complexity originates on the one hand from the underlying technical foundations, which build on distributed and decentralized systems, cryptography, and algorithmic processing [2]. Blockchains such as Ethereum combine these properties for storing transactions in an append-only data structure, where each new block has a cryptographically verifiable link to its predecessor. Thus, users are part of a decentralized network that minimizes the degree of trust required towards other participants who continuously validate the links of the blockchain. In addition, organizational barriers such as the

A. Augusto et al. (Eds.): BPMDS 2022/EMMSAD 2022, LNBIP 450, pp. 205–220, 2022.
https://doi.org/10.1007/978-3-031-07475-2_14

involvement of new regulatory requirements, the development of new skills and competencies, and the availability of financial and human resources may prevent adoption in practice [8].

From the perspective of software engineering, the lack of specialists for programming may today be partly compensated with so-called *low-code* platforms [4,12,31]. These development platforms are typically available as cloud services with visual, diagrammatic interfaces and declarative languages. In our view, they constitute the next step in the industry adoption of academic model-driven engineering (MDE) approaches and its predecessors where models are regarded as primary development artifacts for software engineering [5,10,36]. While *low-code* approaches allow a user to produce results without having to understand source code and there may be an underlying model integrated with features of the platform [4], the model may not conform to an explicit formalization [10]. Further, we consider so-called *no-code* approaches as a subset of low-code approaches that operate at an abstraction level above code, not showing code to the user at all. Today, a large number of such platforms and tools are available that either support the development of complete software applications or focus on providing specific functionality, e.g. for entering data in a form and saving it to a database [26].

For easing the creation of blockchain-based applications it seems obvious to revert to MDE and low-code approaches. These carry the potential to abstract from the technical complexity and enable users to focus on usage scenarios and the organizational embedding. In the following we investigate academic and industrial approaches for realizing blockchain applications using these methods. We will do this along the following three research questions. *RQ1:* Which academic MDE approaches exist for the development of blockchain-based applications?, *RQ2:* Which low-code and no-code platforms permit the realization of blockchain-based applications?, *RQ3:* What are requirements for future blockchain development platforms that are informed by MDE, no-code and low-code?

In particular, we will regard approaches that are already available for creating blockchain-based software applications or offer interfaces to other platforms enabling this. This will permit to describe the state-of-the-art in this area and derive requirements for the development of future approaches. The remainder of the paper is structured as follows. Section 2 will outline related work in the form of previous studies and lead over to our research methodology in Sect. 3. Subsequently, we will present in Sect. 4 our review of academic MDE approaches and in Sect. 5 the review of no-code and low-code development platforms used in industry. Section 6 presents a blockchain use case using state-of-the-art low-code platforms, resulting in the discussion of requirements in Sect. 7.

2   Related Studies

Developing blockchain-based applications requires a high level of expertise and understanding of the underlying technologies. Blockchain-based applications are empowered by smart contracts, i.e. programs executed on the blockchain.

These smart contracts often involve financial transactions or deal with issues related to trust. As such, their correctness is of utmost importance. Due to the immutable nature of blockchains, mistakes in smart contract implementations are difficult to rectify. This can be eased through different visual languages for smart contracts, which have been reviewed and compared in [15]. While visual programming languages aim to reduce complexity and improve accessibility for the programmer, they do not correspond in general to low-code development approaches, which may involve visual programming but also deal with the generation and life-cycle management of software artifacts. Approaches and tools for the analysis and development of smart contracts have been reviewed in [19,33]. While both studies discuss issues related to software engineering, such as code analysis and testing, model-driven or low-code techniques to develop blockchain-based software are not regarded.

The study by Ait Hsain et al. [1] focuses on MDE for Ethereum smart contracts, however the review process is not elaborated. Sánchez-Gómez et al. [29] review model-based testing and development approaches. Since the publication of their study, newer approaches have emerged. A more recent review of MDE methods was conducted by Levasseur et al. [21]. In comparison to their work, we applied a broader search methodology and identified more approaches. None of these studies consider industrial approaches such as platforms and focus predominantly on smart contracts.

In summary, while numerous studies on issues regarding smart contract development have been conducted, to the best of our knowledge, a comprehensive review of the state-of-the-art of MDE and low-code/no-code approaches from both academia and industry in this field is missing so far.

3   Research Methodology

For answering the three research questions we will employ the following research methodology. At first we review existing academic MDE approaches for blockchain applications in the form of a structured literature review (SLR). Thereby we follow the guidelines by Webster and Watson [35] and vom Brocke et al. [6]. The initial corpus of the SLR was generated by searching all keyword combinations from two groups, where group one included 'blockchain, distributed ledger, smart contract' and group two 'enterprise model, conceptual model, business model, model-driven, no-code, low-code'. These keywords were selected based on the domain understanding of the authors. We expected the relevant concepts to be dispersed, thus we chose a broad set of keywords.

For discovering relevant industrial approaches, we reverted to expert knowledge from industry in the field of low-code development combined with our own searches. On this bases, we conducted (1) a survey of available platforms towards suitability for blockchain application development and (2) the implementation of a blockchain use case as an evaluation. This exploratory research approach is directed towards discovering requirements for future platforms that combine blockchain application development with the state-of-the-art from academia and industry.

4   Academic MDE Approaches

In the following subsections, we review approaches of the academic discipline
model-driven engineering in regard to development solutions for blockchains.

Model-driven engineering introduces models as primary artifact to the software development process in order to address numerous challenges of software
engineering [5,27]: First, the common understanding of software artifacts can
be facilitated by domain-specific models, as such models are easier to interpret
for humans than code. Second, model-based reasoning allows the verification
of software, e.g., to determine the fulfillment of security properties. And third,
well-defined models allow developers to create software artifacts in an automated
fashion, which are correct-by-construction, with no or reduced coding effort. To
identify existing MDE approaches that target specifically the development of
blockchain applications, we conducted a systematic literature review as elaborated in the following.

4.1   Review Process

The systematic review process as shown in Fig. 1 follows the guidelines by [35]
and [6]. To obtain an initial corpus of publications, we performed keyword
searches in step (S-1) on ACM, Springer, and IEEE Explore with the search
strings shown in Table 1. From the resulting corpus, duplicates were removed in
step (S-2). Due to the large number of documents, we filtered the publications
by outlets in step (S-3) that typically publish papers in software engineering,
model-driven engineering or information systems. Before the full-text analysis,
the reduced corpus was then screened by titles in step (S-4).

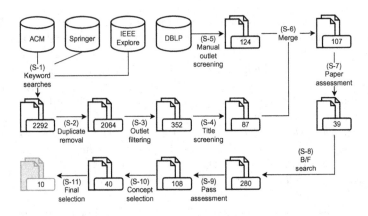

Fig. 1. Academic literature review process

As basis for this fourth step we formulated keyword criteria, whereby the title
should contain one of *"conceptual"*, *"model"*, *"process"*, *"execution"*, *"process"*,

"architecture", *"framework"*, *"design"*, *"development"*, *"pattern"*, *"use case"*, *"supply chain"*, *"database"*, *"storage"*, *"verification"*, *"generation"*, *"language"*, and mention a blockchain-related word, such as *"distributed"*, *"chain"*, *"contract"*. Additionally, we analyzed all titles to capture promising publications. In parallel, we screened in step (S-5) the table of contents of selected outlets in software engineering and related disciplines by applying the same process as in (S-4). That is, we screened all proceedings, workshops, issues, etc., published in one of the following outlets from 2015 to Nov. 2021: *BCCA, BMSD, BPMDS/EMMSAD, BRAINS, COINS, CSIMQ, CVCBT, DAPPCON, DK, EMISA, ER, ICBC, ICBCT, IEEE Blockchain, IEEE ICBC, IJISMD, MoDELS, PoEM* and *SoSyM*. These two sets of publications were then merged and duplicates removed (S-6).

Table 1. Simplified search strings used and results found on ACM, IEEE Explore, and Springer. The concrete syntax of search strings varies for each search portal.

Search string	Results
("blockchain" OR "distributed ledger" OR "smart contract" OR "smart-contract") AND ("All "business model" OR "business modeling") AND (year>2014)	1625
("blockchain" OR "distributed ledger" OR "smart contract" OR "smart-contract") AND ("All "enterprise model" OR "enterprise modeling") AND (year>2014)	40
("blockchain" OR "distributed ledger" OR "smart contract" OR "smart-contract") AND ("All "conceptual model" OR "conceptual modeling") AND (year>2014)	370
("blockchain" OR "distributed ledger" OR "smart contract" OR "smart-contract") AND ("All "model driven" OR "model-driven") AND (year>2014)	181
("blockchain" OR "distributed ledger" OR "smart contract" OR "smart-contract") AND ("All "no code" OR "no-code" OR "low code" OR "low-code") AND (year>2014)	76

In the next step, the publications were assessed by at least reading the abstract and reviewing tables and images (S-7), considering the inclusion criteria that (i) the publication should be directly related to distributed ledger technologies, and (ii) creates, discusses, or presents a modeling approach. Publications using models to only illustrate software, systems, or a use case, e.g., by means of a standard UML use case diagram, were excluded. For the remaining publications, we then performed a recursive backward-forward search, as proposed in [34] (S-8): references and citations were screened, seemingly relevant publications added to the set, and subsequently assessed as in step (S-7). For all relevant new additions, a backward-forward search was again performed.

Eventually, no new relevant publications could be found and the backward-forward search was concluded. Of all thus collected publications, 108 fulfilled the assessment criteria (S-9). We further filtered by contained concepts in step (S-10), i.e., (i) the approach has MDE characteristics, (ii) it must be tool-assisted, and (iii) include generation of code, application artifacts, or some executable specifications. The motivation for choosing these criteria is founded in the commonalities of low-code/no-code and MDE, as elaborated in Sect. 1. Finally, we selected 10 approaches we consider representative for the full spectrum of academic approaches.

4.2   Results

In Table 2, the final selection of academic approaches from (S-11) is shown. We further evaluated the approaches regarding the required user expertise - see column *Expertise*. Approaches where a user must not write any code and only basic understanding of blockchain concepts is required, we consider suitable for *non-technical* users. In contrast, approaches that require understanding of advanced concepts or chain-specific features, e.g. gas costs in Ethereum, we consider suitable for *non-programmers*. Finally, if the user has to write any code, the approach is only suitable for *programmers*.

For the comparison of the academic approaches, we classified them in addition using three layers, which are based on the traditional layers of ArchiMate[1]. This choice is motivated by a previous application of ArchiMate in the context of Blockchain use cases [9]. Approaches on the (i) **business layer** integrate modeling of business concepts, such as use cases from a top-down perspective. The (ii) **application layer** includes approaches which integrate life-cycle and deployment management, or integration facilities. Finally, on the (iii) **technology layer**, we consider approaches whose scope is limited to the generation of smart contract code from models.

Table 2. Selected academic, model-driven approaches for blockchain application development that apply code generation.

Ref.	Name	BP	Modeling language	Layer	Impl. platform	Expertise	OS
[3]	Archi2HC	H	ArchiMate	Business	Archi	●●●	–
[22]	Caterpillar	E	BPMN	Application	custom (Node.js, bpmn-js)	●○○	+
[17]	ChainOps	E	domain-specific	Application	AstraKode Blockchain Modeler	●○○	–
[28]	Das Contract	E,C	DEMO, BPMN, Blockly	Technology	custom (.Net, Node.js)	●●○	○
[25]	iContractBot	MC	domain-specific (iContractML)	Technology	Xatkit	●○○	○
[14]	iContractML	MC	domain-specific (iContractML)	Technology	Obeo Designer (Eclipse Sirius)	●○○	○
[30]	LATTE	E	domain-specific	Technology	custom (Electron)	●●○	+
[32]	LEMMA	E	domain-specific (LEMMA)	Application	LEMMA	●●●	○
[20]	UML2Go	H	UML	Technology	Obeo Acceleo (Eclipse)	●●○	–
[23]	VeriSolid	E	domain-specific (state machine)	Technology	WebGME	●●○	+

Name: Short name of the approach. If none was given by the authors we assigned one. BP: Blockchain platform, E: Ethereum, C: Cardano, H: Hyperledger Fabric, MC: Multi-chain. Expertise: Required experience, ●: non-technical, ●●: non-programmer, ●●●: programmer. OS: open source, +: available, ○: no license specified, –: not available.

In the entire corpus of publications, we could identify only one approach which clearly lies on the **business layer (i)** and simultaneously permits the generation of code artifacts. Babkin et al. [3] propose a mapping between ArchiMate concepts and Hyperledger Composer constructs. From an ArchiMate model, a project artifact for Hyperledger Fabric is generated. However, a programmer must implement the business logic manually. The Das Contract approach [28] applies modeling languages of DEMO to design and generate smart contracts.

---

[1] See https://www.opengroup.org/archimate-forum/archimate-overview.

While DEMO is traditionally used to model organizations, this is however not part of of this approach.

On the **application layer (ii)** lie approaches and tools offering integration and management capabilities for the generated artifacts. Caterpillar [22] is a process execution system, in which processes are modeled as BPMN in a web-based visual editor. The models may be translated to Solidity code or into an intermediate representation to be executed by an on-chain execution engine. Furthermore, the tool offers a model repository and monitoring of processes. In the ChainOps [17] framework, smart contracts are composed visually from pre-defined templates, subsequently validated against domain-specific constraints and policies. Models then are sent to a REST service to be translated and deployed. The vision of ChainOps is to offer a complete and integrated Dapp life-cycle solution for the OntoChain[2] ecosystem. The work of Trebbau et al. [32] is an extension of LEMMA, a modeling framework for microservices. Using the modeling languages of LEMMA, code artifacts for the connection to chain networks and smart contract interaction may be generated. The focus of this approach is the model-based integration of on-chain components.

Most identified approaches focus on the generation of smart contract code without offering additional life-cycle capabilities, and are thus assigned to the **technology layer (iii)**. Suitable for non-technical users are approaches which abstract blockchain and platform-specific concepts. The modeling language iContractML [14] has a visual notation with few elements for the specification of the structure of smart contracts. Models are translated to DAML, which is compatible with various chains. Based on this language, iContractBot [25] allows the user to specify models conversationally. Another approach targeting multiple chains is the aforementioned Das Contract, in which the behavior of a contract is specified in Blockly. Since Blockly contains coding concepts, we do not consider it suitable for non-technical users. Approaches specifically for Ethereum are LATTE [30] and VersiSolid [23]. The former relies on a combination of form-based definition of the structure of Solidity contracts and their implementation, defined visually in a notation similar to flow-charts. In the latter, Solidity contracts are modeled as state machines in visual fashion. This approach focuses on the formal verification of the generated contract. Another platform-specific approach is UML2Go [20] for Hyperledger Fabric. Contracts are modeled as UML class and sequence diagrams and then translated to Go chaincode using model transformation.

The results show that academic approaches predominantly focus on the platform-specific generation of smart contract code, whereas holistic solutions are sparse.

---

[2] https://ontochain.ngi.eu/.

5   Industrial Low-Code and No-Code Approaches

For practitioners, an increasing number of low-code and no-code solutions is available. In an informal compilation by Invernizzi and Tossell[3], solutions from 145 companies were found, such as website and app builders, e-commerce services, and data dashboards. The identified solutions differ substantially in the scope and applications they target. With the aim of assessing the scope and applicability of industrial approaches towards blockchain applications, we conducted a review of state-of-the-art solutions. The data sources for this review are (DS-1): the compilation by Invernizzi and Tossell, (DS-2): practical approaches from prior research [15], and (DS-3): additional research on blockchain-specific no-code and low-code solutions available on the web.

5.1   Review Process

We applied a three-step process, consisting of an initial filtering step (S-1), the evaluation of scope and applicability for blockchains in step (S-2), and the classification of solutions applicable to blockchains (S-3). Initially, 169 solutions were identified. In (S-1), we manually retrieved descriptions from the vendor websites in addition to information provided by (DS-1), followed by filtering out duplicate entries, those that could not be reached on the web, or did not provide sufficient information on their websites (e.g. closed beta software). The remaining 150 solutions were evaluated in (S-2) regarding their scope of blockchain integration. Finally, 40 solutions were identified as applicable for blockchains.

5.2   Results

For discussing available platforms and their blockchain integration, we distinguish between *1st degree* and *2nd degree* integration. A platform supports 1st degree integration if it interacts directly with blockchains through its software or services. 2nd degree integration is supported if an external service could be integrated that offers 1st degree integration. The criteria for the selected platforms (S-3) listed in Table 3 are that they (a) offer blockchain integration of 1st or 2nd degree and (b) were considered a low-code or no-code approach.

Categories with 1st Degree Integration: 1st degree blockchain integration has been found in 17 solutions intended for building websites and apps, workflow automation, and smart contract development. Exemplary integration features in the *app builder* category are the creation of decentralized apps (Dapps) and the integration of cryptocurrency-related data, e.g. price information. App builders such as Outsystems (5) and Bubble (7) support Dapps, where components of a mobile, desktop, or web app can send blockchain transactions and call smart contract functions, e.g. through the MetaMask browser extension.

---

[3] https://pinver.medium.com/decoding-the-no-code-low-code-startup-universe-and-its-players-4b5e0221d58b.

Table 3. Low- and no-code approaches with 1st or 2nd degree blockchain integration.

	Cat.	Name	Website	d_1	d_2	s		Cat.	Name	Website	d_1	d_2	s
1	AM	Adalo	adalo.com	−	+	○	21	SC	DAML	daml.com	+	−	+
2	AM	BuildFire	buildfire.com	−	+	○	22	SC	Simba Chain	simbachain.com	+	−	−
3	AM	Glide	glideapps.com	+	+	−	23	SC	Dappbuilder	dappbuilder.io	+	−	+
4	AM	Axonator	axonator.com	−	+	−	24	SP	Airtable	airtable.com	−	+	−
5	AW	Outsystems	outsystems.com	+	−	−	25	WA	n8n	n8n.io	+	−	+
6	AW	Builder.ai	builder.ai	+	−	−	26	WA	Zapier	zapier.com	+	+	○
7	AW	Bubble	bubble.io	+	+	−	27	WA	Integromat	integromat.com	+	+	−
8	AW	Landbot	landbot.io	−	+	−	28	WA	Process Str	process.st	−	+	−
9	AW	Draftbit	draftbit.com	−	+	○	29	WA	IFTTT	ifttt.com	+	+	−
10	D	Parabola	parabola.io	−	+	−	30	WA	NodeRed	nodered.org	+	+	+
11	D	Gyana	gyana.com	−	+	○	31	WA	Aurachain	aurachain.ch	+	−	−
12	D	Obviously AI	obviously.ai	−	+	−	32	WB	Webflow	webflow.com	+	+	−
13	D	Levity	levity.ai	−	+	−	33	WB	Unstack	unstack.com	−	+	−
14	F	Arengu	arengu.com	−	+	○	34	WB	Squarespace	squarespace.com	−	+	−
15	F	Formstack	formstack.com	−	+	−	35	WB	Linktree	linktr.ee	−	+	−
16	F	Tally	tally.so	−	+	−	36	WB	Pory	pory.io	−	+	−
17	IN	Budibase	budibase.com	−	+	−	37	WB	Softr	softr.io	−	+	−
18	IN	Flowdash	flowdash.com	−	+	−	38	WB	Xooa	xooa.com	+	−	○
19	IN	Jet Admin	jetadmin.io	−	+	○	39	WB	ICME	icme.io	+	−	−
20	IN	Windward	windwardstudios.com	−	+	−	40	WB	Atra	atra.io	+	−	○

Cat.: Category, AM: app builder with mobile focus, AW: app builder with web focus, D: data, F: forms, IN: internal tools, SC: smart contracts, SP: Spreadsheets, WA: workflow automation, WB: website builders, d_1: 1st degree integration, d_2: 2nd degree integration, s: open source, +: applicable, ○: partially applicable, −: not applicable

For *website builders*, blockchain integration has only been found for integrating cryptocurrency-related data, with the exception of ICME (39). ICME is a website builder for creating websites on the Dfinity blockchain. The app and the resulting websites are hosted on Dfinity.

Workflow automation tools allow for the execution of user-defined workflows. A workflow is entered via a visual flow-based editor, showing the subsequent flow of steps for execution along with execution logic, or using dialogs or forms. Exemplary integration features are transactions and smart contract support for the Ethereum blockchain in Zapier (26) and Aurachain (31), and support for the Hyperledger Fabric blockchain in NodeRed (30) and Aurachain (31). Further services support crypto-currency data integrations.

Smart contract development is supported by integration features in Hyperledger Fabric, Hyperledger Sawtooth, Amazon QLDB, and others in DAML (21), a domain-specific language for textual descriptions of smart contracts. The textual language uses a syntax with natural language elements that can be interpreted and deployed for the supported platforms. Smart contract design based on templates and a visual editor is found for Ethereum, Hyperledger Fabric, and others in SimbaChain (22). The editor supports the creation of smart contracts by defining assets and transactions. Dappbuilder (23) offers smart contract creation from pre-defined templates for Ethereum, Polygon, and others. The approach limits applicability to standardized contracts, e.g. issuing tokens according to the Ethereum ERC-20 and similar token standards.

Categories with 2nd Degree Integration: 2nd degree blockchain integration has been found in 30 solutions intended for building websites, apps, or forms, for workflow automation, internal tools for companies, and for data processing and spreadsheets. 7 solutions also offer 1st degree blockchain integration. The integration features across the categories rely on another services providing a direct integration for blockchain applications. Among the no-code or low-code applications, it is typical to integrate other services in the fashion of a composition, for example, creating an application in an app builder with data provided by an external service. Blockchain integration features, due to this capability, rely on other services for blockchain integration.

Notably, 28 of the 30 solutions integrate with Zapier (26), thereby offering support for *interacting with Ethereum smart contracts and transactions*. These concern website and app builders such as Glide (3), which can embed dialogs for smart contracts and transactions in this way, in addition to integrating cryptocurrency data. Similarly, form builders allow defining input fields and the processing of submitted data through integrations. Arengu (14) is a typical example which also supports visualization with a flow-based editor.

Workflow automation tools offer the integration as part of the executable workflow definition. For example, a transaction may be sent after the workflow has been started by another action such as entering data in a spreadsheet. This is often accomplished by integrating AirTable (24). Internal tools include software tools for enterprises, automating typical enterprise resource tasks or operational tasks, e.g. using JetAdmin (19), or business processes as in Flowdash (18). Integrations in this context can be triggered similar to workflow automation tools.

Data processing and spreadsheets tools permit integrating data sources, thereby enabling for example the processing of newly appearing blockchain transactions, filtering for specified criteria, and calculations such as the aggregation of transferred amounts. Examples where this is possible are the spreadsheet tool AirTable (24) and data analytics tools such as Parabola (10).

The results show that the integration possibilities for the creation of websites or apps hinge on few services such as Zapier (26), predominantly found in the workflow automation category. Typical integration features consist of access to blockchain transactions or cryptocurrency data. Further integration possibilities with APIs on a technical level are very common, however, they were not considered no-code or low-code when using using Webhooks, Rest, other forms of HTTP requests or technical API descriptions. For the development of smart contracts, few no-code instances could be found in practice, with all of them requiring expert knowledge in blockchains.

6   Use Case for Low-Code Blockchain Development

For conducting a first evaluation of the state-of-the-art in realizing blockchain applications using low-code and no-code approaches (RQ2), we implemented a blockchain app with a smart contract in the area of supply chain tracking and tracing. For this purpose, we selected the Outsystems low-code platform, which targets developers, together with the SimbaChain platform as an exemplary no-code platform that is directed towards end-users.

The goal was to provide a trusted and up-to-date IT system shared by distributed supply chain participants. In this domain, blockchain-based solutions promise information that is available as a trusted source in near-time or real-time among network participants [7,16]. In particular, the tracking of goods in international shipments is a challenging area, involving the coordination of material flows from suppliers and manufacturers through container and sea freight companies to distributors. Additionally, products and materials need to be traced back to their source. Without a trusted IT infrastructure, shipments are mostly documented using paper documents, with point-to-point communication by e-mail, phone, and siloed IT systems, resulting in high transaction costs [7,37].

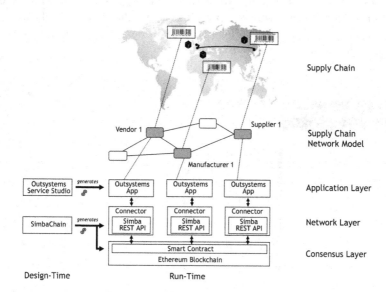

Fig. 2. Blockchain-based architecture for supply chain tracking and tracing.

Figure 2 shows the implemented three-layer architecture with an exemplary network. Using Outsystems studio, an app was designed for registering suppliers, manufacturers, and vendors together with freight forwarding companies, commodities, and shipments. On the application layer, Supplier 1 might scan a shipment through a Global Trade Item Number (GTIN) with a smartphone camera and submit related IDs and attributes. For Manufacturer 1 and Vendor 1, this data becomes available and is updated with shipment events by freight providers and forwarders. Figure 3 shows this data in the app during development. The Ethereum blockchain is integrated for establishing a consistent view of data on the network and consensus layers of the architecture. In Outsystems, a REST API hosted by Simba relays requests to the Ethereum smart contract. Smart contracts and APIs are generated by SimbaChain from the model in Fig. 4.

7 Discussion and Requirements for Future Developments

The review of academic approaches for model-driven engineering for blockchain applications has shown that most approaches focus on the technical level and not all of them support code generation. Rather, many approaches target the formal verification of smart contracts and only some approaches provide working prototypes. Approaches that integrate the business, application, and technical layer have not yet been proposed prominently in the literature. These would however bring benefits in terms of a holistic view on blockchain application design and should be investigated in the future.

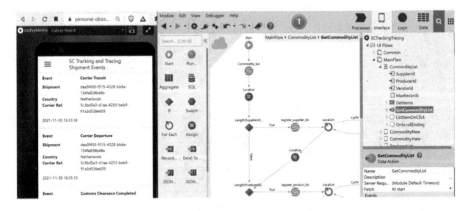

Fig. 3. Design of mobile app (left-hand side) in Outsystems Service Studio (right-hand side) using a flow-based editor for processing commodity data records of shipments.

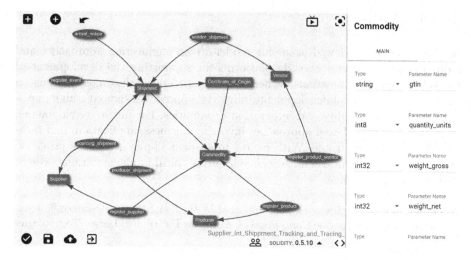

Fig. 4. Smart contract design in SimbaChain using a visual editor for a data model of transactions (blue) and assets (red). (Color figure online)

The reviewed no-code and low-code approaches as used in industry showed the high maturity of these platforms. This concerned in particular the high usability, the availability of a broad range of interfaces for cloud-based and blockchain integrations and the possibility of cross-platform development. On the downside, it is hard to trace errors and debug applications on some low-code platforms as implementation details are hidden. Although some platforms offer the inspection of the generated code, this requires again technical know-how.

The practical use case permitted further insights. Regarding the blockchain implementation through SimbaChain, a major architectural limitation is the generation of APIs used as relay when accessing the smart contract. Additional validation of the blockchain is required for assessing the consistency of data. From a user perspective, the SimbaChain platform requires only high-level knowledge of data types in addition to the visual entity concept documented in the platform. While SimbaChain might thus be considered a *no-code* approach, it is limited to the presented operations and its resulting implementation requires expert knowledge for evaluating implementation trade-offs. The app development with Outsystems allows for a visual modeling of program actions and control structures as shown in Fig. 3. The specification of the individual elements as well as other application components required the knowledge of software development concepts, such as variables, datatypes, event listeners, and HTTP request and, in one case, debugging through the logging and interception of requests. On the other hand, Outsystems might be considered a *low-code* approach with complex capabilities suitable for developers. During development, code consistency, spotting errors visually, discussing and communicating with domain experts, and cross-platform generation have proven beneficial.

8   Conclusion

In this paper we reviewed academic model-driven engineering approaches and industrial low-code and no-code platforms for supporting the development of blockchain-based applications. Whereas academic approaches mostly focus on the technical aspects of development, industrial approaches showed a high maturity in terms of usability and integration capabilities. For future developments, more holistic, cloud-based approaches involving business, application, and technical layers seem desirable. With regard to academic approaches, the provision of integration capabilities and sustainable prototypical implementations present current major challenges.

Acknowledgment. This work was supported by the Swiss National Science Foundation project Domain-Specific Conceptual Modeling for Distributed Ledger Technologies [196889].

References

1. Ait Hsain, Y., Laaz, N., Mbarki, S.: Ethereum's smart contracts construction and development using model driven engineering technologies: a review. Procedia Comput. Sci. **184**, 785–790 (2021)
2. Antonopoulos, A.M., Wood, G.: Mastering Ethereum: Building Smart Contracts and Dapps. O'reilly Media (2018)
3. Babkin, E., Komleva, N.: Model-driven liaison of organization modeling approaches and blockchain platforms. In: Aveiro, D., Guizzardi, G., Borbinha, J. (eds.) EEWC 2019. LNBIP, vol. 374, pp. 167–186. Springer, Cham (2020). https://doi.org/10.1007/978-3-030-37933-9_11
4. Bock, A.C., Frank, U.: Low-code platform. Bus. Inf. Syst. Eng. **63**(6), 733–740 (2021). https://doi.org/10.1007/s12599-021-00726-8
5. Brambilla, M., Cabot, J., Wimmer, M.: Model-driven software engineering in practice, second edition. Syn. Lect. Softw. Eng. **3**(1), 1–207 (2017)
6. vom Brocke, J., Simons, A., Riemer, K., Niehaves, B., Plattfaut, R., Cleven, A.: Standing on the shoulders of giants: challenges and recommendations of literature search in information systems research. Commun. Assoc. Inf. Syst. **37**, 9 (2015)
7. Chen, W., Botchie, D., Braganza, A., Han, H.: A transaction cost perspective on blockchain governance in global value chains. Strateg. Chang. **31**(1), 75–87 (2022)
8. Clohessy, T., Acton, T., Rogers, N.: Blockchain adoption: technological, organisational and environmental considerations. In: Treiblmaier, H., Beck, R. (eds.) Business Transformation through Blockchain, pp. 47–76. Springer, Cham (2019). https://doi.org/10.1007/978-3-319-98911-2_2
9. Curty, S., Härer, F., Fill, H.G.: Towards the comparison of blockchain-based applications using enterprise modeling. In: ER Demos/Posters. CEUR-WS (2021)
10. Di Ruscio, D., Kolovos, D., de Lara, J., Pierantonio, A., Tisi, M., Wimmer, M.: Low-code development and model-driven engineering: two sides of the same coin? Softw. Syst. Model. **21**, 437–446 (2022)
11. Fairley, P.: Ethereum will cut back its absurd energy use. IEEE Spectr. **56**(1), 29–32 (2019)

12. Fill, H.-G., Härer, F., Muff, F., Curty, S.: Towards augmented enterprise models as low-code interfaces to digital systems. In: Shishkov, B. (ed.) BMSD 2021. LNBIP, vol. 422, pp. 343–352. Springer, Cham (2021). https://doi.org/10.1007/978-3-030-79976-2_22

13. Foxley, W., Kim, C.: Valid points: Ethereum's proof-of-stake may happen sooner than you think (2021). https://www.coindesk.com/tech/2021/03/17/valid-points-ethereums-proof-of-stake-may-happen-sooner-than-you-think/

14. Hamdaqa, M., Metz, L.A.P., Qasse, I.: IContractML: a domain-specific language for modeling and deploying smart contracts onto multiple blockchain platforms. In: 12th System Analysis and Modelling Conference, pp. 34–43. ACM (2020)

15. Härer, F., Fill, H.G.: A Comparison of Approaches for Visualizing Blockchains and Smart Contracts. Jusletter IT Weblaw February 2019 (2019)

16. Helo, P., Shamsuzzoha, A.: Real-time supply chain—a blockchain architecture for project deliveries. Robot. Comput. Integr. Manufac. **63**, 101909 (2020)

17. van den Heuvel, W.-J., Tamburri, D.A., D'Amici, D., Izzo, F.O, Potten, S.: Chain-Ops for smart contract-based distributed applications. In: Shishkov, B. (ed.) BMSD 2021. LNBIP, vol. 422, pp. 374–383. Springer, Cham (2021). https://doi.org/10.1007/978-3-030-79976-2_25

18. Holotiuk, F., Moormann, J.: Organizational adoption of digital innovation: the case of blockchain technology. In: ECIS Conference, p. 202 (2018)

19. Hu, B., et al.: A comprehensive survey on smart contract construction and execution: paradigms, tools, and systems. Patterns **2**(2), 100179 (2021)

20. Jurgelaitis, M., Drungilas, V., Čeponienė, L., Vaičiukynas, E., Butkienė, R., Čeponis, J.: Smart contract code generation from platform specific model for hyperledger go. In: Rocha, Ál., Adeli, H., Dzemyda, G., Moreira, F., Ramalho C., Ana M. (eds.) WorldCIST 2021. AISC, vol. 1368, pp. 63–73. Springer, Cham (2021). https://doi.org/10.1007/978-3-030-72654-6_7

21. Levasseur, O., Iqbal, M., Matulevicius, R.: Survey of model-driven engineering techniques for blockchain-based applications. In: Proceedings of the Forum at Practice of Enterprise Modeling 2021, vol. 3045, pp. 11–20. CEUR (2021)

22. López-Pintado, O., Dumas, M., García-Bañuelos, L., Weber, I.: Interpreted execution of business process models on blockchain. In: 2019 IEEE 23rd International Enterprise Distributed Object Computing Conference (EDOC), pp. 206–215 (2019)

23. Mavridou, A., Laszka, A., Stachtiari, E., Dubey, A.: VeriSolid: correct-by-design smart contracts for ethereum. In: Goldberg, I., Moore, T. (eds.) FC 2019. LNCS, vol. 11598, pp. 446–465. Springer, Cham (2019). https://doi.org/10.1007/978-3-030-32101-7_27

24. Nguyen, C.T., Hoang, D.T., Nguyen, D.N., Niyato, D., Nguyen, H.T., Dutkiewicz, E.: Proof-of-stake consensus mechanisms for future blockchain networks: fundamentals, applications and opportunities. IEEE Access **7**, 85727–85745, 100179 (2019)

25. Qasse, I., Mishra, S., Hamdaqa, M.: iContractBot: a chatbot for smart contracts' specification and code generation. In: IEEE/ACM 3rd International Workshop on Bots in Software Engineering, pp. 35–38 (2021)

26. Sahay, A., Indamutsa, A., Di Ruscio, D., Pierantonio, A.: Supporting the understanding and comparison of low-code development platforms. In: SEAA Conference, pp. 171–178. IEEE (2020)

27. Schmidt, D.: Guest editor's introduction: model-driven engineering. Computer **39**(2), 25–31, 100179 (2006)

28. Skotnica, M., Pergl, R.: Das contract - a visual domain specific language for modeling blockchain smart contracts. In: Aveiro, D., Guizzardi, G., Borbinha, J. (eds.) EEWC 2019. LNBIP, vol. 374, pp. 149–166. Springer, Cham (2020). https://doi.org/10.1007/978-3-030-37933-9_10
29. Sánchez-Gómez, N., Torres-Valderrama, J., García-García, J.A., Gutiérrez, J.J., Escalona, M.J.: Model-based software design and testing in blockchain smart contracts: a systematic literature review. IEEE Access 8, 164556–164569, 100179 (2020)
30. Tan, S., S Bhowmick, S., Chua, H.E., Xiao, X.: Latte: visual construction of smart contracts. In: International Conference on Management of Data, pp. 2713–2716. ACM, New York, NY, USA (2020)
31. Tisi, M., et al.: Lowcomote: training the next generation of experts in scalable low-code engineering platforms. In: STAF 2019 (2019)
32. Trebbau, S., Wizenty, P., Sachweh, S.: Towards integrating blockchains with microservice architecture using model-driven engineering. In: Gregory, P., Kruchten, P. (eds.) XP 2021. LNBIP, vol. 426, pp. 167–175. Springer, Cham (2021). https://doi.org/10.1007/978-3-030-88583-0_16
33. Vacca, A., Di Sorbo, A., Visaggio, C.A., Canfora, G.: A systematic literature review of blockchain and smart contract development: techniques, tools, and open challenges. J. Syst. Softw. 174, 110891 (2021)
34. Watson, R.T., Webster, J.: Analysing the past to prepare for the future: writing a literature review a roadmap for release 2.0. J. Decis. Syst. 29(3), 129–147 (2020)
35. Webster, J., Watson, R.T.: Analyzing the past to prepare for the future: Writing a literature review. MIS Q. 26(2) (2002)
36. Whittle, J., Hutchinson, J., Rouncefield, M.: The state of practice in model-driven engineering. IEEE Softw. 31(3), 79–85 (2013)
37. Zeng, F., Chan, H.K., Pawar, K.: The adoption of open platform for container bookings in the maritime supply chain. Transp. Rese. Part E 141(C) (2020)

Eliciting Ethicality Requirements Using the Ontology-Based Requirements Engineering Method

Renata Guizzardi[1]([⊠]), Glenda Amaral[2], Giancarlo Guizzardi[1,2], and John Mylopoulos[3]

[1] University of Twente, Enschede, The Netherlands
r.guizzardi@utwente.nl
[2] CORE/KRDB, Free University of Bozen-Bolzano, Bolzano, Italy
{gmouraamaral,giancarlo.guizzardi}@unibz.it
[3] University of Toronto, Toronto, Canada
jm@cs.toronto.edu

Abstract. The advent of socio-technical, cyber-physical and Artificial Intelligence (AI) systems has broadened the scope of requirements engineering which must now deal with new classes of requirements, concerning ethics, privacy and trust. Unfortunately, requirements engineers cannot be expected to understand the qualities behind these new classes of systems so that they can conduct elicitation, analysis and operationalization. To address this issue, we propose a methodology for conducting requirements engineering which starts with the adoption of an ontology for a *quality domain*, such as ethicality, privacy or trustworthiness, populates the ontology for the system-to-be and conducts requirements analysis grounded on the populated ontology. We illustrate our proposal with ethicality requirements.

Keywords: Requirements elicitation and analysis · Foundational ontologies · Ethical requirements

1 Introduction

In a world where Artificial Intelligence (AI) is pervasive, controlling more services and systems everyday, humans may feel threatened or at risk by giving up control to machines. In this context, many of the potential issues are related to safety and ethics. For example, AI systems may be biased towards a group of people in detriment of others, they may lead to job loss and wealth inequality, and they may make mistakes and even go rogue, by acting against the interests of humanity [4].

Providing a global solution to these problems is a challenging endeavor, but one that has recently been recognized by different organizations, which have proposed guidelines and standards aimed at addressing this pressing matter. Among these, we may cite the IEEE Standard Model Process for Addressing Ethical Concerns during System Design [5] and the European Union Ethics Guidelines

© Springer Nature Switzerland AG 2022
A. Augusto et al. (Eds.): BPMDS 2022/EMMSAD 2022, LNBIP 450, pp. 221–236, 2022.
https://doi.org/10.1007/978-3-031-07475-2_15

for Trustworthy AI [3]. What these works have in common is proposing a set of principles to which the system-to-be must adhere to be considered ethical. The topic targeted in this paper is how to make sure that such principles may effectively guide system development.

We claim that Requirements Engineering (RE) is the Software Engineering area that may exert a bigger impact on developing ethical systems, emphasizing ethical principles in system development from the start. RE is not only responsible for producing the set of requirements that will conduct the design of the system-to-be, but also for validating if such requirements have been properly met, and for monitoring if they are still valid throughout the whole life cycle of the system, even after it becomes operational. However, proposing concepts, tools and techniques that support the incorporation of high-level societal concerns and goals (such as ethicality) into the software development processes as explicit requirements is still a challenge in the RE field.

The solution to the targeted issue involves a deep understanding of what the proposed ethical principles mean and how they can be converted in concrete system requirements, which can then guide system design, besides being validated and monitored. For that, we rely on an ontological approach, based on a novel Requirements Engineering method we name Ontology-based Requirements Engineering (ObRE). The ObRE methodology consists of three activities: 1) adopt or develop an ontology to conceptually clarify the meaning of a class of requirements (in this paper, ethicality requirements); 2) instantiate the ontology for a system-to-be, resulting in a domain model; and 3) use the domain model to guide analysis, resulting in requirements models, such as goal models, requirements tables, user stories etc. Besides presenting ObRE, this paper illustrates its use with an example drawn from the driverless car domain.

Ontological analysis provides a foundation for ObRE as it enables a deep account of the meaning of a particular domain. In turn, such analysis is based on a **foundational ontology** to offer a domain-agnostic set of concepts drawing ideas from Philosophy and Cognitive Science. Domain-agnostic identity and dependency, taxonomic relationships and mereology are examples of concepts offered by foundational ontologies. In turn, ontological analysis uses a foundational ontology to develop **domain ontologies**, i.e., a set of concepts and relationships for a specific domain to be shared by a community of users [19]. It is important to highlight that in our work, an ontology is a reference conceptual framework for conceptualizing a domain, rather than a mere logical specification to support automated reasoning. ObRE is based on the Unified Foundational Ontology (UFO) [20], extended with concepts from the Non-functional Requirements Ontology (NFRO) [23]. The use of NFRO is justified by the fact that the classes of requirements ObRE targets belong to quality domains (e.g. ethicality, trustworthiness and privacy) and, as such, fall into the category of non-functional requirements, as explained in detail in the next section of this paper. ObRE is intended to help a requirements analyst cope with non-functional requirements where the analysts literally doesn't know where to begin in conducting elicitation and analysis, which is the case of ethical requirements, the very focus of this paper. ObRE is intended to help by "semantically unpacking" requirements concepts thereby enabling requirements activities.

The remainder of this paper is structured as follows: Sect. 2 discusses what we mean by ontological analysis, and explains the ontological account of requirements adopted in this work; Sect. 3 presents the ObRE method; Sect. 4 illustrates the proposed method with an example from the ethical AI systems domain; Sect. 5 discusses related works; and finally, Sect. 6 presents final remarks.

2   Research Baseline

2.1   Ontological Analysis

The notions of *ontology* and *ontological analysis* adopted here are akin to their interpretations in philosophy [10]. In this view, the goals of *ontological analysis* are: (i) characterize what kinds of entities are assumed to exist by a given conceptualization of a set of phenomena in reality; (ii) the metaphysical nature of these kinds of entities. An *ontology*, in turn, is a system of categories and their ties (here represented as an artifact) that makes justice to what is uncover by (i) and (ii).

In this sense, an ontology is neither merely a logical specification nor it is mainly concerned with making terminological and taxonomic distinctions. For example, in addressing the domains of risk, one is less concerned with what specific subtypes of risk exist (e.g., physical, biological, financial, electronic), but instead with what exactly *is* risk? (What kind of entity is it? What is its nature?). Is it an object? an event? a relationship? a complex property? If the latter, is a categorical or dispositional property? what is the bearer of such a property?, and so on.

Given the nature of this method of analysis, it must be supported by a domain-independent system comprising the most general categories, hence, crosscuting several domains (e.g., objects, events, relationships, dispositions, etc.), i.e., what is termed a foundational ontology (aka top-level or upper-level ontology). In this article, we adopt the Unified Foundational Ontology (UFO) given its successful track record of supporting the ontological analysis of complex notions such as *value, risk, service, trust, legal relations, money, decisions, economic preferences*, among many others [20,22,29].

2.2   An Ontology for Requirements (NFRO)

The Non-Functional Requirements Ontology (NFRO) is defined as an extension of UFO. As such, it adopts the UFO notion of AGENT, an entity having mental states such as belief, desire and intention and means to act accordingly. Also, the notion of INTENTION that refers to a situation (state-of-affairs) that the AGENT commits to bring about by pursuing goals and executing actions. It is also important to state that according to UFO, AGENT can be categorized into HUMAN (i.e. a person), ARTIFICIAL (i.e. artificial systems, such as information systems, cyberphysical systems, etc.) and INSTITUTIONAL (i.e. organization). A Stakeholder may be a HUMAN or an INSTITUTIONAL agent, while the system-to-be is an ARTIFICIAL one. For reasons of space, we do not include a figure showing this AGENT categorization, but we refer the reader to [21] (chap.3), for details.

Requirements can be functional and non-functional, but the latter are most relevant to ethical requirements, so we focus on them by adopting NFRO [23]. In NFRO, a requirement is a GOAL. Requirements are specialized into NFRs (aka QUALITY GOALS) and FUNCTIONAL REQUIREMENTS (FRs). FRs refer to a FUNCTION (a capability, capacity) that a system can manifest in particular SITUATIONS. NFRs refer to desired qualities taking QUALITY VALUES in particular QUALITY REGIONS. For example, a software system is considered to have good usability if the value associated to its "usability" quality maps to the "good" quality region in the "usability" quality space.

This ontological account delineates different kinds of requirements, and clarifies the nature of NFRs as qualities that map a system artifact into a quality region [23]. Figure 1[1] depicts a selected subset of the NFRO that is relevant here. For an in-depth discussion and formal characterization of QUALITIES, QUALITY UNIVERSALS, QUALITY REGIONS, and QUALITY SPACES, we refer the reader to [19].

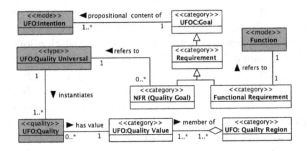

Fig. 1. A fragment of the ontology of non-functional requirements

3   ObRE Method

Figure 2 illustrates the process of the ObRE method, showing the three activities mentioned in Sect. 1.

Fig. 2. The ObRE process

The process starts with **1) Domain Ontology Development**, requirements analysts and ontology engineers perform ontological analysis for a class

---

[1] In all OntoUML diagrams, we adopt the following color coding: types are represented in purple, objects in pink, modes in blue, events in yellow, and abstract entities such as numbers, sets and propositions in white.

of requirements. We emphasize that ObRE does not prescribe that the requirements engineer is versed in the use of ontological analysis concepts. For that, ObRE assumes the presence of an ontology engineer, and the requirements engineer plays a role of a domain expert in the ontology development process. The outcome of activity 1), is an ontology modelled in OntoUML[2] This activity is performed once for each class of requirements and doesn't need to be repeated for each new system development project. For example, in [7], we conducted ontological analysis the notions of *trust* and *trustworthiness* in order to unpack the meaning of trustworthiness requirements. According to the results of our analysis a system is trustworthy if it is believed to have the capability to perform its required functions (Capability belief) and its vulnerabilities will not prevent it from doing so (Vulnerability belief). Moreover, we define trustworthiness as a composition of three other qualities, namely *reliability* in performing its functions, *truthfulness* in presenting its credentials and *transparency* in its operations. To judge how reliable a system is, we must understand how much of the Stakeholder's Capability Belief is actually met by the system's operations. Note that reliability could have been defined in multiple other ways, for instance, it could have been related to accessibility, i.e., how often will the system be responsive to stakeholder needs; or inferred by the system possessing a specific reliability certificate. The trustworthiness ontology has been recently used in a real case study, reported in [8], showing promising results in defining and monitoring trustworthiness requirements for a particular system. In case a new trustworthy system needs to be developed, the same ontology can be fully reused, and instantiated for the new system-to-be.

Having the requirements explicitly defined and understood, the analyst may perform **2) Domain Ontology Instantiation**. Here, the analysts focus on a particular system and instantiate elements of the ontology. For a security ontology, this step would identify stakeholders, vulnerabilities, attack types, etc. for a particular system. This is intended to serve as domain model for conducting requirements analysis. We highlight the importance of this step, since the same class of requirements may lead to distinct concrete requirements for each system. Thus, instantiating the ontology created in 1) helps identify these particular requirements and opens the way for the system-to-be requirements analysis.

In activity **3) Requirements Analysis Method Execution**, analysts use the domain model to define and analyze system requirements. For instance, she may simply define a requirements table, listing the requirements instantiated with the help of the ontology. Or if she prefers a more sophisticated analysis methodology, she may use goal modeling, defining the contribution of different choices to accomplish a particular goal (i.e., requirement), and specifying how goals relate to each other, as well as to relevant stakeholders' resources and tasks. Or yet, she may create user stories based on the identified ontological instances. From this point on, the requirements analysis may progress as the

---

[2] OntoUML is an UML-based language developed to represent UFO's ontological categories, see [19,20] as well as the OntoUML Community Portal https://ontouml.org/.

chosen method prescribes, however, with the benefit of having the ontology and ontological instances as guides.

As depicted in Fig. 2, steps 2) and 3) are intended to be carried out iteratively, as with most RE methods. This supports the analyst in revisiting the previous activities while maturing the requirements elicitation and analysis.

4   Applying ObRE to Ethical Requirements for Intelligent Systems

We illustrate the application of ObRE to ethical requirements. But what is ethics after all? And what are the characteristics of an ethical system?

According to the Markkula Center for Applied Ethics "ethics refers to standards of behavior that tell us how human beings ought to act" while playing different roles, e.g. worker, driver, parent, citizen, friend etc. For each role, there are ethical codes of conduct that capture such standards of behaviour [1]. Ethicists and AI researchers have been studying the interplay of ethics and AI systems where the subjects of ethical codes are systems that play such roles, e.g., worker, driver. Floridi et al. [17] proposes five general principles that underlie ethical codes and are role-independent. These have been adopted by the European Commission in a document concerning trustworthy AI [9]. The principles are: *Autonomy* (respect human dignity), *Beneficience* (do good to others), *Nonmaleficence* (do no harm to others), *Justice* (treat others fairly), and *Explicability* (explainability, transparently).

We can categorize ethical requirements for a system-to-be as types of *Ecological Requirements* [24], in that they are derived from the ecosystem within which the system-to-be is embedded. After all, it is that ecosystem that determine *values* and *risks*" that can lead to ethical behaviours by the system ([24], p. 253). In a nutshell, value and risk are both types of *dispositions* [29], which are properties that heavily dependent on contextual factors for their manifestation [26]. In fact, as mentioned in Sect. 1, the focus on ethics is motivated by the emerging feeling of risk brought by the use of recent technologies. And these risks must be accounted for and analyzed in contrast with the values delivered by systems and services applying such technologies. For the notions of value and risk, we rely on COVER [29] discussed in Subsect. 4.1[3], while Subsects. 4.2 and 4.3 illustrate the application of the ObRE process, the former focusing on the first two ObRE process activities while the latter addresses the last activity.

---

[3] Note that we present COVER here, as opposed to Sect. 2, because the selection of this ontology is attuned to the particular application of ObRE that we choose to illustrate in this section, and the role that *value* and *risk* play in unpacking some of the ethical requirements addressed. Had we chosen a different type of application, e.g., Run-Time Adaptability Requirements [15], a different ontology would have been chosen to play this role.

4.1 The Common Ontology of Value and Risk (COVER)

COVER breaks down VALUE EXPERIENCES into events, dubbed VALUE EVENTS. These are classified into IMPACT EVENTS and TRIGGER EVENTS. The former directly impact a goal or bring about a situation that impacts a goal. While TRIGGER EVENTS are simply parts of an experience identified as causing IMPACT EVENTS, directly or indirectly. Within the category of IMPACT EVENTS we can further distinguish into GAIN EVENT and LOSS EVENT. The difference between them rests on the nature of the impact on goals (positive for GAIN EVENTS and negative for LOSS EVENTS). To formalize goals, COVER reuses the concept of INTENTION from UFO [12].

RISK EXPERIENCES are unwanted events that have the potential of causing losses, and are composed by RISK EVENTS, which can be of two types, namely threat and loss events. A THREAT EVENT carries the potential of causing a loss, intended or unintended. A THREAT EVENT might be the manifestation of: (i) a Vulnerability (a special type of disposition whose manifestation constitutes a loss or can potentially cause a loss); or (ii) a Threatening Capability (capabilities of a threat object that, hence, can dent the goals a Risk Subject). The second mandatory component of a RISK EXPERIENCE is a LOSS EVENT, which necessarily impacts intentions in a negative way. Figure 3 depicts a fragment of COVER, which captures part of the aforementioned ontological notions.

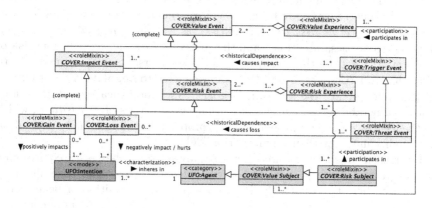

Fig. 3. A fragment of COVER depicting value and risk experiences

4.2 Domain Ontology Development and Instantiation: Ethical Requirements

We apply steps 1) and 2) of ObRE for ethical principles as qualities, and we model ethical requirements as NFR refined into sub-NFRs related to such qualities, following the definitions presented in Sect. 2.2. This is shown in Fig. 4.

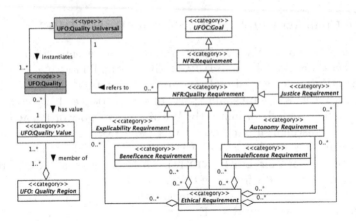

Fig. 4. Ethical requirements

Now, let us interpret ethical requirements in terms of value and risk. Value can be seen as a relational property, emerging from a set of relations between the intrinsic properties of a *value object* (or a value experience) and the goals of a *Value Subject* [29]. The **value** of an object (or experience) measures the degree to which the properties (*affordances*) of that object **positively** contribute (help, make) to the achievement of value subject goals. Mutatis Mutandis, risk is a relational property emerging from a set of relations between the intrinsic properties of an *Object at Risk* (vulnerabilities), as well as *Threat Objects* and *Risk Enablers* (capacities, intentions) and the goals of a *Risk Subject* [29]. The **risk** of an object at risk given threat objects and risk enablers amounts to the degree to which the properties of those entities can be enacted to **negatively** contribute to denting (hurt, break) the risk subject goals. Now, ontologically speaking, affordances, vulnerabilities, capacities, intentions are all types of *dispositions*, which are themselves ecological properties, i.e., properties that essentially depend on their environment for their manifestation [26].

For reasons of space, we are going to analyze two of these sub-requirements here, i.e., those of *beneficience* and *nonmaleficience*. This choice also allows us to contrast these two related NFRs. Considering the definition of beneficience as "doing good to others" [17], we can say that Beneficience Requirements are related to **"creating value"** to stakeholders in the ecosystem in which the system is included. It means that Beneficience Requirements can be seen as goals related to an intention of **positively** impacting the goals of stakeholders in this ecossystem. Analogously, considering the definition of nomaleficence as "doing no harm to others" [17], we can say that Nonmaleficence Requirements are related to **"preventing risks"** to stakeholders. Consequently, Nonmaleficence Requirements can be seen as goals related to an intention of preventing the occurrence of events that may **negatively** impact stekeholders' goals.

Events that impact agents' goals, either positively or negatively, are defined in COVER [29] as Gain Events and Loss Events, respectively. In this sense,

Beneficence Requirements intend to create Gain Events, which positively impact stakeholders' goals. Similarly, Nonmaleficence Requirements intend to prevent the occurrence of Loss Events, which negatively impact stakeholders' goals. Figure 5 represents the OntoUML modeling of Beneficent and Nonmaleficent Requirements.

As presented in Fig. 4, REQUIREMENT is modeled as a GOAL, which is the propositional content of an INTENTION of a stakeholder. We use the notion of agent defined in UFO to model stakeholders. In UFO, agents are individuals that can perform actions, perceive events and bear mental aspects. A relevant type of mental aspect for our proposal is the intention. Intentions are desired state of affairs of which the agent commits to pursuing [11]. In the ontology, INTENTIONS are represented as modes (an externally dependent entity, which can only exist by inhering in other individuals [19]) that inhere in AGENTS. QUALITY REQUIREMENT is a type of Requirement. BENEFICENCE and NONMALEFICENCE REQUIREMENTS are types of QUALITY REQUIREMENTS, which are related to a BENEFICENCE INTENTION and a NONMALEFICENCE INTENTION, respectively. BENEFICENCE INTENTIONS are externally dependent on GAIN EVENTS as their focus of interest is the creation of such events. As previously mentioned, GAIN EVENTS are a type of IMPACT EVENT (as defined in COVER [29]) that positively impact AGENT's goals. NONMALEFICENCE INTENTIONS, in turn, are externally dependent on LOSS EVENTS as their focus of interest is to prevent the ocurrence of such events. As aforementioned, LOSS EVENTS are a type of IMPACT EVENT that negatively impact AGENT's goals.

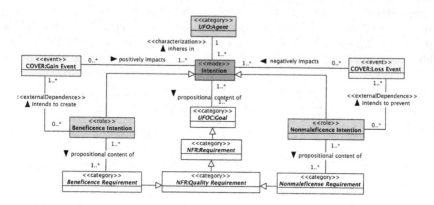

Fig. 5. Beneficence and nonmaleficence requirements

In the sequel, in Fig. 6, we instantiate the ontology with two examples (a Beneficence and a Nonmaleficence Requirement) in the context of driverless cars.

In the first example, the PASSENGER of a driverless car intends "not to be late". In order to address this, we have the BENEFICENCE REQUIREMENT that "the car should choose quicker rout towards destination" related to the INTENTION that the "drivelerless car arrives on time at destination", which is a BENEFICENCE INTENTION that aims at creating a GAIN EVENT. The event "drivelers car arrives on time at destination" is a GAIN EVENT that positively impact the PASSENGER's goal of not being late.

In the second example, the PASSENGER intends "feel safe". In order to address this, we have the NONMALEFICENCE REQUIREMENT that "the car should adopt a defensive driving behavior" related to the INTENTION of "preventing aggressive direction", which is a NONMALEFICENCE INTENTION that aims at preventing the occurrence of a LOSS EVENT. The event "passenger feels nervous as the car drives aggressively" is a LOSS EVENT that negatively impact the PASSENGER's goal of feeling safe.

4.3   Requirements Analysis Method Execution

We exemplify activity 3) of the ObRE process by analyzing the requirements of a driverless car faced with ethical dilemmas.

In particular, we present both a requirements table and a goal model for the driverless car case. We start by presenting Table 1, showing how a requirements table may be enriched with the inclusion of columns representing some of the ontological concepts described in the previous subsections. This facilitates requirements elicitation, by using the right concepts for a particular kind of requirement as guides. In the case of ethical requirements, concepts such as impact event (both positive and negative) and ethical principles. All words highlighted in boldface in Table 1 refer to ontological concepts analyzed in Sect. 4.2, while the ontological instances are written as non-emphasized text.

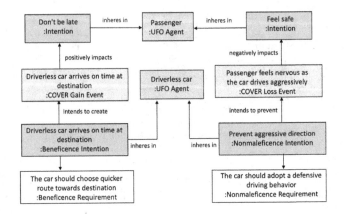

Fig. 6. Ontology instantiation

Note that the ontological analysis of Sect. 4.2 makes very explicit all involved ontological notions used in Table 1, thus supporting the communication and avoiding misunderstandings between the stakeholder and the requirements analyst. For example, having the concepts of GAIN EVENT or LOSS EVENT as well as the specialization of ETHICAL REQUIREMENTS may guide the analyst in asking the right questions during requirements elicitation. This is done by first capturing first the positive and negative impact events concerning Driverless Cars, then relating them with the ethical principles (Beneficence and Nonmaleficence, in this case), and finally coming up with particular requirements for the system-to-be to accomplish such principles. In particular, regarding the latter, these are requirements for the developing of functions and capacities that enable the manifestation of gain events, or that block the manifestation of loss events (e.g., by eliminating the vulnerabilities of the object at risk, or by changing either the intention or the threatening capacities of the threatening agent).

As an alternative, consider a requirements analysis for the Driverless car case using goal modeling. Figure 7 depicts a goal model for this case, using the i^* framework [13][4].

Due to space limitations, this model considers only three of the stakeholders referred to in Table 1, namely, **Passenger**, **Pedestrian** and **Nearby Car**. Moreover, the model depicts the dependency of each of these stakeholders and the **Driverless Car**. Many of the dependencies and goals depicted in this model have been already elicited by using the requirements table. For example, with respect to the Passenger, the **reaching destination on time** goal dependency

Table 1. The result of the application of the proposed process in the driverless car case

Stakeholder	ID	Impact event	Principle	Ethical requirement
Passenger	1	Arrive on time at destination (**positive**)	**Beneficence**	The car should choose quicker route towards destination
	2	Passenger feels nervous when the car drives aggressively (**negative**)	**Nonmaleficence**	The car should adopt a defensive driving behavior
Pedestrian	3	The car runs over a pedestrian (**negative**)	**Nonmaleficence**	The car should stop whenever a pedestrian is crossing the road
	4	Pedestrians waiting by a crossroad have priority to cross it (**positive**)	**Beneficence**	The car should stop before the crosswalk every time there is a pedestrian waiting to cross it
Bystander	5	Be splashed if the car passes by a puddle of water (**negative**)	**Nonmaleficence**	The car should slow down in case there is a puddle of water near a bystander
Nearby cars	6	Be hit (**negative**)	**Nonmaleficence**	The car should slow down when it gets around 20 m in the rear of a nearby car
			Nonmaleficence	The car should make enough distance when overtaking a car
Environment	7	Be polluted (**negative**)	**Nonmaleficence**	The car should turn off the motor every time it stops

---

[4] The model was drawn using the piStar tool, available at https://www.cin.ufpe.br/~jhcp/pistar/.

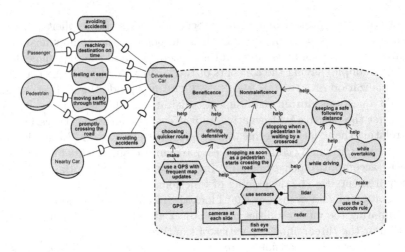

Fig. 7. The driverless car requirements model using i^*

relates to the positive impact event elicited to Passenger (see Table 1, first line), while the ***feeling at ease*** dependency relates to the negative impact captured for this same stakeholder (see Table 1, second line). Nevertheless, new dependencies have been added, for instance, when drawing the model, we realized that avoiding accidents dependency (previously only attributed to the Nearby Car stakeholder, see Table 1, line 6) is also relevant for the Passenger[5].

Besides dependencies, the goal model of Fig. 7 depicts the internal perspective of the Driverless Car, assisting in the analysis of the system's requirements. Note that both ethical principles of Beneficence and Nonmaleficence are represented there by qualities (consistent with our ontological notion of NFR). Then, for each of these qualities, more specific goals and qualities are identified and related to them by contribution links. For instance, the ***choosing quicker route*** quality helps (i.e. partially contributes to) the achievement of Beneficence. Additionally, ***choosing quicker route*** may be indirectly related to the ***reaching destination on time*** goal dependency of the Passenger.

The goal model also allows the requirements analyst to progressively identify more concrete requirements and solutions and the resources needed to accomplish them. For example, the ***use a GPS with frequent map updates*** task makes (i.e. fully accomplishes) the ***choosing quicker route*** quality, and the ***GPS*** itself is a resource needed in this task.

---

[5] We did not update our table on purpose, since although that would make both models more consistent, this is an interesting case in which the visualization of the goal model and its particular constructs (in this case, dependency, goals and qualities) helped us realized a missing requirement for one of the stakeholders. In this paper, the authors are playing the role of the requirements analyst, but cases such as this one may easily happen in practice.

Another task worth clarifying is *use the 2 second rule*. This is a well-known rule for maintaining a safe distance between vehicles. It is adopted in some countries as a good code for driver conduct for human drivers [2], and it can also be adopted as a requirement for driverless cars. Note that this task makes the *keeping a safe following distance while driving* quality. However, to accomplish the higher level *keeping a safe following distance* quality, other tasks and qualities are involved.

The reader may have noticed that each of the RE approaches has its advantages and limitations. For example, the relation between the impact events, principles and ethical requirements are easier to spot in the requirements table, much easier and fast to create in comparison with the goal model. The goal model, however, makes more explicit which intention (and thus which requirement) is related to each of the agents involved in our case. Moreover, it is visual and it allows a much more detailed requirements analysis, in terms of more and less abstract requirements, solutions and needed resources.

We emphasize that ObRE does not subscribe to a specific RE method, leaving this choice for the requirements analyst, based on their particular preference or skill. Another important point is that the choice for the RE approach may be taken based on the approach's underlying modeling languages. For instance, a language offering the concepts of threat, value etc. may be a preferred choice here.

5   Related Works

We examine related works in two directions. First, we take a look at ontology-based methods for RE, especially those targeting NFRs, as these kinds of requirements are the main focus of ObRE. Next, we investigate works that aim at embedding systems with ethics.

ElicitO [6] is an ontology-based tool aimed at providing guidance during requirements elicitation, conducting the requirements analyst in performing a precise specification of NFRs. Taking a similar direction, the work of Veleda and Cysneiros [30] provides an ontology-based tool to help identify NFRs, making explicitly their interdependencies and possible conflicts. Hu et al. [25] also aim at detecting conflicts between NFRs, and conduct a trade-off analysis in case such conflicts arise. This is done by representing NFRs in a softgoal interdependency graph, which is formalized using an ontology. All these works follow a different path in comparison to ours, focusing much more on the automation of requirements analysis by the means of representing NFRs using OWL ontologies. Our work, on the other hand, uses reference ontologies to provide a deep understanding of NFRs whose semantics are usually subjective and complex, by interpreting these NFRs according to the particular domain of the system-to-be. And by the means of this interpretation, our work attempts to guide the requirements analyst in defining requirements that will support the analyzed NFRs.

Nowadays, many researchers have been busy trying to come up with frameworks and approaches targeting responsible AI and the development of systems embedded with ethics. Interesting initiatives are those of Rashid, Moore, May-Chahal and Chitchyan [28], Peters, Vold, Robinson and Calvo [27], Etzioni and Etzioni [16], Dignum [14] and Floridi et al. [17]. The latter has been proposed by several specialists, and has served as basis for the European Union Ethics Guidelines for Trustworthy AI [3]. All these cited research works bring very relevant insight on how to develop ethical systems. However, their proposed frameworks and guidelines are still in an abstract level, and we believe that approaches specifically targeted at Requirements Engineering are still an open issue. Our proposal is proposed with the goal of filling in this gap.

6   Final Remarks

In this paper, we illustrate how a novel RE method named ObRE is able to elicit ethicality requirements. In particular, ObRE precisely defines the concepts that underlie a class of quality requirements (NFRs) through an ontology and offers these concepts for requirements analysis. ObRE aims to address the subjective and ambiguous nature of many classes of requirements, especially the ones that have become prominent recently with the advent of AI systems. As a result, ObRE facilitates the communication between analysts and stakeholders, besides assisting in the identification of requirements.

It is important to note that our approach does not prescribe a specific way to implement the analyzed requirements in the system, for example, by developing a rule-based system, or by having the requirements hardcoded. ObRE focuses solely on the RE activity, supporting the elicitation of requirements, which can then be analyzed, validated and monitored throughout the system's life cycle.

The success of RE activities largely depends on the creation of a shared understanding between stakeholders and analysts for a system-to-be [12,18]. Werner, Li, Ernst and Damian [31] conducted an empirical study to find out why a shared understanding NFRs is so difficult in software organizations. Their study shows that two of the main problems were lack of domain knowledge and inadequate communication. They report on some interesting findings that we believe could be alleviated by the application of ObRE, e.g., i) some NFRs are considered complicated and out of the developers expertise; ii) there is no clear understanding of what particular NFRs mean; and iii) when two or more people are working simultaneously in the same system, even if they communicate, they end up approaching a given NFR in a different way. Ethical requirements, which are the focus of this paper, fit precisely into the situations just described.

Our agenda for the future includes, firstly, a full fledged implementation and validation of the ObRE method, by doing real case studies and having experts evaluate the results. Another interesting research direction is extending the ethical requirements ontology to deal with ethical conflicts. Many problems arise when intelligent systems face situations that involve ethical conflicts. For example, for the driverless car, what happens if the system needs to choose the lesser of two evils, such as either running over a bystander or a pedestrian? The principles we adopted so far in our ontological analysis do not seem to account alone for such cases, and we plan to address this limitation in the near future.

References

1. A framework for ethical decision making (2015). https://www.scu.edu/ethics/ethics-resources/ethical-decision-making/a-framework-for-ethical-decision-making/
2. The 2-second rule. In: Learn the Road Code (2016). https://drive.govt.nz/get-your-learners/interactive-road-code/
3. Ethics guidelines for trustworthy AI (2019). https://digital-strategy.ec.europa.eu/en/library/ethics-guidelines-trustworthy-ai
4. The 7 Most Pressing Ethical Issues in Artificial Intelligence (2019). https://kambria.io/blog/the-7-most-pressing-ethical-issues-in-artificial-intelligence/
5. IEEE standard model process for addressing ethical concerns during system design. IEEE STD 7000-2021, pp. 1–82 (2021). https://doi.org/10.1109/IEEESTD.2021.9536679
6. Al Balushi, T., Sampaio, P., Dabhi, D., Loucopoulos, P.: ElicitO: a quality ontology-guided NFR elicitation tool. In: 13th International Working Conference on Requirement Engineering: Foundation for Software Quality, pp. 306–319 (2007)
7. Amaral, G., Guizzardi, R., Guizzardi, G., Mylopoulos, J.: Ontology-based modeling and analysis of trustworthiness requirements: preliminary results. In: Dobbie, G., Frank, U., Kappel, G., Liddle, S.W., Mayr, H.C. (eds.) ER 2020. LNCS, vol. 12400, pp. 342–352. Springer, Cham (2020). https://doi.org/10.1007/978-3-030-62522-1_25
8. Amaral, G., Guizzardi, R., Guizzardi, G., Mylopoulos, J.: Ontology-based requirements engineering: the case of trustworthiness requirements. In: 40th International Conference on Conceptual Modeling, pp. 257–267 (2021)
9. European Commission High-Level Expert Group on Artificial Intelligence: Draft ethics guidelines for trustworthy AI, draft document (2018)
10. Berto, F., Plebani, M.: Ontology and Metaontology: A Contemporary Guide. Bloomsbury Publishing, London (2015)
11. Castelfranchi, C.: Commitments: from individual intentions to groups and organizations. In: ICMAS, vol. 95, pp. 41–48 (1995)
12. Charaf, M., Rosenkranz, C., Holten, R.: The emergence of shared understanding: applying functional pragmatics to study the requirements development process. Inf. Syst. J. **23**(2), 115–135 (2013)
13. Dalpiaz, F., Franch, X., Horkoff, J.: iStar 2.0 language guide. arXiv:1605.07767 [cs.SE] (2016). http://dalp-fran-hork-16-istar.pdf/
14. Dignum, V.: Responsible Artificial Intelligence: How to Develop and Use AI in a Responsible Way. Springer, Cham (2019). https://doi.org/10.1007/978-3-030-30371-6
15. Duarte, B.B., et al.: Ontological foundations for software requirements with a focus on requirements at runtime. Appl. Ontol. **13**(2), 73–105 (2018)
16. Etzioni, A., Etzioni, O.: Incorporating ethics into artificial intelligence. J. Ethics **12**, 403–418 (2017)
17. Floridi, L., et al.: AI4People-an ethical framework for a good AI society: opportunities, risks, principles, and recommendations. Minds Mach. **28**, 689–707 (2018)
18. Glinz, M., Fricker, S.: On shared understanding in software engineering: an essay. Comput. Sci. Res. Dev. **30**(3–4), 363–376 (2015)
19. Guizzardi, G.: Ontological foundations for structural conceptual models. Telematica Instituut/CTIT (2005)

20. Guizzardi, G., Wagner, G., Almeida, J.P.A., Guizzardi, R.S.S.: Towards ontological foundations for conceptual modeling: the Unified Foundational Ontology (UFO) story. Appl. Ontol. **10**(3–4), 259–271 (2015)
21. Guizzardi, R.: Agent-oriented Constructivist Knowledge Management. Ph.D. thesis, University of Twente, Netherlands (2006)
22. Guizzardi, R., Carneiro, B.G., Porello, D., Guizzardi, G.: A core ontology on decision making. In: Proceedings of the 13th Seminar on Ontology Research in Brazil (2020)
23. Guizzardi, R. et al.: An ontological interpretation of non-functional requirements. In: Proceedings of FOIS, vol. 14, pp. 344–357 (2014)
24. Guizzardi, R., et al.: Ethical requirements for AI systems. In: Proceedings of Canadian AI 2020, pp. 251–256 (2020)
25. Hu, H., et al.: Semantic modelling and automated reasoning of non-functional requirement conflicts in the context of softgoal interdependencies. IET Softw. **9**, 145–156 (2015)
26. Mumford, S.: Dispositions. Clarendon Press, Oxford (2003)
27. Peters, D., Vold, K., Robinson, D., Calvo, R.: Responsible AI: two frameworks for ethical design practice. IEEE Trans. Technol. Soc. **1**(1), 34–47 (2020)
28. Rashid, A., Moore, K., May-Chahal, C., Chitchyan, R.: Managing emergent ethical concerns for software engineering in society. In: 37th IEEE International Conference on Software Engineering, pp. 523–526. IEEE (2015)
29. Sales, T.P., Baião, F., Guizzardi, G., Almeida, J.P.A., Guarino, N., Mylopoulos, J.: The common ontology of value and risk. In: Trujillo, J.C., et al. (eds.) ER 2018. LNCS, vol. 11157, pp. 121–135. Springer, Cham (2018). https://doi.org/10.1007/978-3-030-00847-5_11
30. Veleda, R., Cysneiros, L.M.: Towards an ontology-based approach for eliciting possible solutions to non-functional requirements. In: Giorgini, P., Weber, B. (eds.) CAiSE 2019. LNCS, vol. 11483, pp. 145–161. Springer, Cham (2019). https://doi.org/10.1007/978-3-030-21290-2_10
31. Werner, C., Li, Z., Ernst, N., Damian, D.: The lack of shared understanding of non-functional requirements in continuous software engineering: accidental or essential? In: 28th IEEE International Requirements Engineering Conference, RE 2020, Zurich, Switzerland, 31 August–4 September 2020, pp. 90–101. IEEE (2020)

Agent Responsibility Framework for Digital Agents: Roles and Responsibilities Related to Facets of Work

Steven Alter[✉] (iD)

University of San Francisco, 2130 Fulton Street, San Francisco 94117, USA
alter@usfca.edu

Abstract. This paper presents a new agent responsibility framework designed to help business professionals and IT experts collaborate around the analysis and design of digital agents. The framework emphasizes roles, responsibilities, and capabilities of digital agents in relation to work systems that they support. This paper presents basic concepts related to digital agents, work systems, and facets of work. It uses four examples to illustrate how the new agent responsibility framework helps in visualizing roles and responsibilities of digital agents in relation to work systems that delegate responsibilities to them.

Keywords: Digital agent · Work system · Facets of work · Agent responsibility framework

1 Toward a New Approach for Describing Digital Agents

Current trends toward digitization increase the need for analysis and design approaches that are suitable for business professionals because their appreciation of business and operational realities is essential for designing effective digital agents. That need frequently encounters longstanding difficulties in establishing effective and mutually supportive collaboration of business professionals and IT experts during the analysis and design of computerized systems. Aside from differences in professional interests and concerns, many aspects of this problem involve lack of fit between the interests and concerns of business professionals and the tools, methods, and concerns of IT experts. Many researchers have discussed related problems involving modeling method usage [1, 2], model comprehension [2–4], use of only a subset of the syntactic concepts provided [5], poor fit with modelers' aptitudes and knowledge [6, 7] excessive cognitive load [8], lack of flexibility, dilemmas of control, and excessive prescriptiveness [9]. Part of the problem is that widely used documentation tools and methods (e.g., BPMN and ERD) are often too detailed to support collaborative visualization and discussion related to system design and evaluation.

This paper follows the spirit of a 2018 *BISE* research note [10] that responded to the above issues by promoting ways to move enterprise modeling from an expert discipline toward "grass roots modeling" and "modeling for the masses" by accepting "softened

A. Augusto et al. (Eds.): BPMDS 2022/EMMSAD 2022, LNBIP 450, pp. 237–252, 2022.
https://doi.org/10.1007/978-3-031-07475-2_16

requirements to completeness, coherence and rigor." This paper reflects that spirit while still calling for carefully defined concepts.

This paper's approach for articulating intuitive understandings of systems is largely separate from detailed documentation needed by development efforts. Its new agent responsibility (AR) framework was inspired by Shneiderman's human-centered AI (HCAI) framework [11–13], whose two dimensions are low to high computer automation and low to high human control. The AR framework's horizontal dimension is a spectrum of digital agent roles in relation to specific work systems. The vertical dimension is a series of facets of work to which digital agents might be applied in work systems. This paper explains those ideas and presents four examples to illustrate their potential use. Its emphasis on responsibilities of digital agents might facilitate analysis and design related to increasingly common digital agents even though it will not overcome all known problems related to requirements analysis.

Goal. This paper presents a new agent responsibility framework and explains how its use by business professionals and IT experts might facilitate analysis and design related to digital agents by helping them identify and discuss many types of roles and related responsibilities that work systems might delegate to digital agents.

Organization. This paper builds on a long research stream related to work systems. The next section presents a view of digital agents, which are a type of algorithmic agent. Work system theory (WST) is summarized as the core of a perspective for describing the usage context for digital agents. A hypothetical hiring work system illustrates how digital agents can be treated in designing or evaluating a work system. The agent responsibility (AR) framework is presented with emphasis on its two dimensions: a spectrum of roles and responsibilities and different facets of work. Each of those dimensions is explained in more depth through application to three additional examples of digital agents: an ecommerce platform, a real time advertising auction, and a self-driving car's information system. A concluding section summarizes the overall implication that the use of WST and the AR framework provide a practical approach for understanding and evaluating roles, responsibilities, and capabilities of digital agents in their context of use.

2   Digital Agents as Algorithmic Agents[1]

Digital agents are digital entities whose roles and responsibilities are delegated by work systems (defined later). They are algorithmic agents because they operate by executing algorithms. Those algorithms may be as simple as a decision rule or as complex as an advanced optimization method or an integrated algorithm for driving a self-driving car. Given their nature as abstractions, algorithms cannot do anything by themselves and have effect only when human or non-human actors use them to support, control, or perform actions in the world.

Table 1 lists examples involving digital agents that might or might not use AI-related capabilities. Some of them might be simple decision rules such as allowing no more than

---

[1] This section is an abbreviated and revised version of a section in [14] that discusses algorithms. A subsequent hiring example comes from the same source.

40% of applicants to be classified in category X. Even a simple algorithm like that one can have important and far reaching effects that favor one group of people over other groups, as when category X is treated as qualification for employment or acceptance into college. Digital agents that operate the internet or control autonomous vehicles are more complex and have more far-reaching impacts.

Table 1. Digital agents described based on the activities that they perform

• using facial images to identify people • converting spoken words into text • deciding which applicants should be hired or accepted by a university • deciding whether to alert medical staff about a change in a patient's condition • deciding whether a person is legally entitled to drive a car • deciding whether an autonomous vehicle needs to stop or swerve • controlling the aerodynamics of a rocket • translating from one language to another	• deciding whether to turn off a machine likely to have a mechanical failure soon • suggesting where police should be deployed over the next eight hours • selecting defective items that are being moved on a conveyor belt • combining multiple items in an order to minimize shipping cost • determining the best route for driving from a starting point to a destination • finding the laws that are most relevant to a specific lawsuit

3 Work Systems as the Context for Using Digital Agents

The work system perspective (WSP) is a general approach for understanding systems in organizations by treating those systems as work systems, as explained in [15, 16]. The WSP's core is work system theory (WST), which consists of the definition of work system plus two frameworks for understanding a work system: 1) The work system framework (Fig. 1) is a static view for summarizing how a work system operates. 2) The work system life cycle model (WSLC – Fig. 1) explains how a work system evolves through planned and unplanned change. Earlier confusion about the relationship between core of the work system approach and its various extensions was clarified when [16] identified WST as a conceptual core underlying the work system method (WSM) which had been developed over several decades as a semi-formal systems analysis method for business professionals. Various versions of WSM were tailored to instructional needs of different courses, most of which were for employed MBA and Executive MBA students. Individual students or teams of students used WSM templates to produce over 700 management briefings recommending improvements of problematic IT-reliant work systems during 2003–2017, mostly in their own organizations (e.g., [17]). The goal of a work system-based description or analysis is to understand a situation and often to communicate and collaborate about it with others. When describing and analyzing work systems, the identification and boundaries of the work system are choices that depend on the purpose of the analysis. As discussed in many articles and books about systems approaches (e.g., [18, 19]), different observers may use work system ideas to describe the same system (e.g., a sales system, purchasing system, or management system) somewhat differently even when they pursue similar purposes. Parts of those efforts might document system components using rigorous tools such as BPMN and ERD, even though that level of specificity might be unncessary elsehwhere in those efforts.

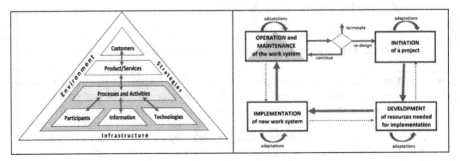

Fig. 1. Work system framework and work system life cycle model

Definition of Work System. A work system is a system in which human participants *and/or* machines perform work (processes and activities) using information, technology, and other resources to produce specific product/services for internal and/or external customers [16]. Terms in that definition are stated in relation to work systems rather than in relation to computer science or other discourses. *Customer* refers to any entity using the work system's outputs; *product/service* avoids distinctions between products and services that are not helpful when discussing work systems; *processes and activities* recognizes that activities in a work system may or may not be structured enough to call a process. The first *and/or* in the definition addresses trends toward service-orientation and automation by saying that work systems may be sociotechnical (human participants perform some of the work) or totally automated (machines perform all of the work).

Information Systems and Projects as Special Cases of Work Systems. Instead   of seeing an IS as a tool, like a laptop or a hammer, the work system perspective treats information systems as work systems most of whose activities are devoted to capturing, transmitting, storing, retrieving, deleting, manipulating, and/or displaying information [15, 16]. An IS may be sociotechnical (e.g., financial analysts creating economic projections with the help of modeling software) or totally automated (e.g., computers generating economic projections automatically after being programmed by people). Projects are another important special case, i.e., work systems designed to produce specific product/services and then go out of existence. Software development is a type of project (and hence, a work system) that can be executed in many ways.

Digital Agents as Information Systems. Digital agents are totally automated information systems whose roles and related responsibilities are delegated by a work system. The roles describe activities that a digital agent executes for the work system. The responsibilities describe the expected level of performance regarding those activities. A digital agent's capabilities determine the extent to which the delegated roles and responsibilities are feasible. A digital agent may be an integral component of the work system or may be completely separate from it, as in outsourcing of work. The somewhat similar idea of delegation to agentic IS artifacts is explained in [20], which discusses many concepts related to delegation, rights, and responsibilities.

Work System Framework: Elements of a Basic Understanding of a Work System. Figure 1 identifies nine elements of a basic understanding of a work system's form, function, and environment during a period when it retains its identity even as incremental changes may occur, such as minor process changes, personnel substitutions, or technology upgrades. *Processes and activities, participants, information,* and *technologies* are completely within the work system. *Customers* and *product/services* may be partially inside and partially outside because customers often participate in activities within a work system and because product/services take shape within a work system. *Environment, infrastructure,* and *strategies* are external to the work system even though they have direct impacts on its operation.

Work System Life Cycle Model (WSLC): How Work Systems Change Over Time. Figure 1 says that work systems (including digital agents, which are work systems since they are information systems) evolve through a combination of planned change via projects and unplanned change via adaptations and workarounds. Significant changes typically affect multiple elements of the work system framework, not just technology. Projects that pursue planned change in business settings traverse three main phases: initiation, development, and implementation. Many aspects of the WSLC remain valid even with nominally agile approaches. Those aspects include the emphasis on work system changes rather than just software development, the focus on evolution over time rather than one-time projects, the simultaneous importance of planned and unplanned change, and the relevance of key responsibilities within each phase.

3.1 A Hypothetical Work System that Uses AI-Based Digital Agents

Table 2 is a work system snapshot (a tool from WSM) summarizing a hypothetical hiring system that is used here to illustrate a work system perspective in a situation that might involve AI. In this example, PQR Corp implemented a new hiring work system two years ago to improve a previous hiring work system that absorbed too much effort inside PQR Corp and operated so slowly that qualified candidates sometimes took jobs at other companies before receiving offers. Also, it hired too many unsuitable candidates who left before becoming productive. The new hiring work system used AlgoComm and AlgoRank, digital agents controlled by software from a cloud-based suite of software tools provided by AlgoCorp. AlgoComm provides capabilities for posting job ads, receiving applications, setting up interview appointments, and performing other communication with candidates. AlgoRank ranks candidates based on job criteria and a machine learning application driven by AlgoCorp's extensive database of job qualifications, salaries, and other information. Both AlgoComm and AlgoRank are digital agents.

Management has become dissatisfied with the current hiring work system. Excessive effort and delays have been reduced, but interviewers and applicants find the AlgoComm interface mechanical, uninviting, and lacking a human feel. Also, three unsuitable hires occurred in the last six months despite use of AlgoRank capabilities. Management wants to launch a new project to upgrade the hiring work system once again. This may involve eliminating the two digital agents, obtaining changes by AlgoCorp, or using either or both digital agents in different ways.

Table 2. Work system snapshot of the current hiring system

Customers		Product/services	
• Applicants • Hiring manager • Larger organization • HR manager (who will use the applications to analyze the nature of applicants)		• Applications (which may be used for subsequent analysis) • Job offers • Rejection letters • Hiring of the applicant	
Major activities and processes			
• **AlgoComm** publicizes the position. • **Applicants** submit resumes to **AlgoComm**. • **AlgoRank** selects shortlisted applicants and sends the list to the hiring manager. • **Hiring manager** decides who to interview. • **AlgoComm** sets up interviews.		• **Interviewers** perform interviews and provide comments about applicants. • **AlgoRank** evaluates candidates. • **Hiring manager** makes hiring decision. • **AlgoComm** notifies applicants. • **Applicant** accepts or rejects job offer.	
Participants	Information		Technology
• Hiring manager • Applicants • Other employees who perform interviews	• Job requisition • Job description • Advertisements • Job applications • Cover letters • Applicant resumes	• Applicant short list • Information and impressions from the interviews • Job offers • Rejection letters	• AlgoComm • AlgoRank • Office software • Internet

A quick glance at Table 2 shows that the hiring work system involves much more than the digital agents AlgoComm and AlgoRank. The transition from the previous hiring system to the current hiring system started with a WSLC *initiation phase* (Fig. 1) in which management decided to improve the existing hiring system by using a vendor's software. The WSLC *development phase* acquired resources needed for implementation in the organization. AlgoCorp was selected as vendor. Developers initialized AlgoCorp's software, set values of parameters to fit PQR Corp's needs, and adapted AlgoCorp's training material for PQR Corp's users. Training during the *implementation phase* occurred quickly. During the *operation and maintenance phase* AlgoCorp used machine learning to update AlgoRank to reflect job market changes. Several incidents during that period involved managers working around the standard process (called *adaptations* by the WSLC) when talented individuals might have gone to a competitor. Management decided that a better hiring work system was needed.

This hypothetical hiring case was designed to illustrate how a work system perspective can help in visualizing and understanding applications of digital agents in real world practice. The main point is that digital agents that affect people typically operate in real world contexts that are fundamentally about work systems achieving real world goals and are not about just about creating or using computerized artifacts.

4 Facets of Work

Facets of work is an extension of WST that supports a deeper understanding of roles and responsibilities of digital agents in work systems. That idea grew out of research trying to bring richer and more evocative concepts to systems analysis and design and to facilitate interactions between analysts and stakeholders, as explained in [21: 342–344]. The notion of facet is an analogy to how a cut diamond consists of a single thing with many facets. The idea of facet has been used with quite different meanings and connotations in disciplines such as psychology, library science, information science, and computer science (e.g., [22–27]).

Most activities in work systems consist of one or more common types of activities such as making decisions, communicating, and processing information. For current purposes, those types of activities can be considered *facets of work* if they are easily understood and widely applicable and if they satisfy a series of criteria: They apply to both sociotechnical work systems and totally automated work systems; they are associated with many concepts that are useful for analyzing system-related situations; they are associated with evaluation criteria and typical design trade-offs; they have sub-facets that can be discussed; they bring open-ended questions that are useful for starting conversations. Table 3 illustrates how the facet *decision making* satisfies those criteria. [21] identifies and provides the same type of information for 18 such facets of work, while recognizing that other researchers might have identified a different number of facets of work that satisfy those criteria. Facets of work often are not mutually independent. To the contrary, the facet *making decisions* often involves other facets such as *communicating, learning,* and *processing information.* The main point is that each facet can be viewed as part of a lens for thinking about where and how work systems might use digital agents.

Table 3. Why *making decisions* qualifies as one of 18 facets of work

Criterion	Illustration of how *making decisions* satisfies a criterion
Applies to socio-technical and totally automated systems	In a sociotechnical work system, marketing managers allocate a corporate advertising budget. In a totally automated work system, an optimization model allocates a corporate advertising budget
Association with many concepts that can be used for analysis	Decision, criteria, alternative, value, risk, payoff, utility, utility function, tradeoff, projection, optimum, satisficing vs. optimizing, heuristic, probability, distribution of results, risk aversion
Association with evaluation criteria	Actual decision outcomes, realism of projected outcomes, ease of implementation, riskiness, decision participation, concurrence

(continued)

Table 3. (*continued*)

Criterion	Illustration of how *making decisions* satisfies a criterion
Association with design tradeoffs	Quick response vs. superficiality, model complexity and precision vs. understandability, brevity vs. omission of important details
Existence of sub-facets for detailed description	Defining the problem; identifying decision criteria; gathering relevant information; analyzing the information; defining alternatives; selecting among alternatives; explaining the decision
Related open-ended questions	How do the available methods and information help in important decisions? What decisions are made with incomplete, inaccurate, or outdated methods or information? How might better methods or information help in making decisions? Where would that information come from?

5   The Agent Responsibility Framework

The hiring example summarized in Table 2 illustrates that digital agents can contribute to activities in work systems. That straightforward observation says little about how to understand roles of digital agents in greater depth. A designer or manager trying to decide whether or how to produce and apply a digital agent could benefit from a framework for identifying and visualizing potential design choices. As noted earlier, the agent responsibility (AR) framework in Fig. 2 was inspired by Shneiderman's 2 × 2 human-centered AI (HCAI) framework [11–13], whose dimensions are low to high computer automation and low to high human control. That framework is useful for discussing human-centered AI but can be expanded to support analysis and design of digital agents with responsibilities delegated by a work system.

The AR framework aims to serve that purpose by characterizing roles and related responsibilities delegated to digital agents by work systems. Clarity about those roles and responsibilities and the capabilities that make them practical requires attention to whether and how a digital agent aims to support specific facets of work in the work system, such as making decisions, communicating, or processing information. A work system's use of a digital agent occurs when that digital agent plays one or more roles (the framework's horizontal dimension) related to one or more of the work system's facets of work (the vertical dimension). The effectiveness of that use depends on the digital agent's capabilities. The brief description of the hiring example implied that roles played by digital agents included providing information and executing activities related to facets of work such as making decisions, communicating, and processing information but that enhanced capabilities might have led to better results.

Figure 2 is a version of the AR framework with six roles that might be performed in relation to any of six facets of work. Combining those two dimensions leads to pinpointing responsibilities delegated to digital agents by work systems. Other versions of the AR framework might include other roles and other facets of work.

		Monitor work system	Provide information	Provide capabilities	Control activities	Coproduce activities	Execute activities
Facet of work >>>	Making decisions						
	Communicating						
	Processing information						
	Coordinating						
	Creating value						
	Maintaining security						

<<<<<<< **Spectrum of roles and responsibilities** >>>>>>>

Fig. 2. Agent responsibility framework with six roles and six facets of work

The AR framework presents the six roles along a spectrum from the lowest to the highest direct involvement in the execution of activities within a work system. The six roles in Fig. 2 were identified based on many iterations of trying to expand the horizontal dimension in Shneiderman's HCAI framework to make it more specific. For example, an early iteration involved only three roles, i.e., support, control, and perform. Here are ways in which those six roles might be performed more effectively in an improved version of the hiring work system.

- **Monitor a work system.** Digital agents might monitor hiring activities to identify important delays and might generate messages to management when aspects of a planned hiring process seem likely to use interviewer resources excessively.
- **Provide information.** Digital agents might scan applications to identify areas of important fit or misfit. Digital agents also might provide comparisons of current applicants with past applicants or even a relevant sample of non-applicants.
- **Provide capabilities.** Digital agents might provide analytical, visualization, and computational capabilities that help interviewers and managers compare applicants and articulate their impressions about how well applicants fit current needs.
- **Control activities.** Digital agents might inspect all informational artifacts generated by hiring activities to make sure that any evidence of bias, unnecessary delays, or mistreatment of applicants is identified and corrected quickly.
- **Coproduce activities.** Digital agents might coproduce with applicants by initiating and conducting screening interviews at times that maximize convenience for interviewees. They might work collaboratively with interviewers by filtering excerpts from voice and video responses that interviewers rate as important.
- **Execute activities.** Digital agents might search professional networks, listings from independent contracting firms, and applications from past applicants to identify potential candidates and send inquiries to those individuals.

The six facets in the vertical dimension are selected from 18 facets of work identified in [21], which showed that all or most of those 18 facets of work are worth considering in many situations. The 12 other facets in [21] include learning, planning, improvising, interacting socially, providing service, and seven others.

Before saying more about the two dimensions in Fig. 2 it is worth noting that the AR framework encompasses ideas that can be used in many ways that do not rely on an exhaustive search of all possible combinations of roles and facets. Simply thinking about the different facets of work could encourage designers or managers to wonder about needs to enhance specific facets of work in the design of specific work systems. Similarly, the spectrum of roles in the horizontal dimension encourages designers or managers to consider different possible roles of digital agents, related responsibilities that might be assigned to them, and capabilities that would be required. There is no reason to consider all or even many of the 36 possible combinations of 6 facets of work and 6 types of roles/responsibilities (or of the 108 combinations based on 6 roles and 18 facets). Instead, practicality implies that designers and managers should look carefully only at the combinations that are important for a specific work system.

6   Application of the AR Framework to Examples

The hiring example in Table 2 was introduced to help in visualizing the relationship between digital agents and work systems. This section applies the AR framework to three other examples to illustrate its potential use in many situations from both provider and user viewpoints. 1) An ecommerce platform is a digital agent for a temporary work system in which an individual or organization uses an ecommerce platform to identify items to buy and complete the purchases. 2) A real time auction of ad placements in online media is a digital agent for a firm's advertising work system that purchases ad placements in online media. 3) The information system in a self-driving car is a digital agent for an individual's temporary work system of driving from one location to another.

The following descriptions of these examples include tables containing a row for each facet in Fig. 2. Each row shows in parenthesis one of the six roles in the AR framework's horizontal dimension and then summarizes how a digital agent playing that role might be applied to that row's facet of work. Table 4 applies the roles in the AR framework in the same sequence in which they appear in Fig. 2. Tables 5 and 6 (for two subsequent examples) use the same sequence but start with the second and third roles, respectively, as a partial illustration that most of the roles can be applied to most of the facets. Associating roles with facets in those different ways is significant only for illustrating that most roles apply to most facets. A more detailed exercise of assigning each role to all 18 facets from [21] would lead to tables containing 108 entries (6 roles × 18 facets) that would not fit within this paper's length limits.

6.1   Example: An Ecommerce Platform as a Digital Agent

This example is an ecommerce platform such as amazon.com or walmart.com that serves as a digital agent for an individual's temporary work system of selecting items to purchase and then purchasing those items. Table 4 shows how the six roles might be applied to the six facets of work in Fig. 2. Table 4 takes the viewpoint of an ecommerce merchant designing or updating a platform to maximize its utility.

Table 4. Applying different digital agent roles in an ecommerce example

Facet	Illustration of how an ecommerce merchant might think about specific digital agent roles (*in parenthesis and italicized*) of an ecommerce platform in relation to a specific facet of work in a typical customer's personal purchasing work system
Making decisions	(*monitor*) The digital agent might *monitor* interim decisions revealed in customer work system's click stream, thus providing clues related to customer goals and priorities and possibly leading to suggestions of plausible options that customers had not yet considered
Communicating	(*provide information*) The digital agent might *provide information* in the form of URLs that would help customer work systems communicate with other information sources that might validate purchasing decisions
Processing information	(*provide capabilities*) To demonstrate the ecommerce site's low prices, the digital agent might *provide capabilities* that customer work systems could use for processing information to find competitor's prices
Coordinating	(*control activities*) Coordination is not significant when an individual uses an ecommerce site. A digital agent might *control* aspects of coordination between multiple platform users in the same organization to avoid duplicative purchases within the same organization
Creating value	(*coproduce activities*) The digital agent might help in creating value for the platform and the customer by *coproducing* the identification of nonobvious buying opportunities that would increase mutual benefits
Maintaining security	(*execute activities*) The digital agent might help in maintaining security for ecommerce customers by *executing activities* that protect the security of email addresses, user names, and other personal information

6.2   Example: A Real Time Advertising Auction as a Digital Agent

A totally automated ecosystem controls the insertion of ads into web-based content such as online news articles. "It is a huge, real-time bidding process, whereby ads are automatically assigned to media spaces across types of media and geographic regions upon an individual user's browser request. … the entire ecosystem's exchange with its hundreds of platforms operates 'on-demand' every time a user's browser opens a publisher website and triggers a real-time request for an ad. The whole exchange is usually completed under 100 ms and remains entirely invisible to the user who may experience a small lag in loading the publisher page." [28]. The digital agent is a real time auction serving an advertiser's work system of buying ad placements in online media. (see Table 5).

Table 5. Applying different digital agent roles during in a real time auction for advertising slots

Facet	Illustration of how a specific digital agent role (*in parenthesis and italicized*) of a real time automated auction might be applied to a specific facet of work in an advertising work system
Making decisions	(*provide information*) The digital agent might <u>provide information</u> about past auctions that would support the buying work system's <u>decision making</u> concerning economically feasible media targets
Communicating	(*provide capabilities*) The digital agent might <u>provide capabilities</u> that increase convenience for the advertisers who need to <u>communicate</u> changing priorities and purchase limits as an auction proceeds
Processing information	(*control activities*) The digital agent might <u>control</u> aspects of the work system's <u>processing of information</u> about current priorities to assure that media choices are not excessively duplicative in advertising targets
Coordinating	(*coproduce activities*) The digital agent might help in <u>coproducing</u> advertising decisions of different groups in the firm by helping them <u>coordinate</u> priorities in data submitted to the online auction
Creating value	(*execute activities*) The digital agent might help in <u>creating value</u> for the customer work systems by providing more complete information about situations where other advertisers won auctions for prized placements
Maintaining security	(*monitor*) The digital agent might <u>monitor</u> bidding on auctions to help customers <u>maintain security</u> by identifying suspicious patterns of auction bidding results

6.3 Example: A Self-driving Car's Information System as a Digital Agent

Self-driving cars are controlled by internal information systems that combine radar, electronic maps, predictive techniques, advanced displays, monitoring of road and traffic conditions, monitoring of the car's internal operation, and automatic braking or swerving. Those information systems help drivers drive safely and sometimes allow drivers to use automatic driving capabilities. The work system is the individual's temporary work system of driving from one location to another. The digital agent is the car's information system that monitors current conditions, communicates with the driver, and takes control under some circumstances (see Table 6).

Table 6. Different digital agent roles for the information system that operates a self-driving car

Facet	Illustration of how a specific digital agent role (*in parenthesis and italicized*) of a self-driving car's information system might be applied to a specific facet of work in a personal driving work system
Making decisions	(*provide capabilities*) The digital agent might *provide capabilities* for making decisions related to avoiding bottlenecks or slow traffic
Communicating	(*control activities*) The digital agent might *control* aspects of the driver's communication with other drivers by activating blinkers, sounding alarms that help the driver and other drivers avoid accidents
Processing information	(*coproduce activities*) The digital agent might help *coproduce* partially manual driving by processing information from the steering mechanism and brakes to make sure that the driver does not accidentally perform dangerous maneuvers
Coordinating	(*execute activities*) The digital agent might automatically *execute* evasive maneuvers to help in coordinating with other self-driving cars that seem to be on a collision course with the car being driven
Creating value	(*monitor*) The digital agent might *monitor* the extent to which the car's displays, heating and air conditioning systems, seating adjustments, and other systems are creating value for the driver and passengers
Maintaining security	(*provide information*) The digital agent might *provide information* that helps in maintaining security by warning the driver that an outside entity is trying to detect electronic signals generated or used within the car

7 Discussion and Conclusions

This paper presented the agent responsibility framework and used examples to explain how it might help managers and designers imagine and evaluate a wide range of possibilities for delegating aspects of the operation of specific work systems to digital agents. It defined digital agent as a type of information system that operates autonomously once launched although it may interact with users, with other digital agents, or with aspects of the surrounding environment. The idea of digital agent may be applied by providers of digital agents (people or organizations that build and deploy digital agents) and by users of digital agents (people or work systems that assign responsibilities to digital agents that their organizations may own or to commercial platforms or other types of digital agents owned by others.

The core of this paper's contribution is the notion that work systems delegate responsibilities to digital agents and that those responsibilities involve performing one or more roles along a spectrum of roles that may apply to one or more facets of work in the work system. That notion leads to many different ways to visualize whether and how a digital agent might be applied beneficially and whether and how its capabilities might be improved to achieve greater benefits. This overall approach is designed to help in articulating a range of concerns that is much broader than the range of concerns uncovered by widely used techniques such as use cases and user stories, which focus more on activities performed by IT users and less on the broader needs of work systems as goal-oriented systems. Similarly, tools such as BPMN and ERD are valuable for documenting details but tend not to reveal many issues related to facets of work such as making decisions, communicating, creating value, and so on.

The version of the AR framework presented here used a matrix of 6 roles × 6 facets of work. As explained earlier, many other facets of work could be considered if those facets of work were important for the work system being analyzed or designed. Those additional facets might be among the 18 identified by [21] or might be other facets of work identified by other researchers (assuming that those facets satisfied the usefulness criteria for facets of work that were illustrated in Table 3).

Limitations. This paper used examples to argue for the practicality of its approach for addressing important problems in real world practice. It did not provide empirical validation. Also, it did not provide a full literature review of requirements engineering or systems analysis and design. That type of literature review would have absorbed too much of the limited space available for explaining this paper's ideas.

Potential Use in Practice. Aspects of the AR framework can be used throughout projects that create and implement both work systems and digital agents used by work systems. Managers and executives can use the AR framework in the initiation phase of the WSLC (Fig. 1) to visualize many aspects of the application situation, e.g., by visualizing the relevant work system and exploring how new or improved digital agents might lead to more successful execution of different facets of work in that work system. In the development phase, developers can consider the extent to which the resources being developed are likely to contribute to better results for important facets of work. In the implementation phase, facets of work can be used to explain or discuss the responsibilities, capabilities, and intended use of digital agents that are being introduced or improved. The operation and maintenance phase can use the roles of digital agents in relation to facets of work to identify possible improvements that might generate better results in the future.

The detailed use of the AR framework and other ideas in this paper can unfold in many different ways that look at how digital agents may have responsibilities related to different roles and may touch multiple facets of work. A simple approach is just to focus on roles in general, i.e., consider the spectrum of roles in the horizontal dimension of the AR framework and think about whether those roles are played well in the work system, regardless of which facets of work are involved. Another simple approach is to focus on facets in a general sense by identifying facets of work that seem important for the work system and evaluate how well those facets of work are performed. In more detail, it is possible to look at responsibilities of a specific digital agent across the spectrum of roles or its responsibilities in relation to various facets of work that seem important. A more focused approach looks at a specific role and a specific facet of work and explores how well one or more digital agents satisfy their responsibilities in relation to that combination of role and facet of work.

All of the above can be done with the 6 × 6 version of the AR framework or with an expanded version that might involve more facets or more responsibilities that are not included in Fig. 2. As noted in Sect. 4, [21] explained how 18 different facets of work meet the criteria for being considered a facet of work, even though it is impractical to look in depth at every imaginable facet in a real world analysis.

Potential Use in Research. The AR framework and related ideas lead to a variety of possibilities for research projects related to digital agents. Conceptual research could compare this paper's view of a work system's delegation of responsibilities to digital agents with the discussion of concepts related to delegation and rights and responsibilities of agentic IS artifacts in [20]. Interesting research topics for empirical study of projects related to the design and implementation of digital agents correspond directly to potential uses in practice: How do managers and executives conceive of digital agent capabilities during the initiation phase? How do developers think about the potential use of digital agent capabilities that they produce? What is the range and rationale of perceptions and beliefs by work system participants concerning roles, responsibilities, and capabilities of digital agent? In what ways do work system adaptations during ongoing operation reflect attention to different facets of work and the adequacy of both capabilities and responsibilities of digital agents?

References

1. Fettke, P.: How conceptual modeling is used. Commun. Assoc. Inf. Syst. **25**(1), 571–592 (2009)
2. Mendling, J., Recker, J., Reijers, H.A., Leopold, H.: An empirical review of the connection between model viewer characteristics and the comprehension of conceptual process models. Inf. Syst. Front. **21**, 1111–1135 (2019)
3. Haisjackl, C., Soffer, P., Lim, S.Y., Weber, B.: How do humans inspect BPMN models: an exploratory study. Software Syst. Model. **17**(2), 655–673 (2018)
4. Johannsen, F., Leist, S., Braunnagel, D.: Testing the impact of wand and weber's decomposition model on process model understandability. In: International Conference on Information Systems (ICIS) (2014)
5. Langer, P., Mayerhofer, T., Wimmer, M., Kappel, G.: On the usage of UML: Initial results of analyzing open UML models. In: Modellierung 2014, pp. 289–304 (2014)
6. Hinkel, G., Kramer, M., Burger, E., Strittmatter, M., Happe, L.: An empirical study on the perception of metamodel quality. In: 4th International Conference on Model-Driven Engineering and Software Development (MODELSWARD). IEEE, pp. 145–152 (2016)
7. Muehlen, M.z., Recker, J.: How much language is enough? theoretical and practical use of the business process modeling notation. In: Bellahsène, Z., Léonard, M. (eds.) Advanced Information Systems Engineering. CAiSE 2008. LNISA, vol. 5074. Springer, Heidelberg (2008). https://doi.org/10.1007/978-3-540-69534-9_35
8. Sweller, J.: Cognitive load theory, learning difficulty, and instructional design. Learn. Instr. **4**(4), 295–312 (1994)
9. Simões, D., Antunes, P., Carriço, L.: Eliciting and modeling business process stories. Bus. Inf. Syst. Eng. **60**(2), 115–132 (2018)
10. Sandkuhl, K., et al.: From expert discipline to common practice: a vision and research agenda for extending the reach of enterprise modeling. Bus. Inf. Syst. Eng. **60**(1), 69–80 (2018)
11. Shneiderman, B.: Human-centered artificial intelligence: reliable, safe and trustworthy. Int. J. Hum. Comput. Interact. **36**(6), 495–504 (2020)

12. Shneiderman, B.: Human-centered artificial intelligence: three fresh ideas. AIS Trans. Hum. Comput. Interact. **12**(3), 109–124 (2020)
13. Shneiderman, B.: Human-Centered AI. Oxford University Press (2022)
14. Alter, S.: Understanding artificial intelligence in the context of usage: contributions and smartness of algorithmic capabilities in work systems. Int. J. Inf. Manage. 102392 (2021)
15. Alter, S.: The Work System Method: Connecting People, Processes, and IT for Business Results. Work System Press, Larkspur, CA (2006)
16. Alter, S.: Work system theory: overview of core concepts, extensions, and challenges for the future. J. Assoc. Inf. Syst. **14**(2), 72–121 (2013)
17. Truex, D., Alter, S., Long, C.: Systems analysis for everyone else: empowering business professionals through a systems analysis method that fits their needs. In: Proceedings of 18th European Conference on Information Systems (2010)
18. Checkland, P.: Systems Thinking, Systems Practice. Wiley, Chichester (1999)
19. Skyttner, L.: General systems theory: origin and hallmarks. Kybernetes **25**(6), 16–22 (1996)
20. Baird, A., Maruping, L.M.: The next generation of research on is use: a theoretical framework of delegation to and from agentic IS artifacts. MIS Q. **45**(1), 315–341 (2021)
21. Alter, S.: Facets of work: enriching the description, analysis, design, and evaluation of systems in organizations. Commun. Assoc. Inf. Syst. **49**(13), 321–354 (2021)
22. Kajonius, P.J., Johnson, J.: Sex differences in 30 facets of the five factor model of personality in the large public (N = 320,128). Personality Individ. Differ. **129**, 126–130 (2018)
23. Hudon, M.: Facet. Knowl. Organ. **47**(4), 320–333 (2020)
24. Broughton, V.: The need for a faceted classification as the basis of all methods of information retrieval. Aslib Proc. **58**(1/2), 49–72 (2006)
25. Wild, P.J., Giess, M.D., McMahon, C.A.: Describing engineering documents with faceted approaches. J. Document. **65**(3), 420–445 (2009)
26. Priss, U.: Facet-like structures in computer science. Axiomathes **18**(2), 243–255 (2008)
27. Opdahl, A.L., Sindre, G.: Facet modelling: an approach to flexible and integrated conceptual modelling. Inf. Syst. **22**(5), 291–323 (1997)
28. Alaimo, C., Kallinikos, J.: Objects, metrics and practices: an inquiry into the programmatic advertising ecosystem. In: Schultze, U., Aanestad, M., Mähring, M., Østerlund, C., Riemer, K. (eds.) IS&O 2018. IFIPAICT, vol. 543, pp. 110–123. Springer, Cham (2018).https://doi.org/10.1007/978-3-030-04091-8_9

A Method for Ontology-Driven Minimum Viable Platform Development

Thomas Derave[1]($\boxtimes$) (ID), Tiago Prince Sales[2] (ID), Frederik Gailly[1,3] (ID),
and Geert Poels[1,3] (ID)

[1] Department of Business Informatics and Operations Management, Ghent University, Ghent, Belgium
{thomas.derave, frederik.gailly, geert.poels}@UGent.be
[2] KRDB Research Centre for Knowledge and Data, Free University of Bozen-Bolzano, Bolzano, Italy
tiago.princesales@unibz.it
[3] FlandersMake@UGent – core lab CVAMO, Ghent, Belgium

Abstract. In this paper a method is proposed for agile digital platform prototype development based on organization-specific ontologies. The resulting prototypes act as minimum viable product of the digital platform that is described by the ontologies. Our method combines the strengths of agile practices, to speed up the development process in a user-oriented manner, with the strengths of ontology-driven development, improving the software structure, single terminology, and communication between stakeholders. The method is demonstrated for the development of the android application 'SafaRide', a digital marketplace for safari ride sharing.

Keywords: Digital platform · Digital marketplace · Ontology-driven software development · MVP · UFO · OntoUML · DPO

1 Introduction

The platform economy refers to activities in business, culture and social interaction that are performed on or are intermediated by digital platforms [1]. These digital platforms like Airbnb, eBay, Etsy, Ticketswap, Tinder, Dropbox and Uber intermediate in the interaction between their users. Digital platforms operating within the platform economy can be categorized by platform type [2] including multi-sided platform, digital marketplace, sharing platform, crowdfunding platform and on-demand platform. These platform types share common functions, but also have substantial differences in functionalities offered and also differ in the type of business model that is supported.

Software development and especially the development of web-based applications is a multidisciplinary and difficult task, time-consuming and highly sensitive to human interaction and team work [3, 4]. Due to the complexity in the platform economy domain, developing platform software that offers the right functionality for the intended digital platform is challenging. Nevertheless, this may be minimized using an efficient software

© Springer Nature Switzerland AG 2022
A. Augusto et al. (Eds.): BPMDS 2022/EMMSAD 2022, LNBIP 450, pp. 253–266, 2022.
https://doi.org/10.1007/978-3-031-07475-2_17

development methodology [4]. Therefore, developers adopted agile approaches that offer fast feedback, are more client-focused, capitalize on continuous improvement, and build on cross-functional teams. For agile prototype deployment, it is advised to launch a Minimum Viable Product [5], or in this case Minimum Viable Platform (MVP) [6], fast and efficient. An MVP is a product with enough features to validate the digital platform idea in an early stage of the development cycle. Existing SaaS tools for developing an MVP, like Sharetribe Go [7] which supports the development of digital marketplaces and Ever Demand [8] which supports the development of on-demand platforms, have the advantage that a developer doesn't need to start from scratch and the MVP can be developed in just a few hours. Unfortunately, these SAAS tools only focus on one specific digital platform type and do not consider the full diversity within the platform domain. Besides, they do not offer enough flexibility to develop a tailer-made MVP to the needs of the digital platform initiative. Furthermore, only a limited number of business model choices are configurable using these tools.

A solution to improve the communication between digital platform initiators and software developers and thus fasten the development of a tailer-made and satisfying MVP could be by using an 'organization-specific' ontology, which is an ontology that describes a specific existing or intended digital platform [9]. In this paper we propose a method for ontology-driven MVP development in the digital platform domain. This method was constructed using the Design Science Research Method (DSRM) of Peffers et al. [10]. Our method uses the Digital Platform Ontology (DPO) [2, 11] and continues on the research of [12] who developed a method for ontology-driven user story development, and the work of [13–15] who developed a method for ontology-driven (relational) database design. We demonstrate the proposed method with the development of an MVP running on Android called 'SafaRide' that intermediates in jeep ride sharing on a safari trip. SafaRide can be categorized as a digital marketplace, as it targets two different types of users and enables transactions between the user of both sides. This makes SafaRide a good case-study to show the advantages of ontology-driven MVP development. In this paper, we propose and demonstrate a first version of our method. In future research, we plan to apply and evaluate our method on a diverse set of digital platforms operating different business models.

This paper will proceed as follows. In Sect. 2 we briefly present the Digital Platform Ontology (DPO), its use in developing organization-specific ontologies for digital platforms and briefly discuss the research process of how our method is constructed. In Sect. 3 we propose our method for ontology-driven MVP development. In Sect. 4 we demonstrate our method on the development of the SafaRide MVP. In Sect. 5 we discuss future work, and eventually we conclude in Sect. 6.

2 Previous Research

In the platform domain there was till recently no existing domain ontology that could be reused and no clear framework to avoid developing an organization-specific ontology (i.e., specific to a particular digital platform) from scratch [16]. This gap was filled by (1) the development of a domain ontology, the Digital Platform Ontology (DPO) which accommodates different digital platforms types [2], (2) a Business Model (BM) extension to the DPO (i.e., Extended DPO) which makes it easier for developers to analyze the influence of business model decisions on the creation of the platform software [11] and (3) a method for developing an organization-specific ontology [9]. Such organization-specific ontology is the result of reusing and combining classes, relationships and constraints of the extended DPO to describe a specific instance of a digital platform for platform software development purposes. Figure 1 represents the organization-specific ontology for SafaRide which is the result of reusing and combining classes, relationships and constraints of the extended DPO specific for the SafaRide business case.

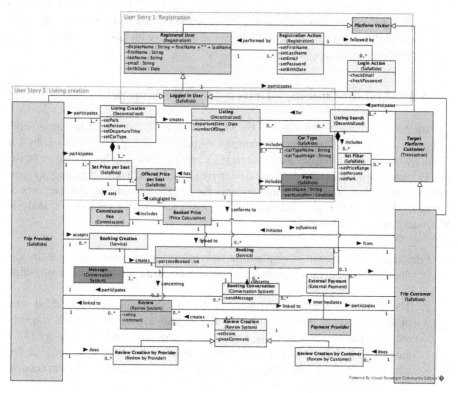

Fig. 1. Organization-specific ontology of SafaRide

The ontology of SafaRide shows that SafaRide intermediates between trip providers and trip customers for a one-time offline service (a free seat in a safari car). After registration, a logged-in user can create a listing specifying the departure time, park, type of car and offering price per seat. Afterwards, another user (called the target platform customer) can search through the listings created using the filters and initiate a booking creation becoming a trip customer. In case the provider accepts this booking creation, the booking comes into existence capturing the booking price including a commission fee. The booking price is transferred via an external provider, and the software allows a conversation via messages between the two users after the booking. After the delivery of the service both a review by the provider and by the customer towards each other are allowed.

In this paper an additional step in this research project is taken by designing a method for the development of an MVP starting from the organization-specific ontology for that platform. The main objectives of the proposed method are improving the shared under-standing of the terminology and functionality during the development of an envisioned digital platform, decrease the perceived complexity of MVP development, improve the quality of the requirements, and improve the flexibility during development. The pro-posed method combines our previous research with some existing methods that use ontologies in the context of agile software development [12–15]. The paper describes the research process of how this method was designed, gives an overview of the steps within the method and finally demonstrates the method with the development of the SafaRide MVP android application.

3 A Method for Ontology-Driven MVP Development

Our method developed following the DSRM of Peffers et al. [10] integrates the methods and guidelines of digital platform organization-specific ontology development by [9], ontology-driven user story development by [12], process modeling based on user stories by [17], and ontology-driven database design by [13–15], and adds UI prototyping and MV* software design as additional elements for MVP development. An overview of our method is given in Fig. 2 and includes four main steps: conceptualization, analysis, MVP development and testing.

1. First, the developers and other platform stakeholders need to conceptualize the idea of what they want to accomplish. This conceptualization is done in three sub steps.

   a. The developers need to understand the domain, the goal(s) and the added value of the envisioned software [12]. For this, significant research efforts might be required just to harmonize the requirements, concepts and terminology [3]. If the project had a previous state, historical project data can be collected [12]. But when no historical data is available, it is possible to conduct brainstorm sessions with different stakeholders.

   b. This domain knowledge is required for the choice of the digital platform type(s) using the typology of [2], and business model of the desired digital platform using the business model taxonomy of [11]. The choice of platform type and business model will influence the relevant ontology modules, and eventually shape the organization-specific ontology modules.

   c. Based on the digital platform type and business model, the developers can reuse and combine the DPO ontology modules that describe parts of the business model that the envisioned platform will deploy into an organization-specific ontology as explained in Sect. 2. This ontology now captures the user roles, required functionality and other domain knowledge of the desired digital platform.

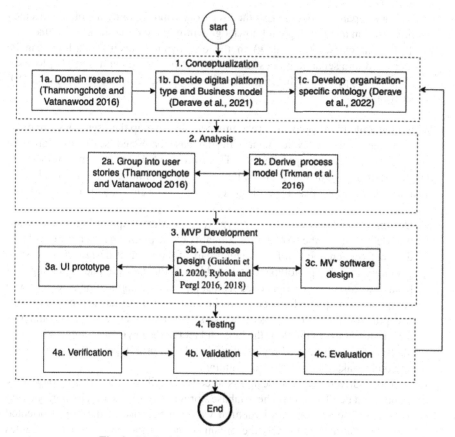

Fig. 2. Method for ontology-driven MVP development

2. After, the developers need to analyze the organization-specific ontology and group the classes and relationships into user stories and a process model that further guides the MVP development process.

a. User stories are a simple narrative illustrating of user goals that a software function will satisfy [18], and articulated in the form of 'As a [role], I want [goal], so that [benefit]'. With [role] specifying a type of user, [goal] describing the (inter)actions that the user wants the software to support, and [benefit] motivating the expected functionality from the user's standpoint. Besides writing them in text, it is also possible to use an object-oriented language like OntoUML for user stories writing [12]. The user stories of the envisioned MVP are already captured in the organization-specific ontology where a certain user role (in red) participates in an event class (in yellow) to create a certain social construct or relator class (in green) between himself and another user or the platform organization. Therefore, grouping a user role, the participating event and the created relator within a separate model grasps the user story while keeping the object-oriented presentation and ontological knowledge within the OntoUML model intact.

b. The event classes (in yellow) in the organization-specific ontology can be reordered in a separate process model following the guidelines of [17] to visualize the happy path or functionality of a single user through the envision MVP software.

3. Within the agile philosophy, it is recommended to develop the user stories in order of importance with the development of the database, back-end (server software) and front-end (UI) software in parallel [19]. Therefore, the MVP should be incrementally developed during sprints of a selection of user stories in three non-sequential steps, with the organization-specific ontology representing the envisioned digital platform.

a. Design a User Interface (UI) prototype (e.g., in MarvelApp or Figma). A prototype demonstrates the basic UI functionality of the platform idea before building the final version and is a fundamental part of the product design. It is possible to demonstrate the prototype to stakeholders as this helps in understanding user behavior [20]. Our experience learns that a prototype application screen or web component is required for each event class in the ontology as the prototype needs to capture the intended actions of the users. Eventually, the prototype should give a clear indication of the flow, the look and feel of the envisioned application. It is advised to do an intermediary validation of the UI prototype with potential users and other stakeholders before continuing.

b. Ontology-driven database design is already described in a series of papers by Rybola and Pergl [13–15]. The database stores and retrieves user, listing, booking and other information in a structural way and because of the object-oriented nature of OntoUML models the organization-specific ontology easily guides the relational database design. The database development is in parallel with the UI prototype and MVP software to guarantee a complete integration of data, information, user functionality and interface.

c. An MVP both requires a backend connecting the application to the database to store and retrieve data, and a UI frontend to interact with the user. For web applications this is typically accomplished using a Model-View-Whatever (MV*) software design pattern [21] that makes code easier to maintain and test with better user experience. The term MV* represents a family of browser-based frameworks that provide support for achieving a separation of concerns in the application's code base. The * in MV* can stand for Controller (MVC), ViewModel (MVVM) or Presenter (MVP) and can be designed by many popular frameworks for application development (Android using Kotlin, Angular using Typescript, WebObjects using Java, Django using Python, Rails using Ruby, .NET using C# and other languages, Flutter using Dart, React using JavaScript, Vue.js using JavaScript). More information on how the organization-specific ontology influences each component of the MV* software design pattern is given during the demonstration of our method in Sect. 4.

4. The last step tests the developed software and includes three non-sequential sub steps named verification, validation and evaluation [4].

   a. Verification is the demonstration of consistency, completeness, and correctness of the MVP. Therefore, we use UI tests, integration tests, unit tests and verify if the goal and benefit of each user story is fully integrated in our MVP software.

   b. Validation is the determination of the satisfaction of the MVP considering user needs and requirements. This can be accomplished by letting the users interact with the UI prototype and MVP software, to make sure the functionality and look and feel is sufficient to their needs.

   c. At last, the goal of the evaluation process is to access the quality, usability, and utility of the MVP from the point of view of those participated in knowledge acquisition phase. This is accomplished by demonstrating the organization-specific ontology, process model, UI prototype and MVP towards the management, financers and other non-user stakeholders. Their feedback will influence the next development iteration and can even adjust the digital platform type and business model of the desired MVP.

Our method has an user-oriented, iterative character as we follow an agile way of development. Through the iterative development process the organization-specific ontology constantly evolves, as flexibility of requirements is a must for agile software development projects [18].

4 Method Demonstration: SafaRide

The envisioned android application for SafaRide is meant for someone who rents a safari car and still has empty seats available, but also for travelers traveling with few and looking for an already booked car to share the ride. Both types of users can be considered as 'peers' or 'prosumers' setting SafaRide within the digital marketplace domain following the definition of [22]. On top of that, the application intermediates in the rental of an under-utilized good (free car seats), also setting SafaRide within the sharing platform domain. The added value for these peers is lower costs and the social advantage of traveling together, creating a win-win situation. The idea of ride sharing during a safari trip is brand new, and no historical data concerning safari trips was available. Therefore, we conducted brainstorm sessions with all stakeholders (in our case the four developers of the application and one African travel expert) to align the idea behind SafaRide. The conceptualization step includes the development of the organization-specific ontology of SafaRide which is already discussed in Sect. 2.

4.1 Analysis

We use the object-oriented user story method of [12] to capture role-event-relator patterns within the relationships and classes of our organization-specific ontology[1]. As an

---

[1] A complete overview of the user stories can be found on https://model-a-platform.com/safaride-user-stories/.

example, we discuss two user stories grouped within the organization-specific ontology of Fig. 1: user story 1 – Registration and user story 3 – Listing creation. In user story 1, a platform visitor can perform a registration action to become a registered user. Only a registered user can perform a login action that enables the creation of listings and bookings. In user story 3, a trip provider can create a listing and set a price per seat, car type, safari park, departure date and number of days within that listing to facilitate a customer finding it during a future listing search.

The events within an OntoUML ontology can also be envisioned as a user activity process using a process model language (e.g., Business Process Model and Notation, BPMN). By placing the event classes (in yellow) within the organization-specific ontology in the right sequence after each other, the happy path from registration until review can be derived. Figure 3 gives part of the process model[2] capturing the event classes within user story 1 and 3. Because a logged-in user can choose the role she wants to play, an OR-gateway was needed to visualize the actions a user of each role can perform.

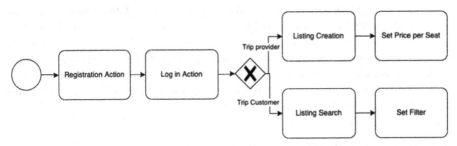

Fig. 3. Part of the SafaRide user process model for registration and listing creation

4.2 MVP Development

We developed the UI prototype using the prototype software 'MarvelApp'[3]. The UI prototype mainly visualizes the flow, look and feel of the envisioned SafaRide software, but doesn't capture the database design, user roles and functionality. For each user activity in Fig. 3, a prototype screen is designed.

In parallel, we constructed a relational database using MySQL as this is still the most popular type of data storage [13]. We copy-pasted the organization-specific ontology into a separate database model and followed the one table per hierarchy approach [15], lifting all relationships and attributes of the child classes into their parent class. For SafaRide, the registered user, trip provider, target platform customer and trip customer attributes and relationships were captured into the parent class called 'User'. After, we only keep the object classes (in red), relator classes (in green) or type classes (in purple) required for data collection and storage. For SafaRide, this was the case for user, listing, car type, park, message, booking and review. We added the mode classes (in blue) as attributes

---

[2] The complete BPMN model of SafaRide can be found on https://model-a-platform.com/saf aride-bpmn-model/.

[3] The UI prototype of SafaRide can be found on https://marvelapp.com/prototype/80ha0ha.

in the related object or relator classes and added indirect relationships between classes through events (e.g., user has a one-to-many relationship with listing through the listing creation event). Finally, we converted the OntoUML model into simple Unified Modeling Language (UML) notation, adding primary and foreign keys to specify the relationships while keeping the multiplicity constraints intact. If required, extra tables need to be included to solve many-to-many relationships, and tables originated from type classes with only one attribute can be included as enumeration types, but this was not the case for the SafaRide model. The final database schema in UML used for the construction of the MySQL database of SafaRide is represented in Fig. 4.

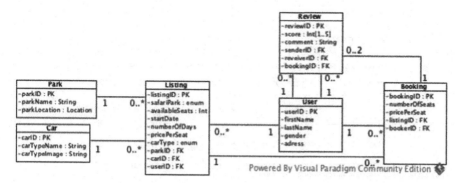

Fig. 4. SafaRide relational database schema in UML

The main contribution of this paper is the improvement of both the back-end and front-end MVP development based on the organization-specific ontology. SafaRide[4] was developed for android[5] using the Kotlin programming language with a Model-View-ViewModel (MVVM) design pattern. An overview of the MVVM design pattern and its components for user stories 1 and 3 of SafaRide is given in Fig. 5.

First, the Model is the application's dynamic data structure, independent of the UI. It is connected to the database(s) and directly manages the data, logic, and rules of the application. For the SafaRide android application, only a local data source, the MySQL database is used. For each table in our database schema (Fig. 4), a data class and repository are created. The main purpose of a data class is to hold data, and no functions are created within the class body as the database fields are used as parameters in the primary constructor. A repository on the other hand provides a clean API for data access to the rest of the application, independent of the database system. It reverses the records in the database to objects within the android application.

Next, the View is represented in a number of view components, and enables the user functionality of the software. Therefore, the event classes within the organization-specific ontology capture the required view components of the intended software. The View in android includes fragments that represent a reusable portion of the app's UI,

---

[4] The latest version of the app can be found on http://model-a-platform.com/safaride-versions/.

[5] For a guide to android app architecture: https://developer.android.com/jetpack/guide#separation-of-concerns.

and activities that are mainly used to construct a single screen of your application [23]. For the SafaRide Android application, the View includes a separate UI folder with an activity or fragment file (in Kotlin) and a layout file (in XML) for each event class in the organization-specific ontology.

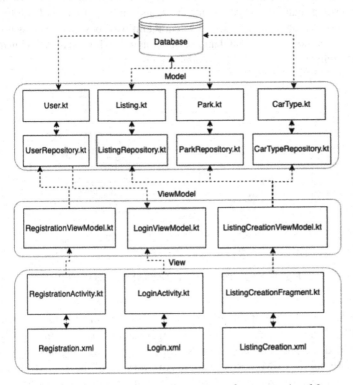

Fig. 5. SafaRide MVVM design pattern of user story 1 and 3

Finally, the ViewModel provides triggering events for changing the state of the Model and the View. This is captured in the relations between the object classes and the event classes within the organization-specific ontology. For the SafaRide Android application, a ViewModel file (in Kotlin) is created within each UI folder and connects the View to the right repositories.

Clear terminology and naming conventions during the MVP development are important; therefore, it is advised to name all classes, variables, and parameters according to the classes in the organization-specific ontology. Good variable names makes the code easier to understand and improves the development [25]. An overview of the conversions from the two user stories in Fig. 1 to SafaRide MVP software is given in Table 1.

Of course, the organization-specific ontology doesn't include all knowledge needed to develop the MVP. Nevertheless, it structures the more complex relationships between different concepts (listing, booking, user roles), improving the efficiency of the development process. The MVP of SafaRide doesn't yet include the commission, payment,

Table 1. Conversions from organization-specific ontology to MVP software

Class	MVP software
Platform Visitor, Registered User, Logged-in User, SafaRide Trip Provider	**Model:** A User data class to define the user objects and a user repository to connect the application to the user table is created
Registration Action	**View:** A registration XML file and registration activity is created **ViewModel:** A registration ViewModel file transfers the user data from the registration activity towards the registration repository
Login Action	**View:** Login XML file and login activity is created **ViewModel:** A login ViewModel checks the username and password with the relevant fields of the database
Listing, Park, CarType	**Model:** A Listing, Park and CarType data class and repository are created to define the objects and connect the application to the tables within the database
Listing Creation, Set Price per Seat,	**View:** ListingCreation XML file and listingCreation fragment is created **ViewModel:** A listingCreation ViewModel transfers the listing data from the listingCreation fragment towards the listing, park and carType repository. This includes the offered price per seat of the listing

booking conversation and review functionality, as these user stories were considered as less urgent and will be developed in future development cycles following our method.

4.3 Testing

During the development of the SafaRide MVP, we designed several UI tests, integration tests and unit tests to assure the quality of the MVP software and verified the completeness of the software with each user story. We also regularly validated the usability of the UI prototype and application with several potential users who are familiar with safari holidays, and evaluated the MVP by demonstrating the organization-specific ontology, process model, UI prototype and MVP towards the African travel expert, and taking his feedback into account during the following development iteration. The SafaRide organization-specific ontology was modified after each sprint to keep the model in line with the (intended) software structure.

5 Discussion and Future Work

In this paper, we proposed a first version of our ontology-driven MVP development method demonstrated by the development of one MVP. Besides being ontology-driven, our method follows an agile approach focusses on the development of an MVP. Software development is known as a complex activity that is highly sensitive to human interaction and team work [3]. Therefore, an agile approach requires fast feedback, is user-focused with continues improvements and cross-functional teams. Our method only considers the happy path of the user process to launch an MVP as fast as possible, with regular validations by users and other stakeholders. However, an agile approach also has a considerable number of downsides. First of all, there is also a fragmented output as teams work on different user stories without a clearly described finite end of the project [26]. Another issue is that teams can work on different user stories with a widespread use of overlapping terminology and conflicting constraints for the components, user roles and functionality of the intended software [9]. On top of that, there is a limited amount of documentation as software companies rapidly develop prototypes without saving complete information or insights acquired in a structured semantic format [27]. Ontology-driven MVP development solves these issues as the organization-specific ontology clearly captures the user stories and their interconnectedness. It describes the boundaries of each user story, and what is required from the MVP before the project ends. It aligns the terminology, improving the communication between teams working on different user stories and helps in understanding how a certain user story fits within the complete project. Besides, the ontology documents the MVP development in an easy, structural, and flexible manner. By regularly updating the requirements within our ontology throughout the development process, our method supports easy comprehension of the project's nature and makes it easier for software reuse in future projects.

In future research, we plan to validate and further improve our method by supporting the development of a diverse set of MVPs of different platform types operating a variety of business models. A test case will be set up with aspiring entrepreneurs who plan to develop an MVP of their platform idea originated from a self-constructed, DPO-based organization-specific ontology. During the development process, the version and improvements of each iteration will be monitored using GitHub classrooms, to visualize and analyze the influence of ontology modifications on the eventual MVP software. In the end, the efficiency and perceived usefulness of our method will be quantified with a questionnaire towards the software developers. Both single developers and teams are composed for the MVP development, to test the efficiency and communication improvements of our ontology-driven approach.

6 Conclusion

In this paper, we proposed a method for ontology-driven, Minimum Viable Platform (MVP) development, constructed using the Design Science Research Method (DSRM) of Peffers et al. [10]. An ontology is not only the collection of concepts, terms, constraints and relationships but also the formal, explicit, conceptual model of object ranges in a computational representation [3]. Our method is ontology-driven, as it uses an organization-specific ontology [9] based on the Digital Platform Ontology (DPO) written in OntoUML as a basis during the development process. A normal UML model only makes distinction between the data classes, while OntoUML models also capture the difference between objects events, social or financial benefit for each user. In the organization-specific ontology, objects and relators portray the required data structure, while events portray the required functionality of the intended software [9]. Therefore, the organization-specific ontology can be divided in user stories with each user story describing a user role, what the user of this role wants and how he benefits from that. The ontology captures the required functionality of these user stories and transformations between the organization-specific ontology and the code are used to construct the final software.

A clear method for MVP development is important, because due to high costs and duration of the project [28], competitors with less diversification but a superior technology are still capable to monopolize a market [29]. Lowering the barrier of digital platform development is therefore vital, as many existing platforms have the tendency to apply a 'winner-takes-all" strategy to create a monopoly. An essential element that creates incentives to enter and isolate the influence of competitors is increasing the differentiation of digital platforms. This way, network effects are mitigated, and divide-and-conquer strategies are less effective, which reduces the monopolization problem at the same time [29].The proposed method helps to increase the knowledge of digital platform design, which triggers the conception of alternatives for monopolistic companies such as Airbnb and Uber, who are criticized for paying low wages, taking high commission fees, and avoiding taxes [30]. This may facilitate the development of diverse, smaller, more alternative, and socially responsible platforms and thus contribute to the creation of a more socially responsible platform economy.

References

1. Kenney, M., Zysman, J.: The rise of the platform economy. Issues Sci. Technol. **32**, 61–69 (2016)
2. Derave, T., Sales, P.T., Gailly, F., Poels, G.: Comparing digital platform types in the platform economy. In: Caise 2021, pp. 5–10 (2021)
3. Clarke, P., et al.: An investigation of software development process terminology. Commun. Comput. Inf. Sci. **609**, 351–361 (2016)
4. Hasan, S.S., Isaac, R.K.: An integrated approach of MAS-CommonKADS, Model-View-Controller and web application optimization strategies for web-based expert system development. Expert Syst. Appl. **38**, 417–428 (2011)
5. Ries, Er.: The Lean Startup. Currency (2011)
6. Gracia, C.: Your marketplace MVP – How to build a Minimum Viable Platform. https://www.sharetribe.com/academy/how-to-build-a-minimum-viable-platform/#:~:text=A Minimum Viable Product (MVP)—or%2C in the, both sides of the marketplace
7. Sharetribe: Sharetribe Go (2019). https://github.com/sharetribe/sharetribe
8. Ever Corporation: Ever Demand (2022). https://github.com/ever-co/ever-demand
9. Derave, T., Sales, T.P., Gailly, F., Poels, G.: Sharing platform ontology development : proof-of-concept. Sustainability **14**, 1–19 (2022)
10. Peffers, K., Tuunanen, T., Rotherberger, M.A., Chatterjee, S.: A design science research methodology for information systems research. J. Manag. Inf. Syst. **24**, 45–78 (2008)

11. Derave, T., Sales, T.P., Gailly, F., Poels, G.: Understanding digital marketplace business models : an ontology approach. In: POEM, pp. 1–12 (2021)

12. Thamrongchote, C., Vatanawood, W.: Business process ontology for defining user story. In: 2016 IEEE/ACIS 15th International Conference on Computer and Information Science ICIS 2016 – Proceedings, pp. 3–6 (2016)

13. Rybola, Z., Pergl, R.: Towards OntoUML for software engineering: optimizing kinds and subkinds transformed into relational databases. Lect. Notes Bus. Inf. Process. **332**, 31–45 (2018)

14. Rybola, Z., Pergl, R.: Towards OntoUML for software engineering: Transformation of Anti-rigid sortal types into relational databases. In: Proceedings of 2016 Federated Conference on Computer Science and Information System FedCSIS 2016, pp. 1581–1591 (2016)

15. Guidoni, G.L., Almeida, J.P.A., Guizzardi, G.: Transformation of ontology-based conceptual models into relational schemas. In: Dobbie, G., Frank, Ulrich, Kappel, G., Liddle, S.W., Mayr, H.C. (eds.) ER 2020. LNCS, vol. 12400, pp. 315–330. Springer, Cham (2020). https://doi.org/10.1007/978-3-030-62522-1_23

16. Mohamad, U.H., Ahmad, M.N., Zakaria, A.M.U.: Ontologies application in the sharing economy domain: a systematic review. Online Inf. Rev. ahead-of-p, (2021)

17. Trkman, M., Mendling, J., Krisper, M.: Using business process models to better understand the dependencies among user stories. Inf. Softw. Technol. **71**, 58–76 (2016)

18. Sh Murtazina, M., Avdeenko, T.V.: The ontology-driven approach to support the requirements engineering process in scrum framework. CEUR Workshop Proc. **2212**, 287–295 (2018)

19. W3schools: What is Full Stack? https://www.w3schools.com/whatis/whatis_fullstack.asp

20. marvel: A guide to creating your first prototype. https://help.marvelapp.com/hc/en-us/articles/360002536038-A-guide-to-creating-your-first-prototype#:~:text=A prototype demonstrates the functionality, also do in Marvel!)

21. Emmit, A.S.J.: SPA Design and Architecture: Understanding single-page web applications. Manning (2015)

22. Täuscher, K., Laudien, S.M.: Understanding platform business models: a mixed methods study of marketplaces. Eur. Manag. J. **36**, 319–329 (2018)

23. geeksforgeeks: Difference Between a Fragment and an Activity in Android. https://www.geeksforgeeks.org/difference-between-a-fragment-and-an-activity-in-android/

24. Srivastava, V.: MVC vs MVP vs MVVM architecture in Android

25. Minnick, C., Holland, E.: Naming JavaScript Variables. https://www.dummies.com/web-design-development/javascript/naming-javascript-variables/

26. Lynn, R.: Disadvantages of Agile (2020). https://www.planview.com/resources/articles/disadvantages-agile/

27. Adnan, M., Afzal, M.: Ontology based multiagent effort estimation system for scrum agile method. IEEE Access. **5**, 25993–26005 (2017)

28. Handgraaf, S.: Five ways to build an online marketplace platform—and how to choose yours. https://www.sharetribe.com/academy/ways-build-marketplace-platform/

29. Sanchez-Cartas, J.M., Leon, G.: Multi-sided platforms and markets: a literature review. SSRN Electron. J. 1–62 (2019)

30. Kenney, M., Zysman, J.: Choosing a future in platform economy: the implications and consequences of digital platforms. J. Chem. Inf. Model. **53**, 1689–1699 (2013)

A Tool for Debugging Unsatisfiable Integrity Constraints in UML/OCL Class Diagrams

Juan Antonio Gómez-Gutiérrez[1]([envelope])[iD], Robert Clarisó[1][iD], and Jordi Cabot[2][iD]

[1] Universitat Oberta de Catalunya, Barcelona, Spain
{juanto,rclariso}@uoc.edu
[2] ICREA, Barcelona, Spain
jordi.cabot@icrea.cat

Abstract. Software models are the basis of the Model-Driven Engineering paradigm. The most popular modeling notation is UML class diagrams, which can be annotated with OCL predicates to describe complex integrity constraints.

When creating and managing UML/OCL models, a challenge for domain engineers is diagnosing faults. Problems like inconsistencies among integrity constraints can render a model useless. While existing verification tools provide ample support for detecting faults, users have less support when trying to understand and fix them. In this paper, we present a tool aimed at helping domain engineers locate, understand and fix faults in UML/OCL class diagrams. This tool is built as a plug-in within an existing UML modeling tool, the UML Specification Environment (USE).

Keywords: UML · OCL · Class diagram · Verification · Integrity constraint · USE · Model debugging

1 Introduction

In the software development process, the relevant characteristics of a system can be captured using a *model*, *e.g.*, a UML diagram. Software models are powerful tools for communication among stakeholders and documentation of design decisions. Moreover, in the Model-Driven Development paradigm, models are the central asset of the software development process, from which other assets like source code are (semi)automatically derived. As a result, the correctness of software models affects the quality of the final software product.

UML class diagrams are a popular notation for modeling structural features. This formalism can be enriched by defining complex integrity constraints using the Object Constraint Language (OCL). OCL is a textual notation that enables the definition of class invariants and pre/postconditions for operations.

As UML/OCL models grow more complex, it may be necessary to check that there are no inconsistencies, *e.g.*, constraints that become unsatisfiable due to

© Springer Nature Switzerland AG 2022
A. Augusto et al. (Eds.): BPMDS 2022/EMMSAD 2022, LNBIP 450, pp. 267–275, 2022.
https://doi.org/10.1007/978-3-031-07475-2_18

the interactions with other constraints. Detecting such errors is a complex task. Furthermore, it is even harder to understand their causes in order to repair the model, rewriting the incorrect constraints in a proper way.

In this paper, we present MVM (Model Validator Mixer)[1], a modeling tool for domain engineers that helps them locate, understand and fix consistency problems in UML/OCL class diagrams. To this end, MVM computes and organizes information about groups of inconsistent constraints and sample instances that satisfy most (but not all) integrity constraints. MVM is implemented as a plug-in for the UML Specification Environment (USE) [4], a modeling tool offering advanced features for the verification and validation of UML/OCL models.

2   Related Work

Several works have considered the formal verification of UML class diagrams annotated with OCL constraints, e.g., PLEDGE [12], USE Model Validator [7], UMLtoCSP/EMFtoCSP [2,5] or AuRUS [9], among others. These tools can check correctness properties like *finite satisfiability*, *i.e.*, whether there is a finite instance of the class diagram that satisfies all UML and OCL integrity constraints simultaneously. If the property holds, an example instance is computed as output, otherwise the method warns about the lack of satisfying instances. Other tools such as the Alloy Analyzer [6] or VIATRA [10] can check equivalent properties for closely related conceptual modeling formalisms.

Nevertheless, these tools focus on either detecting faults efficiently or generating high quality example instances (realistic, diverse, . . .) [11,12]. Thus, once a fault has been detected there is little support to help the designer locate, understand and fix the problem(s). In the following, we discuss three approaches that work in this direction: *unsatisfiable cores*, *max-satisfiabilty* and *model repair*.

An unsatisfiable core is a subset of integrity constraints that is unsatisfiable. If the class diagram is inconsistent, it is possible to compute a small (or even minimal) unsatisfiable core of integrity constraints, helping to locate the fault [8,9,13]. These techniques can be used for *model debugging* (also called *fault localization*): identifying the fragment(s) of a specification that are causing the fault [14,17]. Conversely, using a maximum satisfiability algorithm it is possible to compute the largest set of constraints that can be satisfied simultaneously [15,16].

A final set of techniques aim to generate repairs, *i.e.* small (or even minimal) changes to a model that fix a particular fault. Some of these methods have targeted Alloy specifications [1,14,17] and UML/OCL class diagrams [3]. As a drawback, the catalog of fixes (mutation operators) has to be established a priori and, in some cases, additional predicates to validate the fix must be defined. Instead, our approach aims to help the designer locate, understand and fix faults. That is, it does not assume that the model is almost correct and can be fixed with small updates. Information such as unsatisfiable cores and max-satisfiability is combined with examples and useful feedback to help the designer understand the fault.

---

[1] You can download the tool at: https://github.com/juanto2021/MVM#readme.

3   Presentation of MVM

3.1   Context

Our goal with MVM is helping domain engineers debug problems with their UML/OCL class diagrams. Rather than offering a stand-alone tool with yet another syntax and GUI for creating model, we have aimed at extending an existing toolkit. Thus, we have integrated MVM inside the UML Specification Environment (USE).

USE already offers several features for the verification and validation of UML/OCL class diagrams. First, it uses a textual syntax for enconding both the class diagram and the OCL constraints. Then, it offers GUIs to visualize the class diagram, instances (object diagrams) and constraints. Moreover, it can check whether an object diagram satisfies all or some integrity constraints. And, finally, it includes a plug-in called Model Validator [7] that can determine if the constraints are satisfiable or not. To this end, it uses a bounded verification solver that constructs a valid instance of the class diagram (satisfiable) or reports its absence within the bounded domains (unsatisfiable). When the result is unsatisfiable, no further feedback is provided by USE (see Sect. 2 for the feedback provided by other extensions).

MVM will supply feedback aimed at helping domain engineers diagnose and fix the problem. It will use USE's notation to describe the UML/OCL class diagrams and USE's GUI to visualize sample instances.

3.2   Feedback

A UML/OCL class diagram may contain one or more consistency errors that need to be fixed. All of them will exhibit the same symptom (the model is unsatisfiable), but their causes should be fixed independently.

Each consistency error may be caused by a single incorrect invariant or an unintended interaction between several invariants. To this end, we will provide the following information to the domain engineer:

– *Minimal unsatisfiable cores:* Sets of OCL invariants that cannot be simultaneously satisfied and that become satisfiable if any member of the set is removed. While each unsatisfiable core is potentially an independent error, several cores that share some constraints may indicate a problem in the constraints included in their intersection.
– *Max-satisfiable constraints and instances:* Sets of OCL invariants that can be satisfied as a whole, together with sample instances satisfying only those max-satisfiable constraints. The goal is showing the domain engineer what such instances would look like, in order to help him have a better idea of how the current constraints should be modified.
– *"What-if" scenarios:* Sample instances that would be legal if one constraint in the unsatisfiable core is dropped. Again, the rationale is helping the domain engineer figure out whether such instances should be made valid by rewriting

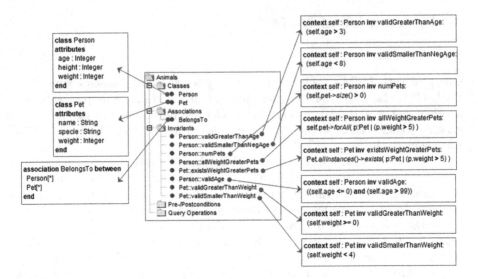

Fig. 1. Model animals.

the corresponding constraint. For example, in Fig. 2 you can see in the right-most tab which combinations are satisfiable if you eliminate this invariant. Also, double-clicking on any of the proposed combinations creates an object diagram with a sample valid instance.

The central idea is presenting this information in a cohesive and usable way that helps the user understand the consistency problems that need to be addressed, their causes and candidate repairs.

3.3 Running Example

In order to illustrate the operation of MVM, we will use the UML class diagram in Fig. 1 as our running example. It contains 2 classes (Person and Pet), each with different attributes, several invariants and an association. This model fragment could reflect work in progress to add new features to an existing system.

This class diagram has two separate consistency issues. First, invariant `validAge` cannot be satisfied. Age was probably intended to be in the range from 1 to 99 years, but the relational operators got reversed by mistake:

```
context Person inv validAge:              -- Invariant 5
    self.age <= 0 and self.age > 99
```

The second problem affects invariants related to the weight of pets: one (`validSmallerThanWeight`) establishes an upper bound of the weight of pets, while two others require the existence of a heavier pet (`existsWeightGreaterPets`) or require the pets owned by some person to be heavier (`allWeightGreaterPets`). Intuitively, the upper bound for the weight should be increased, or the requirements on heavier pets be lowered.

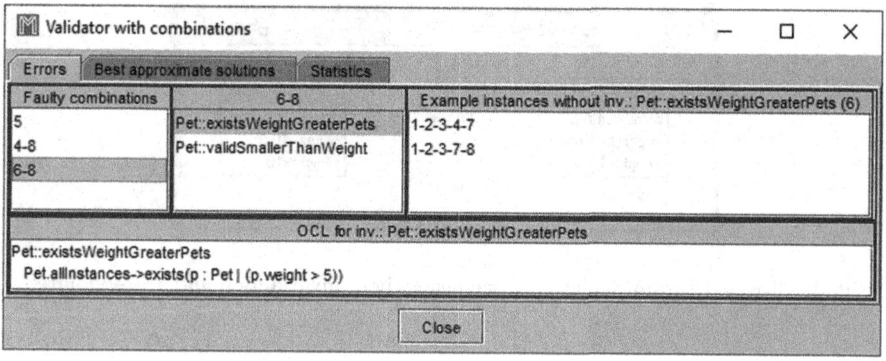

Fig. 2. Errors tab in the MVM dialog box.

```
context Person inv allWeightGreaterPets: -- Invariant 4
    self.pet→forAll(p|p.weight>5)

context Pet inv existsWeightGreaterPets: -- Invariant 6
    Pet.allInstances()→exists(p:Pet|p.weight>5)

context Pet inv validSmallerThanWeight:  -- Invariant 8
    self.weight < 4
```

In the following, we will show how MVM can be used to identify these issues and help domain engineers come up with potential solutions.

3.4 User Interface

MVM displays the information about consistency errors in a dialog box consisting of three tabs: *Errors*, *Best approximate solutions* and *Statistics*.

Errors. In this tab, we show the minimal combinations of invariants that are unsatisfiable (minimal unsatisfiable cores). It consists of the following panels:

– Faulty combinations: The leftmost panel shows the minimal unsatisfiable core. When a combination is selected in this list, the following two views are synchronized.
– Example instances without the selected invariant: This panel shows examples of satisfiable combinations that do not contain one invariant from the core. Double-clicking a combination (each excludes one invariant from the core) creates an object diagram that satisfies the invariant in that combination.
– OCL for inv: For convenience, this panel displays the OCL definition of the selected invariant.

Figure 2 depicts this user interface for the running example. In this dialog box you can see in the upper left part, a list that shows three faulty combinations of invariants that cannot be satisfied:

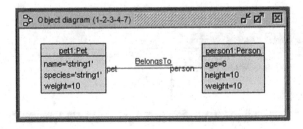

Fig. 3. Object diagram depicting a scenario where invariants 5 and 7 are violated.

- 5 (validAge): This single invariant is unsatisfiable on its own.
- 4–8 (allWeightGreaterPets, validSmallerThanWeight): Even though each invariant is satisfiable on its own, the combination of both is unsatisfiable.
- 6–8 (existsWeightGreaterPets, validSmallerThanWeight): Same as before.

The first core is disjoint from the rest, so this is a separate error that should be repaired independently. Regarding the last two cores, their intersection suggests a potentially shared cause within invariant 8 (validSmallerThanWeight). In order to understand these faults, the domain engineer can inspect instances that violate only one of the constraints in this unsatisfiable core, using the rightmost panel. For instance, if we are studying invariant 5 (validAge), we can inspect an instance that satisfies the combination of invariants 1-2-3-4-6-7 (which excludes 5). Figure 3 shows the object diagram depicting such instance, as shown in USE.

Best Approximate Solutions. This tab shows the satisfiable combinations with the highest number of invariants:

- Invariants: The leftmost panel shows the list of satisfiable combinations with the highest number of invariants.
- Combination panel: When clicking on a combination, the invariants that compose it are shown in the upper right panel.
- OCL for inv: When clicking on a specific invariant, the definition of that invariant is shown in the lower panel.

Figure 4 shows the information this tab. In a similar way to that described for the "Errors" tab, when clicking on a combination, the invariants that compose it will be shown in the upper right list and, when clicking on a specific invariant, its definition will be shown in the lower part.

Statistics. The computation of unsatisfiable cores relies on USE's Model Validator to check if a given combination of invariants is satisfiable or not. If a combination of invariants is deemed unsatisfiable, supersets of this combination will also be unsatisfiable. Similarly, if a combination is found to be satisfiable, it is not necessary to explore subsets of this combination. Thus, it is not necessary to invoke the Model Validator for *each* combination: many calls can be pruned.

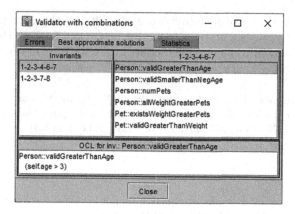

Fig. 4. Best approximate solutions.

Validator with combinations	— □ ✕
Errors Best approximate solutions Statistics	
Execution time	566 milliseconds
Number of calls to the solver	16
Number of satisfied calls	8
Number of unsatisfied calls	8
Total number of combinations	128
Total number of combinations satisfiable	79
Total number of combinations unsatisfiable	49
	Close

Fig. 5. Statistics

This tab shows information about the computation of unsatisfiable cores and sample instances. It describes the CPU time spent searching for combinations, the number of calls to the solver, and the number of calls that produced a satisfiable/unsatisfiable result. Figure 5 depicts this panel.

4   Conclusions and Future Work

In this paper we have presented MVM, a tool for debugging consistency errors in UML/OCL class diagrams. This tool complements existing UML/OCL tools such as USE by detailing which are the unsatisfiable invariants and the best possible combinations, giving feedback to the user in the form of potential instances for relevant scenarios.

As future work, we will improve the usability of the user interface, *e.g.*, providing step-by-step suggestions to fix the model; and improve the efficiency of the calculation, by introducing different strategies for enumerating unsatisfiable cores and proposing heuristics tailored for OCL invariants.

Acknowledgements. This work is partially funded by the Spanish Agencia Estatal de Investigación through the project "LOw-COde development of Smart Software" (LOCOSS, PID2020-114615RB-I00/AEI/10.13039/501100011033).

References

1. Brida, S.G., et al.: Bounded exhaustive search of Alloy specification repairs. In: ICSE 2021, pp. 1135–1147. IEEE (2021)
2. Cabot, J., Clarisó, R., Riera, D.: On the verification of UML/OCL class diagrams using constraint programming. JSS **93**, 1–23 (2014)
3. Clarisó, R., Cabot, J.: Fixing defects in integrity constraints via constraint mutation. In: QUATIC 2018, pp. 74–82. IEEE (2018)
4. Gogolla, M., Büttner, F., Richters, M.: USE: a UML-based specification environment for validating UML and OCL. Sci. Comput. Program. **69**, 27–34 (2007). https://doi.org/10.1016/j.scico.2007.01.013
5. González, C.A., Büttner, F., Clarisó, R., Cabot, J.: EMFtoCSP: a tool for the lightweight verification of EMF models. In: FormSERA 2012, pp. 44–50 (2012). https://doi.org/10.1109/FormSERA.2012.6229788
6. Jackson, D.: Software Abstractions: Logic, Language, and Analysis. MIT Press, Cambridge (2012)
7. Kuhlmann, M., Hamann, L., Gogolla, M.: Extensive validation of OCL models by integrating SAT solving into USE. In: Bishop, J., Vallecillo, A. (eds.) TOOLS 2011. LNCS, vol. 6705, pp. 290–306. Springer, Heidelberg (2011). https://doi.org/10.1007/978-3-642-21952-8_21
8. Przigoda, N., Wille, R., Drechsler, R.: Analyzing inconsistencies in UML/OCL models. J. Circuits Syst. Comput. **25**(03), 1640021 (2016)
9. Rull, G., Farré, C., Queralt, A., Teniente, E., Urpí, T.: AuRUS: explaining the validation of UML/OCL conceptual schemas. Softw. Syst. Model. **14**(2), 953–980 (2013). https://doi.org/10.1007/s10270-013-0350-8
10. Semeráth, O., Nagy, A.S., Varró, D.: A graph solver for the automated generation of consistent domain-specific models. In: ICSE 2018, pp. 969–980 (2018)
11. Semeráth, O., Varró, D.: Iterative generation of diverse models for testing specifications of DSL tools. In: FASE 2018, vol. 18, pp. 227–245 (2018)
12. Soltana, G., Sabetzadeh, M., Briand, L.C.: Practical constraint solving for generating system test data. ACM TOSEM **29**(2), 1–48 (2020)
13. Torlak, E., Chang, F.S.-H., Jackson, D.: Finding minimal unsatisfiable cores of declarative specifications. In: Cuellar, J., Maibaum, T., Sere, K. (eds.) FM 2008. LNCS, vol. 5014, pp. 326–341. Springer, Heidelberg (2008). https://doi.org/10.1007/978-3-540-68237-0_23
14. Wang, K., Sullivan, A., Khurshid, S.: Automated model repair for Alloy. In: ASE 2018, pp. 577–588. IEEE (2018)

15. Wu, H.: MaxUSE: a tool for finding achievable constraints and conflicts for inconsistent UML class diagrams. In: Polikarpova, N., Schneider, S. (eds.) IFM 2017. LNCS, vol. 10510, pp. 348–356. Springer, Cham (2017). https://doi.org/10.1007/978-3-319-66845-1_23
16. Zhang, C., et al.: AlloyMax: bringing maximum satisfaction to relational specifications. In: ESEC-FSE 2021, pp. 155–167 (2021)
17. Zheng, G., Bagheri, H., Nguyen, T.: Debugging declarative models in Alloy. In: ICSME 2020, pp. 844–848. IEEE (2020)

Domain-Specific and Knowledge Modeling (EMMSAD 2022)

Towards Simplification of ME-Maps

Azzam Maraee[1,2(✉)] and Arnon Sturm[1]

[1] Ben-Gurion University of the Negev, Beer-Sheva, Israel
mari@cs.bgu.ac.il, sturm@bgu.ac.il
[2] Achva Academic College, Arugot, Israel

Abstract. As knowledge increases tremendously each and every day, there is a need for various means to manage and organize it, so to utilize it when needed. For example, for finding solutions to technical and engineering problems. An alternative for achieving these goals is through knowledge mapping that aims at indexing the knowledge. Recently, we devised an approach called ME-MAP for mapping out know-how, so to facilitate knowledge indexing. However, the challenge of handling large maps still exists. In this paper, we address this challenge by proposing a simplification mechanism for ME-maps. In particular, we define the meaning of simplification in ME-MAP, set simplification rules, and develop an algorithm for simplifying ME-maps. In addition, we confirm the correctness of the algorithm and its scalability, as well as its support for understanding domain maps through a preliminary user study.

Keywords: ME-MAP · Know-how · Simplification · Reasoning

1 Introduction

Knowledge, especially in technology and engineering domains, is developing at a tremendous pace. In such domains, we are especially concerned with know-how, the kind of knowledge that guides action towards practical objectives, prescribing solutions to technical problems, and evaluating alternative solutions [24]. Know-how management can provide various benefits such as: domain review, trade-off analysis, and support for decision making. While there is almost instant access to published know-how on-line, to the best of our knowledge, there has been little advance in how a body of know-how is organized for easier access, understanding, and reasoning.

One way of addressing the know-how management challenge is through knowledge mapping. "A knowledge map - whether it is an actual map, 'yellow pages' or cleverly constructed database - points to knowledge but it does not contain it. It is a guide not a repository" [6]. The need to refer to explicit knowledge structures for complex information seeking situations has been discussed in e.g., [9], in which the authors refer to the case of exploratory search which cannot be achieved through simple keyword search. Other usages of knowledge maps also include enhancing the results of search engines [4] and increasing the efficiency of creativity and invention [20].

This research was partially supported by the Israel Science Foundation (Grant No. 495/14).

A. Augusto et al. (Eds.): BPMDS 2022/EMMSAD 2022, LNBIP 450, pp. 279–294, 2022.
https://doi.org/10.1007/978-3-031-07475-2_19

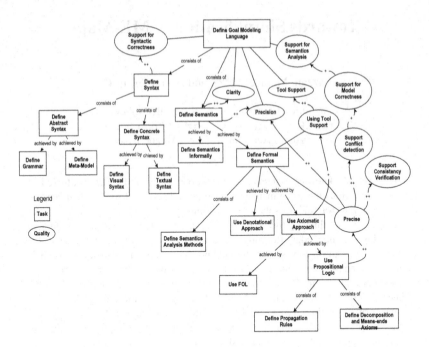

Fig. 1. A partial ME-map for the Goal Modeling Language specification domain.

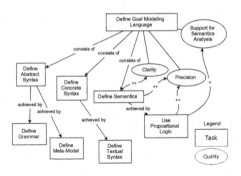

Fig. 2. A simplification of the map appears in Fig. 1.

We believe that know-how mapping will increase knowledge accessibility and its utilization, improve exploratory search, facilitate exploratory reading, and assist in decision making processes.

Following the advantages mentioned above, we devised a mapping approach, ME-MAP (Means-End Map), that leverages on Goal-Oriented Requirements Engineering (GORE) conceptual structure to organize and manage a body of know-how for technology and engineering domains. The ME-MAP approach has been evaluated both for the ease of construction [28] and for the ease of understanding [22] of maps and found to be useful in both cases. An example of such a map appears in Fig. 1 that partially maps out the domain of defining a goal modeling language. In constructing the map, we consult several works in the GORE domain.

A major problem that arises during know-how modeling/mapping is that the maps become increasingly large and complex. Therefore, it becomes difficult to understand, inspect and modify such maps due to the potentially many inter-relationships and elements that may exist. In the ME-map in Fig. 1, although represents a fraction of the domain, there are a lot of elements and inter-dependencies, which make it difficult to grasp and understand the domain. To address these concerns, there is a need for a "zoom-out" technique that executes simplification operations over the maps and transforms the maps into *high-level* ones. Figure 2 presents a simplification of the ME-map in Fig. 1.

Simplification can be used for two major purposes: (1) **Understandability**: The accuracy of comprehending the domain. (2) **Reasoning efficiency**: A simplified map that keeps the reasoning properties under interest, improves the efficiency of the reasoning process, as there are fewer elements to deal with. *Our conjecture is that the simplification would indeed improve the understandability and reasoning.* It should be noted that by simplification we refer to a view over the map rather than to its modification. Thus, the users can navigate within the various views.

In this paper we elaborate on the simplification of ME maps and provide algorithms for generating simplified maps (views) that preserve the original semantics. We further evaluate the simplification for its performance and usability.

The paper is organized as follows. Section 2 details the simplification task and presents the algorithms. Section 3 details the implementation and evaluation of the simplification algorithms. Section 4 reviews related works and positions those with respect to this study. Finally, Sect. 5 concludes and outlines plans for future research.

2   Simplification of ME-Maps

The ME-MAP approach draws its core concepts from the goal-oriented requirement engineering (GORE) paradigm [31]. A main objective of ME-MAP is to take advantage of the inherent means-ends relationship that characterizes know-how, where the identification of problems and development of feasible solutions is a key concern. The approach aims at presenting problems identified in a domain, properties of problems that are particularly relevant in the domain, and offers a systematic review of proposed solutions. Formally, a ME-map is a tuple $ME = \langle \mathcal{E}, \mathcal{L}nk \rangle$, where $\mathcal{E}$ is a non-empty set of elements such that $\mathcal{E} = \mathcal{T} \cup \mathcal{Q}, \mathcal{T} \cap \mathcal{Q} = \emptyset$, where $\mathcal{T}, \mathcal{Q}$ are set of tasks and qualities, respectively. $\mathcal{L}nk$ is a set of pairs of elements representing the links between them. The semantics of the ME-MAP language is defined as the set of all alternative solutions to the main problems. The detailed syntax and semantics of the ME-MAP appear in [17]. It is important to note that achieved-by links indicate alternatives from which only one of these can be selected for a legal instance (XOR) whereas consists-of links indicate parts that are required to be selected for a legal instance (AND).

Simplification deals with the reduction of information by retaining essential properties and removing insignificant details deemed unimportant by the user [8]. Map simplification helps in dealing with the map complexity, scalability, improves the map understandability, and might also support the validation tasks compared to existing larger ME maps. For example, assume that for the ME map in Fig. 1, we are only interested in the tasks (called *initial user tasks*), *Define Grammar*, *Define Meta-Model*, *Define Textual Syntax*, *Use Propositional Logic*. Then, removing the other tasks and "collapsing" the links between the selected tasks produces the ME map in Fig. 2. This simplified map explicates that the *Use Propositional Logic* task contributes positively to the qualities *Support for Semantics Analysis* and *Precision*.

The ME-Map simplification procedure involves identifying a set of tasks that should remain on the map. Based on this set, the simplification is performed. Egyed in [8] showed that a major challenge in simplification is recomputing the *hiding information* in the context of the remaining, *non-hidden* map elements. For example, removing contribution links between two non-hidden qualities may require adding a new link whose label is the composition of the labels of the removed links. Egyed uses a set of abstraction rules to remove classes and group relationships into one relationship. In this paper, we adopt a similar approach. In the following we refer to simplification validity, simplification rules, the simplification method and finally the simplification algorithm.

2.1 Valid Simplification

Simplification uses a set of *initial tasks* provided by the user. The simplification process creates a partial, concise map that includes the initial tasks and possibly additional tasks between the root and the initial tasks. Simplification should preserve semantic properties we will discuss later (soundness and completeness). Otherwise, the simplified map may be misleading and not preserve reasoning properties such as consistency. Consider a simplification of the ME-map in Fig. 3a with initial tasks X, T_7, T_8, T_9. Figures 3b, 3c present possible simplifications. Figure 3b presents $achieved - by$ relationships between T and X, T_7, T_8 and T_9 respectively. However, the ME-map in Fig. 3a does not include $achieved - by$ paths between T to these three tasks. The map can mislead the user because X, T_7, T_8, and T_9 are not alternatives (direct or indirect) for achieving T. In addition, the semantics enforce an xor constraint on the $achieved - by$ relationships. A legal instance of the simplified map can include only one task. On the other hand, in the original ME-map, a legal instance might include both tasks T_7 and T_9. Task X is inconsistent in Fig. 3a but is consistent in Figs. 3b, 3c. The simplification in Fig. 3b loses semantic properties that existed in the original model. Thus the use of the maps in Fig. 3b for consistency verification is incorrect. The ME-map in Fig. 3d introduces an improvement over the incorrect version in Fig. 3c. Any relationship between two tasks in the simplified map also exists in the original map directly or indirectly. For example, for the $achieved - by$ relationship between T_1 and T_7, there exists a path of relationship $T \xrightarrow{achieved-by}^{+} T_7$ in the original map.

Based on these observations we require the simplified map to satisfy the following properties:

Soundness requires that any relationship implied by the simplified map must also be implied by the original map.

Completeness requires that any relationship between the root and an initial task in the original map must be implied by the simplified map.

Removing any task requires ensuring that the removed task does not alter map soundness and completeness properties. The removal of tasks requires adding new links

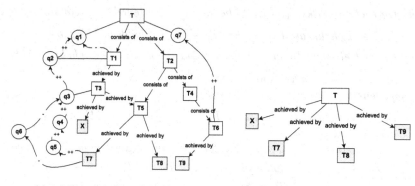

(a) A ME map before simplification

(b) A wrong simplification for the ME map in Figure 3a

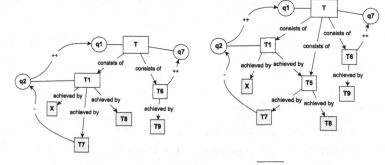

(c) A wrong simplification for the ME map in Figure 3a

(d) A possible right simplification for the ME map in Figure 3a

Fig. 3. A map with three possible simplifications

that preserve the implied relationships between the remaining tasks. For instance, an $achieved - by$ sequence $T_1 \xrightarrow{achieved-by} T_2$, $T_2 \xrightarrow{achieved-by} T_3$, might be replaced by one "achieved-by" link $T_1 \xrightarrow{achieved-by} T_3$. Nevertheless, its implied semantics is unchanged: , T_1 is "achieved by" T_3. A contribution link sequence $elm_1 \xrightarrow{cont_1} q_1$, $q_1 \xrightarrow{cont_2} q_2$, might be replaced by a single contribution link $elm_1 \xrightarrow{cont} q_2$ in which $cont$ reflects the implicit contribution of $cont_1$ with $cont_2$.

Definition 1 (Valid simplification). *A valid simplification of* $ME = \langle \mathcal{E}, \mathcal{L}nk \rangle$ *and initial tasks* S *is a ME-Map* $ME_{\downarrow[S]} = \langle \mathcal{E}' \subseteq \mathcal{E}, \mathcal{L}nk' \rangle$ *that satisfies the following properties:*

1. *The initial tasks* S *are the leaf tasks of* $\mathcal{E}'$.
2. *Soundness*

(a) *For each two tasks T_1, $T_2 \in \mathcal{E}'$ being $lnk = achieved - by/consists - of$, if $T_1 \xrightarrow{lnk} T_2$ holds in $ME_{\downarrow[S]}$, then $T_1 \xrightarrow{lnk}^{+} T_2{}^1$ holds in ME too.*

(b) *For each element elm and quality q in $ME_{\downarrow[S]}$ if elm $\xrightarrow{cont}$ q holds in $ME_{\downarrow[S]}$, then elm $\xrightarrow{cont}^{+}$ q holds in ME too.*

3. **Completeness**

(a) *For each two tasks T_1, $T_2 \in \mathcal{E}'$, if $T_1 \xrightarrow{lnk}^{+} T_2$ holds in ME, then $T_1 \xrightarrow{lnk}^{+} T_2$ holds in $ME_{\downarrow[S]}$ too.*

(b) *For each tasks T_1, $T_n \in \mathcal{E}'$, for each interleaved path of $achieved - by/consists - of$ relationships between T_1 and T_n, $T_1 \xrightarrow{\alpha_1}^{+} T_2$, $T_2 \xrightarrow{\alpha_2}^{+} T_3, \ldots, T_{n-1} \xrightarrow{\alpha_n}^{+} T_n$ in ME where $\alpha_i \in \{achieved\text{-}by, consists\text{-}of\}$, $i = 1, n$ and $\alpha_i \neq \alpha_{i+1}$, there exists a similar interleaved path (possibly shorter) with same tasks $T_1, T_2, \ldots, T_n$ and the same interrelationships $T_1 \xrightarrow{\alpha_1}^{+} T_2$, $T_2 \xrightarrow{\alpha_2}^{+} T_3, \ldots, T_{n-1} \xrightarrow{\alpha_n}^{+} T_n$ in $ME_{\downarrow[S]}$.*

(c) *For each element elm and quality q in $\mathcal{E}'$ if elm $\xrightarrow{cont}^{+}$ q holds in ME, then elm $\xrightarrow{cont}^{+}$ q holds in $ME_{\downarrow[S]}$ too.*

2.2   Simplification Rules

The simplification cannot be applied without considering the context in which the paths belong. If the task T belongs to two paths of different types, $\alpha_1 = T_1 \xrightarrow{achieved-by} T, T \xrightarrow{achieved-by} T_2$ and $\alpha_2 = T_3 \xrightarrow{consists-of} T, T \xrightarrow{consists-of} T_4$, then T is therefore an intermediate task of an interleaved path of $achieved - by$ and $consists - of$ links $T_1 \xrightarrow{achieved-by} T, T \xrightarrow{consists-of} T_4$. Therefore T is not eliminated and the later two paths α_1, α_2 will not be reduced even though they are paths of links of the same type. Based on these observations we present the notion of a mandatory task and a mandatory quality.

Definition 2 (Mandatory tasks and qualities). *Let $ME = \langle \mathcal{E}, \mathcal{L}nk \rangle$ be a ME-map and $S \subseteq \mathcal{E}$ a set of initial tasks.*

*(1) Mandatory task. A task T is called a **mandatory** task if it satisfies one of the following conditions*

1. *T is the root task or $T \in S$*
2. *There exists a sequence $< T_1 \xrightarrow{consists-of} T, T \xrightarrow{achieved-by} T_2 >$ or a sequence $< T_1 \xrightarrow{achieved-by} T, T \xrightarrow{consists-of} T_4$ that belongs to some path of $achieved - by$ and $consists - of$ links between the root and a task in S.*

*A task that does not satisfy any of the above conditions is called **non-mandatory** task or alternatively **removable** task.*

---

^{1} $\xrightarrow{lnk}^{+}$ denotes a path of $achieved - by$ or $consists - of$ relationships.

(2) Mandatory qualify. *A quality q is called a **mandatory** quality if its owner task [17] is a **mandatory** task. It is called a **non-mandatory** quality or removable quality if its owner is non-mandatory or it is not a quality of any task.*

Let $T_{removable}$ and $q_{removable}$ be removable task and quality respectively. Then:

R1. $source \xrightarrow{achieved-by} T_{removable}, T_{removable} \xrightarrow{achieved-by} target \Rightarrow source$
$\xrightarrow{achieved-by} target$

R2. $source \xrightarrow{consists-of} T_{removable}, T_{removable} \xrightarrow{consists-of} target \Rightarrow source$
$\xrightarrow{consists-of} target$

R3. $elment_{source} \xrightarrow{cont[l_1]} q_{removable}, q_{removable} \xrightarrow{cont[l_2]} q_{target} \Rightarrow$
$elment_{source} \xrightarrow{cont} [min(l_1, l_2)^2] q_{target}$

Listing 1: Simplification rules

Algorithm 1: SimplifyMap

Input: A ME map ME and a set of important task elements S
Output: A ME map $ME_{\downarrow[S]}$
begin

1   **Step 1: Adding the** $achieved - by$ **and** $consists - of$ **links**
2   marks all mandatory tasks and qualities in ME according to Definition 2
3   initialize $ME_{\downarrow[S]}$ by all mandatory tasks in ME
4   select a task $t \in S$:
5   **for** *each path π_i of achieved $-$ by or consists $-$ of of links from the root task to t* **do**
    begin
6   initialize π_i' by π_i
        apply recursively rule 1 and 2 on π_i'
    end
7   **for** *for each link (achieved $-$ by or consists $-$ of) lnk $\in \pi_i'$* **do**
8   add a corresponding link in $ME_{\downarrow[S]}$
    end
    end
9   **Step 2: Adding the association and contribution links**
10 insert to $ME_{\downarrow[S]}$ all mandatory qualities in ME with thier associations
11 **for** *each pair of mandatory tasks $T_1, T_2 \in ME_{\downarrow[S]}$* **do**
12   **for** *each path π of contribution links from T_1 to T_2* **do**
13   initialize π' by the result of applying rule 3 recursively on the successive links in π
14   for each contribution link $e \xrightarrow{cont[l_1]} q$ in π',
15   **if** *there exists a contribution link $\alpha = e \xrightarrow{cont[l_1']} q$ in $ME_{\downarrow[S]}$* **then**
16   updates label of α to $min(l_1, l_1')$
        end
        else
17   add α to $ME_{\downarrow[S]}$
        end
    end
    end
end

---

[2] Here we take a conservative approach, yet, the min function can be replaced by other functions.

The Simplification Algorithm

Algorithm 1 produces a simplified map based on an initial set. It includes two major steps, as we have already shown. Step 1 produces a simplified map without the qualities while the second step updates the map from step 1 with qualities, association and contribution links.

Contribution links can only differ in their labels; therefore, two successive contribution links can be reduced to a single link. The new link must, however, have a new label that represents the combined contribution labels of the two links. In addition, when a new contribution link $elm \xrightarrow{cont} q$ is created between some element elm and some quality q, no other additional contribution link between elm and q is created. But rather, the label $cont$ is updated to reflect the contribution of the two links together (aggregation operation). The way we combined the joined contribution labels was by choosing the minimum label. We have adopted a conservative approach by placing greater weight on the lowest value of contribution links in a series of successive labels or groupings of labels than on the higher values. This is, however, a domain-specific problem, and other joined contribution policies can be used.

3   Implementation and Evaluation

We implemented the simplification algorithm together with other reasoning methods presented in [17] within a *MEMapReasoner* prototype tool we developed [18]. The tool gets as an input a *JSON* file exported from the *ME Map* web-based tool [27] and *MEMapReasoner* provides the related output as a *JSON* file.

Based on the implemented prototype, we evaluate the work with respect to its two purposes. The first refers to the algorithm scalability and reasoning efficiency and the second to the impact of ME-map simplification on understandability.

3.1   Scalability Evaluation

To evaluate the simplification algorithm we test it with several maps following different characteristics in terms of elements and related links. As mentioned earlier, the graph-based techniques used in our paper have exponential worst-case time complexity. Therefore, we need to show that in actual maps, this method scale well. Thus, it is appealing to test the method on large-scale maps. However, currently, such maps are not available. To address this, we follow solutions proposed in other domains and generated large maps automatically. In the following, we report on the evaluation setup, the execution, and the results of the evaluation we performed.

Setup and Execution. First, we performed the tests on four limited-size ME-maps. The advantage of these maps is that they represent real domains. They were built by our group and their size range from 20 to 30 tasks on each map. Second, we generated synthetic ME-maps. The sizes of these maps were 500–2000 tasks. To generate the maps, we started with a seed of tasks and links, and iteratively generated layers of child tasks with randomly selected *achieved − by* and *consists − of* links. Moving backward on the paths of the generated map, we added qualities, association links,

Table 1. Average time for the simplification tasks

Domain	Metrics						%Dec	Abst. (msec)
	Ta	Qu	AB	CO	Con	El		
Data mining domain	13	4	10	2	6	35	0.57	28
Goal modeling domain	18	10	10	9	11	58	0.65	39
Sentiment analysis domain	27	2	13	13	7	62	0.67	32
DPSL domain	19	5	14	5	20	63	0.42	36
Synthetic map - 500	500	11	243	259	90	1103	0.80	521
Synthetic map - 1000	1000	11	490	513	90	2103	0.55	1300
Synthetic map - 1500	1500	11	763	739	105	3119	0.86	1521
Synthetic map - 2000	2000	12	990	1012	105	4119	0.79	3414

and contribution links so to develop realistic maps. Although the number of qualities is much lower than the number of tasks, we believe that the way the maps were built enforces the algorithm to consider the implications of abstracting qualities as well.

For each of the tested maps we apply the simplification algorithm. For the initial user (important) tasks, we selected randomly 30% of the leave tasks. The independent variables are: *number of tasks, number of qualities number of achieved − by number of links, number of consists − of links* and *number of contribution links*, whereas the dependent variables are the decreased percentage of elements and the time needed to perform the simplification. We executed each task 5 times and computed the average of all runs. The evaluation was performed on a A*acer* computer laptop, Windows 10 64 bits, Intel(R) Core^{TM} i5-1035G1, 8GB RAM and 512GB SSD.

Results and Discussion. Table 1 introduces the results of the evaluation. The left-hand side of the table provides descriptive information about the maps: number of Task (Ta), number of Qualities (Qu), number of achieved-by links (AB), number of consists-of links (CO), number of contribution links (Con) and the total number of Elements (El). The right-hand side of the table details the decreasing percentage of the number of elements in the simplified maps (%Dec) and the time in milliseconds it took to perform the simplification. The table shows that applying the simplification algorithm reduces over 55% of the elements in most maps. In addition, it shows that the algorithm works efficiently and we got results in less than four seconds even for a large map with 2000 tasks. The results also indicate that the overall number of elements is not enough to analyze performance. The domains of *Sentiment Analysis* and *DPSL* have almost the same number of elements, with sizes of 62 and 63, receptively. However, there are differences in the overall performance. The performance of the simplification task in the *Design Patterns* map is about 12% higher than the *Sentiment Analysis* map. Since the maps are actually graphs, the performance of the algorithm is significantly affected by the number of contribution paths. As shown in the table, the number of contribution links in the *DPSL* map is around triple more than the *Sentiment Analysis* map.

To check the implication of the simplification results, we execute a consistency check [17] over the maps and their corresponding simplifications. The column **Cons-**

Before in Table 2 shows the times in milliseconds of running the consistency algorithm on the synthetic maps evaluated in the previous section augmented with a consistency problem. The results show that the performance is expensive and the consistency check lasted between 11 s for the map of 500 tasks and 15 min for the map with 2000 tasks. The column **ConsAfter** in the table shows the time it last to apply the same consistency check on the simplified maps. The results show significant improvements (Improvement column) compared to the performance of the algorithm on the original maps. Note that in both cases for each map the same consistency problems were identified.

Table 2. Improvement in applying consistency check

ME-Map	ConsBefore (MS)	ConsAfter (MS)	Improvement
500	10929	1575	0.86
1000	275409	80171	0.71
1500	310165	21881	0.93
2000	924655	226889	0.75

Threats to Validity. The results of the experiments we conducted should be taken cautiously due to the following threats to validity. First, we perform the experiments on a small number of maps. In addition, as we develop the maps, it might be that the way the maps are constructed is biased. Yet, the "real" domain maps were carefully reviewed by several of our group members to reflect the actual domain knowledge. Nevertheless, these maps were relatively small and larger "real" domain maps are required.

3.2   Understandability

To check the support of the ME-map simplification with respect to understanding a domain, we conducted a user study by means of a preliminary controlled experiment. In the following we shortly elaborate on the experiment design, execution, and results.

Hypotheses. We checked the comprehension of a domain by means of question answering, in which we checked the correctness, the time to answer the questions, and the confidence we had in their answers.

Our conjectures are that using simplification would lead to more correct answers as many unrelated details are avoided and thus the quest for answers is easier. For that reason, we also believe that the confidence in the answers will increase. As for time to answer the questions, there is a trade-off between finding all answers in one place and the need to navigate over or execute multiple simplifications. Yet, when the number of simplifications is limited we believe that the time to answer the questions will be shorter than when searching for the answer in a complete/unified map. In case of many simplifications, finding the right one may take time. Similarly, deciding on the appropriate simplification may also take time.

Design. We next describe the variables, the participants, and the tasks.

The independent variable in the experiments is the way the domain map was presented. Either as a unified map or two separated simplified maps that jointly represent the entire domain. We decided upon this design to make sure that the answers were achieved by following the provided simplifications. The independent variables are the following: (1) the correctness of the answers, measured by their relative alignment with the gold standard on a scale of 0-1. We classified the questions into three categories of task identification, screening, and analysis. These categories refer to different capabilities required by the participants. (2) the time it takes to answer the question, measured in minutes; and (3) the confidence a participant had in her answers, measured on a scale of 1 to 7 (indicates the highest confidence). We also checked the perception of the participants.

The participants in the experiment were nine senior undergraduate and graduate students at Ben-Gurion University of the Negev. They were recruited by a call for participation posting and were offered monetary compensation. They were not familiar with the domain and with the ME-MAP approach.

The experiment form consists of three parts: (1) a pre-questionnaire that checks the background and knowledge of the participants; (2) the main task, in which participants received either a single domain ME map or two simplified ME maps and were required to answers a set of questions regarding the domain; (3) the last part of the form reflects upon the participants' perception on ME map and their form. The domain that was introduced in the experiment is the domain of Software Design Pattern Specification Languages (DPSL) and consisted of knowledge extracted from [15]. The experiment forms can be found in [19].

Execution. The execution of the experiment took place in a special session that lasts approximately 1 h. Before the experiment started, we briefly introduced ME-MAP and its semantics for about 10 min. Then, the participants were asked to sign the consent form detailing their rights. They were randomly divided into two groups. Form A in which the subjects received a unified ME map of the DPSL domain was assigned to 4 subjects. Form B in which the subjects received two simplified ME maps of the DPSL domain was assigned to 5 subjects. In both forms the students were asked the same 9 questions. For each question, they wrote their answer, the time it took them to arrive at that answer, and the confidence they had in that answer. Next, they filled out the post questionnaire.

Results. In Table 3 we present the results of the main task performed by the participants. We present the results in four categories: Total, which accumulates all answers; Task identification, which accumulates the answers to questions 1–2; Screening, which accumulates the answers to questions 3–4 and refers to comparison among tasks; and Analyze Concrete Contributions, which accumulates the answers to questions 5–9. The $\bar{x}$ columns indicate the average and the σ indicate the standard deviation. In terms of correctness, it seems that using the simplified maps achieved better results, in particular, in comprehending complex tasks such as trade off analysis. The same hold for the confidence the participants had in their answers, in particular, when analyzing specific contributions. A deviation from that trend refers to the time it took the participants to arrive at their answers. It appears that the screening task took much more time when using the simplified maps.

Table 3. Descriptive statistics

	Correctness		Confidence		Time	
	$\bar{x}$	σ	$\bar{x}$	σ	$\bar{x}$	σ
Total						
Unified map	0.48	0.2	4.5	0.88	3.26	0.9
Simplified maps	_0.63_	0.23	_5.08_	0.9	_3.22_	0.39
Task identification						
Unified map	0.63	0.32	5.38	1.38	3.28	1.35
Simplified maps	_0.64_	0.42	_5.4_	1.14	_2.8_	0.76
Screening						
Unified map	0.33	0.42	4.00	1.47	_5.13_	2.29
Simplified maps	_0.67_	0.32	_4.1_	1.78	6.8	1.04
Analyze concrete contributions						
Unified map	0.49	0.23	4.35	1.00	2.5	1.16
Simplified maps	_0.61_	0.17	_5.35_	1.02	_1.96_	0.61

From analyzing the participants' subjective preferences, we found out that there are benefits of having both the unified view (to see all the details) and the simplified views (to focus on specific aspects).

Discussion. The results indicate that for simple comprehension questions, there is no difference in using either the unified or the simplified maps in both correctness and confidence. This is probably due to the minimal cognitive effort required for detecting related tasks. Nevertheless, in most cases the time to reach the answers is shorter when using the simplified maps. This is probably due to the focused information appears on those maps. The most observable difference between the two representations occurs in the complex task of analyzing concrete contributions. Here, using the simplified maps results in more correct answers that gain higher confidence. It also took less time to reach these answers. We attribute these differences to the way the simplified maps are organized in terms that they presented concise information which was easy to grasp with respect to the same information that was spread all over the unified map.

Another issue that requires further attention is the time it took to perform the screening tasks. It seems that the participants who use the simplified maps switched among the maps trying to answer the questions as it was not clear, where the relevant information can be found. This is actually quite important. In the experiment, we defined the simplification in advance. However, in a regular situation, we expect the users of a knowledge map to perform their own simplification based on their searching and exploration needs (using the proposed algorithm), and thus they would skip the need to navigate across multiple simplifications to allocate the relevant information.

Threats to Validity. Here again, the results of our study need to be considered in view of several threats to validity. First, we examined two alternatives for knowledge representation. As the experiment is quite simple in its design, there might be a chance for mono operation bias, in which we did not explore or test a range of simplifications. Second, in the experiment we used a hard copy of the maps, whereas in reality we expect the participants to work with an on-line platform that ease the search and simplifications. Third, the conclusions we arrived at should be taken with caution, as we got no statistical support for their validity. Yet, they provide an indication of the supremacy of the simplification. Fourth, we had a limited number of participants, thus, it is challenging to draw a definite conclusion. In addition, we experiment with only one domain a fact that also challenges the generalization of the results.

4   Related Work

Abstraction plays a crucial role in dealing with model complexity. It deals with simplifying information by retaining essential properties and removing insignificant details. Indeed, numerous works on reducing model complexity have been presented in various modeling languages and domains and for various purposes like increasing comprehension or verification purposes [5,7,8,14,25,30].

de Lara et al. [7] identified four types of abstractions: (1) Merge techniques in which one element of the same type replace a set of model elements, collecting the merged elements' properties [8]; (2) Aggregation techniques which suggest grouping low-level model elements into higher-level elements, e.g., [25]; (3) Delete techniques that delete elements which are not considered relevant or modify some observed properties of a model. e.g., [30]; and (4) View techniques in which a new model is created (called view) using the same language or a different one and that discard the original model features that are irrelevant for the desired abstraction, e.g., [11].

Egyed presented in [8] an algorithm for abstraction (simplification) of UML class diagrams. The presented algorithm uses abstraction rules to remove intermediate classes and group intermediate relationships (such as associations and class hierarchies). The author evaluated the abstraction technique on over a dozen real-world case studies ranging from in-house-developed models to third-party models. Other approaches used a set of rules for class model simplification presented in [1,12].

Shoval et al. presented in [25] a method for creating a hierarchy of entity-relationship diagrams (HERD) from a "flat" ER diagram. The method uses packaging operations that aggregate entities and relationships into higher-level ER diagrams called structures. A structure is a partial ER diagram with external relationships to related structures that might group two or more specific relationships (Aggregate). Other approaches in ER that use the aggregation can be found in [3,13,21,29]. Villegas and Olive present in [30] a method that uses a set of elements provided by the user (called *user focus set*), and the method filters (simplifies) the conceptual schema by producing a subset of the elements of the original schema taking into account the importance of each entity type in the schema and its closeness to the entity types the user focuses on. The method might create new entities and use the hierarchy to produce a more abstract model.

Other modeling languages have used different abstraction techniques such as aggregation into higher-level elements or removing unnecessary elements to reduce the model's complexity, such as workflow languages [23,26]. Some of these languages use already built-in hierarchical primitives that enable element aggregation.

As the language we are using in this paper is a subset of i^* [31] we refer to studies dealing with its complexity management. We found out that scalability is considered one of the important challenging problems that have been treated only to a limited extent [2, 10, 16]. Most solutions focus on increasing the modularity of the i^* language by providing modularization mechanisms. These approaches require extending the languages with new modeling constructs that encapsulate the internal structures of the model. A detailed survey can be found in [16]. In contrast to the works presented by the i^* community, in this work we chose to remain with the existing language and not extend the language with new constructs that naturally require a steeper learning curve. Our aim is to simplify the maps to enable better understanding, inspecting, and managing the maps while preserving their semantics. In that sense, we adopt a similar direction to the work of Egyed who introduced abstraction rules for class models and an algorithm for applying them [8].

5   Conclusion and Future Work

We develop a simplification algorithm for know-how maps and found it improving knowledge reasoning efficiency as well as knowledge understandability. We examined the reasoning efficiency and scaleability using large scale maps and the understandability via a controlled experiment. The importance of the map simplification is high as knowledge, in particular know-how, is developing at a fast pace, so the need to manage and reason about it is increased. Even know-how maps that index the existing knowledge are complex and tend to scale fast, and thus required further simplification. We believe that by applying the simplification algorithm over the maps, stakeholders can better manage and navigate throughout the maps, and better be supported for decision making.

In the future, we plan to further investigate and evaluate the mechanism we developed and look for additional mechanisms that facilitate various simplification capabilities, so to better manage ME maps. We also plan to test the simplification of ME maps for industrial/practical purposes. In particular, as the ME-MAP approach is derived from GORE, we plan to apply the simplification mechanism to goal modeling techniques.

References

1. Abdulganiyyi, N., Ibrahim, N.: Semantic abstraction of class diagram using logical approach. In: 4th World Congress on Information and Communication Technologies, pp. 251–256. IEEE (2014)
2. Alencar, F., et al.: Towards modular i* models. In: Proceedings of the 2010 ACM Symposium on Applied Computing, pp. 292–297 (2010)
3. Campbell, L.J., Halpin, T.A., Proper, H.: Conceptual schemas with abstractions making flat conceptual schemas more comprehensible. Data Know. Eng. **20**(1), 39–85 (1996)
4. Carvalho, M.R., Hewett, R., Canas, A.J.: Enhancing web searches from concept map-based knowledge models. In: Fifth Multiconference on Systems, Cybernetics and Informatics, pp. 69–73 (2001)

5. Caughlin, D., Sisti, A.F.: Summary of model abstraction techniques. In: Enabling Technology for Simulation Science, vol. 3083, pp. 2–13 (1997)
6. Davenport, T., Prusak, L.: Working Knowledge: How Organizations Manage What they Know. Harvard Business Review Press, Boston (1998)
7. De Lara, J., Guerra, E., Cuadrado, J.: Reusable abstractions for modeling languages. Inf. Syst. **38**(8), 1128–1149 (2013)
8. Egyed, E.: Automated abstraction of class diagrams. ACM TOSEM **11**(4), 449–491 (2002)
9. Falke, T.G.I.: GraphDocExplore: a framework for the experimental comparison of graph-based document exploration techniques. In: Conference on Empirical Methods in NLP, pp. 19–24 (2017)
10. Franch, X.: Incorporating modules into the $i*$ framework. In: Pernici, B. (ed.) CAiSE 2010. LNCS, vol. 6051, pp. 439–454. Springer, Heidelberg (2010). https://doi.org/10.1007/978-3-642-13094-6_34
11. Guerra, E., de Lara, J., Malizia, A., Díaz, P.: Supporting user-oriented analysis for multi-view domain-specific visual languages. Inf. Soft. Tech. **51**(4), 769–784 (2009)
12. Guizzardi, G., Figueiredo, G., Hedblom, M.M., Poels, G.: Ontology-based model abstraction. In: 13th International Conference on Research Challenges in Information Science (RCIS), pp. 1–13. IEEE (2019)
13. Jaeschke, P., Oberweis, A., Stucky, W.: Extending ER model clustering by relationship clustering. In: Elmasri, R.A., Kouramajian, V., Thalheim, B. (eds.) ER 1993. LNCS, vol. 823, pp. 451–462. Springer, Heidelberg (1994). https://doi.org/10.1007/BFb0024387
14. Jimenez-Pastor, A., Garmendia, A., de Lara, J.: Scalable model exploration for model-driven engineering. J. Syst. Softw. **132**, 204–225 (2017)
15. Khwaja, S., Alshayeb, M.: Survey on software design-pattern specification languages. ACM Comput. Surv. **49**(1), 1–35 (2016)
16. Lima, P., et al.: An extended systematic mapping study about the scalability of i* models. CLEI Electron. J. **19**(3), 6:1–6:23 (2016)
17. Maraee, A., Sturm, A.: Reasoning methods for ME-maps-a CSP based approach. In: 12th Conference on Research Challenges in Information Science (RCIS), pp. 1–11 (2018)
18. Maraee, A., Sturm, A., Prokofiev, D.: MEMapReasoner (2019). https://bit.ly/2WOGGtL
19. Maraee, A., Sturm, A.: ME-map simplification (2021). https://tinyurl.com/y7wdl2yc
20. Menaouer, B., Nada, M.: The relationship between knowledge mapping and the open innovation process: the case of education system. Arti. Intell. Eng. Design Analy. Manuf. **34**(1), 17–29 (2020)
21. Moody, D.L., Flitman, A.: A methodology for clustering entity relationship models — a human information processing approach. In: Akoka, J., Bouzeghoub, M., Comyn-Wattiau, I., Métais, E. (eds.) ER 1999. LNCS, vol. 1728, pp. 114–130. Springer, Heidelberg (1999). https://doi.org/10.1007/3-540-47866-3_8
22. Nassour, J., Elhadad, M., Sturm, A., Yu, E.: Evaluating the comprehension of means-ends maps. Softw. Syst. Model. **18**(3), 1885–1903 (2018)
23. Polyvyanyy, A., Smirnov, S., Weske, M.: Business process model abstraction. In: vom Brocke, J., Rosemann, M. (eds.) Handbook on Business Process Management 1. IHIS, pp. 147–165. Springer, Heidelberg (2015). https://doi.org/10.1007/978-3-642-45100-3_7
24. Sarewitz, D., Nelson, R.R.: Progress in know-how: its origins and limits. Innov. Technol. Gov. Glob. **3**(1), 101–117 (2008)
25. Shoval, P., Danoch, R., Balaban, M.: Hierarchical entity-relationship diagrams: the model, method of creation and experimental evaluation. Req. Eng. **9**(4), 217–228 (2004)
26. Smirnov, S.: Business process model abstraction. Ph.D. thesis, Universitätsbibliothek der Universität Potsdam (2012)
27. Sturm, A.: Knowledge Map Tool (2017). http://khmap.ise.bgu.ac.il/map/

28. Sturm, A., Gross, D., Wang, J., Yu, E.: Means-ends based know-how mapping. J. Knowl. Manag. **21**(2), 454–473 (2017)
29. Teorey, T., Wei, G., Bolton, D., Koenig, J.: ER model clustering as an aid for user communication and documentation in database design. Commun. ACM **32**(8), 975–987 (1989)
30. Villegas, A., Olivé, A.: A method for filtering large conceptual schemas. In: Parsons, J., Saeki, M., Shoval, P., Woo, C., Wand, Y. (eds.) ER 2010. LNCS, vol. 6412, pp. 247–260. Springer, Heidelberg (2010). https://doi.org/10.1007/978-3-642-16373-9_18
31. Yu, E., Giorgini, P., Maiden, N., Mylopoulos, J.: Social Modeling for Requirements Engineering. MIT Press, Cambridge (2011)

A Semi-automated Method
for Domain-Specific Ontology Creation
from Medical Guidelines

Omar ElAssy⬤, Rik de Vendt⬤, Fabiano Dalpiaz⬤,
and Sjaak Brinkkemper(✉)⬤

Department of Information and Computing Sciences,
Utrecht University, Utrecht, The Netherlands
{o.omarihabelsayedelassy,r.devendt,f.dalpiaz,s.brinkkemper}@uu.nl

Abstract. The automated capturing and summarization of medical
consultations has the potential to reduce the administrative burden in
healthcare. Consultations are structured conversations that broadly follow a guideline with a systematic examination of predefined observations
and symptoms to diagnose and treat well-defined medical conditions. A
key component in automated conversation summarization is the matching of the knowledge graph of the consultation transcript with a medical
domain ontology for the interpretation of the consultation conversation.
Existing general medical ontologies such as SNOMED CT provide a taxonomic view on the terminology, but they do not capture the essence of the
guidelines that define consultations. As part of our research on medical
conversation summarization, this paper puts forward a semi-automated
method for generating an ontological representation of a medical guideline. The method, which takes as input the well-known SNOMED CT
nomenclature and a medical guideline, maps the guidelines to a so-called
Medical Guideline Ontology (MGO), a machine-processable version of
the guideline that can be used for interpreting the conversation during a
consultation. We illustrate our approach by discussing the creation of an
MGO of the medical condition of ear canal inflammation (Otitis Externa)
given the corresponding guideline from a Dutch medical authority.

Keywords: Domain ontology · Method engineering · Knowledge
graph · SNOMED CT · Medical Guideline Ontology

1   Introduction

The automated summarization of conversations may save time and cost, especially in domains where dialogues are structured based on predefined guidelines.
Medical consultations are a prime example, as they broadly follow a systematic
examination of predefined symptoms and observations to diagnose and treat well-
defined conditions affecting fixed human anatomy [11]. The potential of automated
conversation summarization depends on the readiness of the structured representations of domain-specific knowledge in a machine-processable format [15]. In
particular, rule-based conversation summarization grants explainability that is

© Springer Nature Switzerland AG 2022
A. Augusto et al. (Eds.): BPMDS 2022/EMMSAD 2022, LNBIP 450, pp. 295–309, 2022.
https://doi.org/10.1007/978-3-031-07475-2_20

unachievable with machine learning approaches, thus, ontologies can efficiently represent domain guidelines in such rule-based applications [22].

Medical consultations typically last 5–10 min in which about 1,000–1,500 words are spoken by care provider and patient. Medical reports contain between 20 and 40 highly standardized terms with abbreviations for frequent words (e.g., pt for patient) [16]. In our Care2Report research project [15,16], we combine *domain ontology learning* with the concept of *ontological conversation interpretation* in a two-layered architecture (Fig. 1). The semantic interpretation of the consultation conversation requires the availability of a domain-specific ontology, that binds spoken words to formally defined medical concepts. Input are medical guidelines and clinical practice guidelines for the patient's ailment type that are available from medical professional associations. Many ontology learning techniques (linguistic analysis, inductive logic programming, and statistical learning [6]) can be applied to generate a domain-specific ontology, in our case the Medical Guideline Ontology (MGO). As medical conversations require optimal precision, we prefer linguistic parsing analyzers (see Sect. 5). The SNOMED CT medical glossary [5] serves for the medical concept identification and linking.

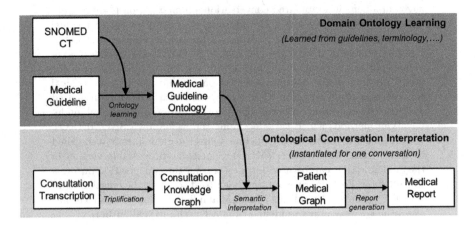

Fig. 1. Ontological conversation interpretation in Care2report [16], with the Medical Guideline Ontology supporting semantic interpretation.

The *ontological conversation interpretation pipeline* enables the consultation summarization in four steps: (1) transcribing the audio file by utilizing an automated speech recognizer (ASR), (2) generation of OWL triples (aka triplification) into a complete consultation knowledge graph, (3) semantic interpretation of these triples by means of the Medical Guideline Ontology to a significantly smaller patient medical graph [16], and (4) the generation of a medical report that is presented to the care provider for editing, approval and uploading into the Electronic medical file of this patient.

We adopt the distinction of Ehrlinger and Wöß [9]: the medical ontology acts as a schema on a generic layer serving multiple similar consultations, whereas the knowledge graph represents an instantiated fact base as spoken during the consultation. In the context of conversation summarization, the ontology represents the diverse and primarily textual domain knowledge (e.g., human anatomy and medical guidelines) in a machine-processable fabric of concepts and relationships. Manually building a domain ontology is time consuming and error prone; thus, it should be carried out using ontology learning: constructing and integrating a machine-readable semantic-rich ontology (semi-)automatically [24].

However, tools and techniques for ontology learning primarily aim to extract knowledge from general data corpora as it was, and still is, driven by the necessity of linking either openly available data (e.g., DBpedia [13]) or corporate-specific business data (e.g., Google Knowledge Graph [2]). Therefore, research is needed to develop a method that enables the systematic representation of domain guidelines in machine-processable ontologies. This paper introduces the notion of *ontological conversation interpretation* (Fig. 1) by presenting a method for developing ontologies in the medical domain to support the expansion of the automated conversation summarization system Care2Report [15].

Care2Report's summarization pipeline [15] relies on an ontology embodying the domain's vocabulary and guidelines that act as the structured container to be filled with the multimodal information from the medical consultation. The information extracted from the conversation populates the ontology to generate the rule-adhering report that the physician checks before uploading to the Electronic Medical Records system (EMR) [16]. This paper investigates elements of the second stage of the Care2Report pipeline: the definition of a Medical Guideline Ontology, a machine-processable version of a medical guideline.

To illustrate, we use a medical guideline for ear canal inflammation (Otitis Externa) from the Dutch College of General Practitioners [3]. The medical domain knowledge is assembled from the terminology in the Systematized Nomenclature of Medicine - Clinical Terms (SNOMED CT) [5].

This paper addresses the two aspects of the ontology learning method: the notational side represented by the Medical Guideline Ontology (MGO), and the procedural method expressed in a Process-Deliverable Diagram (PDD) model and by an algorithm. The design science research cycle, as described by Wieringa [23], is fitting to answer the research question: *How to systematically construct ontologies from the human anatomy and medical guidelines?*

The paper makes three contributions:

- We introduce and formalize the Medical Guideline Ontology (MGO), a domain ontology that constitutes a machine-readable version of a medical guideline and that describes the relevant aspects concerning the patient's anatomy, symptoms, physician's observations, diagnosis, and treatments.
- We define a procedural method to develop such ontologies in the form of a Process-Deliverable Diagram model, refined into an algorithm that can be at the basis of automated tooling.
- We illustrate the MGO and the procedure to the case of the external ear canal inflammation.

Paper Organization. After reviewing the related work in Sect. 2, we introduce the MGO in Sect. 3 and its formalization in Sect. 4. We then present our method in Sect. 5 and its application in Sect. 6. Finally, we draw conclusions in Sect. 7.

2   Guidelines and Nomenclature in Medical Informatics

Medical Guidelines. A medical guideline is a document with recommendations that aim to optimize patient care based on a systematic review of evidence and on weighing the benefits and harms of alternative care options [18]. It consists of definitions and procedural instructions for executing an anamnesis, diagnosis and treatment in care provisions that aim to advance care quality, improve the patient's health and well-being, and support medical decision-making. Many (inter)national medical authorities publish and maintain medical guidelines [17].

In the Netherlands, both the Dutch College of General Practitioners (Nederlands Huisartsen Genootschap - NHG) and the Dutch Federation of Medical Specialists (Federatie Medisch Specialisten - FMS) publish numerous guidelines [1,3], only the former is used in this paper. The guidelines include sections about prognosis, common causes and background, physical examination and diagnosis guidelines, treatment policy, consultations and referral guidelines (if any), and control and future patient check-ups.

The symptoms and observations indicating a condition and the treatments recommended for such condition by the guidelines are relevant to the construction and population of the Medical Guideline Ontology (MGO) and the related sub-ontologies, as will be detailed in the coming sections. The MGO, the consultation knowledge graph, and the consultation report aim to serve as a representational artifact, rather than supporting the physician's decision making; thus, the reasoning behind which treatment to choose is beyond our scope. Therefore, the MGO should contain all treatment possibilities as options, while the physician's discretion will decide which ones to use.

Medical Nomenclature: SNOMED CT. The Systematized Nomenclature of Medicine - Clinical Terms (SNOMED CT) is currently the world's most extensive clinical terminology system [7]. This paper uses SNOMED CT as an ontology source representing human anatomy and terminology hierarchy to identify relevant medical concepts from all the potential concepts in the textual medical guidelines. The terminology structure is in hierarchical formations of concepts defined and connected to each other by relationships, with identifiers for machine use and descriptors for human readability. The top node of the SNOMED CT hierarchy is occupied by the root concept *SNOMED CT concept*, and nineteen direct subtypes of it are the *top level concepts* that provide the structure of the SNOMED CT. Different conditions and medical consultations use a subset of the available concept hierarchies.

3   Medical Guideline Ontology

The Medical Guideline Ontology (MGO) is a domain ontology that represents a medical guideline in a machine-processable format. In the context of the considered guideline, the MGO represents the relevant patient's anatomy and symptoms, the physician's observations, diagnosis and prescribed treatments. Note that symptoms are subjective abnormalities that the patient perceives, while observations are objective abnormalities detected by the physician [12]. The schema of the MGO is illustrated in Fig. 2.

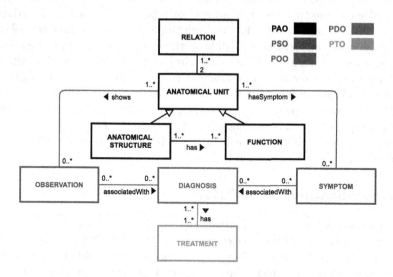

Fig. 2. Schema of the Medical Guideline Ontology

The MGO consists of five (sub)ontologies. The Patient Anatomy Ontology (PAO) depicts the human anatomical structures and functions (within the context of the guideline). The Patient Symptoms Ontology (PSO) represents the complaints and anomalies (symptoms) that a patient may report. The Patient Observations Ontology (POO) represents all the observations that the physician may make about the patient's condition. The Patient Diagnosis Ontology (PDO) describes the physician's diagnosis of a patient's condition. Finally, the Patient Treatment Ontology (PTO) describes all the treatments prescribed by the physician, including medications, instructions, referrals, or additional medical tests.

The Patient Anatomy Ontology (PAO) is the foundation for the knowledge representation in the MGO. The PAO can be built based on existing resources like the Foundational Model of Anatomy [20], or it can utilize an existing hierarchical terminology structure like SNOMED CT, as in this research. Within the SNOMED CT hierarchies, the human anatomy is represented in one section: *SNOMED CT concept ⇒ Body structure ⇒ Anatomical or acquired body structure* [5]. The key concepts in the PAO are those of ANATOMICAL UNIT and RELATION. The former is specialized by ANATOMICAL UNIT (e.g., ear, left eye) and FUNCTION (e.g., hearing), with the HAS relationship linking the two, e.g., 'an ear has the function of hearing'. The RELATION is meant to represent other types of links between anatomical units, such as part-of, next-to, etc.

The medical report produced by the automated conversation summarization system Care2Report to upload into the EMR follows a predefined structure [8] of four sections: (i) Subjective: what the patient reports; (ii) Objective: what the physician identifies; (iii) Evaluation: assessment and diagnosis by the physician; and (iv) Plan for treatment and follow up.

Following the same arrangement, the MGO consists of a composite of four sub-ontologies reflecting the four aspects of reporting and a fifth foundational ontology for human anatomy. Each of the those (anatomy, symptoms, observations, diagnosis, and treatment) builds on the previous one(s) to include further knowledge into the resulting MGO shown in Fig. 2. The MGO provides the notational aspect of the ontology development method proposed in this paper.

The MGO and its instantiation into a consultation knowledge graph with information from a specific consultation (with a concrete patient) provide a graphical representation of ontology-based knowledge where every two concepts and the relationship between them form a triple. Examples of such triples are introduced in the coming sections.

4   Formalization of the MGO

The structure and the interaction between the various ontologies are relatively intuitive for simple conditions concerning comparatively simple body structures. However, adding the complete human anatomy and the guidelines from several medical authorities can make the ontologies less intuitive to understand and communicate. Therefore, it is essential to introduce formal descriptions of the ontologies and their components; this section introduces a few of these descriptions. Formally defining the MGO requires the definition of the following sets:

Set	Description
B	anatomical structures of the body.
F	anatomical functions of the body.
A	anatomical units ($A = B \cup F$).
S	medical symptoms (reported by a patient).
O	medical observations (observed by a physician).
V	possible values to be assigned to symptoms $s \in S$ or observations $o \in O$.
E	explicit diagnoses.
I	implicit diagnoses.
D	medical diagnoses: $D = E \cup I$.
T	medical treatments.

The elements in these sets may vary depending on the scope of the ontologies. Defining the comprehensiveness of these sets depends on the goal of the medical reporting and on the number and complexity o the guidelines. We leave the investigation of this aspect to future research.

The definitions of the ontologies comprising the MGO are defined with respect to a patient p (the subject of the guideline, which is also the most comprehensive anatomical unit) as follows:

Ontol.	Vertices	Edges
PAO	$A = B \cup F$	$\{(b_1, b_2)|b_1, b_2 \in B \wedge b_1$ is a direct anatomical sub-part of $b_2\}$ $\cup$ $(\{b, f)|b \in B \wedge f \in F \wedge b$ has an anatomical function $f\}$
PSO	$A \cup S \cup V$	$\{(a, s), (s, v) \mid a \in A \wedge s \in S \wedge v \in V\}$ i.e., the symptoms
POO	$A \cup O \cup V$	$\{(a, o), (o, v) \mid a \in A \wedge o \in O \wedge v \in V\}$ i.e., the observations
PDO	$\{p\} \cup D$	$\{(p, d) \mid d \in D\}$ i.e., the possible diagnoses of a generic patient
PTO	$\{p\} \cup T$	$\{(p, t) \mid t \in T\}$ i.e., the possible treatments of a generic patient

As per Sect. 3, the MGO is a domain ontology representing the guideline's contents in terms of patient anatomy and symptoms as well as physician's observations, diagnosis and treatments: MGO = PAO $\cup$ PSO $\cup$ POO $\cup$ PDO $\cup$ PTO.

Finally, some of the rules that need to be coded into the system to define the relationships between the entities are listed below, consulting domain experts is expected to add to this list. We provide some examples, but note that the creation of a comprehensive list of rules is domain-specific and goes beyond the purpose of this paper:

1. Each anatomical structure (b) is a part of another anatomical structure (b) unless it is the complete body structure (b*).
   $\forall b_1 \exists b_2 : \text{isPartOf}(b_1, b_2)$ $\qquad\qquad\qquad b_1, b_2 \in B, \neg (b_1 = \text{b*})$
2. Each function (f) is assigned to one or more anatomical structure (b).
   $\forall f \exists b : \text{hasFunction}(b,f)$ $\qquad\qquad\qquad\qquad\qquad b \in B, f \in F$
3. Each symptom (s) is associated with one or more anatomical unit (a).
   $\forall s \exists a : \text{hasSymptom}(a,s)$ $\qquad\qquad\qquad\qquad\qquad s \in S, a \in A$
4. Each observation (o) is associated with one or more anatomical unit (a).
   $\forall o \exists a : \text{hasObservation}(a,o)$ $\qquad\qquad\qquad\qquad\qquad o \in O, a \in A$
5. Patients are diagnosed with at least diagnosis (d).
   Given p, $\exists d : \text{diagnosedWith}(p,d)$ $\qquad\qquad\qquad\qquad\qquad d \in D$
6. Patients are treated with a treatment (t). A treatment encompasses any physician's prescription, including medications, instructions for the patient to follow, referral to a specialist, further tests, or any other procedure.
   Given p, $\exists t : \text{treatedWith}(p,t)$ $\qquad\qquad\qquad\qquad\qquad t \in T$
7. An explicit diagnosis (e) is associated with a symptom (s) or an observation (o).
   $\forall e \exists s \, \exists o: \text{associatedWith}(s,e) \vee \text{associatedWith}(o,e)$ $\qquad e \in E, s \in S, o \in O$
8. An implicit diagnosis is not explicit. That is, an implicit diagnosis (i) is neither associated with a symptom (s) nor an observation (o).
   $\forall i \forall e: \neg (i = e)$ $\qquad\qquad\qquad\qquad\qquad\qquad\qquad i \in I, e \in E$

5 Method for Systematic Creation of Medical Ontologies

While the previous section introduced the MGO for representing a medical guideline in a machine-processable format, this section introduces the procedural method perspective outlined in a Process-Deliverable Diagram (PDD) model. The PDD illustrates the activities and artefacts of a specific process [21]. The model emphasizes the relationships between the activities and their deliverables by connecting them with dotted arrows across the diagram [21].

5.1   Ontology Creation PDD

Figure 3 shows the used PDD, in which the process is broken down into eight main activities. For simplicity, activities three to seven are illustrated (and manually performed) sequentially; however, they can also be executed in parallel.

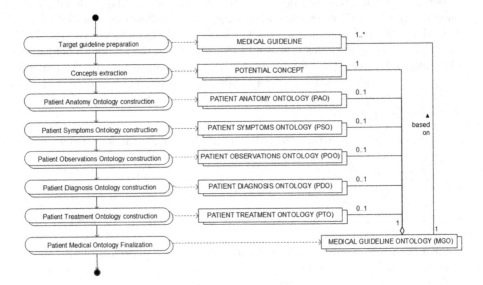

Fig. 3. PDD of the ontology creation process

1. **Target guideline preparation**: The guideline of the medical condition is selected from the medical authority's website, translated (if necessary), scraped, and prepared for the following concept extraction activity.
2. **Concept extraction**: The relevant sections of the guidelines are identified, including sections describing symptoms, physical examination, and treatment plans. As nouns are the natural language representation of things, ideas and notions, they identify the concepts to be extracted. Thus, the potential concepts to extract are all nouns and noun phrases in the relevant sections that will be mapped in the next steps against the SNOMED CT to identify the constituent concepts of the ontology (e.g., anatomical units, symptoms, observations, and treatments). Some potential concepts will not be used in the ontology as they represent general nouns used in the text.
3. **Patient Anatomy Ontology (PAO) construction**: The guideline concepts corresponding to SNOMED CT *anatomical concepts* are identified and converted into a hierarchy from which the PAO is constructed.

4. **Patient Symptoms Ontology (PSO) construction**: The concepts identified in the medical guideline sections describing symptoms are mapped against the corresponding SNOMED CT hierarchies (*findings* and *disorders*) to build the PSO.

5. **Patient Observations Ontology (POO) construction**: Similar to the previous activity except dealing with physician observations instead of patient-described symptoms. Thus, the relevant guideline sections are different.

6. **Patient Diagnosis Ontology (PDO) construction**: The medical condition or disease discussed in the guideline is the diagnosis associated with symptoms and observations to construct the PDO.

7. **Patient Treatment Ontology (PTO) construction**: The concepts identified in the treatment-related sections of the guideline are mapped against the corresponding SNOMED CT hierarchies (*procedure, substance, dose form,* and *physical object*) to build the PTO.

8. **Medical Guideline Ontology Finalization**: All the previous (sub)ontologies are combined along with needed information (e.g., prefixes) to construct the complete MGO. This activity also includes checks to validity by confirming the lack of disjoint concepts.

5.2 A Detailed Look on Ontology Creation

Figure 4 expands the PAO construction activity to show the various subactivities and the resulting deliverables. The PDD activities constructing the remaining ontologies follow the same general high-level pattern to build the relevant ontology based on the list of extracted potential concepts from the guidelines. Potential concepts are mapped at each stage to both the relevant sections of the guidelines (e.g., physical examination and treatment policy) and the relevant hierarchies of the SNOMED CT (e.g., findings and disorders). Thus, the

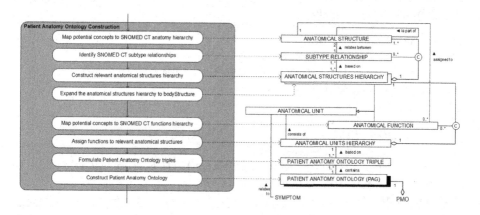

Fig. 4. Patient Anatomy Ontology (PAO) construction

concepts that show in both relevant modules are the appropriate candidate concepts for the ontology at hand (e.g., symptom concept, observation concept or treatment concept). An anatomical unit (that can have symptoms, observations, diagnosis, or treatment) can be either an anatomical structure or a function. An *anatomical structure* is "a physical anatomical entity and a physical object, ... it consists of parts that are themselves anatomical structures", anatomical structures are "...localized to a specific area or combine and carry out one or more specialized [anatomical] *functions* of an organism." [19].

For a detailed illustration of the complete PDD and a description of all the (sub)activities and concepts, refer to the technical report [10].

5.3   Algorithm

Algorithm 1 refines the PDD in Fig. 3 by explaining the derivation of an MGO from a medical guideline MG for a disease D, and from a human anatomy graph HA. This algorithm is at the basis of our current Care2Report pipeline.

Algorithm 1. Medical Guideline Ontology Generation

Input: MG a Medical Guideline for disease D,
  HA the standard complete human anatomy graph,
Output: a generic ontology MGO for this medical guideline

```
 1: function BUILDONTOLOGYBYTRIPLES(MG, D, HA)
 2:    for all sent ∈ MG do
 3:      P_sent ← EXTRACTNOUNPHRASES(sent)
 4:      for all cs ∈ P_sent do
 5:        if cs ∈ HA then
 6:          AnatD ← AnatD ∪ {cs}
 7:    PAO ← SUBGRAPH(AnatD, HA)          ▷ The concepts in AnatD and their links
 8:    MGO ← ∅, PSO ← ∅, POO ← ∅, PDO ← ∅, PTO ← ∅,
 9:    for all ae ∈ PAO do
10:      for all sent ∈ MG do
11:        P_sent ← EXTRACTNOUNPHRASES(sent)
12:        for all cs ∈ P_sent do
13:          if cs ∈ SNOMED.symptom then
14:            PSO ← PSO ∪ {⟨ae, hasSymptom, cs⟩, ⟨cs, associatedWith, D⟩}
15:          if cs ∈ SNOMED.observation then
16:            POO ← POO ∪ {⟨ae, hasObservation, cs⟩, ⟨cs, associatedWith, D⟩}
17:          if cs ∈ SNOMED.diagnosis then
18:            PDO ← PDO ∪ {⟨patient, diagnosedWith, cs⟩}
19:          if cs ∈ SNOMED.treatment then
20:            PTO ← PTO ∪ {⟨patient, treatedWith, cs⟩, ⟨D, hasTreament, cs⟩}
21:    MGO ← PAO ∪ PSO ∪ POO ∪ PDO ∪ PTO
22:    return MGO
```

The algorithms iterates over all sentences in the medical guideline (lines 2–6). Each sentence is parsed to extract the noun phrases (e.g., Otitis, ear canal) that are mentioned in the text (line 3). These noun phrases are analyzed (lines 4–6) so that only those corresponding to elements of the human anatomy graph are retained and stored into the variable *AnatD*. The *PAO* is defined (line 7) as the subgraph of the *HA* that includes only the concepts in *AnatD*, their descendants in the part-of hierarchy, and the relationships between the retained concepts.

After their initialization as empty sets (line 8), the remaining ontologies *MGO, PSO, POO, PDO, PTO* are populated in lines 9–21. The elements added to the *PAO* are iterated over (lines 9–20): the sub-cycle starting in line 10 iterates again over the medical guidelines, which are again parsed by extracting the noun phrases (line 11). Each of these noun phrases contributes to populating the various ontologies, depending on whether the noun phrase is a symptom (lines 13–14), observation (lines 15–16), diagnosis (lines 17–18), or treatment (lines 19–20). Finally, the MGO is defined (line 21) as the union of the five ontologies.

6   Application to the Otitis Externa Case

To illustrate the MGO and apply the derived procedure to create an ontology, we use the NHG guideline for the inflammation of the external ear canal (Otitis Externa) [4]. The condition is chosen as an example for the relative simplicity of the associated guidelines and the lack of complicated medical procedures, terminology, or differential diagnosis. Otitis Externa is an inflammation caused by a disturbance in the acidic environment of the ear canal and it is usually associated with swimming. The symptoms reported by the patient may include ear pain, ear itching, fluid drainage from the ear, and hearing loss. In addition, the physician examines both the complaint-free ear and the affected ear for signs of scars, swelling, flaking, redness, the state of the eardrum, etc. [4].

Some symptoms (e.g., hearing loss) are not required for an Otitis Externa diagnosis, indicating that while the MGO representation of the condition should include it as a possible symptom, some specific consultations might have this symptom present while others do not. Also, the guidelines indicate that the physician should check the eardrum; however, Otitis Externa is not associated with any observations regarding the eardrum, suggesting that any observation of the eardrum (e.g., rapture) might indicate a different diagnosis. As for the treatment, the guideline recommends that the physician should instruct the patient on how to clean the infected ear properly, and prescribe ear drops. Also, referral to a specialist is recommended if the condition does not improve promptly or if the patient is from a specific vulnerable group (e.g., elderly and diabetic).

As an example, we consider a fictitious consultation for an Otitis Externa patient suffering from ear pain (no indication of itching, fluid drainage, or hearing loss), and the examination shows swelling, redness, and skin flaking in the external ear canal. Figure 5a represents the general MGO of the Otitis Externa condition with indication of the guideline sections forming it, while Fig. 5b is the consultation-specific knowledge graph for the fictitious patient.

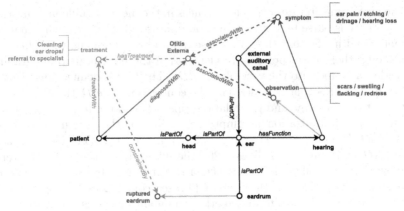

(a) MGO of the Otitis Externa Condition [4]

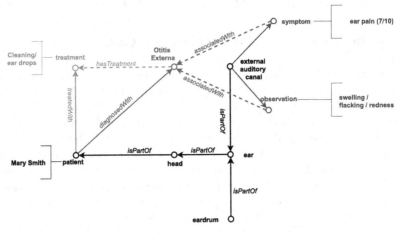

(b) Example Consultation Knowledge Graph of an Otitis Externa patient

Fig. 5. Otitis Externa representation

The MGO can be represented in triples for machine processing; for example, some of the triples portrayed in Fig. 5b are explained below:

– The human anatomy is represented in a hierarchy of anatomical structures connected to their parent structures using *isPartOf* relationship. For example, ⟨externalAuditoryCanal, isPartOf, ear⟩.
– The second part of the PAO is the assignment of anatomical functions to the anatomical structures performing them as in ⟨ear, hasFunction, hearing⟩.
– Symptoms and observations triples define the PSO and the POO. For example, the following triples refer to a pain symptom: ⟨externalAuditoryCanal, hasSymptom, symp_2⟩, ⟨symp_2, symptom, earPain⟩, ⟨symp_2, hasValue, 7/10⟩.

– The patient diagnosis and treatments are expressed in triples; for example: ⟨patient, diagnosedWith, OtitisExterna⟩, ⟨patient, treatedWith, earDrops⟩.

Applying the procedure in the PDD to Otitis Externa produces the ontology shown in Fig. 6 using the WebVOWL web application [14]. For conciseness, the ontology does not visualize the top-level classes (e.g., anatomy, symptom) and the is-a relationship linking the other concepts to them. More details on ontology construction and the resulting ontology can be found in the technical report [10].

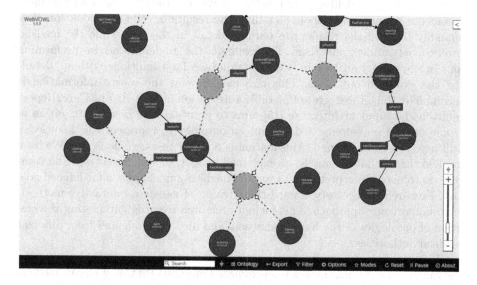

Fig. 6. Partial WebVOWL visualization of the Otitis Externa Ontology

The method was applied manually, requiring substantial time investment. The full potential of the Care2Report system relies on developing an automatic process to generate ontologies of all medical conditions using guidelines from various countries and in different languages. The ontology development relies on data from two sources: SNOMED CT, which can be easily mapped to an OWL ontology; and the text-based medical guidelines that pose the real challenge for knowledge extraction and structuring to be tackled in future research.

7   Conclusion

We introduced *ontological conversation interpretation* by creating a method for the systematic creation of medical ontologies from the SNOMED CT terminology and anatomical hierarchies, combined with the medical guidelines of different medical conditions. The resulting MGO is a formalized notation, and the PDD is a procedural guide to systematically create ontologies and enrich them by connecting new guidelines to the existing definitions of anatomy, symptoms, observations, and treatments; and adding more if the existing concepts are insufficient to represent the guideline fully. Furthermore, we have applied our approach to the case of Otitis Externa to illustrate its application and feasibility.

Limitations and Future Directions. The method needs to be validated on guidelines of more complex and varying conditions. For example, the NHG guideline for "Non-traumatic knee complaints" details a method for differentiating between various similar conditions and thus does not follow the typical sections in most NHG guidelines. This may require an evolution of our MGO. Moreover, some guidelines only point the physician towards the tests and measurements to monitor without detailing the results or values to look for, presumably because the results are hard to detail in the text while the medical professionals understand them. For example, the guidelines advise performing an electrocardiogram test in several cardiovascular conditions without detailing the expected outcomes. This is a challenge as the source information is incomplete; thus, the degree of possible automation is limited. The Care2Report multi-modal input architecture [15] aims to eventually allow the integration of (some of) the measurement data, but an ontology to represent this knowledge still needs to be developed. Automation is another research challenge. We have applied the method manually, as explained in Sect. 6, and the correct and complete automated interpretation of textual medical guidelines is a far-fetched goal [18]. Research is necessary toward the creation of assisted, interactive methods that support our approach. This includes research towards automating the creation of ontologies of the human anatomy and medical guidelines from different medical authorities.

This research aims to foster research in a societally-relevant field: increasing the quality of healthcare via semi-automated methods that may relieve medical professionals from their administrative burden. We make a step in this direction by laying down the formal foundations for the construction of semi-automated systems that support the interpretation of conversations using ontologies.

References

1. Federatie Medisch Specialisten FMS - Richtlijnen (Guidelines of The Dutch Federation of Medical Specialists). https://richtlijnendatabase.nl/. Accessed 11 Mar 2022
2. Introducing the knowledge graph: things, not strings. https://blog.google/products/search/introducing-knowledge-graph-things-not/. Accessed 11 Mar 2022
3. Nederlands Huisartsen Genootschap NHG - Richtlijnen (Guidelines of The Dutch College of General Practitioners). https://richtlijnen.nhg.org/. Accessed 11 Mar 2022
4. NHG Otitis Externa Guidelines. https://richtlijnen.nhg.org/standaarden/otitis-externa. Accessed 11 Mar 2022
5. SNOMED CT Basics. https://confluence.ihtsdotools.org/display/DOCSTART/4.+SNOMED+CT+Basics. Accessed 11 Mar 2022
6. Asim, M.N., Wasim, M., Khan, M.U.G., Mahmood, W., Abbasi, H.M.: A survey of ontology learning techniques and applications. Database **2018** (2018)

7. Bodenreider, O., Cornet, R., Vreeman, D.J.: Recent developments in clinical terminologies: SNOMED CT, LOINC, and RxNorm. Yearb. Med. Inform. **27**(01), 129–139 (2018)

8. Cameron, S., Turtle-Song, I.: Learning to write case notes using the SOAP format. J. Couns. Dev. **80**(3), 286–292 (2002)

9. Ehrlinger, L., Wöß, W.: Towards a definition of knowledge graphs. SEMANTiCS (Posters Demos SuCCESS) **48**(1–4), 2 (2016)

10. ElAssy, O., Dalpiaz, F., Brinkkemper, S.: Developing Ontologies of Medical Guidelines for Automated Conversation Summarization, April 2022. https://doi.org/10.5281/zenodo.6469617

11. Latif, S., Qadir, J., Qayyum, A., Usama, M., Younis, S.: Speech technology for healthcare: opportunities, challenges, and state of the art. IEEE Rev. Biomed. Eng. **14**, 342–356 (2020)

12. LeBlond, R.F., et al.: DeGowin's Diagnostic Examination. McGraw-Hill Education, New York (2015)

13. Lehmann, J., et al.: Dbpedia-a large-scale, multilingual knowledge base extracted from Wikipedia. Semant. Web **6**(2), 167–195 (2015)

14. Lohmann, S., Negru, S., Haag, F., Ertl, T.: Visualizing ontologies with VOWL. Semant. Web **7**(4), 399–419 (2016)

15. Maas, L., et al.: The Care2Report system: automated medical reporting as an integrated solution to reduce administrative burden in healthcare. In: Proceedings of HICSS (2020)

16. Molenaar, S., Maas, L., Burriel, V., Dalpiaz, F., Brinkkemper, S.: Medical dialogue summarization for automated reporting in healthcare. In: Dupuy-Chessa, S., Proper, H.A. (eds.) CAiSE 2020. LNBIP, vol. 382, pp. 76–88. Springer, Cham (2020). https://doi.org/10.1007/978-3-030-49165-9_7

17. World Health Organization. WHO handbook for guideline development. World Health Organization (2014)

18. Peleg, M.: Computer-interpretable clinical guidelines: a methodological review. J. Biomed. Inform. **46**(4), 744–763 (2013)

19. Rosse, C., Mejino, J.L., Modayur, B.R., Jakobovits, R., Hinshaw, K.P., Brinkley, J.F.: Motivation and organizational principles for the digital anatomist symbolic knowledge base: an approach toward standards in anatomical knowledge representation. J. Am. Med. Inform. Assoc. **5**, 17–40 (1998)

20. Rosse, C., Mejino Jr., J.L.V.: A reference ontology for biomedical informatics: the foundational model of anatomy. J. Biomed. Inform. **36**(6), 478–500 (2003)

21. van de Weerd, I., Brinkkemper, S.: Meta-modeling for situational analysis and design methods. In: Handbook of Research on Modern Systems Analysis and Design Technologies and Applications, pp. 35–54. IGI Global (2009)

22. Wang, M., Wang, M., Fei, Y., Yang, Y., Walker, J., Mostafa, J.: A systematic review of automatic text summarization for biomedical literature and EHRs. J. Am. Med. Inform. Assoc. **28**(10), 2287–2297 (2021)

23. Wieringa, R.J.: Design Science Methodology for Information Systems and Software Engineering. Springer, Heidelberg (2014). https://doi.org/10.1007/978-3-662-43839-8

24. Zhou, L.: Ontology learning: state of the art and open issues. Inf. Technol. Manag. **8**(3), 241–252 (2007)

Towards Access Control Models for Conversational User Interfaces

Elena Planas[1]([✉]) [iD], Salvador Martínez[2] [iD], Marco Brambilla[3] [iD],
and Jordi Cabot[1,4] [iD]

[1] Universitat Oberta de Catalunya, Barcelona, Spain
eplanash@uoc.edu
[2] IMT Atlantique, Nantes, France
salvador.martinez@imt-atlantique.fr
[3] Politecnico di Milano, Milan, Italy
marco.brambilla@polimi.it
[4] ICREA, Barcelona, Spain
jordi.cabot@icrea.cat

Abstract. Conversational User Interfaces (CUIs), such as chatbots, are becoming a common component of many software systems and they are evolving in many directions (including advanced features, often powered by AI-based components). However, less attention has been paid to their security aspects, such as access-control, which may pose a clear risk. In this paper, we apply Model-Driven techniques to define more secure CUIs. In particular, we propose a framework to integrate an Access-Control protocol into the CUI specification and implementation through a set of policy rules described using a Domain-Specific Language (DSL) integrated with the core CUI language.

1 Introduction

Nowadays, user interfaces that allow fluid and natural communication between humans and machines are gaining popularity [11]. Many of these interfaces, commonly referred as Conversational User Interfaces (CUIs), are becoming complex software artifacts themselves, for instance, through AI-enhanced software components that enable the adoption of Natural Language Processing (NLP) features.

CUIs are being increasingly adopted in various domains such as e-commerce, customer service, eHealth or to support internal enterprise processes, among others. Many of these scenarios are susceptible to arise security risks of both the user and the system. For instance, we may need to add security when we need:

- To disable potential queries depending on the user (e.g. a bot for a Human Resource Intranet must be careful not to disclose private data, such as salaries, unless the request comes from an authorized person).

This work has been partially funded by the Spanish government (LOCOSS project - PID2020-114615RB-I00 and BODI project - PDC2021-121404-I00).

A. Augusto et al. (Eds.): BPMDS 2022/EMMSAD 2022, LNBIP 450, pp. 310–317, 2022.
https://doi.org/10.1007/978-3-031-07475-2_21

- To execute different behaviours depending on the user. For instance, a CUI embedded into an e-learning system will provide different answers depending on the user who queries the marks (teacher or student).
- To provide different information precision for the same query depending on the user privileges. For instance, a weather or financial CUI may provide a more detailed answer to paying users.

Several works [7,12,16] emphasize the importance of considering security, and especially access-control as highlighted in the above scenarios, in the CUI definition though no concrete solution is proposed.

In this line, this work proposes to enrich CUI definitions with access-control primitives to enable the definition of more secure CUIs. Our solution is based on the use of model-driven techniques to raise the abstraction level at which the CUIs (and the access-control extensions) are defined. This facilitates the generation of such secure CUIs on top of different development platforms. In particular, we extend our generic CUI language [15] with new access-control modeling primitives adapted to the CUI domain and show how this extended models can be enforced as part of a policy evaluation component. As an example, we discuss such implementation on top of the Xatkit open source framework [6].

The rest of the paper is structured as follows: Sect. 2 provides the background about CUIs and access-control; Sect. 3 describes the framework we propose to provide model-based access-control for CUIs; Sect. 4 summarizes the related work; and finally Sect. 5 concludes.

2   Background

Conversational User Interfaces (CUIs) aim to emulate a conversation with a real human. The most relevant examples of CUIs are the chat*bots* and voice*bots*. A bot wraps a CUI as a key component but complements it with a behavior specification that defines how the bot should react to a given user request. The conversation capabilities of a bot are usually designed as a set of *intents*, where each intent represents a possible user's goal. The bot awaits for its CUI front-end to match the user's input text (called *utterance*) with one of the intents the bot implements. The matching phase may rely on external Intent Recognition Providers (e.g. DialogFlow, Amazon Lex, Watson Assistant). When there is a match, the bot back-end executes the required behaviour, optionally calling external services; and finally, the bot produces a response that it is returned to the user. For non-trivial bots, the behaviour is modeled using a kind of state-machine expressing the valid interaction flows between the users and the bot.

Access-control [18] is a mechanism aimed at assuring that the resources within a given software system are available only to authorized parties, thus granting *Confidentiality* and *Integrity* properties on resources. Basically, access-control consists of assigning *subjects* (e.g., system users) the *permission* to perform *actions* (e.g., read, write, connect) on *resources* (e.g., files, services). Access-control policies are a pervasive mechanism in current information systems, and may be specified according to many different models and languages, such as Mandatory Access-Control (MAC) [2], Discretionary Access-Control (DAC) [2], Attribute-Based Access-Control [9], and Role-based Access-Control (RBAC) [17]. In this work we focus on RBAC, where permissions are not directly assigned to users (which would be time-consuming and error-prone in large systems with many users), but granted to roles. Then, users are assigned to one or more roles, thus acquiring the respective permissions. To ease the administration of RBAC security policies, roles may be organized in hierarchies where permissions are inherited and possibly added to the more specific roles.

3   Access-Control Framework for CUIs

Figure 1 summarizes our framework to integrate access-control on CUIs, consisting of: (1) a **design time component** (*RBAC Policy rules* in the figure) to enable the specification of the bot authorization policy (see Sect. 3.1); and (2) a **runtime component** (*PEP* and *PDP* in the figure) in charge of evaluating and enforcing that policy upon the resource's access from users (see Sect. 3.2).

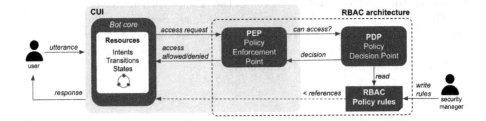

Fig. 1. Framework overview.

3.1   Policy Specification

The authorization policy is expressed via a policy language. To this end, in this paper we propose to extend a generic CUI language [15] with new modeling primitives adding access-control semantics to CUIs. As any DSL, this extended *access-control-CUI* DSL is defined through two main components [10]: (i) an *abstract syntax* (metamodel) which specifies the language concepts and their relationships, and (ii) a *concrete syntax* which provides a specific (textual or graphical) representation to specify models conforming to the abstract syntax.

Figure 2 depicts our proposal for the language metamodel, combining all the RBAC basic concepts with CUIs specific elements. In the following, we detail its main concepts.

CUI Metamodel. The CUI-specific metamodel (coloured in grey in Fig. 2) is a simplified version from the metamodel previously defined by the authors in [15] and describes the set of concepts used for modeling the intent definitions of a bot and its execution logic. The main elements of this metamodel are:

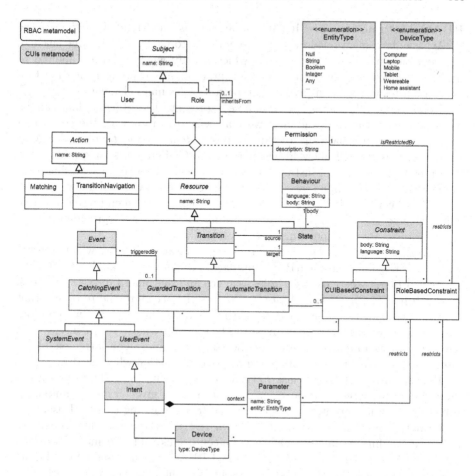

Fig. 2. Access-control CUIs metamodel.

Intents. The metaclass *Intent* represents the possible user's goals when interacting with the CUI. Intents, which are a specific type of *Event* (as bot interactions can also be triggered by external events), can optionally have *Parameter*s which allow defining specific characteristics of the *Intent*. On the other hand, intents can be triggered using several devices.

States. Following the state-machine formalism, this metaclass models a particular behavioral state in which the bot stays until a new intent triggers a transition to another state.

Transitions. The metaclass *Transition* represents the potential bot changes from one state to another. We distinguish two types of *Transition*s: *AutomaticTransitions* (triggered automatically) and *GuardedTransitions* (triggered when a specific guard holds). A *GuardedTransition* may be triggered by one or more *Event*s and include a *Constraint* to be satisfied for the transition to occur. This allows a fine-grained control over the firing of the *Transition*.

RBAC Metamodel. The RBAC metamodel is an extended version of the RBAC standard mentioned in Sect. 2 to adapt it to CUIs. This is done through the definition of a set of permissions which specify which roles are allowed to perform a specific action (a match to an intent or a transition navigation to a state) on a resource (intent, transition, or state). Its main elements are:

Resources. The metaclass *Resource* represents the objects that can be accessed within the CUI and that we may want to protect. In the context of CUIs, resources are basically of three types: *Intents*, *Transitions*, and *States*. Protecting intents will allow hiding part of the CUI's intents to specific roles. This may be necessary, for instance, to prevent specific users from accessing some intents. On the other hand, protecting transitions and states will allow, once an intent has been matched, to execute different behaviors depending on the role who triggered the intent. This may be useful, for instance, to provide different answers for an intent depending on the role of the user.

Subjects. The metaclass *Subject* represents the active entities which interact with the CUI. Following a RBAC approach, we define two kinds of subjects: *Users* and *Roles*, where users get roles assigned and role inheritance is supported.

Actions. The metaclass *Action* represents the access to the resources that may be performed by the subjects of the CUI. In this context, we consider the possible actions performed by subjects are *Matchings* (to an intent) and *TransitionNavigations* (to a state of the state machine). The latter enables a more fine-grained control to the potential user interaction when needed.

Permissions. The metaclass *Permission* represents the right to perform a given *action* (a match or a transition navigation) on a given *resource* (an intent, transition or state) granted to a specific *role* (corresponding to a CUI user).

Constraints. The metaclass *Constraint* restricts the permission to execute the corresponding action only when certain conditions hold. The metaclass *RoleBasedConstraint*, which extends the original RBAC standard model combining a concept from the ABAC model, represents specific context-based constraints (such as geographic location or the used device) to restrict the permissions.

Concrete Syntax. In order to complete the definition of our DSL, we could provide a textual concrete syntax, a graphical one or a combination. We show an example of a textual syntax in Sect. 3.3.

3.2   Policy Evaluation and Enforcement

Given an RBAC policy, our framework needs to combine a number of runtime components to enforce it. The recommendation in the implementation of modern policy frameworks is separating the infrastructure logic from the application logic by using a reference monitor architecture [1]. This architecture consists in two basic components: a **Policy Enforcement Point** (PEP) and a **Policy Decision Point** (PDP). Every access action requested by an user is intercepted by the PEP that, in turn, forwards it to the PDP to yield an access decision.

Our framework follows this architecture. As Fig. 1 shows, access requests to the bot resources (intents, transitions and states) are intercepted. These requests are then forwarded to the PDP, which reads the policy rules to resolve the access. The access decision yielded by the PDP is returned to the bot through the PEP.

3.3   Proof of Concept

In order to show the feasibility of our approach, we discuss in this section a prototype implementation of our framework on top of the Xatkit framework [6] and illustrate it with a simple weather chatbot example[1].

We have first added the textual concrete syntax extensions needed to model the new CUI metaclasses as part of a Xatkit specification. Listing 1.1 shows a snippet of the authorization policy specification which describes that the intent *Get Historical Weather* can be only matched by registered users. To simplify the definition of more complex CUIs we could provide default permission configurations (i.e. enabling or disabling access unless explicitly stated otherwise) and define GRANT ALL level permissions (i.e. authorization to match all available intents). Proper parsing of these textual *syntactic sugar shortcuts* would be translated into equivalent metamodel instantiations.

```
 1  Permission p1 (
 2       Role unregisteredUser
 3       Resource GetHistoricalWeatherIntent
 4       Action matching
 5  ) -> Deny
 6  Permission p2 (
 7       Role registeredUser
 8       Resource GetHistoricalWeatherIntent
 9       Action matching
10  ) -> Allow
```

Listing 1.1. Policy example for a weather chatbot.

We have then implemented the policy evaluation and enforcement. There are several possible strategies to this end, also depending on whether the chatbot designer has internal access to the chatbot engine.

When modifying the execution logic of the chatbot engine is possible, we could embed the security checks as part of the engine itself. These checks would be added as standard elements of the chatbot execution logic and be implicitly verified upon every single intent matching or transition navigation request. But in most scenarios, chatbot designers will not have this option as most chatbot platforms are not open source or are *hidden* behind an API offered to deploy the bot and interact with the engine. In these cases, access-control must be explicitly added to the individual chatbot logic. Authorization verification becomes now explicit but, on the other hand, it can be easily added on top of many more chatbot engines.

This is the strategy shown in Listing 1.2. In this example, we show how the transition from an initial *Awaiting input* state to the *Print historical weather* state will only be triggered when the user utterance matches the *Get Historical Weather* intent above and the user is authorized to match such intent.

---

[1] https://github.com/elenaplanas/xatkit-RBACBot.

```
1  awaitingInput
2   .when(intentIs(GetHistoricalWeatherIntent)
3   .and(c -> policyRules.checkPermission(user.getRole().getName(),
4   "matching","GetHistoricalWeatherIntent"))).moveTo(printHistoricalWeather)
```

Listing 1.2. Policy Enforcement Point (PEP) implementation.

Note that, even if access-control evaluation and enforcement is now explicit, it could still be automatically added to the concerned transitions. Given a security policy such as the one in Listing 1.1 and a plain chatbot definition, we could automatically instrument all relevant transitions with the proper access-control checks based on the policy definition.

4   Related Work

Several authors have expressed the need to secure chatbots, especially in critical domains such as banking [12] or health [16]. In the same line, [7] even proposes chatbot providers to attach an SLA to their chatbots, including security aspects. Indeed, as pointed out in [4,5,8,19], chatbots are concerned by (and should be tested against) a number of security concerns. While these works highlight the need to integrate security aspects, they do not propose concrete and actionable solutions. Even for industrial tools (like DialogFlow, Amazon Lex or Watson Assistant) access-control is focused on the management of the permissions to collaborate in the bot definition. At most, you can also define who can execute the bot, with no further fine-grained permission levels.

This limitation is shared by proposals focusing on chatbot definition languages, such as [6,14,15], which do not include modeling primitives to define the access-control policies even if modeling of access-control policies is a subject with a long tradition in the MDE community [3], with some notable examples like SecureUML [13] which extends UML with an RBAC metamodel that serves as inspiration for our own proposal. To sum up, we believe ours is the first approach to integrate access-control as first-class citizen in a bot definition language.

5   Conclusions

In this paper we have proposed a new model-driven framework for enhancing the security of CUIs by integrating and adapting the semantics of the Role Based Access-Control (RBAC) protocol to Conversational User Interfaces (CUIs). In particular, we have extended a generic CUI metamodel with RBAC primitives that enable the definition of fine-grained access control policies for all key CUI elements (such as intents, states and transitions). We also provided a preliminary proof of concept to demonstrate the feasibility of our approach.

As further work we plan to enrich the framework with other access-control models and improve the validation and tool support of the approach. Moreover, we see this work is a first step towards the modeling of other security-related aspects for CUIs, such as DDoS, privacy, encryption, and so on.

References

1. Information technology - Open Systems Interconnection - Security frameworks for open systems: Access control framework (ISO-10181-3/X.812) (1996)
2. 5200.28-STD, D: Trusted Computer System Evaluation Criteria. DOD Computer Security Center (1985)
3. Basin, D., Clavel, M., Egea, M.: A decade of model-driven security. In: Proceedings of the 16th ACM Symposium on Access Control Models and Technologies, pp. 1–10 (2011)
4. Bozic, J., Wotawa, F.: Security testing for chatbots. In: Testing Software and Systems (2018)
5. Cabot, J., Burgueño, L., Clarisó, R., Daniel, G., Perianez-Pascual, J., Rodríguez-Echeverría, R.: Testing challenges for NLP-intensive bots. In: 3rd IEEE/ACM International Workshop on Bots in Software Engineering. IEEE (2021)
6. Daniel, G., Cabot, J., Deruelle, L., Derras, M.: Xatkit: a multimodal low-code chatbot development framework. IEEE Access **8** (2020)
7. Gondaliya, K., Butakov, S., Zavarsky, P.: SLA as a mechanism to manage risks related to chatbot services. In: 2020 IEEE 6th International Conference on Big Data Security on Cloud (BigDataSecurity) (2020)
8. Hasal, M., Nowaková, J., Ahmed Saghair, K., Abdulla, H., Snášel, V., Ogiela, L.: Chatbots: security, privacy, data protection, and social aspects. Concurr. Comput. Pract. Exp. **33**(19) (2021)
9. Hu, V.C., Ferraiolo, D., et al.: Guide to Attribute Based Access Control (ABAC) Definition and Considerations (draft), vol. 800, issue 162. NIST Special Publication (2013)
10. Kleppe, A.: Software Language Engineering: Creating Domain-Specific Languages Using Metamodels. Pearson Education (2008)
11. Klopfenstein, L.C., Delpriori, S., Malatini, S., Bogliolo, A.: The rise of bots: a survey of conversational interfaces, patterns, and paradigms. In: Conference on Designing Interactive Systems, ACM (2017)
12. Lai, S.T., Leu, F.Y., Lin, J.W.: A banking chatbot security control procedure for protecting user data security and privacy. In: Advances on Broadband and Wireless Computing, Communication and Applications (2019)
13. Lodderstedt, T., Basin, D., Doser, J.: SecureUML: a UML-based modeling language for model-driven security. In: UML 2002. LNCS, vol. 2460, pp. 426–441. Springer, Heidelberg (2002)
14. Pérez-Soler, S., Guerra, E., de Lara, J.: Model-driven chatbot development. In: Conceptual Modeling (2020)
15. Planas, E., Daniel, G., Brambilla, M., Cabot, J.: Towards a model-driven approach for multiexperience AI-based user interfaces. Softw. Syst. Model. **20**(4), 997–1009 (2021)
16. Roca, S., Sancho, J., García, J., Álvaro Alesanco: microservice chatbot architecture for chronic patient support. J. Biomed. Inf. **102** (2020)
17. Sandhu, R., Ferraiolo, D., Kuhn, R.: The NIST model for role-based access control: towards a unified standard. In: RBAC 2000. ACM (2000)
18. Sandhu, R.S., Samarati, P.: Access control: principle and practice. Commun. Magaz. IEEE **32**(9) (1994)
19. Ye, W., Li, Q.: Chatbot security and privacy in the age of personal assistants. In: 2020 IEEE/ACM Symposium on Edge Computing (SEC) (2020)

Evaluation of Modeling Approaches (EMMSAD 2022)

Exploratory Study on Students' Understanding of Multi-perspective Modelling

Charlotte Verbruggen$^{(\boxtimes)}$ ⓘ and Monique Snoeck ⓘ

Research Centre for Information Systems Engineering, KU Leuven, Naamsestraat 69, 3000 Leuven, Belgium
{charlotte.verbruggen,monique.snoeck}@kuleuven.be

Abstract. Computer Science education programs often include courses on both UML and BPMN to teach students the methodology and the principles behind information systems development. While these modelling languages are typically taught in separate courses or course sections, in practice, the UML Class diagram and the BPMN process model provide different perspectives of the same information system. Therefore, students should be taught how to differentiate between these perspectives and maintain consistency between them. The goal of this exploratory study is to determine the effect that actively modelling both the UML Class diagram and the BPMN process model for a same case has on the students' understanding of multi-perspective modelling. This is done by means of an observational study with 6 students. The students were asked to think out loud while first creating a UML class diagram and then creating a BPMN process model for a given case. At the end of the study, the students filled in a questionnaire about their experience. The most important result from this experiment is that there is a potential correlation between the understanding of multi-perspective modeling and overall model quality. The study highlights points of consideration for future studies, such as time constraints and modelling experience of the participants, and prompts new research questions for further research.

Keywords: Exploratory study · UML class diagram · BPMN process model · Multi-modelling

1 Introduction

Both UML and BPMN are frequently used in education to teach students the methodology and the principles behind information systems development. UML Class diagrams are often used for teaching database or software structure while BPMN provides the business process perspective. These languages would be typically taught in different courses or course sections, and would be illustrated with cases and exercises tailored to illustrate specific features of the language. In practice, however, the UML Class diagram and the BPMN process model provide different perspectives of the same information system. It is therefore important that students learn to differentiate between the perspectives (i.e. know what to capture in what perspective) while maintaining consistency

© Springer Nature Switzerland AG 2022
A. Augusto et al. (Eds.): BPMDS 2022/EMMSAD 2022, LNBIP 450, pp. 321–335, 2022.
https://doi.org/10.1007/978-3-031-07475-2_22

between these two perspectives. In other words, learning the individual languages is not enough: a skilled modeler needs to integrate the knowledge of both languages so as to be able to co-model the data and process perspective of a given process-aware information system. Although there are many courses on UML Class diagrams and BPMN process models and these languages may be taught in a single course addressing enterprise modelling (e.g. teaching ARIS, 4EM, MEMO), devoting specific attention to teaching the integration of both can instill important insights in students on the overall design of a process-aware information system.

The course "Architecture and Modelling of Management Information Systems" at the KU Leuven fulfils this need by teaching the MERODE approach, with multi-modelling being the most important learning objective. The approach is structured in three layers, each encapsulating one or more perspectives. The first layer is the enterprise layer (EL) which contains two sub-layers: the domain layer (DL) and the event handling layer (EHL). The DL consists of a UML Class diagram where each association must express existence dependency. Each Business Object in the DL is further completed with an Object Life Cycle (OLC). The events that trigger transitions in the OLCs of the Business Objects, are captured in the EHL. The EHL contains an Object Event Table (OET) that maps each business event to the Business Objects it affects. The second layer is the Information System Services Layer (ISL). This layer captures the input and output services that provide access to the EL. Finally, the third layer is the Business Process Layer (BPL) where the input and output services from the ISL can be invoked.

Currently, the learning goals of the course include "Upon completion of this course, the student is capable of organizing requirements in a layered architecture", "Upon completion of this course, the student is capable of performing a requirements analysis to create an enterprise model" and "Upon completion of this course, the student is able to relate the enterprise model and the information system services to a business process model." In other words, students have to identify which requirements belong to the business process model, but they don't have to create this model. The course thus sets a step towards the integration of domain modelling and BP modelling, but there is still a significant gap towards a true integrated multi-modelling approach. The goal of this paper is to investigate students' understanding of multi-perspective modelling, more specifically, the integration of the domain model and the business process model. This is done by means of an observational study with 6 students. The goal of the observational study is to determine whether students' understanding of which requirement is relevant for what layer is improved by modelling the business process in combination with the domain model, instead of only modelling the enterprise layer.

This paper is structured as follows. In Sect. 2, we provide an overview of related work. Section 3 describes the methodology used for the experiment. Section 4 reports the results of the experiment, which are discussed in Sect. 5.

2   Related Work

When querying Google Scholar and Web of Science, we searched on the keywords (multi-modelling OR "integrated modelling" OR "integrated modeling") AND (teaching OR education OR learning OR instruction). In web of science, we looked in all relevant categories for software and information systems modelling, and in google scholar, we filtered on articles published in the SoSyM journal. We found zero publications in in Software and Information Systems Modelling conference proceedings or journals that focus on the topic of teaching multi-perspective modelling. Although a lot of research exists on teaching modelling techniques, most papers report on teaching of an individual modelling language or perspective, not an integrated approach with multiple perspectives. Rosenthal et al. [1] provide a literature review on conceptual modelling in education. Their selection consists of 121 published papers from 1986 until 2017. The majority of papers where published after 2004. They classified the publications in distinct groups based on the modelling purpose they focus on. Object-oriented modeling is the biggest topic, with 51% of the papers focusing on this topic. The other categories identified by Rosenthal et al. are data modeling (27%), conceptual modeling in general (11%), business process modelling (8%) enterprise modelling (2%) and goal modelling with i* (1%). While Object-oriented modeling and enterprise modelling can capture multi-perspective modelling approaches, this was not discussed as an emerging research theme. The literature review provides an overview of the learning paradigms, learning approaches, learning theories and teaching methods mentioned in these publications. It is notable that not many publications discuss these aspects. However, the publications that discus a learning paradigm mostly mention the constructivism paradigm, where "the learner is viewed as independently constructing her own subjective representations and understandings of reality through critical reflection" [1]. The publications mentioning a learning approach focus on collaborative learning. Finally, Rosenthal et al. identify four emerging research themes. The most important research theme is "Learning tool support", especially learning support built into object-oriented modelling tools and data modelling tools. The second research theme is "Feedback", with 22 publications reporting on process-oriented feedback and 10 publications reporting on outcome feedback. The other two research themes are "Learning Analytics" and "Gamification/Serious games". Regarding learning analytics, Rosenthal et al. [1] observe that learning analytics in conceptual modelling education is mostly focused on datamining of logging data from modelling tools. They identify the limitation that this approach neglects other aspects of the learning process, such as "learner motivation and willingness-to-learn or the use of additional tools outside of the modelling tool, e.g., paper-based modeling". They suggest thinking-out-loud experiments to fill this gap.

While teaching conceptual data modelling is the topic of many studies, there is still a lack of understanding what makes modelling a difficult task, and how the learning of conceptual modelling can be supported. Rosenthal et al. [2] study the difficulties that experienced modelers face in Data Modelling. They investigated the modelers' experience using a mixed-method approach, including recording the modelers while they think aloud. They contrast this with the experiences of novice modelers. Bogdanova and Snoeck [3] present a framework for the education of conceptual data modelling based on Bloom's taxonomy. The aim of this framework is to link the assessment of students to the related learning outcomes of the course, and to provide appropriate feedback as a means to support leaning. The framework can be used to automate the process of providing personalized feedback, as demonstrated in [4, 5]. Besides feedback, also prototyping can be a useful tool for helping the learning to understand the meaning of a model better [6–8]. Amongst the most frequently occurring difficulties mentioned in [2] and [9] is the modelling of relationships. Nevertheless, when a case description is intentionally cluttered with information relating to other aspects, the research in [9] demonstrates that (unless specific training is provided) up to 30% of the solutions contain superfluous classes, part of which are due to attempts to capture too many aspects in a single perspective. A sequel research mapping errors to learning objectives [4], reveals that out the four errors appearing in more than 60% of the tasks, three are related to the learning objective of distinguishing between EL, IS and BP layer requirements.

Process modelling is also a prevalent topic in Computer Science education, as indicated by the large amount of studies done about the cognitive aspects of process modelling. For example, Figl et al. [10] analyzed the influence of notational aspects on the comprehension of process models. In a different study, Figl and Laue [11] looked at the comprehensive complexity of relationships between elements in a process model. Burattin et al. [12] developed a machine learning approach to automatically identify the different phases a modeler goes through when creating a process model. In the area of process modelling, the integration of full-fledged data modelling is still under development [13], and research analyzing modelling errors related to a multi-modelling has not been found.

When considering research on students understanding of modelling languages or on recurring difficulties in teaching modelling, all of the afore-mentioned research papers address only one modelling language (e.g., BPMN, UML Class diagrams, ER, etc.). To the authors' best knowledge, research that addresses the learning or teaching of a multi-modelling approach is inexistent. The goal of the research presented in this paper is to study to what extent the co-modelling of different perspectives of a single case study can shed light on the problems faced by students, in view of creating better support for learning multi-modelling.

3   Methodology

The methodology used in this paper is inspired by [2] and aims to capture the cognitive process of novice modelers by means of a thinking-out-loud experiment. The aim of the experiment is to determine whether modelling the business process in combination with the domain model, improves the understanding of the layered structure of MERODE, compared to just modelling the enterprise layer.

In the experiment, a number of students are given a case description (see Appendix 2) and asked to model the enterprise layer as a UML class diagram and the business process layer as a BPMN process model (see Appendix 1 for model solutions). The selected case description for this exercise is adapted from [14], as that case lends itself to multi-perspective modelling: it contains ingredients for both a process model and a data model and the ingredients are not separated. So, the students have to filter out themselves what is relevant for the process model and what is relevant for the data model.

The participants are all students in the course "Architecture and Modelling of Management Information Systems". At the time of the experiment, the participants have just finished week 3 of the course, meaning they were introduced to the layered approach of MERODE and had seen Sect. 1 to 3 of the handbook "Enterprise Information Systems Engineering" [15]. The students following this course also have had a prior course on database management, and most followed at least one course where the BPMN notation is taught. The call for participation included the prerequisite that participants should have some experience with UML class diagrams and BPMN process models. Before starting the experiment, the participants were sent a short demo of the tool Signavio.

3.1 Experiment Set-up

Based on the recommendation by Rosenthal et al. [2], we use a multi-modal approach, combining

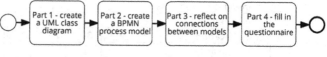

Fig. 1. Experiment process

several methods of data collection. The cognitive processes of the participants are recorded in various ways in order to capture as much information as possible. Participants are asked to think out loud which is audio-recorded, their modelling actions are captured via screen recording, and an over-the-shoulder video-recording captures the annotations they make to the case description provided on paper. The experiment consists of 4 parts, as shown in Fig. 1. In the first part, the participants create a domain model for the given case by means of a UML class diagram. Then, they model the process for the same case in a BPMN process model. In the third part, they indicate at which places in the BPMN model it is necessary to access the information from the UML class diagram. Finally, they are asked to fill a questionnaire on their experience during the experiment.

4 Results

4.1 Measured Performance

In first instance, we analyzed the models created by the participants by listing the mistakes found in the models. Each mistake is grouped into a mistake type (e.g. "missing task"). These mistake types are then categorized again into one of four mistake groups: "BPMN model", "UML class diagram", "layer allocation", and "notation". The "layer allocation" category consists of mistakes where a certain requirement was accounted for in the wrong model. For example, when "HR Department" was modelled as a class in the UML class diagram, while it is the user of the system, and thus needs (only) to appear as actor in the BPMN diagram. The category of "notation" deals with notational issues (i.e. syntactical issues), either for BPMN models or for UML class diagrams, for example, an exclusive-or gateway in the BPMN model that has only one incoming flow and only one outgoing flow.

Table 1. Overview of mistakes made by the 6 participants

	Participant						Total	Total %
	1	2	3	4	5	6		
BPMN model	12	10	8	7	16	16	69	55,2%
missing path	4	1	1	1	5	3	15	
missing task	4	2	2	2	6	7	23	
missing timer	2	2		1	2		7	
multiplicity of task	1	1			1	1	4	
Universe of discourse as pool		1					1	
overspecification of task	1	1	1	1	1	1	6	
task in wrong pool		2	2			1	5	
missing pool			2	1	1	1	5	
unneeded subprocess				1		1	2	
unneeded pool						1	1	
layer allocation	3	4	2	1	0	3	13	10,4%
attribute as task		1					1	
actor as class	2	3				3	8	
class as task	1		1	1			3	
input form as class		1					1	
notation	5	5	3	5	1	4	23	18,4%
BPMN - event is not atomic	1	2					3	
BPMN - loose task	1					1	2	
BPMN - missing end event	2	1				1	4	
UML - association as attribute			1	1			2	
BPMN - missing message flows		1		1		1	3	
BPMN - pool name missing						1	1	
BPMN - unneeded gateway				1	1		2	
UML - missing multiplicity			2	2			4	
UML - unconnected diagram	1	1					2	
UML class diagram	3	6	1	3	3	4	20	16,0%
wrong attributes		1					1	
association multiplicity		2				2	4	
missing association		1					1	
missing class	2	1	1	1	2	2	9	
unneeded class	1			1	1		3	
Universe of discourse as class		1					1	
class as attribute				1			1	
Total	23	25	14	16	20	27	125	100,0%

In total, the models contain 125 mistakes, both syntactic and semantic (see Table 1). More than half of the mistakes were found in the BPMN models. The UML class diagrams account for 16% of the mistakes, and 18.4% of the mistakes are related to notation. The smallest group are "layer allocation" mistakes, accounting for 10.4% of the mistakes. However, they might have repercussions on the quality of the model that represent the distinct perspectives. Therefore, we discuss them in more detail below.

The most frequently occurring error in the UML class diagram is the missing class. Of the four classes that were expected (Job Vacancy – Candidate/Application – Review – Interview), Candidate was the only class present in all solutions. Job Vacancy was part of three solutions. Review and Interview each appeared only once in a different solution, even though we made sure to include sentences in the case description that suggest modelling these as classes: "All reviews [...] should be filed within four weeks of being requested" and "[...] interviews are registered in the system".

The most frequently occurring errors in the BPMN model are the missing task and the missing path. Often this is due to an incomplete model, see the discussion section.

The group of "layer allocation" mistakes consists of four types of mistakes. The mistake type that occurs most often is **"actor as UML class"**, meaning that, in the scope of a small application, an actor such as "HR Department", "Professor" or "International Office" is unnecessarily modelled as a class in the UML class diagram. This mistake is made by three out of six participants and each of those participants makes this mistake multiple times. It is notable that in seven out of eight cases where this mistake is made, the actor is modeled both as a class in the UML class diagram and as a pool in the BPMN model. In the other case, the participant ran out of time. The second mistake type is **"class as task"**, meaning that the BPMN model contains tasks like "review the candidate" and "register interview", while the corresponding classes where the information is stored are missing from the UML class diagram. This mistake occurs once in three different solutions. The other two mistake types occur only once each: **"attribute as task"** and **"input form as class"**. On average, participants made two layer allocation mistakes and only one participant did not make any layer allocation mistakes.

Our sample of six participants is too small to make a statistical analysis, but overall, the ratio of layer allocation mistakes to total mistakes seems fairly consistent around 13% (not counting the participant that didn't make any layer allocation mistakes).

4.2 Recordings

We can inspect the time spent on each part of the exercise. Each participant was given a timeslot of one hour to work on the exercise and fill in the survey. However, four of the six participants were unable to finish the exercise in the allocated time. This explains that 58% of the mistakes are related to missing elements. Noticeably, the two participants that did not run out of time, spent about 30% of their time on the UML class diagram, while the other four participants spent 50%-60% on the UML class diagram (see Table 2). Those two 'faster' participants have a low number of layer allocation mistakes. They also have the lowest ratio of total mistakes to total number of elements and they spent noticeably more time explaining the connection between the models. They are the only two students that made changes to their models in the third part of the exercise.

By analyzing the video recordings, we can conclude that the three participants that have the least amount of layer allocation mistakes (0, 1 or 2) were able to connect their models to each other to some extent. The other three participants made more mistakes (3 or 4) and did not understand how to connect their models.

Finally, we look at the type of notes participants make on the case description. Participants were given a pen and a set of markers. All participants highlighted words (this includes underlining or circling in pen) while reading the case for the first time.

Table 2. Division of time over models

Participant	1	2	3	4	5	6
% time UML	52%	50%	29%	34%	52%	59%
% time BPMN	42%	49%	57%	55%	44%	35%
% time explaining connections	6%	1%	15%	12%	5%	6%

Only three participants continued making notes, highlights or sketches while they were modelling. We did not find any meaningful correlations between note taking and the understanding of multi-perspective modelling.

4.3 Questionnaire

The first two questions of the questionnaire are about previous experience with UML class diagrams and BPMN models. Half of the participants (1, 2, 3) indicate that they have some experience with UML class diagrams, and half indicate that they have a reasonable amount of experience (e.g. active participation in a course). For BPMN, participant 2 has some experience, the others indicate having a reasonable amount.

The questionnaire also investigates their perceived understanding of the layers during the creation of the UML model, and how this evolved over the next parts of the exercise. Half of the participants (3, 4, 6) indicate that they have some issues allocating requirements to layers during the creation of the UML class diagram. The only participant experiencing no layer allocation problems (5) indeed did not include superfluous classes in the UML diagram. However, the process model was highly incomplete. Half of the participants (1, 3, 4) also agree that creating the BPMN model helped them to identify to which layer each requirement belongs. Two of these (3, 4) are the faster modelers, who also made the lowest number of errors overall. In a follow-up question, the participants can clarify how creating the BPMN model helped or didn't help. Of the three participants that don't agree that the BPMN model is helpful, two explain that they didn't think about the layers while solving the exercise, and one only discusses the BPMN model instead of the connections between both models. Those three participants (2, 5 and 6) have the highest numbers of errors overall. All participants who agree that the creation of the BPMN model was helpful for layer allocation also agree that the third part of the exercise (thinking about the connections between the models) is helpful to understand the interaction between the layers. In a follow-up question, the others indicate that they either didn't see the relation, didn't think of the layers while modelling, or have a lack of experience. All six participants agree that they have a better understanding of the case after finishing part 2 and part 3 of the exercise, and four out of six (1, 3, 4, 5) indicate that they have a better understanding of the layers in general.

The final two questions of the questionnaire investigate whether students think additional similar exercises and code generation for the business process layer would be helpful when studying the course "Architecture and Modelling of Management Information Systems". The same group of participants that indicate that part 2 and part 3 of the exercise were helpful (1, 3, 4), agree that including this type of exercise in the course would be beneficial. Five out of six participants (all but 4) believe that code generation for the business process layer would help them.

5 Discussion

This exploratory study is a first step in investigating the use of multi-perspective modelling in computer science education. Although the experiment is small-scale, the results already indicate that more research in this domain could lead to some interesting insights. In this study, the data was gathered at the start of the course "Architecture and Modelling of Management Information Systems". As the students progress through the course, we will be able to gather more data and perform a more in-depth analysis.

5.1 Analysis of Mistakes

The type of mistakes that occurs the most (23 times in total) is a missing task in the BPMN model. In each solution, at least two tasks were missing, but generally speaking many more were missing, leading also to missing paths (15), etc. The third type of mistake is a missing class in the UML class diagram. This occurred at least once in each solution and nine times in total. The high number of missing tasks can be explained by the fact that four out of six participants spent quite some time on creating the UML class diagram and then ran out of time for modelling the business process. However, while the participants were instructed to start with the UML class diagram, they were free to decide themselves when the diagram was finished. Therefore, the time constraint does not explain the missing classes. The participants' inability to identify review and interview as potential classes, and not even including these as attributes could be explained by the participants' limited experience with data modelling.

The fourth type of mistake that occurred often, was a layer allocation mistake: "actor as class". Three participants (3, 4, 5) did not make this mistake, the other three made the mistake multiple times. We can make two observations concerning this mistake. First, the three participants that made this mistake were also unable to reflect on the connections between both models in part 3. Two of these participants said that they didn't know what the connections were and one participant only talked about the BPMN process model. This could indicate that the interaction between the layers is a complex concept to grasp for students. Second, two out of the three students that did not make this mistake (3, 4), made less mistakes overall. Even when we discard the layer allocation mistakes, these two students made the least number of mistakes. This could indicate that once students understand the interactions between layers, the overall quality of their models improves. Participant 5 also didn't make this mistake, however, the process model was highly incomplete, thus leading to a large number of mistakes overall. The other layer allocation mistakes were less frequent, showing that, at least in this case, the modelling of actors in a system is one of the main challenges of layer allocation. For another case this could turn out to be different.

In this analysis, we did not consider the amount of correctly modelled aspects of the case. This also influences the quality of a solution. For example, participant 2 made the most mistakes, however, their models were more complete than for example the models of participant 5. The ratio of mistakes to total number of elements in the models could account for this discrepancy. As shown in Table 3, this ratio suggests that the solution of participant 2 is better than the solutions of participants 1, 5 and 6, despite having the highest number of mistakes.

Table 3. Total mistakes vs Total number of elements

Participant	1	2	3	4	5	6	Total
total mistakes	23	25	14	16	20	27	125
total number of elements	20	50	36	37	21	21	185
Total mistakes / Total number of elements	1,15	0,50	0,39	0,43	0,95	1,29	0,68

5.2 Analysis of Recordings

As indicated in the results, there seems to be a correlation between the number of layer allocation mistakes and the time spent on the UML class diagram, at least for the better performing participants 3 and 4. It would be interesting to study whether there is a causal relation between the understanding of the interaction between layers and ease of identifying classes for the UML class diagram, reducing the time spent on this task. Alternatively, spending more time on the business process layer could improve the understanding of the interaction between layers, resulting in less mistakes.

Another interesting observation from the recordings is that one of the participants who understands the interaction between the layers well, explicitly mentioned that they would prefer to switch between the models and not follow the instructed order. This was the only participant who explicitly modelled the connections between the models by including in the BPMN model datastores representing the classes of the UML class diagram. Repeating the experiment where students are allowed to determine the order themselves, could provide more insight into the cognitive process of novice modelers.

5.3 Analysis of Survey Results

A first observation regarding the questionnaire, is that the level of experience in UML class diagrams was lower than expected. Since the participants were all students of the program "Master of Information Management" or "Master of Business and Information Systems Engineering", we assume they have all taken the courses "Business Information Systems" and "Principles of Database Management", as these courses are mandatory in both programs that are planned before the "Architecture and Modelling of Management Information Systems" course. Both courses include UML class diagrams. However, three participants indicated they only have some experience with UML class diagrams, instead of choosing the option "*I have a reasonable amount of experience (e.g. active participation in a course about UML class diagrams)*".

The second observation is that there is a slight discrepancy between the answers to some questions. More specifically, only half of the participants indicated that Part 2 and 3 where helpful for understanding the interaction between the layers, but all participants agreed that Part 2 and Part 3 contributed to their overall understanding of the case. Apparently, understanding the case is different from understanding the different layers and perspectives present in the case description. This could indicate a mismatch between the actual issues novice modelers have (understanding to which perspective a requirement relates), and their perception of the issues that they face (understanding a requirement).

Finally, our third observation is related to the last two questions, which measure the perceived usefulness of these types of exercises and prototyping of the business process layer. While not all participants agreed that these would be useful additions to the course material, no participant showed disagreement, instead choosing for the option "Neutral". So overall, we can expect a positive response to these additions.

5.4 Reflection on Methodology

In this study, we used a multi-modal data collection method in order to capture as much information as possible. Out of the different modes that were used for the collection of data, the correction of the participants' solutions, the screen and voice recordings and the questionnaire yielded interesting information. However, the recordings of the notation did not bring any additional insights. To simplify the experiment, we might consider leaving this out. In view of repeating the experiment with larger groups, and considering the amount of time needed for processing all the data, in future repetitions of this study we will consider focusing on correcting mistakes, data gathering while observing and a well-designed survey. Data gathering while observing would significantly reduce the time spent on transcribing recordings, since the recordings would serve mostly verification for the gathered data and not as a primary source.

5.5 Limitations

The exploratory nature of this study comes with a number of limitations. The first limitation is the small number of participants. With only six participants, the results of this study are only an indication of the understanding that novice modelers have of multi-perspective modelling. Nevertheless, the insights gathered in terms of timing, order of tasks, etc., provides useful insights in how to set up experiments with larger groups of participants to obtain more significant results.

As the participants come from an international group of students, none of them were native English speakers, and they had differing levels of fluency in the English language. Also, not all participants were accustomed to thinking-out-loud exercises. This likely led to a loss of information about their cognitive process. Despite this loss of information, some interesting insights could already be captured from this observational study.

A third limitation, as indicated in the previous section of the discussion, is that some participants had limited experience with UML class diagrams. Also, some participants seemed to have limited experience with Signavio, despite receiving a demo beforehand and using this tool in a previous course. This probably led to the fact that most participants needed more time than we anticipated, resulting in incomplete BPMN diagrams. For future experiments, we can consider providing tool training beforehand.

A fourth limitation is that the students were only given one case. It would be interesting to investigate if the results of this experiment persist when students are given different cases. That way, we could eliminate the wording and specific aspects of a given case as cause for issues.

A fifth limitation of the study is that there is always room for interpretation when creating a model based on a case description. This was taken into account when correcting and comparing the solutions in the following way: we didn't penalize for sub-optimal naming of model elements, missing conditions on gateway paths or missing attributes. To further mitigate for this problem, we use a case from another researcher, for which we created an own solution that turned out to be almost identical to the original solution. Both the original solution [14] and our own variant [13] were published in the context of papers that underwent a review process. In this sense, we can consider the case and its solution as validated by several experts.

6 Conclusion

This exploratory study is a first step in the investigation of novice modelers' understanding of multi-perspective modeling. The study uses a combination of participant's solutions to the exercise, recordings and a survey to gather data. The inclusion of the recordings and the survey added meaning to the overview of mistakes made. The study shows promising results including a potential correlation between the understanding of multi-perspective modeling and overall model quality, and between the understanding of multi-perspective modeling and the time distribution over the two models. Further research is needed to confirm these findings and to investigate if there is a causal relation. Another result is that the modelling of actors in the system can be a challenge for novice modelers. The study highlights points of consideration for future studies, such as time constraints and modelling experience of the participants, and prompts new research questions for further research.

Appendix 1 – Model Solution

The model solution consists of a UML Class diagram (Fig. 2) and a BPMN process model (Fig. 3).

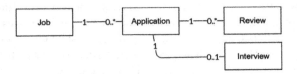

Fig. 2. UML class diagram - model solution

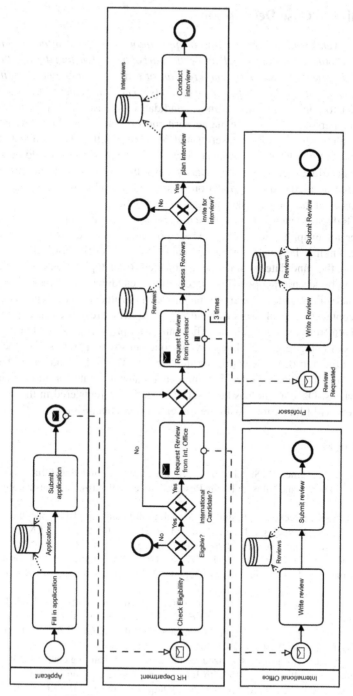

Fig. 3. BPMN process model - model solution

Appendix 2 – Case Description

The KU Leuven wants to develop a web application for the recruitment of new PhD candidates. In this exercise, you will model the part of the system that deals with entering and reviewing new applications. The creation of a new vacancy and deciding which candidate to hire are out of scope for this exercise. The requirements are stated below:

In order to apply for a job vacancy, candidates have to fill in a form where they specify their personal information (name, surname, e-mail address, birthday, nationality) and they upload their grades transcript and motivation letter. The application can be saved and submitted when the applicant is ready. The application should be submitted before the deadline specified in the vacancy. Once the application is submitted, the HR department is notified and the application is assigned to an HR officer. After submission, the candidate can no longer make changes to the application.

The HR department will then make a first assessment of the application. They decide whether or not an application is eligible based on the obtained degree, grades transcript, university ranking, language certificates, and GMAT or GRE-score. If an application is ineligible, the candidate is immediately rejected. If an application is eligible, it must be reviewed by several people. First, international candidates will be reviewed by the international office. Once the international office has written a review, the HR department will then contact three professors with the request to write a review of the application. All reviews, both from the international office and from professors, should be filed within four weeks of being requested. Each review concludes with a proposal for the next step in the recruitment process: rejection, or an interview. When the deadline of the vacancy is passed, the HR office will decide which candidates to invite for an interview based on the reviews. Once a date has been set, interviews are registered in the system. The interviewers will fill in a form with their comments & conclusions.

References

1. Rosenthal, K., Ternes, B., Strecker, S.: Learning Conceptual Modeling: Structuring Overview, Research Themes and Paths for Future Research, June 2019. https://aisel.aisnet.org/ecis2019_rp/137
2. Rosenthal, K., Strecker, S., Pastor, O.: Modeling difficulties in data modeling. In: Dobbie, G., Frank, U., Kappel, G., Liddle, S.W., Mayr, H.C. (eds.) ER 2020. LNCS, vol. 12400, pp. 501–511. Springer, Cham (2020). https://doi.org/10.1007/978-3-030-62522-1_37
3. Bogdanova, D., Snoeck, M.: CaMeLOT: An educational framework for conceptual data modelling. Int. J. Appl. Earth Obs. Geoinf. (2019). https://doi.org/10.1016/j.infsof.2019.02.006
4. Bogdanova, D., Snoeck, M.: Use of personalized feedback reports in a blended conceptual modelling course. In: 2019 ACM/IEEE 22nd International Conference on Model Driven Engineering Languages and Systems Companion (MODELS-C), pp. 672–679 (2019). https://doi.org/10.1109/MODELS-C.2019.00103
5. Bogdanova, D.: Towards personalized feedback in a smart learning environment for teaching conceptual modelling. In: 2019 13th International Conference on Research Challenges in Information Science (RCIS), pp. 1–5 (2019). https://doi.org/10.1109/RCIS.2019.8876983
6. Sedrakyan, G., Snoeck, M., Poelmans, S.: Assessing the effectiveness of feedback enabled simulation in teaching conceptual modeling. Comput. Educ. **78**, 367–382 (2014). https://doi.org/10.1016/j.compedu.2014.06.014

7. Sedrakyan, G., Poelmans, S., Snoeck, M.: Assessing the influence of feedback-inclusive rapid prototyping on understanding the semantics of parallel UML statecharts by novice modellers. Inf. Softw. Technol. **82**, 159–172 (2017). https://doi.org/10.1016/j.infsof.2016.11.001

8. Ruiz, J., Serral, E., Snoeck, M.: A fully implemented didactic tool for the teaching of interactive software systems. In: Proceedings of the 6th International Conference on Model-Driven Engineering and Software Development - MODELSWARD, pp. 95–105 (2018). https://doi.org/10.5220/0006579600950105

9. Bogdanova, D., Snoeck, M.: Learning from errors: error-based exercises in domain modelling pedagogy. In: Buchmann, R.A., Karagiannis, D., Kirikova, M. (eds.) PoEM 2018. LNBIP, vol. 335, pp. 321–334. Springer, Cham (2018). https://doi.org/10.1007/978-3-030-02302-7_20

10. Figl, K., Mendling, J., Strembeck, M.: The influence of notational deficiencies on process model comprehension. J. Assoc. Inf. Syst. **14**(6), 312–338 (2013). https://www.proquest.com/scholarly-journals/influence-notational-deficiencies-on-process/docview/1470423062/se-2?accountid=17215

11. Figl, K., Laue, R.: Cognitive complexity in business process modeling. In: Mouratidis, H., Rolland, C. (eds.) CAiSE 2011. LNCS, vol. 6741, pp. 452–466. Springer, Heidelberg (2011). https://doi.org/10.1007/978-3-642-21640-4_34

12. Burattin, A., Kaiser, M., Neurauter, M., Weber, B.: Learning process modeling phases from modeling interactions and eye tracking data. Data Knowl. Eng. **121**, 1–17 (2019). https://doi.org/10.1016/j.datak.2019.04.001

13. Snoeck, M., De Smedt, J., De Weerdt, J.: Supporting data-aware processes with MERODE. In: Augusto, A., Gill, A., Nurcan, S., Reinhartz-Berger, I., Schmidt, R., Zdravkovic, J. (eds.) Enterprise, Business-Process and Information Systems Modeling, pp. 131–146. Springer, Cham (2021). https://doi.org/10.1007/978-3-030-79186-5_9

14. Künzle, V., Weber, B., Reichert, M.: Object-aware Business Processes: Fundamental Requirements and their Support in Existing Approaches (2011)

15. Snoeck, M.: Enterprise Information Systems Engineering. Springer, Cham (2014). http://www.springer.com/series/8371

Experiences from Developing a Web Crawler Using a Model-Driven Development Tool: Emerging Opportunities

David Mosquera[✉] [iD], Anastassios Martakos, and Marcela Ruiz[iD]

Zürich University of Applied Sciences, Gertrudstrasse 15, 8400 Winterthur, Switzerland
{mosq,ruiz}@zhaw.ch, martaana@students.zhaw.ch

Abstract. Model-driven development (MDD) tools aim to increase software development speed and decrease software time-to-market. Available MDD tools in the market state that software development teams can fast and easily develop "any" software by using them. So, the following research question arises: what is the perception of a software developer in using an MDD tool to create software he/she is used to develop without models? We selected Mendix, a user-friendly and easy configurable MDD tool, to address such a question and develop a domain-specific software artifact. We propose a use case collaborating with a Swiss company that allows users to compare insurances based on web crawling. Therefore, we ask a software developer at the Swiss company to develop a simplified version of a web crawler using the selected MDD tool. The software developer has extensive experience with developing web crawlers. However, for the software developer using MDD tools was a new paradigm of software development. We observe that the software developer successfully developed the web crawler using the MDD tool. However, he/she perceived some difficulties during the development, arising opportunities such as decreasing modeling complexity, increasing the MDD tool integrability, and improving modeling assistance. Finally, we conclude the experience report by drawing next research endeavors to generalize the results and discover new opportunities for improving MDD tools.

Keywords: Model-driven development · Web crawling · Experience report

1 Introduction

Model-driven development (MDD) tools promise to increase the productivity of software development teams and decrease software time-to-market [1]. Thus, software development teams invest their effort in creating conceptual models that describe the under-development software application rather than coding. Then, an MDD tool allows them to automatically transform such conceptual models into code using automatic model-to-model and model-to-text transformations.

Several MDD tools are available in the market [2–6] and literature [7–10] aiming to achieve the MDD "promise." These tools state that software development teams can fast and easily develop software by using them. Based on such a statement, a software

A. Augusto et al. (Eds.): BPMDS 2022/EMMSAD 2022, LNBIP 450, pp. 336–343, 2022.
https://doi.org/10.1007/978-3-031-07475-2_23

developer should be able to develop most of the functionalities as he/she uses to develop using other approaches. So, the following research question arises: what is the perception of a software developer in using an MDD tool to develop software he/she is used to developing without models?

We design a use case collaborating with a Swiss company to address our research question. This company allows users to compare insurance premiums from several insurance providers using web crawling. Web crawling allows for automatically extracting data from websites using software [11]. As a result, web crawlers gather details from web pages in near real-time to present them to the user in a single source summarized way. Developing web crawlers require domain-specific knowledge, making it a relevant domain for addressing our research question. Moreover, we select Mendix—one of the MDD tool market leaders—to develop the use case [6] and test our research question.

We ask an experienced software developer at the Swiss company to develop the designed use case using Mendix. The software developer has extensive experience with developing web crawlers. However, for the software developer using MDD tools was a new paradigm of software development. We document all the use case development, observing that the software developer successfully developed a simplified web crawler using Mendix. However, he/she perceived some difficulties using Mendix. Based on such remarks, we identified three main opportunities for improvement: decreasing modeling complexity, increasing MDD tool integrability, and improving modeling assistance. These identified opportunities for improvement are helpful and relevant to model-driven engineers—i.e., who develop MDD tools—although more extensive data gathering is required to validate and generalize the results. In future work, we expect to replicate this experience with several web crawling and other domain software developers to validate and improve the identified opportunities.

This experience report is structured as follows: in Sect. 2, we review the available MDD tools in the market and we motivate our research question; in Sect. 3, we introduce the use case designed in collaboration with the Swiss company; in Sect. 4, we report the results and the identified opportunities for improvement based on the software development perception using Mendix; and, finally, in Sect. 5 we discuss conclusions and future work.

2   MDD Tools Overview and Motivation

Software specifications are created by conducting analysis, requirement specification, and design. Conceptual models are used throughout this process to represent the software under-development. In code-centric approaches, software developers manually turn these conceptual models into code. MDD tools propose to go one step further by using the models as blueprints to automatically generate the code based on such conceptual models [1, 12, 13]. As a result, software development teams improve their productivity and decrease the software time-to-market.

To support such a transformation process, several MDD tools have been developed and are now available in the market to develop software based on conceptual models. For instance, OutSystems [2] offers a domain-specific language (DSL) as a fourth-generation language that provides a graceful fullback to third-generation programming languages such as C#. Microsoft PowerApps [3] allows companies to create software using a drag-and-drop editor, integrating such software into the Microsoft ecosystem. Appian [4] enables businesses to automate their processes, producing mobile-ready applications integrated into cloud systems without programming. WebRatio [5, 14] offers an Eclipse-based [15] developing environment for creating web and mobile software applications by using IFML (Interaction Flow Modeling Language) models. Finally, Mendix [6] uses a visual editor with its own modeling language to represent business logic workflows, generating web-based applications.

We observe these MDD tools state that "any" software can be developed by using them, making statements such as: "anyone with an idea can make powerful apps [6]," "we accelerate customers' business by discovering, designing, and automating their most important processes [4]," "automate your business processes and bring them online [5]," among others. We observe that the MDD tools delimit the "any" software idea to specific domains, such as business processes. However, the MDD tools promise that software developers can develop the software they are used to developing using models in such specific domains. Therefore, the following research question arises:

> **(RQ)** What is the perception of a software developer in using an MDD tool to develop software he/she is used to develop without models?

3   The Use Case: Web Crawling and MDD Tools

We plan to ask a software developer to use one of the MDD tools reviewed in Sect. 2 and develop a domain-specific use case to address our RQ. We had the opportunity to collaborate with a Swiss company that offers online services for comparing insurances based on web crawling. Therefore, we select web crawling as our domain-specific use case. We introduce such a use case in the following paragraph.

The Swiss company uses web crawling to automatically retrieve data about insurances, allowing users to compare them in a single source summarized web page. The web pages where the Swiss company extracts data are named *targets* [11]. Sometimes, the web crawler needs to be rewritten when a new *target* appears. Therefore, the Swiss company proposes crawling new *targets* as soon as is required as the use case. As a result of developing this use case, the web crawler must collect the data from such a new *target* and store it in the database for further processing, as shown in Fig. 1.

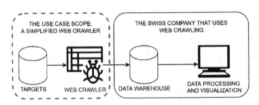

Fig. 1. Use case overview.

Having proposed the use case, the next step is selecting an MDD tool to develop it. As a proof of concept, we selected Mendix from the reviewed MDD tools since it is a user-friendly tool that allows software developers to kick-start modeling quickly. We considered other MDD tools; however, they were not that easy to configure and run the software as Mendix. For instance, Mendix has a web environment that allows software developers to use the tool as soon as they login into the Mendix website, without any additional configuration. Other tools, such as WebRatio, require the software developers to download an IDE (Integrated Development Environment) software and configure external elements such as databases and web servers, hindering their configuration. Moreover, Mendix is one of the MDD tool leaders in the market based on the Gartner Magic Quadrant (see Fig. 2).

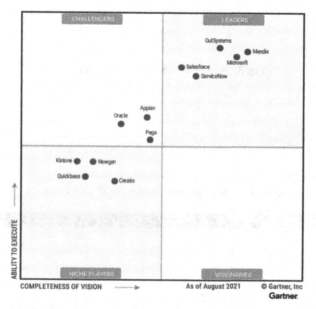

Fig. 2. Gartner Magic Quadrant on enterprise low-code application platforms, taken from [16].

4   Results on Developing the Use Case

We ask a software developer from the Swiss company to use Mendix to develop the use case introduced in Sect. 3. The software developer has more than four years of industrial experience, working two years at the Swiss company. The software developer has enough expertise to develop a web crawler, making him/her a feasible subject to create a web crawler using Mendix. The software developer invested approximately 40 working hours in developing the use case using Mendix, including learning how to use the tool itself since it was her/his first time using an MDD tool. As a result, the software developer created: a domain model containing the information of the web crawler targets (see Fig. 3); a set of microflow models comprising the business logic (see Fig. 4); and a graphic user interface for managing the web crawler targets (see Fig. 5).

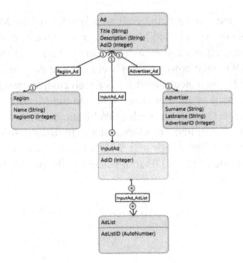

Fig. 3. Web crawler Mendix's domain model.

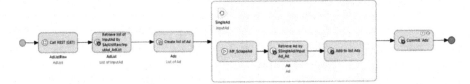

Fig. 4. Excerpt of the web crawler Mendix's microflows.

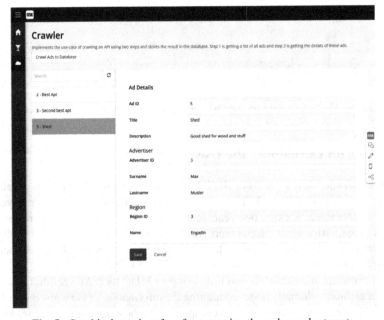

Fig. 5. Graphical user interface for managing the web crawler targets.

We asked the software developer to report on his perception while using Mendix to conduct the use case, including the design, the development process, and the improvement remarks. Based on the provided information, we concluded that Mendix allowed the software developer to implement a simplified web crawler based on the results. That means, although Mendix is a general-purpose MDD tool, the MDD tool provides enough functionalities to implement domain-specific software, as is a web crawler. Such a result is an insight for answering our RQ. However, we collected the software development improvement remarks about developing software using the MDD tool based on her/his experience. We analyzed such comments to compile them as opportunities in the following paragraphs.

Decreasing Modeling Complexity: The software developer stated that developing a simple feature requires several models, increasing the software development complexity. Based on his/her practical experience, the use case functionalities could be developed in a few lines of code (between 10 to 30 lines of code) on a general-purpose programming language such as JavaScript or C#. Therefore, we identified that providing MDD tools with general-purpose programming languages that allow software developers to write code and integrate them with the models can overcome such a complex issue.

Increasing MDD Tool Integrability: The software developer stated that several technologies and tools are usually integrated in practice to develop software such as web crawlers. Such integration allows software developers to increase development speed using tested and already-implemented functionalities. However, the software developer state that Mendix has no support for integrating domain-specific technologies and tools such as Puppeteer [17], a contemporary web crawling tool. Therefore, we identified that providing MDD tools with integration mechanisms can exploit the benefits of already-implemented technologies and tools, increasing the software development speed.

Improving Modeling Assistance: The software developer stated that he/she perceived some difficulties during modeling in Mendix. Finding references between models, debugging the microflows, and understanding the modeling syntax are examples of such problems. Although Mendix has modeling assistants to assist in creating models such as automatic completion, the software developer state that the modeling assistance in MDD tools is behind programming assistance in IDEs (Integrated Development Environment). This lack of well-designed and complete modeling assistance negatively affects the "developer" experience with the MDD tool. Therefore, we identify that improving modeling assistance in MDD tools by creating more complete and user-oriented modeling assistance can overcome such difficulties.

5 Conclusions and Future Work

Several MDD tools are available in the market, promising that software development teams can fast and easily develop any software by using them. However, what is the perception of a software developer in using an MDD tool to create software he/she is used to develop without models? We propose a use case in collaboration with a Swiss company that allows users to compare insurances based on web crawling to address this question. We reviewed a set of available MDD tools and selected Mendix, a user-friendly and easy to configure MDD tool, to develop such a use case. Then, we ask an experienced software developer at the Swiss company to develop the use case. Although the software developer had no experience using MDD tools, we observed he/she successfully developed a simplified web crawler using Mendix. These results provide data for answering our RQ since, at least in this context, the selected MDD tool has enough functionalities to implement a web crawler. Finally, we collect the software developer remarks during the use case development using the MDD tool. As a result, we outlined three opportunities for improvement based on his/her experience: decreasing modeling complexity, increasing MDD tool interoperability, and improving modeling assistance.

Although this experience report's results are helpful, we know it is not feasible to generalize them based on just one software developer's perception, one specific domain, and one specific MDD tool. Thus, we plan to replicate this experience with other software developers, including domain-specific use cases in collaboration with other industrial partners. Currently, we have industry partners that can bring such domain-specific use cases to us, mainly focused on: software testing, data-centric applications, and car racing simulators. These efforts will bring us data for generalizing our results, arising new opportunities to improve the MDD tools.

Acknowledgments. Our research is supported by the Zürich University of Applied Sciences (ZHAW) – School of Engineering: Institute for Applied Information Technology (InIT); and the Innosuisse Flagship Initiative - Project SHIFT.

References

1. Sendall, S., Kozaczynski, W.: Model transformation: the heart and soul of model-driven software development. IEEE Softw. **20**, 42–45 (2003)
2. OutSystems Home Page. https://www.outsystems.com. Accessed 04 Mar 2022
3. PowerApps Home Page. https://powerapps.microsoft.com/en-us/. Accessed 04 Mar 2022
4. Appian Home Page. https://appian.com. Accessed 04 Mar 2022
5. WebRato Home Page. https://www.webratio.com/site/content/es/home. Accessed 04 Mar 2022
6. Mendix Home Page. https://www.mendix.com. Accessed 04 Mar 2022
7. Jia, X., Jones, C.: AXIOM: a model-driven approach to cross-platform application development. In: ICSOFT 2012 - Proceedings of the 7th International Conference on Software Paradigm Trends, pp. 24–33 (2012)
8. Acerbis, R., Bongio, A., Brambilla, M., Butti, S.: Model-driven development of cross-platform mobile applications with web ratio and IFML. In: Proceedings - 2nd ACM International Conference on Mobile Software Engineering and Systems, MOBILESoft 2015, pp. 170–171 (2015)
9. Rieger, C.: Business apps with MAML. In: Proceedings of the Symposium on Applied Computing, pp. 1599–1606. ACM, New York, NY, USA (2017)
10. Rosales-Morales, V.Y., Sánchez-Morales, L.N., AlorHernández, G., Garcia-Alcaraz, J.L., Sánchez-Cervantes, J.L., Rodriguez-Mazahua, L.: ImagIngDev: a new approach for developing automatic cross-platform mobile applications using image processing techniques. Comput. J. **63**, 732–757 (2020)

11. Khder, M.: Web scraping or web crawling: state of art, techniques, approaches and application. Int. J. Adv. Soft Comput. App. **13**, 145–168 (2021)
12. Liddle, S.W.: Model-driven software development. In: Embley, D., Thalheim, B. (eds) Handbook of Conceptual Modeling, pp. 17–54. Springer, Heidelberg (2011). https://doi.org/10.1007/978-3-642-158650-0_2
13. Sahay, A., Indamutsa, A., di Ruscio, D., Pierantonio, A.: Supporting the understanding and comparison of low-code development platforms. In: 46th Euromicro Conference on Software Engineering and Advanced Applications (SEAA), pp. 171–178. IEEE (2020)
14. Brambilla, M., Butti, S., Fraternali, P.: WebRatio BPM: a tool for designing and deploying business processes on the web. In: Benatallah, B., Casati, F., Kappel, G., Rossi, G. (eds.) Web Engineering. LNCS, vol. 6189, pp. 415–429. Springer, Heidelberg (2010). https://doi.org/10.1007/978-3-642-13911-6_28
15. Geer, D.: Eclipse becomes the dominant Java IDE. Computer (Long Beach Calif). **38**, 16–18 (2005)
16. Gartner, I.: Gartner Magic Quadrant for Enterprise Low-Code Application Platforms (2021)
17. Puppeteer GitHub Repository. https://github.com/puppeteer/puppeteer. Accessed 06 Mar 2022

Posters

Process Mining for Time Series Data

Tobias Ziolkowski[1]([⊠]), Agnes Koschmider[2], René Schubert[1],
and Matthias Renz[3]

[1] GEOMAR Helmholtz Centre for Ocean Research Kiel, Kiel, Germany
{tziolkowski, rschubert}@geomar.de
[2] Group Process Analytics, Kiel University, Kiel, Germany
ak@informatik.uni-kiel.de
[3] Group Data Science, Kiel University, Kiel, Germany
mr@informatik.uni-kiel.de

Abstract. Process mining is an established technique to automatically discover a descriptive model of the execution of a process based on event data. Commonly, the event data is recorded by information systems referring to business events and typically tracked at a higher activity abstraction. Disciplines like economics, engineering, life and natural sciences could gain high benefits from process mining in terms of identifying anomalies in the process or supporting predictive analytic in what is being measured. In this way, process mining based analysis give more insights into data than traditional approaches do setting the focus on data correlations. However, these domains mainly rely on sensor data producing time series information, where the event data does not directly relate to high-level business process concepts. This paper suggests an approach for process discovery on "raw" time series data by leveraging clustering to raise the abstraction level of events. As a use-case, we applied our approach on ocean science data where we used raw sensed time-series data from a simulated seasonal coastal upwelling system. In this way, we can give new insights into the data in terms of the identification of anomalies in the process flow aiming to prevent unintended consequences.

Keywords: Process mining · Time series · Clustering · DTW

1 Introduction

Process mining in terms of discovering processes from data recorded by information systems and identifying bottlenecks or deviations in these processes can provide valuable insights into data sets of other disciplines like engineering, natural and life science. These disciplines collect high volume of data and have a high demand for a structured approach [1] to answer process related questions like (a) what unknown processes are acting (i.e., did we found all processes that exist) and (b) whether the found processes actually work as thought. Process mining can provide answers to both questions. The purpose of this paper is to suggest an approach to discover processes from "raw" time series data. The approach consists of the following steps: first, we split the time series in segments, use Dynamic Time Warping (DTW) to measure similarities between the temporal sequences, apply hierarchical clustering to identify patterns and

A. Augusto et al. (Eds.): BPMDS 2022/EMMSAD 2022, LNBIP 450, pp. 347–350, 2022.
https://doi.org/10.1007/978-3-031-07475-2

map each cluster to (process) activities to obtain an event log. By discovering the known physical process through the application of our approach, we show that our approach works. In addition, our approach gives the following two advantages that traditional approaches in ocean science analysis did not allow so far: Our approach allows understanding temporal pattern/trend in what is being measured. In natural science like ocean science it can even give an early indication on the overall direction of a typical ocean cycle, which is hard to predict with traditional approaches in ocean science. Outliers detected in a dataset can help prevent unintended consequences and point to new processes. A data-oriented detection of new processes (i.e., concept drift) is challenging to foresee when limiting the analysis purely on data mining uncovering patterns in data. In our approach outliers are detected through the analysis of the occurrence frequency of process instances.

2 Traditional Analysis

Traditional approaches in ocean science focus on describing physical relationships between different variables with the purpose to explain ocean processes. A *process* is, however, a physical model and not a process chain as it is discovered with process mining. Generally, following traditional approaches two common analysis techniques to these time-series are applied: filtering and lag-correlation.

We analyze a seasonal upwelling system, as the seasonality itself reveals the connection of the involved variables. In seasonal coastal upwelling systems, stronger winds in particular parts of the year push the warm surface water offshore leading near the coast to a rise (upwelling) of colder and nutrient-rich waters from below.

The term of "process" is limited to a correlation analysis of variables and the comparison of correlation coefficients is used to explain effects. The next section presents a process mining approach to study seasonal upwelling systems. It presents an approach to efficiently bridge the gap between "raw" time-series data and process mining.

3 Process Mining-Based Approach

To provide added value of process mining for this domain in terms of giving new insights into the data analysis, we use "raw" time series data as input for our technique. In this way, our approach should be generic enough to be used in any discipline producing raw sensor data in terms of time series. Particularly, we use time series data from a simulated seasonal coastal upwelling system VIKING20X [2]. Please note that in natural and life sciences it is a common way to use simulated data since none data-driven analytics approaches exist yet. Figure 1 shows our technique to discover a process model from time series data and relies on the notions as introduced before. We carried out the following sequential steps: Time series data is used as input. Data transformation is applied. Concretely, the data is split into subsequences to ease the analysis. In Step 3, we measure similarity between subsequences with applying DTW. Clustering is applied to identify patterns that can be mapped onto a (process) activity

Input   **Output**

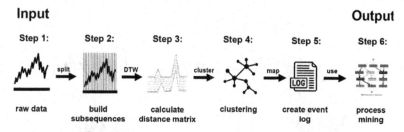

Step 1:   Step 2:   Step 3:   Step 4:   Step 5:   Step 6:

raw data   build   calculate   clustering   create event   process
                 subsequences   distance matrix   log   mining

Fig. 1. The steps from raw sensor data (i.e., time-series) to process mining.

(i.e., each cluster is mapped onto a (process) activity. An event log is created including the timestamp, caseID and activity. Finally, Process Discovery is applied on the event log.

In general, these six steps can be applied to "raw" physical time-series data to transform the data into a process model. When analyzing "raw" data (i.e., time series, sensor data, video data) always the following challenges need to be addressed: sample size, data quality (i.e., incomplete data, missing entries, etc.) and mapping uncertain time-series data on process activities. To handle sample size, we selected a representative data. Then, we split all data into subsequences and we use DTW to measure similarity between subsequences to reduce the impact of incomplete samples. DTW allows to measure distance between subsequences of different lengths, so, if one subsequence includes incomplete samples and therefore has a different length than other subsequences, DTW nevertheless calculates the correct distance.

4   Results and Generality of the Approach

In this approach we have shown that process mining can be applied to time series data and thereby opens up new perspectives for ocean sciences. Based on these findings, the framework can also be used for analyzing other physical processes. This approach would also be conceivable for questions from biology or medicine. In principle, this framework is able to give new insights to all research disciplines that have time series data as input. Beside the expected relationship between the physical variables (see Sect. 2), the process model in Fig. 2 also shows additional behavior. Although the wind does not change, the westward current occasionally increases. In Fig. 2 this is the path from "Windstress stays" to "Westward Current raises". Although the upwelling drops, the surface temperature occasionally does not increase. In Fig. 2 this is the path from "Upward Current drops" to "Temperature stays". Both insights cannot be spotted with traditional analysis in ocean science. Thus, process mining provides an added value. To evaluate the generality of our approach, we plan to apply it on additional data sets from other sciences. A limitation identified in our approach is that the cluster names and the subsequence sizes are defined manually. This requires domain knowledge, so a selection of suitable names for all clusters is not possible without it. In order to meet this challenge, we plan to evaluate a trend analysis and classification algorithm in order to name the clusters automatically.

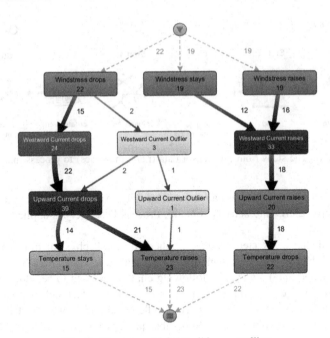

Fig. 2. Process model describing upwelling.

5 Conclusion and Future Research Directions

This paper introduces an approach for the discovery of processes from "raw" time series data. Specifically, the proposed approach focuses on the main challenge of identifying sequences of events mapped to activities used to construct event-based processes. As a use case, we applied our process mining pipeline on ocean science data where we used raw sensed time-series data from a simulated seasonal coastal upwelling system. To further advance the field and to support process discovery from raw sensor data requires to bridge several assumptions that traditional process mining techniques enforce on the structure of recorded event data. For this, new techniques are required that do not assume one single event log nor an isomorphic relation to activity executions [3].

References

1. van Zelst, S.J., Mannhardt, F., de Leoni, M. et al.: Event abstraction in process mining: literature review and taxonomy. Granul. Comput. **6**, 719–736 (2021). https://doi.org/10.1007/s41066-020-00226-2
2. Biastoch, A.: Regional imprints of changes in the Atlantic meridional overturning circulation in the eddy-rich ocean model VIKING20X. Ocean Sci. Discuss. 1–52 (2021)
3. Janssen, D., Mannhardt, F., Koschmider, A., van Zelst, S.J.: Process model discovery from sensor event data. In: Leemans, S., Leopold, H. (eds.) ICPM 2020. LNBIP, vol. 406, pp. 69–81. Springer, Cham (2021). https://doi.org/10.1007/978-3-030-72693-5_6

Towards an Information Systems-driven Maturity Model for Industry 4.0

Francesco Leotta(✉) [ID], Jerin George Mathew [ID], Flavia Monti [ID], and Massimo Mecella [ID]

Sapienza Universitá di Roma, Rome, Italy
{leotta,mathew,monti,mecella}@diag.uniroma1.it

Abstract. The term Industry 4.0 is used to denote the last evolution of manufacturing, concerning the large employment of information technologies, Internet-of-Things (IoT) and Artificial Intelligence (AI) to reduce the costs and produce high quality products. Even though many manufacturers declare themselves Industry 4.0-compliant, in order to attract public investments or to simply emerge among competitors, often only very limited aspects of the production comply with the definition. In this paper, we introduce the technologies involved in Industry 4.0, and, according to those ones, we propose the idea of a framework to assess the maturity of a company as an Industry 4.0 player.

Keywords: Industry 4.0 · Maturity model · Information system · Artificial intelligence

The term Industry 4.0 is used to denote the last evolution of manufacturing. Whereas the employment of interconnection technologies is common in industry since several decades, they have been mainly employed to instruct machines and to acquire limited information from them (e.g., alarms and operating conditions). Industry 4.0 aims instead at a full understanding and control of the industrial processes, where information is not only limited to the manufacturing line, covering instead all of the phases of the production, from design to so-called de-manufacturing, with a level of granularity ranging from the specific produced item (which can be specifically tracked) to the whole company management processes.

This revolution brings to the development of several reference architectures (e.g., RAMI 4.0, IIRA, IBM Industrie 4.0 Architecture, NIST) providing a common understanding to devise appropriate systems and approaches in a digital factory [1]. Indeed, they identify resources, components, functions, activities and interconnections necessary to fit Industry 4.0 requirements.

In order to pursue these objectives, Industry 4.0 strongly relies on three main ingredients: *process management systems*, *communication protocols*, and *complementary technologies*.

© Springer Nature Switzerland AG 2022
A. Augusto et al. (Eds.): BPMDS 2022/EMMSAD 2022, LNBIP 450, pp. 351–354, 2022.
https://doi.org/10.1007/978-3-031-07475-2

Process Management Systems. Processes of a company are assisted by a set of different software systems.

- Computer Aided Design (CAD) and Computer Aided Manufacturing (CAM) software are used respectively to design a product and to determine the manufacturing processes (machine operations).
- Customer Relationship Management (CRM) and Supply Chain Management (SCM) are the systems supporting customers and suppliers respectively. A CRM facilitates a better communication with clients by offering solutions to their requests. A SCM provides supply chain features such as inventory management, support to suppliers, logistics, shipping and delivery.
- The Product Life-cycle Management (PLM) system creates a product knowledge environment. It accurately analyzes the product during its entire life, from the design, to the deployment and maintenance, up to disposal. And it offers product data to all the actors in the organization for production improvements.
- The Enterprise Resource Planning (ERP) system supports many of the processes common to any kind of company. These functions include sales, marketing, purchasing, production planning, inventory, finance, and human resources. With respect to manufacturing, modern ERP systems also include planning functionalities in the form of Material Resource Planning (MRP) and Manufacturing Resource Planning (MRP II) [2].
- A Manufacturing Execution System (MES) is commonly associated with the ERP system, to monitor and interact with the production process and assembly lines. It interfaces with the ERP system and the production lines, storing data from both sources. Information collected is aggregated to produce the best decisions to optimize the production. Functionalities of MES include production management, quality check, human resources, data collection, real time understanding and system integration. Also, the MES is interconnected to the other components in the company to support interoperability between them and enable autonomous decisions [3].

Communication Protocols. Several communication protocols are actually in use (even simultaneously [4]) in the industrial domain and each of them has different capabilities in terms of latency, fault-tolerance and security.

According to [4], three main classes of communication protocols can be defined: *Fieldbuses*, *Real Time Ethernet* and *industrial wireless protocols*.

- Fieldbuses were the first kind of communication protocol developed for the industrial domain and were introduced to overcome the limitation of the early cabling systems developed in the industrial setting. Representative examples of fieldbus networks include Modbus, CANopen, PROFIBUS and DeviceNet.
- Then, the increasing popularity of Internet has paved the way to a variety of Ethernet-based protocols. These protocols are commonly referred to as Real Time Ethernet (RTE) and represent a natural evolution of legacy fieldbuses. Protocols falling under this category include EtherCAT, PROFINET, Modbus TCP, to name a few.

- Finally, in recent years, the popularity of wireless protocols started to draw increasing interest also in the manufacturing domain, since they can significantly reduce the amount of required cabling. Popular protocols include Zig-Bee, 6loWPAN and Bluetooth Low Energy (BLE).

Complementary Technologies. A variety of cutting-edge technologies have been successfully adapted and employed in the manufacturing domain.

In particular, *big data* techniques are becoming increasingly popular to manage and process the sheer amount of data produced in the industrial environment, by using highly distributed and parallel processing pipelines to increase the processing throughput as the size of data grows.

Big data techniques are tightly coupled with the increasing use of *cloud computing*, a paradigm that enables leasing of computing and storage in a flexible and transparent way without the need for a careful dimensioning and forecast of needed resources

Industry 4.0 also led to an unprecedented availability of data and computing resources, leading to a growing interest in the adoption of *artificial intelligence* techniques in the manufacturing domain. Many of those techniques revolve around ingesting past data to learn models which are then deployed to predict future outcomes.

Data generated by all the systems in the factory (e.g. ERP, MES) can be fed into *process mining* algorithms for monitoring, conformance checking and process enhancement [5]. Also, many companies include *Robotic Process Automation* (RPA) technology in their systems to support automation on repetitive tasks performed by humans [6].

Finally, we also want to mention the growing interest in the notion of *digital twin* (DT) in the manufacturing domain. A DT is a digital representation of a physical asset which is mainly used for simulation purposes both at design time and at run-time. In addition, it is also used for monitoring and retrieving data for maintenance tasks [7].

An existing company can gradually shift to Industry 4.0, by embracing digitalization, automation and intelligence (the term *smart manufacturing* is sometimes used) to improve different aspects of the production and of the final product lifespan. However the plethora of available solutions outlined above, combined with their different use cases and requirements, might represent a challenge for a company in scheduling and planning the investments required to correctly shift towards Industry 4.0. Moreover, it is increasingly difficult for a company to understand how much it is Industry 4.0 compliant; even though many manufacturers declare that, often only limited aspects of the production comply with the definition.

The availability of a *maturity model* can be useful for companies to self-evaluate strengths and weaknesses and to define a roadmap of investments towards a more Industry 4.0-compliant business. In addition, a maturity model enables comparisons across companies, which can be helpful to companies themselves but also to investing and regulatory authorities as a benchmark.

We are currently working to define, introduce and validate a model to assess the maturity of a company as an Industry 4.0 player according to different dimensions, where scores are defined depending on the complexity and type of software and hardware installed and their usage. The rationale here is that any progress towards Industry 4.0 in a factory requires the adoption of new information systems or to adapt existing, even traditional ones.

Acknowledgments. This work has been partly supported by the projects H2020 FIRST (id: 734599), H2020 DESTINI (id: 857420) and Italian MISE Electrospindle (id: F/160038/01-04/X41).

References

1. Moghaddam, M., Cadavid, M.N., Kenley, C.R., Deshmukh, A.V.: Reference architectures for smart manufacturing: a critical review. J. Manufact. Sst. **49**, 215–225 (2018)
2. Kletti, J.: Manufacturing Execution Systems – MES. Springer, Heidelberg (2007). https://doi.org/10.1007/978-3-540-49744-8
3. Jaskó, S., Skrop, A., Holczinger, T., Chován, T., Abonyi, J.: Development of MESs in accordance with Industry 4.0 requirements: a review of standard and ontology-based methodologies and tools. Comput. Ind. **123**, 103300 (2020)
4. Wollschlaeger, M., Sauter, T., Jasperneite, J.: The future of industrial communication: automation networks in the era of the Internet-of-Things and Industry 4.0. IEEE Ind. Electron. Mag. **11**(1), 17–27 (2017)
5. SteStertz, F., Mangler, J., Scheibel, B., Rinderle-Ma, S.: Expectations vs. experiences – process mining in small and medium sized manufacturing companies. In: Polyvyanyy, A., Wynn, M.T., Van Looy, A., Reichert, M. (eds.) BPM 2021. LNBIP, vol. 427, pp. 195–211. Springer, Cham (2021). https://doi.org/10.1007/978-3-030-85440-9_12
6. Rinderle-Ma, S., Mangler, J.: Process automation and process mining in manufacturing. In: Polyvyanyy, A., Wynn, M.T., Van Looy, A., Reichert, M. (eds.) BPM 2021. LNCS, vol. 12875, pp. 3–14. Springer, Cham (2021). https://doi.org/10.1007/978-3-030-85469-0_1
7. Catarci, T., Firmani, D., Leotta, F., Mandreoli, F., Mecella, M., Sapio, F.: A conceptual architecture and model for smart manufacturing relying on service-based digital twins. In: 2019 IEEE International Conference on Web Services (ICWS), pp. 229–236. IEEE (2019)

Author Index

Ahmeti, Engjëll 91
Alter, Steven 237
Amaral, Glenda 221

Brambilla, Marco 310
Brinkkemper, Sjaak 295

Cabot, Jordi 267, 310
Chen, Qifan 108
Clarisó, Robert 267
Corradini, Flavio 63
Curty, Simon 205

Dalpiaz, Fabiano 295
de Camargo, João Vitor 43
de Moreira Bohnenberger, Nicolas Mauro 43
de Vendt, Rik 295
Derave, Thomas 253

ElAssy, Omar 295

Fill, Hans-Georg 205
Fredericks, Chezre 79
Furrer, Frank J. 29

Gailly, Frederik 253
Gómez-Gutiérrez, Juan Antonio 267
Guizzardi, Giancarlo 221
Guizzardi, Renata 221

Hacks, Simon 139
Härer, Felix 205
Hornsteiner, Markus 18
Hülsmann, Tom-Hendrik 173

Jablonski, Stefan 91

Kaczmarek-Heß, Monika 157
Kampik, Timotheus 123
Käppel, Martin 91

Katsikeas, Sotirios 139
Koschmider, Agnes 347

Leotta, Francesco 351
Lu, Yang 108

Maraee, Azzam 279
Martakos, Anastassios 336
Martínez, Salvador 310
Mathew, Jerin George 351
Mecella, Massimo 351
Monti, Flavia 351
Moreira de Oliveira, José Palazzo 43
Mosquera, David 336
Mylopoulos, John 221

Nolte, Mario 157

Pegoraro, Marco 173
Pfeiffer, Jérôme 139
Planas, Elena 310
Poels, Geert 253
Polančič, Gregor 43
Poon, Simon K. 108
Prince Sales, Tiago 253

Re, Barbara 63
Rencelj Ling, Engla 139
Renz, Matthias 347
Roelens, Ben 188
Rossi, Lorenzo 63
Ruiz, Marcela 336

Schönig, Stefan 18
Schubert, René 347
Seymour, Lisa F. 79
Skouti, Tarek 29
Snoeck, Monique 321
Sosa-Sánchez, Encarna 43

Stein Dani, Vinicius   43
Stoiber, Christoph   18
Strahringer, Susanne   29
Sturm, Arnon   279

Thom, Lucineia Heloisa   43
Tierens, Louise   188
Tiezzi, Francesco   63

Uysal, Merih Seran   173

van der Aalst, Wil M. P.   173
Verbruggen, Charlotte   321

Weber, Barbara   3
Weske, Mathias   123
Wortmann, Andreas   139

Xiong, Wenjun   139

Zerbato, Francesca   3
Zimmermann, Lisa   3
Ziolkowski, Tobias   347

Printed in the United States
by Baker & Taylor Publisher Services